Readings In

PROFESSIONAL EDUCATION

An Interdisciplinary Approach

Allyn and Bacon, Inc.
Boston
1963

Readings In

PROFESSIONAL EDUCATION

An Interdisciplinary Approach

Aubrey Haan

Chairman, Division of Education
San Francisco State College

Norma Haan

Institute of Human Development
University of California

Library of Congress catalog card number: 63-15332

Printed in the United States of America

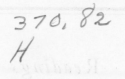

For permission to quote from published material the authors are indebted to the Teacher College Record, Soviet Education, Comparative Education Review, the National Education Association, Yale University Press, Oxford University Press, Guidance and Personnel Journal, John Wiley and Sons, Inc., Holt, Rinehart and Winston, Inc., University of Kansas Press, Free Press of Glencoe, University of Chicago Press, Journal of Abnormal and Social Psychology, American Orthopsychiatric Association, Harvard University Press, Buttenheim Corporation, the Elementary School Journal, and the Arya Press.

Table of Contents

II

The Function of Education in a Society

III

Contributions of the Behavioral Sciences

IV

Explorations in Modern Education

Readings In

PROFESSIONAL EDUCATION

An Interdisciplinary Approach

Introduction to

Contributors to section one:

E. Afanasenko

Irma Salas

L. J. Lewis

Charles H. Dobinson

Edmund King

Educational decisions i

section one:

In all societies in world history, education has been one of the basic social functions carried on by the group. In the simplest and most unchanging societies, education involved imitation and direct indoctrination into the ways adults behaved and worked. As societies became more complex, provisions for education also became more varied and specialized. The highly technological societies of modern times with their rapid rates of change are continually involved in making and remaking decisions about the purposes and means of education. It is clear that these decisions are of the utmost importance in the democratization of societies and in their political and economic development. The decisions as to who shall be educated, the content of education, and the interdependence of education and the economy are therefore the subjects of intense interest and conflict. The public school is at the very center of its society's greatest concerns. In this Section and the following sections, the nature and process of educational decision-making is shown in various societies. The selections are intended to furnish the reader with descriptions of these varied decisions and with scientific bases from the various disciplines for evaluating their effectiveness.

Developments throughout the world—economic development, literacy, political democratization and the end of colonialism—are placing great emphasis on the need for more education. The immense cultural disjunctions experienced by groups everywhere in the world as technological and ideological changes im-

n various societies

SECTION I

pinge on old value systems will put freedom in peril for new and old societies alike, perhaps for a world society in the making. It will be difficult to educate people fast enough to enable them to meet new aspirations and constitute stable, open societies.

A world society, pluralistic and basically free and open, will be aided by the growing knowledge of the science of man, by research into mental health, and by research in how children learn. The teacher as a professional person is a necessary factor in this development. The five readings that follow have been selected to provide the reader with knowledge of some of the important educational decisions, philosophies, and general developments in Russia, Africa, South America, France, and England. Aurobindo's essay in Section II also gives the reader an insight into Indian educational philosophy. Education is carried on in each of the cultures and societies represented by the papers in the light of values important in the culture. In a pluralistic universe such as we have, schools will vary basically in the curriculum experiences they offer children. Of course, as more of a science of man is developed these differences will tend to narrow, but, hopefully will never disappear.

Soviet education

Afanasenko, the author of this selection, is Minister of Education of the Russian Soviet Federal Socialist Republics. This selection is his speech before the 22nd Congress of the RSFSR and was intended primarily for domestic audiences. It is a relatively frank appraisal of the problems facing the Russian educational system and a review of progress. It is interesting to read not only because it reflects the current developments in Russia but because the problems faced by their school systems are so similar to those in all world societies facing up to the demands for universal compulsory education. Shortages of classrooms, the problems of repeaters and dropouts, the need for more character education, teacher shortages, the lagging of certain aspects of vocational educational behind technological developments, orientation of new teachers, the problems of employment for youth and the universal search for effective methods of learning all sound much like problems facing education everywhere in the world.

African education

The article by L. J. Lewis sketches the basic problems faced by African nations as they achieve independence and are confronted by the upsurge of increased demands for education. Money to be spent for schools out of total national income is in short supply. The economies of most of the nations are weak; there is a crying need for more schools and more trained people who will in the long run help strengthen these economies, but this cycle (of better trained people—more productive economies—more money for education—more trained people—more varied economy) needs priming from the outside; this, of course, is what is occurring through the United Nations, UNESCO, England, France, the United States, Belgium and other nations and agencies. Everything needed for the necessary expansion of the school system is in short supply, except children. Africa is experiencing the most rapid population increase in its entire history. The control of disease, of infant and maternal mortality, and of sanitation generally has resulted in rapid growth. Lewis points up the problems of the lack of balance between technical training and the needs of these economies. The modern economy with its complex relationships between education, production of goods and services, and social and political institutions is only beginning in most of Africa; the vital connection between schools and welfare is easily seen here.

Latin American education

The author of this selection, Dr. Salas, is Professor of Education at the University of Chile. Her analysis of the educational problems of Latin American countries reveals some problems peculiar to these societies; the problems arising from the inflexible class society inherited from Spain and Portugal are most pervasive. This has delayed democratization of education until comparatively recently; it has also led to lacks in technical education—work with the hands being considered beneath the dignity of some classes. As in Africa, Latin America faces a rapid population expansion amounting to more than 160% of the world rate. Inadequate economic development and the lack of technical education to sustain it leave these nations without enough money to furnish schools now required for modern development. Some of the nations here spend as much as 34% of the national budget on schools; the lowest expenditure is 8%, still more than twice the percentage spent by the United States. As Dr. Salas points out, the problem of more education here is complicated by old traditions bearing on the privileges of a supposed elite.

French educational reform

Nowhere has the struggle to break the restrictions of traditional education been more difficult or more dramatic than in France. The disastrous capitulation of France to Germany in 1940 launched bitter criticism against the educational system. The selection of the school system as one of the chief objects for condemnation was to a degree irrational; in this respect it was similar to the outcry against American education after the Soviet triumph with their first Sputnik. Education reflects the culture in which it exists. The reader will want to turn to Wolfenstein's article on "French Parents Take Their Children to the Park" to get some further insight into the way in which aspects of a culture can contribute to the lack of aggressive concern on the part of the individual for social purposes. The French proposals for reforms will provide for more attention to total personality development and therefore for time for the child to work through his developmental problems. These proposals are in line with the basic philosophy of education in the United States.

Comprehensive schools in England

Nothing has been more significant in recent educational developments in Western Europe than the adaptation of the American comprehensive school to new European needs. The adoption of many aspects of the comprehensive school reflects the increasing democratization of education and also the accumulated evidence that the decisions about children's future were being made too soon and too rigidly under the old system. King makes clear that the development of the comprehensive school in England, as elsewhere, is taking shape according to the particular values and structures of English society.

To the reader

The reader is invited to compare the problems and philosophies of the various cultures as they reveal themselves in their educational systems. He is also urged to read Sections III and IV in order to provide himself further with scientific bases for judgment.

See Section Bibliographies, page 361.

1-1 Soviet school reorganization*

THE JANUARY PLENUM OF THE PARTY CENTRAL COMmittee was a major event in the life of our Party and nation.

The 22nd Party Congress will sum up the results of the constructive labor of the Soviet people in fulfilling the decisions of the 20th and 21st Congresses and will adopt a new Party program—the program for the victory of communism in our country.

Preparation for the Congress is proceeding with exceptional enthusiasm throughout the country.

Zonal, regional and territorial conferences of advanced workers in agriculture, as well as regional and territorial Party plenums, all held after the January Plenum, revealed inexhaustible reserves for the creation of an abundance of consumption goods in our country and defined concrete means applicable to local conditions for solving the problems involved in the further development of agriculture. At the conferences, along with advanced workers in agriculture, secondary school pupils, who have made an appropriate contribution to agricultural development, shared their experience in cultivating high yields of corn and other grain crops and in working successfully on live-

* E. Afanasenko, "Let us Greet the 22nd Congress with Further Progress in the School Reorganization," *Soviet Education*, Vol. IV, No. 2 (Dec., 1961), pp. 3–17. The author is Minister of Education of the RSFSR.

E. Afanasenko

stock farms. This testifies to the fact that our rural school has tied in its work closely with the life and labor of the nation, that it has become an active participant in the struggle for higher yields and increased productivity in animal husbandry. Experience has shown that the opportunities of the schools in this respect are still far from exhausted.

There is special significance for all of us in the instructions of the January Plenum of the Central Committee on the need to devote ourselves to agriculture, basing our work on the data of science and the achievements of advanced experience, on improving the methods of leadership, on a responsible attitude toward the fulfillment of planned targets and obligations assumed, on resolute struggle against careerism and whitewashing, on instilling truthfulness and integrity in each communist, each Soviet individual, as integral qualities.

The Soviet teacher has always been a faithful helper of the Party in all of its pursuits. And now he is taking an active part in the truly national effort to extend a worthy greeting to the 22nd Party Congress; he is striving to make his contribution to the cause of building communism.

The best way for workers in the field of public education to greet the 22nd Party Congress with new achievements is to make substantial progress in the implementation of the school reform law. Two years have passed since the law was adopted, and it is now our duty to survey the work which has been done, to examine the unresolved problems and to map out the ways of solving them quickly so that we can report real progress to the Party Congress in the creation of the new school.

Realize Eight-Year Universal Compulsory Education

Universal compulsory eight-year education is one of our immediate tasks. In the 1959–1960 school year, 1,706 eight-year schools were opened in the Russian Federation; another 6,594 are to be established during the current school year. All in all there are at present 8,300 eight-year schools (boarding schools included), of which 5,756 are situated in rural areas. While this indicates that a good deal of work has been done in the localities, it can hardly satisfy us.

The point is that in the two years that remain we must reorganize 21,307 seven-year schools into eight-year schools, that is, many more than we have managed to reorganize in the past two years. We must not forget that until now we have been reorganizing seven-year schools which had the necessary material facilities; in the next two years we shall have to transform into eight-year schools some institutions which lack such a material base.

In 1961 we must reorganize the bulk of our seven-year schools into eight-year schools. Unless this is done we shall jeopardize the fulfillment of the law on eight-year universal education. This must be stated in view of the impermissible procrastination which is occurring in a number of places. In the Smolensk Region, for example, only 59 eight-year schools have been established, with almost 600 more still to be reorganized. Of the 524 seven-year schools in the Kursk Region, only 90 have been reorganized thus far; in the Krasnoyarsk Territory—only 90 out of 583. The reorganization is moving slowly in the Daghestan and Mordovian Autonomous Republics, the Altai Territory, and the Briansk, Voronezh, Kalinin, Omsk, Saratov and several other regions.

It should be noted that certain departments of public education (in the cities of Orekhovo-Zuevo in the Moscow Region and Kaluga and Obninsk in the Kaluga Region, etc.) have already, with the help of Party and government bodies and the broad public, completed the reorganization of their seven-year schools. The transformation of the seven-year schools into eight-year schools will be finished this year in Vologda and Cherepovets, in the Sokolsky and Verkhnevazhsky Districts of the Vologda Region, the Tarussy District of the Kaluga Region and elsewhere.

In reorganizing the public education system we must not under any circumstances allow the slightest deterioration in the educational services provided the population. Therefore the reduction of the number of elementary, and in some cases even incomplete secondary, schools in the Altai Territory, the Kirov, Kemerovo, Novosibirsk and other regions creates serious apprehension and just complaints on the part of the population.

The newspaper *Uchitel'skaia Gazeta* has raised the question of reorganizing the elementary schools as branches of the secondary or eight-year schools. I do not think that we should do this now. Experience has shown that many principals of eight-year and secondary schools do not adequately control and guide the instructional and character-training work of the 1st to 4th grade teachers of their own schools. The elementary schools that are located two, three and more kilometers from the eight-year and secondary schools find themselves in a particularly difficult situation. At the same time it is essential for the eight-year and secondary schools to become genuine methods centers for the elementary school teachers of their districts.

To ensure the transition to universal compulsory eight-year education, it is not enough to have the required network of elementary and eight-year schools; we must also see to it that not a single child or adolescent is left without schooling and that pupils do not drop out of school.

Dropouts

Three years ago, in a note to the Presidium of the Party Central Committee, Nikita S. Khrushchev pointed out that although seven-year education was at that time compulsory a substantial number of young people were not even finishing the 7th grade, let alone the full secondary-school course. Unfortunately we have still not put things in order in this respect. Although the number of pupils dropping out of school has fallen off in the past few years it is still very large.

We can no longer put up with this situation. We must examine in detail the causes for pupil dropouts in every school of every autonomous republic, territory, region, district and city; we must determine why some children are left without schooling. We must contact each child before the beginning of the school year and take concrete steps to ensure that all children and adolescents report for studies on September 1st. We must put an end to pupils dropping out before they finish the eight-year school.

Repeaters

As has been said many times before, one of the chief reasons for the failure to achieve universal education is the large number of repeaters. In the schools of the RSFSR this year a great many repeaters in the elementary as well as 5th to 7th grades did not attend classes. The number of repeaters who dropped out of school in the Daghestan and Mordovian Autonomous Republics, the Krasnoyarsk and Maritime Territories, and the Irkutsk, Gorky and Kemerovo Regions was particularly high.

It should be emphasized once again that universal education today is less an organizational than a pedagogical problem, and that the struggle for its realization demands above all a radical improvement in the conduct of instructional and character-training work. Most important of all is a sensitive approach to each child, the ability to come to his aid in time and not to let him get behind in his studies, to instill in each child a love for school and studying and to make the school seem like his own home. This is precisely the direction in which the teaching staffs of all the schools must work in order to achieve universal education.

In our Federation there are now almost one and one-half million pupils in schools situated three and more kilometers from their homes; only 40 per cent of such children have been placed in boarding schools. Regular transportation for the children is not provided in many cases. This leads to large-scale absenteeism during the spring thaws and autumn rains, the winter snow storms and frosts, which in turn results in pupils' lagging behind in their studies, and often to their leaving school. In the new school year effective measures must be taken to carry out the requirements of the law on regular transportation for pupils.

In 1959 a decision was adopted on the creation of a special universal education fund in each school. However these funds are not being fully utilized in many places. This has been the case in the Khabarovsk, Maritime and Krasnoyarsk Territories, the Vologda, Kostroma and Sverdlovsk Regions and in a number of other areas. School principals who display such an attitude toward utilization of the special universal education funds should be called strictly to account.

Creation of prolonged-day schools and groups has a very important role to play in implementing eight-year universal education. Our republic began the current year with 248 such schools and in addition, over 9,000 such groups in 6,127 schools. The prolonged-day schools and groups have an enrollment of over 300,000 children.

It is intolerable that there is still not a single prolonged-day school in the North Ossetian Autonomous Republic, the Amur, Arkhangelsk, Belgorod, Lipetsk and Leningrad Regions.

It is equally impermissible that in certain prolonged-day schools and groups all of the work comes down to fulfilling homework assignments. Outdoor games, walks, interesting excursions or other out-of-class activities are not organized.

Public education bodies must improve the direction of the prolonged-day schools and groups by drawing on the experience of the best of them as well as of the most advanced boarding schools.

Achievement of universal education requires that the schools enroll all physically and mentally handicapped children. Yet in many cases the public education bodies do not take the necessary measures to increase the number of special schools. This situation must unquestionably be corrected in the shortest possible time.

We have all of the prerequisites to do away with the shortcomings in universal education. This is borne out by the experience of the 360 districts and cities in the Russian Federation which achieved universal seven-year education.

The Ministry of Education held a conference of the heads of those district and city education departments which have attained full attendance by all children and adolescents of school age. The valuable experience of the participants in that conference permits us to draw a number of highly instructive conclusions.

In the districts and cities where universal education has been achieved, the schools work under the usual conditions and encounter the same difficulties that arise everywhere. The secret of the success of the educators in these districts and cities lies in their lofty sense of responsibility, their truly statesmanlike approach to their work, in their ability to draw on the daily help of Party, government, trade union and Komsomol organizations, the parents and the Soviet public as a whole in the fight for universal education.

An example

The experience of the Mil'kovo District Education Department of the Kamchatka Region in achieving universal education is of considerable interest. The department is headed by Leonid N. Verin.

The district is over 300 kilometers long. Communication with the schools is effected only by air or by dog sleighs, or, in the summer, by water transport. The five elementary schools of the district are situated 60 to 105 kilometers from the nearest secondary or eight-year schools. But for two years now all children in the Mil'kovo District have been attending school.

Considerable attention is given there, first of all, to a correct census of all the children who come under compulsory education. In the district public education department one can find not only the ordinary statistics on the number of children, but also lists of those who for one reason or another may be absent from school or have dropped out.

In all of the schools of the district the class teachers make a careful study of the living conditions of their pupils, as well as of children about to enter school. Special note is taken of those who encounter difficulties in attending school, and special work is carried on with them. For instance, at the end of the past school year six pupils in the Shapkinskaia Secondary School were singled out for special consideration because of the possibility that they might discontinue their studies. To prevent their leaving school, it was decided to maintain contact with them all summer long. The boys were drawn into a team doing preparatory work for the new school year. They worked for 18 days, after which, as a reward for their good work, they were taken on a hiking trip to the Kluchevskaia Hill along with a group of older boys. Those girls with poor health were placed in a Young Pioneer Camp for the entire summer, where they were kept under regular medical observation.

The schools in the Mil'kovo District follow the excellent practice of making the last week in August a week for preparing the children for school. During the week all of the teachers, older pupils and members of the parents committees visit the children and check up on their readiness for school. The question of helping those who need help is settled quickly. Before school opens a festive assembly of all pupils is held, attended by heads of enterprises, government and Party personnel and parents.

All children in the Mil'kovo District who live in remote areas are accommodated in boarding schools. The enrollment of the children in the boarding schools is also made a festive event: newcomers are presented with gifts and the older children acquaint them with the established regime in the boarding school. Every December the District Executive Committee decides on expanding the boarding schools for the next year if the need arises.

School meals are well organized in all schools of the district. The universal education funds are fully and wisely spent, and as a result all children in need of material help receive it in good time.

The excellent work carried on by the teaching staffs with repeaters also helps to keep them in school. The teacher keeps an eye on repeaters from the day the term begins, calling on them often, assigning them extra lessons, and doing everything to bolster their confidence in the possibility of finishing school.

Teachers, older pupils and parents help children who are ill at home with their studies. On recovering these children are usually able to keep up with the rest of the class.

In the Mil'kovo District public organizations have been drawn into the work of achieving universal education. The district newspaper makes a substantial contribution by publishing interesting articles frequently on school life, on the importance of knowledge, on the parents' role in implementing universal education.

It goes without saying that if such comprehensive and purposeful work were carried on in every district and school all children and adolescents would be in school.

Bringing Order Into the Secondary Schools With Production Training

The law provides, as everyone knows, that the reorganization of the secondary schools is to be completed in the 1963–1964 school year.

By the beginning of the current school year, 4,541 secondary ten-year schools (or 38%) out of a total of 12,811 such schools had been reorganized as secondary schools with production training—2,798 in the cities and workers' settlements and 1,743 in rural localities.

Whereas the network of secondary schools with production training is being established more quickly in the cities and workers' settlements than the national economic plan envisaged, the process is extremely slow in the rural localities.

It is especially slow both in the cities and rural areas of the Daghestan, Kalmyk and Yakut Autonomous Republics, the Maritime Territory, and the Ivanovo, Kaliningrad, and Yaroslavl Regions. There is no justification for this.

In carrying out the reorganization of the secondary schools, many departments of public education repeat the same mistake made in establishing the network of elementary and eight-year schools: they close some of them. This is contrary to the School Law, which provides for the extension of secondary education in our country.

The heads of some public education departments evidently forget that in the next few years the number of pupils in the upper grades, which is now insignificant, will grow rapidly. The number of 8th grade classes has already increased appreciably, and in two or three years' time there will be so many pupils in the upper grades that there will be serious difficulties in accommodating them, even if the network of secondary schools is maintained.

There are still many instances of the secondary schools being reorganized without the proper preparation. For example, the Loktinskaia Secondary School of the Chashinskii District, Kurgan Region, was reorganized as a secondary school with production training this year, but it has neither the necessary material base nor the qualified teachers to provide production training for the pupils.

We must greatly accelerate the reorganization of the ten-year schools into secondary schools with production training, but this does not justify reducing the reorganization to a mere formality.

We must be more bold in establishing secondary schools with

production training in the 9th to 11th grades. In such schools it is easier to create well-equipped rooms for the general education and special subjects, and it is easier to find skilled teaching personnel for them. The problem of vocational training and the combining of instruction with productive work is more readily solved in these schools; the entire instructional and character-training process can be conducted more purposefully; the pedagogical leaders of these schools can concentrate their attention on the upper classes which are receiving specialized training.

One of the most important and difficult tasks in setting up the secondary schools with production training is the organization of vocational training for the pupils of the 9th to 11th grades. In solving this problem we have still not overcome the primitiveness about which Comrade N. S. Khrushchev spoke at the All-Russian Teachers' Congress.

The School Law made the local planning bodies, economic councils, agricultural administrations and departments of public education responsible for deciding in what trades the pupils of each secondary school with production training shall be trained, for determining how many pupils shall be accepted in the 9th grade in each of the trades, and also for finding employment for graduates of the secondary school. But as of now these questions are still decided in the majority of cases by the school, which must base its decisions on its possibilities for providing vocational training and productive work at some nearby production enterprise. In doing this the needs of the economic area for workers in specific trades are not taken into consideration everywhere, nor the possibility of finding employment for the graduates of the secondary schools.

Let us take Perm Region as an example. This year the Novo-Il'inskaia Secondary School of the Nyt'vinskii District began to train lathe operators at a house-building factory. But in the next few years the factory will not need lathe operators but electric-saw operators, electricians and assembly men. School No. 65 in Perm is training gauge-makers, but the enterprises near the school do not need people in that line. Although many large construction enterprises in the region are greatly in need of workers, all of the secondary schools with production training are training less than 100 pupils in the building trades.

Often one and the same school offers production training in many diverse specialties. School No. 200 in Leningrad, for instance, gives production training in 16 trades, and School No. 203 in Moscow —in 15 trades. It is impossible to organize the educational process correctly under such circumstances.

Detailed instructions were issued last September by the State Planning Commission and the RSFSR Ministry of Education concerning the drawing up of a plan for training skilled workers in the secondary schools with production training for various branches of the national economy and culture during the period 1961 to 1965. This work must be completed without further delay in conformity with the instructions given.

In selecting the trades for each secondary school with production training, we must proceed from the premise that as a rule one school can provide training in no more than three or four trades, and one class can offer one or two trades.

There are now 270,000 pupils receiving vocational training in the secondary schools with production training of the Russian Federation. Most of them (over 160,000) are being trained for industrial trades, and this is only natural and correct. But only some 56,500 pupils are receiving training in agricultural trades, and this will far from satisfy the demand for mechanics, livestock breeders and other agricultural workers. Everyone knows what a large and continually growing need there is for construction personnel, and yet only 9,000 pupils are getting production training in this field.

Only 3,500 pupils are being trained for work in trade or public catering enterprises, despite the very great demand for workers in these lines.

In concretizing the plans for vocational training, they must be made to conform to the requirements of the national economy and culture of the given economic area. In doing this it is particularly important to give careful thought to the question of trades for girls. There would be nothing reprehensible in taking into consideration the specific nature of women's work and organizing some classes for girls only and others for boys only in the secondary schools with production training; the schools as a whole would remain coeducational.

It is not unusual for pupils to be assigned to production training classes without regard for their leanings or abilities. Thus in a number of Moscow schools girls were enrolled in classes training kindergarten teachers although they did not have an ear for music and had speech and other physical defects which prevented them from working in this field. A subsequent check revealed that some of them agreed to take the training without intending to work in pre-school institutions.

The Stavrovskaia Secondary School in the Vladimir Region trains livestock breeders, but not one of the graduates of the 11th grade last year went to work on the farm, or even remained in his collective farm.

The haste shown in selecting the trades for the secondary schools with production training and the serious shortcomings in their work often engender in some pupils the desire to transfer to other educational institutions.

The secondary schools with production training must be judged by the results of their work, by how they cope with the task of training roundly developed, educated people with communist convictions, and by whether their graduates go to work in the trades they have selected.

Particular attention must be given to ensuring that the young person who has finished the rural secondary school with production training remains on a collective or state farm. The decisions of the January Plenum of the Party Central Committee require this of us.

Education Through Study and Labor—the School's Main Task

We are now fully justified in saying that the most important result of the reorganization of the schools is that they have become truly schools of labor.

Every year labor enters increasingly into the life of the school and is more closely linked with the content of their instructional and character-training work. The schools are developing a definite system of labor education which makes it possible from an early age to instill in the pupils respect for those who toil and prepares them psychologically for labor for the benefit of society.

N. S. Khrushchev has repeatedly stressed in his speeches that the chief significance of the pupils' labor lies not in its material results but in its tremendous educational effect on them.

The labor of pupils in the 1st to 4th, and 5th to 8th grades is in the nature of educational, socially useful labor, training for productive labor. It was in this spirit that the syllabus for labor training and socially useful work was drawn up for the pupils of the 1st to 8th grades.

If the pupils are overloaded with labor tasks, and if they are asked to perform monotonous or overly-demanding tasks, it is possible that they may not develop a love for labor; they may develop a distaste for it. For this reason we do not agree with the proposals made by a number of colleagues in our press to the effect that young schoolchildren should be drawn into systematic work in the production workshops to fill orders from enterprises, trade organizations, etc. But we do favor labor training for the pupils of the 1st to 4th and 5th to 8th grades which is socially useful in character and is suited to their strength. Experimental work in cultivating agricultural crops, participation by the children in planting greenery and improving the public services of their cities, in making visual and other educational aids for the schools, kindergartens, etc., have proved their worth.

Nor do we agree with the negative view some heads of the public education departments and school principals have taken of the social-production practice introduced in the eight-year schools last year in accordance with the new curriculum. The experience of the schools of the Belgorod, Lipetsk, Kuibyshev and Briansk Regions, the city of Leningrad and other places where such practice work has been properly organized has shown that it helps to fix the work habits acquired by the pupils and facilitates the efficient application of those habits in socially useful work, and that it has great educational value. The RSFSR Ministry of Education, after having studied last year's experience with social production practice, has issued instructions concerning its most efficient organization.

In organizing the productive labor of upper grade pupils, we must not allow the mistakes of past years to be repeated. We must substantially improve the forms of production training in the industrial enterprises. At the present time pupils receive vocational training for the most part through individual instruction. What happens is that the workers, who are anxious to fulfill their own production quotas, do not have the time to teach the pupils assigned to them. It is not unusual, consequently, for the pupils to spend the day observing the worker, or doing an auxiliary job for him from time to time. Such a system of training does not allow the pupil to acquire the practical skills of his trade, and undermines his interest in productive work.

In the city secondary schools with production training we must go over to the group method of training pupils, and to the organization of productive work at permanent places. The recent decision to organize training shops and sections in the factories and at building sites for the production training of secondary school pupils will facilitate this change. The decision points out that the training shops and sections must consist of a class set up for theoretical instruction and of a production section for practical training with one work bench for the use of three pupils a day, so equipped as to guarantee their training in advanced methods of work.

Haste in awarding pupils skill categories must be avoided. Such haste fosters a "light" attitude toward work, and disarms them for the difficulties they will encounter in their later work activities. Pupils must be given to understand that the skill category is a serious matter and can only be earned through hard work and study. That will instill in them respect for the trades they are acquiring.

In the rural schools the main form of organizing productive work must be pupils' teams in the collective and state farms. Their importance in the communist upbringing of pupils has been stressed repeatedly by Comrade N. S. Khrushchev. In his recent speech at a meeting of advanced agricultural workers of the North Caucasus, N. S. Khrushchev said: "The main and most important thing is that in the pupils' teams the children learn to respect agricultural production and to love labor. In them there is an excellent combination of education and of instilling in the youth the desire to be useful to the nation, to participate in the production of the material values needed by society. The pupils' teams are a school for the upbringing of active builders of communism. The example of the Stavropol schoolchildren deserves to be copied and popularized on the widest scale."

At the end of March the Bureau of the Party Central Committee examined the experience of the pupils' teams' in the state and collective farms of Stavropol and adopted a decision that it be widely introduced into school practice. It is our job to ensure the speediest possible implementation of this decision.

While we accept the pupils' teams as the basic form of production training and productive work in agriculture for pupils, there is no reason to reject such other forms as the experimental training plots in situations where such forms of organizing the labor of rural schoolchildren are well suited to local conditions.

Experimental agricultural work

The general education polytechnical schools giving labor training have the mission of instilling in the pupils a desire for innovation, a creative attitude toward labor. Experimental agricultural work is of inestimable value in achieving this task. A great deal has been done to organize such work in the schools of the Russian Federation during the past few years.

Recently the Collegium of the Ministry of Education discussed the preliminary results of the experimental agricultural work of the schools of Gorky Region. It is noteworthy that this experimental work in the region was set up as a matter of importance to the state. Not only were teachers involved in its direction, but many prominent scientists and associates of research institutions as well. The Party Regional Committee and the Executive Committee of the Regional Soviet of Working Peoples' Deputies kept a constant check on its progress.

This experimental work has also attained great scope in the schools of the Rostov, Kuibyshev, Leningrad, Yaroslavl, Saratov, Riazan, Omsk and Ulianovsk Regions and the Stavropol and Krasnodar Territories.

Many schools have been pioneers in introducing new varieties of plants and better methods of cultivating agricultural crops in the farms of their districts. N. S. Khrushchev gave the pupils' experimental work high praise when, at a meeting of advanced agricultural workers in the Kurgan Region, he held up the children who had achieved success in raising corn for seed under the difficult climatic conditions of Siberia as an example to the famous innovator and agronomist Maltsev.

However there are still many shortcomings in the experimental agricultural work of pupils: far from all of the schools have joined in this work; many of the schools still organize only learning experiments which do not have any practical significance.

Agricultural experimentation must become part of the practice of all the schools and must become one of the basic elements of the socially useful productive work of schoolchildren in agriculture.

In some cases the heads of rural schools expand the plots of land attached to the schools endlessly or increase the size of the number of livestock entrusted to the care of the children too much. In the Mikhailovskii District of the Stalingrad Region, for instance, some of the children have as much as 1,600 hectares of arable land. It would be difficult to expect one school to care for such a farm while observing the standards of advanced agriculture. The Stavrovskaia Secondary School in the Vladimir Region has undertaken to provide complete care for a collective farm herd of over sixty head of cattle. Its pupils work on the farm every day from five in the morning, and finish their work late in the evening. This system of organizing the pupils' work has a negative effect on their education and character training, on their rounded development.

Of course it is impossible to organize production training on small plots which do not really allow for drawing the pupils into productive work. A sense of measure, a pedagogical approach to these problems, is essential.

The size of the plot of land assigned for the pupils' team, for the experimental training farm, must be related to the number of pupils, the duration of the working day, the norms of output established for schoolchildren, the amount of labor expended in growing the given crop, the degree to which the work is mechanized, and also the climatic conditions in each zone. This question was discussed at the All-Russian Conference of Staffs of Rural Secondary Schools With Production Training. The delegates to the conference agreed that as a rule the size of the plot attached to the school should average 0.05 to 0.1 hectare per pupil when labor consuming crops are being grown, and from 0.5 to 1 hectare per pupil for grain crops. But even these approximate norms must be made more precise in each school.

Experience has shown that it is not advisable to place maintenance of livestock farms entirely in the hands of the schools, as this leads to great overworking of the pupils. It is more correct to assign the pupils of the rural secondary schools to collective and state farms and to organize their work according to a schedule that conforms to the curriculum and syllabuses for production training.

The point is often made that every rural school with production training should be completely equipped with its own modern farm machinery. We think that it would be wrong to turn over to the school a large number of agricultural machines, since they could not be rationally utilized there. Every rural school with production training needs farm machinery for its educational purposes, but for their productive work the pupils should use the machines that belong to the collective and state farms.

Remuneration

It is also very important to decide correctly the question of paying for the pupils' productive work in factories, at construction sites, on collective and state farms. There has been a good deal of discussion on this question. We hold that the productive work of the pupils must be remunerated, but it is impossible to establish privileged conditions for them. Schoolchildren should have reduced output quotas corresponding to their age, but their work should be paid for according to the rates set for adult workers and collective farmers, in accordance with the quantity and quality of the product.

It would be expedient, in our opinion, for the class, the unit or the team itself to distribute the sum earned among the schoolchildren who have participated in the work. This would not exclude the possibility of allocating a certain part of the earnings for collective needs, such as the arrangement of excursions, hiking trips and other cultural or athletic undertakings. It seems to us that such a system of payment for the pupils' work would help instill in them a communist attitude toward labor.

The struggle to give the pupils profound and firm knowledge of the fundamentals of the sciences was and still is the chief task of the school. Under the conditions of the comprehensive building of communism in our country, the pupils' work and studies are inseparable. The closer we draw to communism, the greater will be the social significance of education in our country.

Speaking at a meeting of advanced agricultural workers of the Caucasus, Comrade N. S. Khrushchev said: "Education used to be what you might call the capital of a man. Getting an education was like acquiring a certain amount of capital which could then be exploited for one's personal aims. Now everyone in our country receives an education, and he gets it mainly in order to work better for the good of society."

The combining of education with productive work opens up new possibilities for raising the pupils' level of knowledge. We can cite as an example the Rostov School No. 1, which is ably organizing the pupils' labor, and at the same time is successfully solving the task of raising the level of the entire instructional and character-training process and the quality of the pupils' knowledge. There are hardly any repeaters in this school.

It would be wrong to close our eyes to the apparent defects in the general educational training of pupils in a number of schools. Although the number of repeaters has fallen somewhat in the past few years, there are still many of them. What is more, a good many are found in the 1st and 2nd grades where, given correct organization of the learning process, there should be no failures.

We also cannot pass over the fact that the most predominant mark among pupils remains the "3." This shows that a considerable portion of the children have not mastered the fundamentals of the sciences deeply enough, and that there are serious shortcomings in the content, organization and methods of school work.

Low teaching levels

We must stress again and again that one of the biggest reasons for the inadequate level of pupils' knowledge, for their unsatisfactory progress in their studies, for the large number of repeaters is the imperfection of teaching methods and the low level of teaching of a considerable portion of the teachers.

Universal compulsory education requires that the teacher concern himself with each of his pupils; the methods and techniques employed by the teacher must make it possible for all pupils without exception to assimilate the syllabus material and at the same time give scope for the development of their individual inclinations and abilities. Such an approach to teaching presupposes the broad development of diverse forms of independent work and resorting in some cases to individual assignments.

Comrade Darskii, a teacher in one of the schools of the Moscow Region, was right when, in his article for the newspaper *Pravda* entitled "How to Put an End to the Overloading of Pupils," he demonstrated convincingly that many teachers "lack the pedagogical skill and ability to give their pupils firm knowledge and to instill all the necessary habits in them at the right time." As a result the children do not have "the proper preparation at the moment of transition from elementary school into the seven-year school and then the 8th grade of secondary school." From this there follows the overloading of pupils with school work. Therefore, Darskii concludes, "the primary means of putting an end to the overloading of pupils is to struggle persistently and continuously for the inculcation of lasting knowledge and habits at every stage of learning. The main role in this belongs to the teacher."

The Academy of Pedagogical Sciences has still not acquitted itself of its duty to the teaching profession in solving the problem of raising the quality of teaching, for it has still not provided a methodology for teaching the different subjects that measures up to the demands of the Soviet school.

The pupils' proficiency in the Russian language and mathematics is particularly low. The reason is that the inadequacy of the existing teaching methods is most sharply felt in the teaching of these two subjects.

In order to read well, write correctly, solve arithmetical tasks and problems, count quickly, it is not enough to memorize formulas and rules; the pupil must understand well what he has studied and be able to apply it in practice. But in the teaching of Russian and mathematics in the school the verbal method still predominates, and this method devotes too little time to independent work by the pupils and the development of practical habits.

From the above one conclusion can be drawn: the teaching profession and pedagogical science still face the acute task of overcoming formalism, the verbal method of teaching all curriculum subjects, and above all, Russian and mathematics. In doing this particular attention must be paid to elementary education, for that is the foundation without which the pupils will not be able to successfully master the foundations of the sciences in the secondary school.

It will be possible to perfect our methods of teaching all the curriculum subjects only if the teachers in every school are given leeway for creative thinking and searching. The school principals and public education department personnel must give the utmost support to the teacher's initiative in improving the educational process, be attentive to his suggestions, check them carefully in practice and apply those that prove worthy on a wide scale in all the schools. At the same time it is necessary to avoid implementing schemes that are poorly thought out and often unrealistic, and can do nothing but harm.

N. S. Khrushchev's instruction on the need to improve agriculture, drawing from the achievements of science and advanced experience, has particular significance for improving public education and its leadership.

We must strongly condemn the nihilistic attitude towards pedagogical science which still exists, and help all teachers master the scientific foundations of the pedagogical process, without knowledge of which intelligent innovation is impossible. At the same time it is necessary to organize the study and introduction of advanced pedagogical experience in a statesmanlike way. This is now the main task in the direction of the schools.

There is still a good deal of formalism in supervising the teacher's work. School principals and directors of studies give most of their attention to the form of the lesson and not to checking on the quality of the pupils' learning. Of course it is easier to remark upon the way the lesson has been organized and to express judgments on individual methods used by the teacher. In order to really evaluate the pupils' knowledge the school principal and director of studies must themselves know the syllabus material well. In our opinion we must keep this in mind now in striving to raise the qualifications of the heads of the schools. We must demand of them that they check the pupils' knowledge systematically and judge the teacher's work by that criterion.

In checking on the realization of the School Reorganization Law, we must pay the most serious attention to the pupils' level of knowledge, skills and habits; all attempts to reduce our demands on the pupils must be suppressed. At the same time we must put an end to the attempts to solve the problem of repeaters by administrative measures, and no pressure must be exerted on the teachers when they evaluate the pupils' knowledge and mark their proficiency.

It is not unusual for the work of the school and the teacher to be judged, as before, by the percentage of good marks, without examining the actual level of the pupils' knowledge, skills and habits. This is a vicious path, the path of reviving percentage-mania, long condemned by our Party. Those heads of schools and public education departments who revive the percentage-mania in any form whatever must be called strictly to account for it.

In this connection it might be well to take up the question of socialist competition in the schools.

We are in favor of extensive socialist competition among the pupils in their socially useful work, in their cultural and athletic activities. But their study activity must not under any circumstances be made an object of socialist competition. The Ministry of Education deems it necessary to again stress the impermissibility of socialist competition in studies, no matter what form it may take.

Non-Russian schools

Among all of the measures being carried out now, much attention is being given to reorganizing the work of the non-Russian schools.

The ministries of education of the autonomous republics have drawn up new curriculums for the eight-year and secondary non-Russian schools which will make it possible to ensure the same level of general knowledge as the Russian schools provide.

The teaching of the native and Russian languages in the non-Russian schools has been put in order. Much work is being done to provide them with new syllabuses and textbooks.

Nevertheless it must be said that the non-Russian schools have the same shortcomings in the organization, content and methods of instruction as do the Russian schools. The state of instruction and the pupils' knowledge in the native and Russian languages warrant particularly serious apprehension.

The public education bodies and the principals of the non-Russian schools must give their most serious attention to raising the quality of teaching the native and Russian languages and the pupils' knowledge of these subjects, carrying out the national principle of education in strict conformity with the Law on the School.

Simultaneously, changes must be introduced in the curriculums of the secondary schools of certain autonomous republics, primarily the Bashkir and Tatar Autonomous Republics, for the purpose of improving the production training and productive work of the pupils in the upper grades of these schools.

Improvement of the educational process and, consequently, of the quality of learning and the pupils' proficiency depends to a great extent upon the Ministry of Education and the Academy of Pedagogical Sciences.

This year the task of compiling and endorsing the new curriculums for all types of schools has been completed. They were adopted after wide discussion by the members of the teaching profession, and are unquestionably a step forward in comparison with the syllabuses in use until now. But they still have faults, the most serious of which is that they are over-loaded with material. The Ministry of Education has found it necessary just the same to stabilize them for the next few years; it has decided not to make any changes in them unless there is a special need.

During the current school year we have published model syllabuses for production training and productive work in 44 trades; by the beginning of the 1961–1962 school year the syllabuses for another 15 trades will also be distributed.

The present textbooks are being reviewed and new ones written. By the beginning of the 1961–1962 school year the schools will receive 15 revised and 11 new textbooks for the 1st to 7th grades. There are, however, serious defects in this work. A decision to improve the publication of school textbooks was recently adopted. It will unquestionably help the Ministry of Education to supply the schools with good, stable textbooks in the near future.

The reorganization of the schools has introduced much that is new in the content and forms of educational work in the schools.

The latter are now confronted with the task of educating the new man of communist society. The whole tenor of school life, all its instructional and character-training activity must be subordinated to the solution of this task.

As the experience of many schools has shown, the combining of learning with life, with work, with the practice of building communism creates favorable conditions for the formation of a Marxist-Leninist world outlook and a lofty communist morality among the schoolchildren.

A positive phenomenon worth mentioning is that the pupils, especially the upper-grade pupils, have a greater love for work and a growing respect for those who work, as well as a growing desire to be of use to the people and to participate in the production of the material values necessary to society. They have a more conscientious attitude towards their studies.

The combining of learning with socially useful labor enriches the content of the work of the Young Pioneer and Komsomol organizations in the schools.

During the Second National Expedition of Young Pioneers and Schoolchildren in 1960, the pupils fulfilled tasks set by the economic councils, agricultural departments and cultural and educational institutions having to do with the search for useful minerals, the collection of historical materials, and study of the geography of the country. Interesting work is also being done in connection with the Two-Year Plan of the Young Pioneer Organization.

The introduction of production training and productive work in the secondary schools has promoted close ties between the pupils and the young workers in the factories, collective and state farms. Pupils in the upper grades participate in production conferences in the factories, join in their amateur art and athletic activities, and help the workers put out their factory wall newspapers. Many upper-grade pupils help the young workers in evening and correspondence schools with their studies.

This does not mean that we can ignore the serious shortcomings in the education of the pupils.

In many schools the content of the lessons is not properly utilized to further educational purposes. Every teacher has a duty to present his subject in such a way that the pupils do not merely learn a certain sum of knowledge; their knowledge must be transformed into profound convictions; noble impulses and the desire to serve their country honorably must be awakened in them. The educational impact of the lesson and other forms of study activity must be increased, and learning must be put at the service of forming the character of the man of communist society.

The content and forms of work with the junior and senior groups of Young Pioneers must be carefully differentiated. As a rule there are no Komsomol organizations in the eight-year schools. For this reason the Young Pioneers studying in the 7th and especially the 8th grades must be active leaders and organizers of all socially useful undertakings of the pupils, and serve as the mainstay of the monitors councils and the Young Pioneer leadership.

Reorganization of the work of the Komsomol organizations in the schools must be directed towards raising their responsibility for the studies and work achievements of the whole community of pupils. Komsomol members must be active helpers of the teachers in shaping correct ideas and views and healthy, vital interests among the pupils of the upper grades. Much of the organizational work that is now carried out by the class teachers should be assigned to the Komsomol organizations, which should be shown much more confidence.

The Komsomol and Young Pioneer organizations enjoy unlimited opportunities for independent activity and initiative in our schools. Principals and teachers should encourage the development of their initiative in every possible way.

Innovations must be made in the work of the class teacher. He should be regarded primarily as the organizer of the pupils' collective. In conducting the many-sided educational work of the classroom, the class teacher should involve all teachers, parents and the public; he should draw support from the more active pupils. This will guarantee the success of his work.

This year all the schools have for the first time followed the model program for educational work. Their experience in applying the program should be studied and suggestions should be made as to how it can be further improved.

The reorganization of the schools also calls for a decided improvement in the organization of out-of-class and out-of-school work. The content of that work must contribute to the rounded development of the pupils and the satisfaction of their inclinations and interests. Particular attention must be given to their esthetic and physical education.

More Attention to the Evening (Shift) Secondary Schools

The Communist Party and the Soviet Government are greatly concerned that all men and women workers and collective farmers obtain a secondary education. The practical realization of this task depends to a great extent upon expanding the network of evening (shift) and correspondence schools, and on the improvement of their work.

During the past two years the Central Committee of our Party and the Soviet Government have adopted a number of decisions aimed at further improvement of evening and correspondence school education in our country. A study we have made of the evening (shift) schools of Sverdlovsk Region and the general conclusions drawn concerning the best work done there have been of great help. A great deal more attention is being given the evening schools by local Party, government and economic organizations, the trade union, Komsomol and other public organizations of the factories, the collective and state farms. The change-over to the seven- and six-hour working day for all factory and office workers has also helped a good deal in increasing the enrollment of worker and rural youth in the evening and correspondence schools. The movement of those seeking the title of shock worker or communist work team, whose motto is to work, live and study in a communist manner, is the source of young people streaming into the evening (shift) and correspondence schools.

In the current school year there are more than 4,500 schools for working youth and more than 2,000 schools for rural youth operating in the Russian Federation. This means an increase of over 1,500 in the number of such schools in the past two years. More than 1,500,000 persons are enrolled in them. The national economic plan for enrollment in the evening schools has been fulfilled by 100.3 per cent. There has been a marked increase in the number of evening schools and in their enrollment in the Tatar Autonomous Republic, the Stavropol Territory, and the Belgorod, Voronezh, Kursk, Novgorod, Rostov, Sverdlovsk and Riazan Regions.

The educational and character-training work of many of the evening (shift) and correspondence schools has been noticeably improved.

A great many places this year are offering classes to enable students of evening (shift) schools to increase their job skills. The Cheliabinsk Regional Executive Committee and Economic Council, for instance, have jointly adopted a special decision on the forms and methods of increasing job skills. Such classes are being held in 102 evening schools of the region at the present time.

Nevertheless many grave shortcomings and unresolved problems are still to be found in the work of the evening (shift) and correspondence schools. The average figures on overfulfillment of the plan for the enrollment of pupils conceal defects in the work of the schools of many regions and territories, among them the Vologda, Gorky, Kirov and Kuibyshev Regions.

In the Kursk Region the extensive organizational work carried out by the public education bodies has resulted in significant overfulfillment of the plan for enrollment in the evening schools. The neighboring Orel Region has not lived up to its plan for the development of the network of evening schools and the enrollment of students in them, although conditions there are the same.

One of the great defects of many of the evening (shift) and correspondence schools remains the large number of students who drop out. Also, the level of learning is not high and the students' progress is poor.

We have the immediate task of definitely overcoming all these defects in the work of the evening (shift) and correspondence schools. Practice has revealed that this task can be solved only with the help of the broad public.

As before, the question of increasing the job skills of the students of the evening (shift) schools must receive special attention.

The Ministry of Education ratified this year new syllabuses for the 3rd to 8th grades of the secondary evening schools. The publication of textbooks in the general education subjects for these schools has begun—six of them should be ready for distribution by the beginning of the new school year. The experiments in accelerated completion of the eight-year school course by adults in the evening (shift) schools will continue in the 1961–1962 school year.

The decisions of the January Plenum of the Party Central Committee require that more attention must be paid to the studies of agricultural workers carried on without leaving their jobs. The task N. S. Khrushchev has set us of fearlessly giving leadership positions to the best workers among the rural youth can only be solved if we help them to raise their general educational level. Of course it is harder in rural localities than in cities to organize studies for the youth which do not take them away from productive work. But where this task is given the proper attention by Party and government organizations, and by the leaders of the collective and state farms, it is successfully solved. This year, for instance, 130 young collective farmers are studying in the Korovinskaia School for Rural Youth in the Kursk Region. Of that number, 42 live in the district center, 31 live five kilometers away in the village of Ivanovka, 11—four kilometers away in the village of Malovatka, 24—five kilometers away in the village of Zuyevka, 19—three kilometers away in the village of Nikolskoe, and so on. They all attend school regularly. This has been facilitated by the regular transportation to and from studies provided by the collective farms, by the constant supervision exercised by the collective farm boards over attendance, and also by the combination of general education and vocational training in the schools.

Along with the evening schools, correspondence courses for the agricultural workers must also be more extensively developed. This applies in particular to districts where the settlements, individual farms and collective farm sections are widely dispersed.

Improve the Direction of the Boarding Schools

In implementing the decisions of the 20th Party Congress, local Party and government bodies and the public education departments have done considerable work in setting up boarding schools. Over the past five years, 976 boarding schools with an enrollment of about 300,000 children have been established in the Russian Federation.

Many boarding schools have made substantial progress in their educational and character-training work and can serve as models for the mass of general education schools.

The boarding schools have received unanimous acceptance by our people; their status as the prototype of the school of the future grows with each year. Unfortunately serious defects exist in the work of some of these schools.

The national economic plan for the number of such schools and their enrollment has not been fulfilled year after year. The situation is particularly bad in the Altai Territory and the Novosibirsk and Irkutsk Regions with respect to fulfilling the plan for developing the network of boarding schools. The main reason is the lag in the construction of school buildings and dormitories for these schools.

When the boarding schools were first being established they were placed, in many regions, in buildings that were not suited for their needs, and they lacked the necessary educational equipment. The result has been that some of the boarding schools still lack the proper conditions for normal organization of the educational and character-training process and the children's daily life. Quite a few schools in the Penza Region, for instance, do not have study rooms or workshops. In 1959 the Tula Regional Department of Public Education opened the Gremiachevskaia Boarding School, but in 1960 it had to be closed and the children transferred to another school.

Such an approach to the creation of boarding schools tends to discredit this new type of educational and character-training institution in the eyes of the public and greatly harms an undertaking of tremendous importance to the state.

Important omissions and shortcomings have been revealed this year in the organization and operation of the boarding schools of the Tula Region. It is not only the Tula Regional Executive Committee and Public Education Department which must draw serious conclusions for themselves from the survey conducted there. All public education departments must bear its results in mind in deciding questions connected with the development of the network of boarding schools.

We must shortly examine the affairs of each and every boarding school, with the help of Party and government bodies, to determine how the material and study facilities can be strengthened in those cases where the school does not have the required conditions for conducting properly its educational and character-training work and organizing the life of the children. The construction of new buildings for the boarding schools must be speeded up so that the capital investments allocated are utilized at the proper time. The boarding schools must be opened, as a rule, at the beginning of the school year.

Eight-year boarding schools will be developed primarily in the next few years, but this does not imply that we need to "hold back" the opening of secondary boarding schools.

In our view it is most advisable to open eight-year boarding schools for 240 to 480 pupils, and secondary boarding schools for 330 to 570 pupils. The proposal to open boarding schools for the 9th to 11th grades with three or four parallel classes is worth considering.

In selecting the trades in which the pupils of the secondary boarding schools with production training shall specialize, the same principles that guide all the secondary schools with production training must be followed. It would be wise, however, for the boarding schools of this type to offer vocational training in fields for which not every town or district has the facilities to train personnel, and to see to it that their graduates are placed in jobs within the boundaries of the territory, region or republic where the schools are situated.

Our main efforts right now must be directed towards further improvement of the educational and character-training work of the boarding schools, taking into consideration their specific nature. The experience of our foremost schools shows that excellent results in the education of the children can be acheived quickly, their progress increased, work habits instilled, and they can be drawn into various kinds of cultural and public activities.

We must free the pupils, especially those in the upper grades, of excessive protection, and provide for intelligent initiative and independent activities; the routine in the school must allow them free time.

Solution of the educational tasks of the boarding schools necessitates a closer relationship between the teaching staffs and parents; the parents' assistance must be utilized as much as possible.

The success of the boarding schools depends primarily on their personnel. In the first years of their existence, the schools devoted a good deal of attention to selecting principals, teachers and supervisors, but this attention has slackened, unfortunately, in a number of regions. There are even cases where individuals are casually given positions as teachers in the boarding schools; nor is it rare for "teachers" who have been ousted from the regular schools to find a situation for themselves in the boarding schools. It is not surprising therefore that the level of instruction and character training in some of the boarding schools does not answer the demands made of them.

We need a system by which the best teachers are selected for the boarding schools—teachers who have proved themselves in practical work in the regular schools, who can not only present knowledge very skillfully but also have a talent for character training, for drawing the children close to them, for forming and guiding children's groups.

The direction of the boarding schools must be improved. The experience of the best schools must be carefully studied and introduced. The Academy of Pedagogical Sciences must show greater speed in completing its scientifically substantiated recommendations on the basic problems of educational and character-training work in the boarding schools. All of this will help to raise the work of the boarding schools to the level demanded of them by the Party and government.

At the same time our concern for the children of the children's homes must not slacken. The instructions of the Party Central Committee and the USSR Council of Ministers on the reorganization of the children's homes into boarding schools must be carried out systematically.

Show Constant Concern for the Teacher

It is the teacher who will determine whether the reorganization of the schools will be successful, and it is consequently a matter of major public importance for the schools to be staffed with qualified teachers and for regular work to be conducted with them to raise their qualifications.

This year, in comparison with the last, there are 28,000 more teachers with a higher education in the 5th to 7th grades of the seven- and eight-year and secondary schools. The number of teachers who do not have a higher education and are working in the upper grades of the secondary schools has dropped slightly. The teaching personnel of the evening (shift) schools for worker youth has improved, thanks no doubt to the government decision adopted last year which establishes the same pay for teachers there as in the secondary schools for children.

In the 1961–1962 school year a great many young teachers will find positions in the schools in connection with the great increase in pupil enrollment. According to the statistics of the local education departments, 18,200 young teachers are needed for work in the elementary grades, and another 46,000 for the 5th to 11th grades.

The public education bodies must show the highest sense of public responsibility in the way in which they use the young people sent to work in their schools. We can no longer put up with the instability of teaching staffs, which is especially great in the regions and territories of Siberia and the Far East.

In many cases when teachers leave their jobs it is because proper attention has not been paid to their living and working conditions.

The heads of the education departments must do all that they can to provide the proper living and working conditions for each teacher. They must decide quickly and accurately the school and teaching load for each new teacher and inform him of it. The young teachers must be welcomed in an organized manner, and told about their tasks and working conditions. They must be surrounded with attention.

The reception given young teachers in the Griazovetskii District of the Vologda Region deserves commendation. Last year 39 young teachers arrived in this district. Immediately after the August Teachers Conference (which they attended), the young teachers were invited to the Party District Committee for a talk. There they also met a number of veterans of the teaching profession, honored teachers, whose speeches bolstered their self-confidence and above all bore witness to the kindly, sensitive attitude towards them of their future colleagues. This interest in the young teachers does not diminish after they arrive. This explains why the young teachers of the Griazovetskii District remain at the schools to which they are sent.

The same reception must be given to young teachers in all of the rural districts without exception, and solicitude must be shown all of them from the very first day of their arrival.

Strengthen the Material Facilities of the School to the Utmost

The Law on the School calls for the further consolidation of the material facilities of the schools. In the solution of this task we enjoy the daily asssistance of the Party Central Committee and the USSR and RSFSR Councils of Ministers.

During the past few years there has been a slight improvement in the work of the local soviets and education departments in school construction. In 1960 the plan for the commissioning of new school buildings, including those built with local and collective farm funds, was fulfilled by 103.6 per cent.

All in all, 576,300 places for pupils were made available in 1960 through government capital investment, or 28 per cent more than in 1959. The collective farms have given substantial help in building new schools. Schools seating 251,300 pupils were built with their funds and other resources in 1960, almost 100,000 seats more than during the preceding year. As a result the schools of the Russian Federation had another 827,600 places in 1960.

The school construction plan for 1960 was successfully fulfilled in the Chuvash, Mari and North Ossetian Autonomous Republics, the Khabarovsk Territory, and the Astrakhan, Belgorod, Vologda, Kaliningrad, Kalinin, Lipetsk, Magadan, and Pskov Regions, as well as the Tuva Autonomous Region and the city of Leningrad. At the same time many territories, regions and autonomous republics did not fulfill their tasks satisfactorily. Kirov Region, for example, only fulfilled its plan for the commissioning of new school buildings by 70 per cent, and Orenburg Region—by 56.5 per cent. Many regions, territories and autonomous republics have not kept to the dates set for the completion of school buildings. The quality of the construction work is still low, and there is still substantial dissipation of funds and labor.

A large school construction program is to be carried out in 1961. To avoid increasing the practice of studying in shifts, we must not only ensure the timely fulfillment of the school construction plan, but we must also begin to think right now about additional resources for increasing the space available to our schools—by transferring office buildings to the schools or by building extensions to the existing schools. In particular we must make correct use of the supplementary allocation in 1961 of 40 million rubles by the Council of Ministers of the republic for the purpose of eliminating multiple shifts.

Every year more buildings are being placed at the disposal of the evening schools. This year 1,950 evening schools for worker youth occupy their own premises. Of that number, 748 buildings were provided by industrial enterprises. We must be more insistent in raising with the economic councils and executive committees of the local soviets the question of giving buildings to the evening (shift) schools which can be used for educational purposes.

Reorganization of the work of the schools calls for well-equipped study rooms and workshops. Over the past two years the number of study rooms in the schools has increased by 6,000, and the number of school workshops by more than 4,500. More than 50,000 machine tools were added during the same period, while the number of movie cameras was more than doubled. Nevertheless the general situation as regards school equipment remains difficult.

In the coming year the schools of the republic will receive over 20,000 lathes of all kinds, 40,000 work benches, 24,000 sewing machines, and almost 7,000 movie cameras. By the end of the Seven-Year Plan period every eight-year school should have at least four lathes, and every secondary school from six to eight; all eight-year and secondary schools will be supplied with movie cameras.

Besides supplying the schools with industrial equipment for training purposes, such equipment must be produced on a wide scale in the school workshops, the training shops of the factories, and the production workshops of the secondary schools with production training. The Academy of Pedagogical Sciences must more quickly compile an album of blueprints of training equipment for all the curriculum subjects which can be made by the pupils themselves.

Measures are being taken to supply the schools with better furniture, especially modern desks. By the new school years industry will supply the schools with more than 500,000 such desks.

In accordance with decisions on the subject, 15 house-building and wood-working enterprises are soon to go over to the production of 42 million rubles worth of new furniture for the day and boarding schools. This will meet fully the need for school furniture.

This year, as in previous years, the RSFSR Ministry of Education and the Trade Union Committee are organizing a socialist competition for the best preparation of schools for the new school year. The competition must be conducted in an organized manner so that it is a worthy greeting to the 22nd Party Congress.

Improve Radically the Style of Directing Public Education

Successful reorganization of the schools depends to a great extent on the leadership exercised by the public education bodies in this reorganization.

In the decisions of the January Plenum of the Party Central Committee and in N. S. Khrushchev's speech at the Plenum, as well as in his speeches at the area conferences of advanced agricultural workers, we can find exhaustive instructions as to how the style of leadership of any sector of the economic or cultural life of our country must be changed. Those instructions fully apply to leadership in the field of public education.

In order to direct the work of public education correctly we must rely on the findings of pedagogical science, be well acquainted with the situation in the schools, maintain close contact with the teachers and constantly seek their advice. Only then will our supervision and direction prove effective and help the school staffs to improve daily their instructional and character-training work.

The successful work of many public education departments can be explained by the fact that their heads have drawn on the many-sided support of Party and government bodies, pay constant attention to the opinions of the teachers, and draw the community into the work of building the new school.

The work of the Rostov Regional Department of Public Education, headed by Comrade Ivanenko, is of interest in this connection.

The excellent relationship between the Rostov Regional Department of Public Education and the local Party, government and economic organizations and the schools themselves enabled it to draw heavily on the help of the community in all of its activities. The Public Education Council of the Department has become a real organ of collective leadership, an excellent means of drawing the community into the solution of all the basic tasks of public education.

As a result the situation in the region has improved each year. Twenty-nine of its 49 districts have already achieved universal education and the national economic plan on school enrollment has been fulfilled. The number of students in the schools for working youth is 2,000 in excesss of the plan. The quality of learning and the pupils' proficiency are rising.

The Rostov Region devotes considerable attention to the or-

E. AFANASENKO

ganization of the students' productive work and the development of agricultural experimentation in the schools. Construction of schools and other aspects of strengthening the material base of the schools are being handled well.

But there are still many regional, district and city public education departments which cannot part with their armchair style of leadership, which confine themselves to mailing directives and collecting all kinds of statistics. They do not concentrate on organizational work, on solving the fundamental problems of public education.

The January Plenum of the Party Central Committee teaches us that leadership must be concrete. We can no longer content ourselves with issuing directives of a general nature. School principals and teachers must be told clearly what is expected of them, how they are to reorganize the schools, what concrete tasks must be solved to that end, and how they are to be solved, utilizing the experience of the advanced schools and teachers. At the same time we must constantly raise our demands on workers in the field of education, instill in them a responsible attitude toward their duties and toward the fulfillment of the planned targets and the obligations they have assumed. This can be ensured by systematic and thorough check-ups on the solution of the concrete tasks arising from the Law on the Reorganization of the Schools by the local public education bodies and the schools. The work of each department of public education and school and of their heads and teachers must be appraised not in terms of the number of measures they have carried out, or on the basis of summaries and reports, but by the results.

We must instill in our personnel a spirit of integrity and honesty, teach them to speak frankly and openly of their shortcomings, and firmly put an end to any attempts at deception and sugar-coating. Unfortunately some leaders of schools and education departments, anxious to create the impression that all is well, conceal serious shortcomings in their work and try to attribute their failures and neglect to a variety of "objective" factors.

A good deal of sugar-coating still occurs in the appraisal of the state of universal education. In the Menzelinskii District of the Tatar Autonomous Republic only one pupil was listed as not attending school, whereas a check-up revealed that the number was actually much greater. In the Biliarskii District, the impression was that all the children were going to school, but a check-up showed that several children were not attending school.

Non-objective appraisals of the results of the school's educational work are also encountered. In January of 1961 written tests in mathematics were given in the 5th grades of a number of schools in the Kursk Region. The tests were taken by 1,162 pupils. Approximately one-fourth of them received unsatisfactory marks, although according to the official statistics of these schools only 8.2 per cent of all pupils in the 5th grade had not received passing marks in mathematics. Even more striking disparities between the results of the tests and the official statistics issued by the schools on the pupils' proficiency were brought to light in the Daghestan Autonomous Republic.

In order to improve the work of our public education bodies and schools, we must raise our demands on their staffs. We must be consistently guided by the instructions given by N. S. Khrushchev at the January Plenum of the Party Central Committee concerning the necessity of replacing leaders who were obviously not coping with their responsibilities. We cannot teach such people indefinitely and wait patiently for the day when they will improve their work. The work suffers by it.

There must be more boldness in promoting young teachers who know their work and are capable of solving our public education tasks at the level of present-day standards to responsible positions in the schools and the district and city public education departments.

The new Party program to be adopted at the 22nd Party Congress will undoubtedly define the role of the Soviet school in the further building of communism, and will raise new and complicated tasks for the development of public education in our country. We must all prepare for the successful solution of those tasks. To do this, we must make every effort and lose no time in remedying the shortcomings in our work of fulfilling the decisions of the 20th and 21st Party Congresses and the Law on the School.

There can be no doubt that the Soviet teachers and public education workers will do everything in their power to greet the 22nd Party Congress worthily, with further progress in the education of the coming generations as roundly developed and active builders of the Communist society.

1-2 Education in Latin America*

A DIRECT HEIR OF SIXTEENTH CENTURY SPAIN AND Portugal, Latin America, by virtue of homogeneity of race, language, religion, and culture, constitutes a distinct civilization, although with important national variations. Within the pattern of its common culture, Latin America shows great diversity—in geography, climate, population, wealth of natural resources, etc. Such differences give a unique character to each of the nations of the region.

The Social Structure

The Spanish and Portuguese *conquistadores* brought to the New World the rigidly stratified and inflexible class society which existed in the Iberian peninsula in the sixteenth century. Class distinctions remain strong in spite of the advance of democratic ideas. In education, the class orientation still has effects that are incalculable. It markedly limits educational facilities at the elementary level, resulting in high proportions of children between the ages of 7 and 14 who do not attend school. This selectivity as a function of class membership also accounts for much of the failure of youngsters who start school to attain the

---

* Irma Salas, "Education in Latin America," *Teachers College Record*, Vol. 63, No. 5 (February, 1962), pp. 337–342.

Irma Salas

higher grades. More than 80% of elementary school children discontinue their attendance during the six years called for by the present curriculum, and a similar but slightly smaller loss occurs in the secondary schools. Entrance to the university is restricted to an infinitesimal proportion of even those who have an opportunity to enter the elementary grades.

Naturally, this state of affairs most strongly affects the weaker socio-economic groups. In 1930, the percentage of students from lower class origins attending secondary schools in Chile was only 13.6, and out of 23 such students enrolled in the first year of high school, only four were graduated. In 1950, improvements were attested to by the fact that nearly one-fourth of those graduating from secondary schools belonged to the working classes. Even so, the process of democratization has far to go, and it has not yet touched the Latin American universities, where the proportion of students from the less privileged strata of society is minuscule.

A further indication of class consciousness is reflected in the considerable growth of Latin American private schools, especially at the secondary level. In many countries, 40% of the high school enrollment is accounted for by the independent schools. While it is true that many of these institutions belong to various Roman Catholic Orders and that many parents send their children to them for religious reasons, it is also true that a decided sense of social class influences their decision.

In general, members of the upper classes send their children to private schools, which, besides the fees paid by parents, are subsidized in some countries by the state. As a result, they usually enjoy superior buildings, facilities, and faculties. As a consequence, upper class interest in the improvement and extension of public education is difficult to mobilize.

Still another effect of the class system is the existence of an unspoken assumption that the secondary schools belong to the middle and upper classes, whereas the common elementary school has been the province of the working classes. In many instances, this point of view results in a dual system of elementary education funded by the state. On the one hand, there is the common elementary school; on the other, there is the elementary school attached to the high school or the elementary preparatory school. Although graduates of the common school have, in principle, the right to be admitted to the first year of the secondary school, they can rarely exercise it because of a lack of vacancies. Students who have attended the other two types of elementary school, however, have automatic access to the high school.

From the point of view of the curriculum, this situation means a lack of articulation between elementary and secondary school programs. As the educational home of working class children, the elementary school teaches the basic instruments of learning and the basic information in the various fields of knowledge. The high schools, charged with the instruction of the upper classes, are concerned essentially with transmitting a humanistic and scientific culture and preparing their students for the university. Even now, the elementary and secondary schools are looked upon not as stages in the total process of education, but as the vehicles for providing different types of education to different types of people.

Under such conditions, it is not surprising that elementary teachers receive very inferior salaries in comparison with the incomes of their secondary school colleagues, and their training in Latin American normal schools is sharply different from that provided for high school teachers. For the same reasons, technical education in Latin American schools has been slow to take hold and is still far from the rate of expansion and efficiency demanded by the economic needs of the region. Parallel to the academic high school and requiring an elementary school certificate for admission, the technical school was designed to train the children of working class people for the job market and to supplement the education of high school graduates who, because the secondary schools tend to exclude utilitarian and vocational considerations in their curricula, had no direct preparation for making a living. In some countries, this pattern is changing, but the traditional scorn of the *caballero* for manual labor is still vigorous and influential in many places.

In the universities, designed to train leaders in the professions, the sciences, literature, and the arts, the same selective and class-related forces are at work. In each nation, approximately only 10% of those who finish secondary school (themselves a remarkably small fraction of the total adolescent population) enroll in college.

State Influences

If we turn from the structure of society to the character of the state itself, we find the same heritage of the *conquistadores*. Public administration is typically highly centralized, affording little opportunity for local groups to participate effectively in the study and solution of their own problems. Governmental authority is conceived in absolutistic terms, and its influence pervades almost every aspect of Latin American life.

In the administration of the schools, the same principles and patterns prevail. In each of the 20 republics, there is a Ministry or Secretariat of Education, a governmental agency which regulates and controls the schools, whether public or private. Even in those countries where a federal form of state government permits the decentralization of school administration, the provinces, although they may create their own elementary schools, are dependent on the federal power for funds and are technically and administratively responsible to the ministry. With few exceptions, Latin American secondary schools are maintained and administered directly by the central government, and the universities are generally state institutions, autonomous in principle but nationally financed and subject to the national laws that create and regulate them.

This centralized, authoritarian conception of the state has far-reaching educational influences, perhaps the most important of which is local apathy. With little or no likelihood of influencing the nature and quality of their schools, local communities characteristically show little interest in education, and the schools themselves tend in most countries to become isolated and unresponsive to the needs and aspirations of the locales in which they are situated. They contrast sharply with those cultures in which education has a vitality and a compelling aspect that grow out of the fact that it is a community enterprise of great and direct local moment.

In Latin America, the curriculum, the methods of teaching, the system of examinations, the internal organization, and virtually all details of school procedure are prescribed by the central authority. Occasionally, there is consultation with representatives of the teachers' organizations, but generally there is none. The schools therefore show a degree of uniformity that correctly points toward formalism, a lack of regard for local conditions and needs, and an unsusceptibility to change which, in this rapidly changing world, can leave stagnation as the only alternative.

Such a situation reflects, of course, a culturally based tendency to seek inspiration predominantly in the past and a belief in the static quality of a heritage that should be preserved and transmitted but not enriched and modified by a grappling with new circumstances. Teachers themselves, lacking the opportunity through either their training or their experience to develop initiative, grow readily accustomed to following the prescriptions of the centralized authority. In general, they even oppose those reforms that the system itself occasionally requires, and they hardly look with favor on novelty and change.

It is within such a social context that Latin American education has been shaped. Some aspects of it will undoubtedly alter, although slowly. Some are essential to the culture and must remain. The challenge is to find within this matrix the opportunities to create new structures that will make it possible for education to become one of the directive agencies of the social development through which all of Latin America must soon pass.

Educational Access

In all Latin American countries, national laws establish free and compulsory education for children from six or seven years of age to some period from age 12 to 15. The modal age range covered is from seven to 14. Secondary, technical, and higher public education are also practically free, and children from low income families are exempt from the payment of school fees, which are generally quite low.

In spite of these legal provisions, however, access to education in the entire region has been, until very recently, remarkably low. In 1950, 49% of the Latin American population aged 15 or over had either not attended school at all or had abandoned it before completing the *first* grade. Forty-four per cent had received some elementary education, but only about 8% had fulfilled the period of "compulsory" education. Similarly, although 6% had had the benefit of some secondary or technical schooling, no more than 2% had completed it. Only one per cent had begun or finished any form of higher education.

In consequence, the level of education in 16 Latin American countries in 1950, defined by the number of school years completed by the adult population, averaged 2.2. It fluctuated from 3.6 as the average in the most educated nations, to less than 2.0 in an intermediate group of countries, to 1.0 for the least educated cluster of national units. For the adults who had had an opportunity to attend school at all (51%), the average educational level was 4.4 school years, with very little difference among the groupings by country. The number of people who have had educational experience beyond the elementary school is only 16% of those who *complete* the elementary grades.

To understand these facts, it is necessary to comprehend the rate of growth in Latin American population. The average yearly increase in population in the region is about 2.6% as against a world average of 1.6%. Among other things, this means that the nations concerned must make an effort roughly 60% greater than the average effort of the rest of the world to increase their educational services merely to keep pace with their growing numbers. Because population increase is correlated with economic underdevelopment, those countries that can least afford it must face the heaviest expense in maintaining schools.

How well this problem has been dealt with can be estimated by taking enrollment trends against an index of educational need, the extent of national illiteracy.

Latin America can be roughly divided into three groups of countries on the basis of illiteracy rates. The first (Argentina, Uruguay, Chile, Costa Rica, and Cuba) has an average rate of illiteracy of 17%. The group accounts for 20% of the region's population with 40% of its own people located in rural areas. Sixty-six per cent of the population in these five nations are 15 years of age or older, and the per capita income lies between $300 and $349. The second group of countries (Panama, Paraguay, Colombia, Mexico, Ecuador, Venezuela, Brazil, and Peru) has an average rate of illiteracy of 49%. Accounting for 70% of the Latin American people, it has a rural population equal to 62%; and with 58% of its people 15 or over, the group has a per capita income of from only $100 to $149. Finally, the third group (Dominican Republic, El Salvador, Nicaragua, Honduras, Bolivia, Guatemala, and Haiti) shows an illiteracy rate of 70% among 10% of the regional population. Where 74% of these people are rurally located and 59% 15 or older, the per capita income is less than $100.

When one examines elementary school enrollments in these three groups of nations for 1956, one finds that 63.2% of the children between the ages of five and 14 in the first group were actually in school; in the second group, the figure was 43.9%, and in the third, 36.6%. The *increase* in enrollment from 1950 to 1959 was 15% for the nations of the first group, 46% for those of the second, and 70% for the third set of countries. Secondary school enrollments for the same period increased four times faster than elementary registrations in the first group, showed the same rate of inrcease as elementary enrollments in the second, and represented only two-thirds of the elementary increase in the third group. As for higher education, there were less than a half million students in universities throughout Latin America in 1956, about 23.5 for every 10,000 of population. Even so, it marked a rise from the 1950 figure of only 15.9 per 10,000 inhabitants of the region.

Enrollments at various educational levels by women reflect a curious pattern. In the elementary schools, girls account for approximately 49% of registrations. At the secondary level, however, they represent only 38% of the total enrollment. In higher education, omitting teacher training, women's enrollments reach 24%, almost the same as in more highly developed countries than those of Latin America.

As one would expect from this portrait of Latin American schools, the financial investment is low in absolute terms. The per capita expense per year is less than $5, whereas more advanced nations average better than $15 per inhabitant per year on education. In terms of budgetary proportions, however, the appropriations for education annually average about 17.7% of the general national budget, ranging from 8% to 34%. Again, a central problem is that of mounting expense in a region least able to bear increasing costs.

Effort and Progress

Despite the magnitude of Latin America's problems, including the stratified social system and the traditions of centralized and authoritarian government inherited from the Spain and Portugal of the sixteenth century, the region has made considerable progress in coping with its educational difficulties during the past three or four decades. Almost all the nations of the region have made important efforts to extend their services in spite of the drain on resources and energy created by concurrent heavy demands for accelerated development socially, politically, and economically, as well as educationally.

In all countries, the segments of the population that enjoy the highest class status have educational opportunities that often equal those in far better developed parts of the world. It is among the lower classes, particularly in rural areas, that greater effort must be expended and an enlarged access to schools created. That progress is occurring on this score is indicated by the increased elementary school enrollments in 1959 over 1950, primarily concentrated in the most needful nations (those with the most virulent rates of illiteracy) and in rural sectors of the region. Increments in attendance at the secondary schools and in higher education have also kept reasonable pace with the expanding population.

While educational opportunities for women are somewhat inferior to those available to men, they tend to equal them or even slightly to surpass them as the average educational level of the population improves generally.

All these developments, although often heartbreakingly small, represent an effort by the Latin American countries and their people to pull themselves up by their bootstraps. Improving education is only a part, if a central and vital part, of an urgent attempt to deal with a long history of poverty, poor health, economic dependency, and political instability, the seamy side of the Iberian legacy to the New World. But that heritage also includes sources of proud strength that, under the stimulus of the modern world as it has impinged upon the region through new developments in communication and transportation, are beginning to respond in new ways to the needs of the people. The spasms of Latin America dealing with its grave educational concerns are essentially the stirrings of a giant who has slept too long.

1-3 Education and political independence in Africa*

It is no use rushing matters or pretending that political decisions are an adequate substitute for planning and partnership for education and economic development.

THOSE WORDS, TAKEN FROM THE LEADING ARTICLE OF *The Times* (London) of July 9, 1960, are the theme of this paper. Toward the end of that article the writer draws comparisons between the events leading to independence and those accompanying the attainment of independence in Ghana and the Belgian Congo. Lest English readers might prove complacent about British achievement the article concludes with a warning that in parts of British East Africa the situation is "none too good."

The first point to make is that while there is a close relationship between educational policy and attainment of satisfactory forms of political independence, this does not mean that one particular educational policy is necessarily the only one. The educational policies followed in the past in Africa by the major colonial powers have differed considerably in character. All

---

* L. J. Lewis, "Education and Political Independence in Africa," *Comparative Education Review,* Vol. 4, No. 1 (June, 1961), pp. 39–49.

L. J. Lewis

generalizations are inadequate, but there are essential differences in the policies followed by the French, Belgian, and British governments which can be expressed in general terms. The French, until very recently, assumed that French civilization was the best of all possible civilizations and visualized France Metropolitan and France D'Outre Mer as a unity. In educational terms this was expressed in the concept of Africans and Asians learnings to be French. Education was planned, on the one hand, to provide for the vocational needs of trade, industry, and administration, and, on the other hand, to ensure that the necessary élite should be truly French.

Belgian policy was much more parental in concept and assumed a long-term period of tutelage, during which the attainment of material well-being was the first priority. In consequence, until very recently, provision of educational facilities omitted serious consideration of anything other than training for subordinate vocational responsibilities.

British policy, less logically thought out than the other policies, since the 1920's has been governed by the assumption that political independence was a foreseeable end point, but at the same time it has been much influenced by economic and social considerations.

If these generalizations are valid, it would follow that British policy would most likely have prepared the Africans for political independence. But the best that can be said about it is that political independence has come more smoothly in British West Africa than elsewhere. Whether this will continue to be so is open to question. As regards the French territories, though some of the newly independent ones are in difficulties, such as the Cameroons and the Congo Republic, certainly some of them—Mali, Sudan, for example—are managing well with their immediate problems. One thing can be said with a reasonable degree of authority: Whatever the educational policy that has been pursued, those territories that have the longest enjoyed educational systems attempting to provide education at all levels are most likely to survive the difficulties of assuming political, economic, and social responsibilities consequential upon attaining political independence.

Expansion of primary education

Having indulged in that degree of generalization, let us examine in some detail the educational provisions in various parts of Africa. Whether a government has come early or late to recognizing that political independence is the goal of its African peoples, there is general appreciation that democratic independence, in the Western sense, is dependent upon a franchise that has sufficient education to participate intelligently in the running of public affairs at local, national, and international levels. The acceptance of this has resulted in attempts everywhere to provide some form of basic education, of four to six years' duration, for every child, and to intensify efforts to make the adult members of the community literate.

The approach has varied. In Ghana and in Western and Eastern Nigeria, the attainment of universal, free primary education has been made an absolute priority. In other English-speaking territories this objective has been accepted in principle. In French-speaking Africa, the principle is accepted, the rate and method of working out its application being left to local interpretation.

The consequences have been, in every instance, a phase of rapid expansion, which has strained the resources in respect of the provision of buildings and equipment, produced serious dilution of the quality of the teaching, and reduced the effectiveness of supervision. Even where no attempt has been made on political grounds to provide free primary education, most African communities have shown in recent years so strong a desire for education for their children that rapid expansion has been inevitable. Between 1946 and 1956 school enrollment in most territories expanded over 100 per cent. In the former French Equatorial Africa territories, the increase in enrollment was 314.5 per cent. In the Western Region of Nigeria, where a system of free and universal primary education was set up in 1955, the increase in the primary school enrollment was 142 per cent in five years. In Ghana, the primary school enrollment rose from 154,360 in 1951 to 455,053 in 1958.

Political decisions to expand the provision of primary education, whether taken by dependent or independent governments, have been in every case motivated by two considerations. In the first place there has been appreciation of the fact that political responsibility in democratic terms is dependent upon an informed electorate. Second, that social and economic development are dependent upon the intelligent and understanding cooperation of the community to implement plans, and upon an adequate supply of skilled manpower.

It is less easy to determine the major sources of drive for the educational expansion. While it is true to say that the climate of political change contributed to the acceleration of the expansion of primary education, it must be recognized that plans for expansion were being prepared before the full significance of the nature of the political developments had become clear. It is equally difficult to determine to what extent local politicians were responsible for stimulating the demand for education, by giving it priority in their policy statements and in their electioneering campaigns, and to what extent they were giving explicit expression to the desire of the demos they sought to represent and to lead. In some respects, the sudden expansion of primary education in the late forties and fifties was the outcome of the work of missions and governments in the previous quarter of a century.

Resultant problems

The rapid expansion of primary education has resulted in a number of problems of great moment. The number of teachers required has risen far beyond the resources available for training them; at the same time the number of children capable of benefiting from secondary education has increased far beyond the facilities available. Moreover, there was not and could not be enough money for building and equipping more schools. The enormous response to the provision of primary school facilities has resulted in a general lowering of the age of admission. In consequence large numbers of children are now completing the formal primary course at too early an age, and at too early a stage of physical maturity, to be able to enter gainful employment, even when there are opportunities available.

Before considering these problems it would be wise to get some measure of the present provision of primary education. The picture presented in twenty-two territories is shown in Table 1-1.

Excluding the Lagos figures, as representing an arbitrary unit within a territory, the highest ratios of enrollment are Eastern Region, Nigeria, approximately 80 per cent; Ghana, approximately 60 per cent; Belgian Congo, approximately 55 per cent; and Nyasaland, approximately 50 per cent. By contrast, the Northern Region of Nigeria has approximately only 5 per cent of the children of school age attending the primary school, and former Italian Somaliland has approximately 6 per cent.

Now the significance of these figures is that except for a few isolated areas such as Lagos and the Northern Rhodesia industrial area, every country is still faced with a formidable task in providing facilities for primary education for every child of school age, and this despite the tremendous expansion that has taken place. The task is seen to be all the more formidable when it is recognized that coupled with it is the need to expand and improve facilities for the training of teachers for the schools.

In all countries there is a lack of teachers to fill the new posts, and in most countries, except at the lowest level of unqualified and untrained teacher, there are difficulties in meeting the need. Indicative of the dimension of the problem is the situation in the Northern Region of Nigeria, where pressure for expansion is still low, and where

TABLE 1-1. PRIMARY EDUCATION, POPULATION AND ENROLLMENT

Territory	*Year*	*School Age Population **	*Primary School Enrollment*
Central and West Africa:			
Belgian Congo	1957–58	2,711,800	1,572,824
Cameroons (French)	1958	640,000	293,977
Ivory Coast	1958	618,000	125,727
Dahomey	1959	345,000	81,107
Gabon	1958	82,000	39,763
Gambia	1958	58,000	6,465
Ghana	1958	967,200	540,921
Upper Volta	1959	694,000	40,923
Liberia	1959	250,000	53,232
Nigeria			
Lagos	1958	67,400	56,688
Northern Region	1957	3,608,600	205,769
Western Region	1957	1,347,200	982,755
Eastern Region	1957	1,585,400	1,209,167
Republic of the Congo	1958	156,000	78,962
Senegal	1958	460,000	80,473
Sierra Leone	1958	428,000	69,276
Sudan	1958	740,000	42,052
Togoland	1959	220,000	78,689
East Africa:			
Ethiopia	1958–59	4,000,000	158,005
Federation of Rhodesia and Nyasaland			
Northern Rhodesia	1958	444,000	243,926
Nyasaland	1958	520,000	269,693
Kenya	1958	1,198,000	601,410
Madagascar	1959	1,010,000	364,217
Uganda	1957	1,153,000	418,179
Somaliland (Italian)	1958–59	264,000	16,485
Tanganyika	1958	1,733,067	403,301

SOURCE: *On the Needs of Tropical Africa in the Field of Primary and Secondary Education* (Unesco/Ed/Africa/2, Paris, 15 January 1960).

* Estimated at 20 per cent of the total population.

only one child in eighteen is enrolled at the primary school, while five hundred teachers (5 per cent of the total primary teaching staff) need to be enrolled each year in order to fill existing vacancies. Only in Ghana and in Northern Rhodesia can it be said that the supply of teachers for primary schools is beginning to approximate to needs in terms of numbers of persons with satisfactory minimum qualifications.

Apart from questions of policy about the recruitment and conditions of service of teachers, political changes have exercised a profound influence on the status of the teaching profession. Where steps have been taken to prepare for political independence, great demands have been made upon teachers as the most important pool of persons with suitable educational qualifications for service on committees as elected or nominated representatives, for leadership in political organizations, and for membership of parliamentary and local authority political machinery. In consequence the schools have suffered on two counts. At all levels of political activity, participation by teachers has resulted in much absenteeism from school duties, and the more able or the more politically active members of the profession have left for full-time public or political service. This, however, is not the total story. Political independence is invariably accompanied by an expansion of the public services, the development of diplomatic services, and a deliberate policy of reduction in the number of expatriate employees. Since the teaching profession is the main source of educated persons, it is exploited by government, commerce, and industry to meet their more urgent staffing needs.

This has produced a disastrous situation which up to the present has not received the serious attention it warrants. Various stopgap measures have been attempted, such as a temporary lowering of standards of academic and professional qualification, and less demanding conditions of training. But a satisfactory solution requires an examination of the total educational process; in particular, there is need for a reassessment of schooling in terms of the current social and economic conditions, and a reappraisal of the methods of recruiting and training teachers. The primary school curriculum is still in all essentials that portion of the traditional curriculum that can be covered in four or six years. It is a curriculum devised essentially to lead on to the conventional western type of secondary school. It is true that some effort has been made to give a rural bias to the content, but in no instance has the curriculum been reviewed in the light of changing circumstances. Because in the past the primary school has been regarded as the first stage in the process of formal education, it has been dominated by the qualifications required for admission to the secondary school. But the majority of children attending the primary school receive no opportunity of further formal education. The best percentage of general secondary school enrollment from the primary school is 15.4 per cent in Ghana. Of the twenty-two territories listed in Table 1-1, only six have a percentage enrollment of between 5 and 10 per cent, and six have a percentage enrollment of less than 1 per cent.

The vast majority of children can expect nothing more than a short period of formal education, in most cases four to six years, and yet, shortly, will have to assume immense political, economic, and social responsibilities in conditions of great strain. In these circumstances it is obvious that the content and the treatment of the primary school needs drastic revision. Such revision is likely to result in the need for a new approach to the training of teachers.

Another aspect of the problem of providing enough teachers to meet the increase in the primary school enrollment is that of expanding the training facilities and providing adequate salaries. In the foreseeable future none of the countries can hope to find sufficient money to meet all the costs from their own resources. Yet something must be attempted if the economic and social status of the teachers is not to deteriorate at a time when the provision of education is so important to general development.

It will not be easy to solve these problems. Whatever financial assistance may be forthcoming from the former metropolitan countries, either directly or through international machinery, there will have to be a radical revision of the content of primary education and of the methods of training teachers.

At the same time the taxpaying community must be educated politically. Here the newly independent governments have failed as completely as did their predecessors, despite the existence of official information services. In Ghana, the failure to prepare the community for the idea of dispensing with a middle school leaving examination made it necessary to resuscitate the examination two years after it had been dropped. Failure to prepare the people for the increase in local rates to meet the rescinding of the payment of fees in the primary school had equally unfortunate consequences. In the Western and Eastern Regions of Nigeria there were similar failures.

Unless the members of a free society understand the nature of changes and developments taking place they are unlikely to cooperate or accept financial responsibility for education. This lesson is not yet fully appreciated by many of the political leaders. It is a lesson that must be learned if genuine local responsibility is to develop.

Problems of expansion of secondary education

Turning to secondary education and to technical and vocational education at the secondary level in these same countries, the factual picture is as presented in Table 1-2.

Arthur Lewis, Principal of the University College of the West Indies, estimates that the proportion of the population that should receive secondary education, if the needs of a country for educated manpower are to be met, is 4 per cent of each generation. Whether one accepts this or not, it is clear from the figures in Table 1-2 that the existing provision for secondary education is everywhere inadequate.

The supply of qualified secondary school teachers is even less satisfactory than is the supply of primary school teachers. In Ghana, for instance, ten years after the opening of an Institute of Education to give professional training to university graduates, the number of candidates put forward for the first postgraduate professional examination was thirteen.

Here the political leaders are faced with a serious dilemma. For prestige reasons, as well as for less emotional reasons, it is necessary to recruit local graduates as quickly as possible into the administration and into overseas services. Similarly, to a lesser but still significant extent, commerce and industry are anxious to obtain the services of local graduates. The demands of these avenues to employment are being met at the expense of the secondary schools and colleges. The gaps thus created in the staffing of secondary schools can be filled, in part, by recruiting expatriates. There are not the political objections, at least not to the same degree, to employing expatriates for teaching as there are to employing them in administrative posts. Unfortunately, recruitment of expatriates has been made difficult by a number of developments, all of which add up to reduced security, reduced opportunities of promotion, and conditions of service which do not compete favorably with those in other forms of employment.

Curricula

One feature in which modifications might have been expected in consequence of political independence, namely, the content of the curriculum, has received scarcely any attention. In every territory almost all the secondary schools follow the traditional academic curriculum which is so familiar. Technical and "modern" curricula have received little attention. For instance, in Ghana, the only major change that has been made in the secondary school curriculum is the introduction of French. This decision was political, reflecting the "island" nature of Ghana in relation to the French-speaking territories around it and Dr. Kwame Nkrumah's concern for Pan-Africanism. In the French-speak-

TABLE 1-2. SECONDARY EDUCATION, POPULATION AND ENROLLMENT

Territory	*Year*	*School Age Population **	*Secondary Enrollment*	*Technical and Vocational Enrollment*
Central and West Africa:				
Belgian Congo	1957–58	2,711,800	12,158	28,677
Cameroons (French)	1958	640,000	6,645	3,344
Ivory Coast	1958	618,000	4,310	794
Dahomey	1959	345,000	2,881	737
Gabon	1958	82,000	1,025	131
Gambia	1958	58,400	674	47
Ghana	1958	967,200	83,096	4,979
Upper Volta	1959	694,000	1,841	502
Liberia	1959	250,000	3,046	592
Nigeria				
Lagos	1958	67,400	4,591	1,578
Northern Region	1957	3,608,600	3,651	872
Western Region	1957	1,347,200	46,810	220
Eastern Region	1957	1,585,400	12,242	3,100
Republic of the Congo	1958	156,000	1,975	1,284
Senegal	1958	460,000	5,066	1,036
Sierra Leone	1958	428,000	5,904	333
Sudan	1958	740,000	1,790	959
Togoland	1959	220,000	1,847	526
East Africa:				
Ethiopia	1958–59	4,000,000	4,496	2,450
Federation of Rhodesia and Nyasaland				
Northern Rhodesia	1958	444,000	1,890	1,840
Nyasaland	1958	520,000	1,169	927
Kenya	1958	1,198,000	3,922	1,114
Madagascar	1959	1,010,000	19,116	6,314
Uganda	1957	1,153,400	21,599	3,807
Somaliland (Italian)	1958–59	264,000	822	915
Tanganyika	1958	1,733,067	3,499	1,366

SOURCE: *On the Needs of Tropical Africa in the Field of Primary and Secondary Education* (Unesco/Ed/Africa/2, Paris, 15 January 1960).

* Estimated at 20 per cent of the total population.

ing territories themselves, political independence has not produced any immediate radical changes in the curriculum, except that in Guinea English is now taught on the same footing as French. The urge to attain full expression of the "African personality" has led to a desire to adjust the balance between the use of French and African languages in the schools, but it is realized that for the time being French must continue to be the main vehicle of education until an adequate supply of material in the accepted African languages is available. Incidentally, while considering language as a medium of instruction and as part of the content of the curriculum at both the primary and secondary levels, it is important to note that it is loaded with political implications. Undue emphasis upon the significance of the mother-tongue can become a divisive influence in territories where no single African language or language group is dominant. At the same time, whatever the merits of an African language, political independence tends to increase the range of international contacts and activities; while technological development almost of necessity involves the use of one or other of the major Western languages. The problems are further complicated by the lack of indigenous linguistic authorities to guide political decisions. One of the chief defects in the newly established university institutions is the failure up to the present to develop vigorous faculties and departments for the study of African languages.

The development of vocational secondary education has been more marked under French and Belgian auspices than under British. This in part reflects the differences of general policy, in part the differences in the development of primary and secondary education. One factor that may bring about fairly rapid changes in this direction is the changing emphasis upon the value of the technician as opposed to the white-collar worker that is an inevitable concomitant of economic development, especially if the latter is planned and the planning is accompanied by effective manpower surveys. The most potent influences in this respect are likely to be the World Bank (the International Bank for Reconstruction and Development), the International Monetary Fund, the C.I.A., and the United Nations Special Fund. The latter, the most recent agency in the field, is engaged in three types of project; (1) preparing surveys of material resources; (2) conducting research programs leading to expanded use of local materials; and (3) establishing training institutes. The expansion of the activities of the United Nations Special Fund puts a premium upon the enlistment of local effort and upon local financial support for the projects undertaken. This is an approach likely to appeal to political leaders in the newly independent territories and to encourage a critical examination of the content and the balance of technical and vocational training at the secondary school level.

University and postsecondary education

In the sphere of University and postsecondary technological education, there is greater diversity. Apart from Fourah Bay College, Sierra Leone, Gordon College, Khartoum, and minor provision of university teaching facilities at Achimota (Gold Coast), Yaba Higher College, Nigeria, and Makerere College, Uganda, the provision of local facilities for higher education is virtually a postwar development. In the British territories the postwar development was based upon common principles and common machinery. While allowing for local variations, all the planning was guided by the advisory and administrative services of the Inter-University Council for Higher Education (in the Colonies) Overseas for university institutions and by the Council for Overseas Colleges of Arts, Science and Technology for technical education. The University of London accepted responsibility for the granting of university degrees under a scheme of special relationship, and the Council for Overseas Colleges of Arts, Science and Technology assisted the institutions under its auspices to negotiate schemes to gain recognition of their qualifications by the appropriate professional and educational bodies in the United Kingdom.

The overriding policy was the establishment of autonomous institutions similar in character and standard to those existing in the United Kingdom. No timetable was drawn up for reaching independent status, but the tendency has been for the university institutions to take independent status with or soon after attainment of political independence.

Governments have shown considerable generosity toward these institutions and on the whole have fully respected their autonomy. However, in Ghana, Prime Minister Nkrumah has recently made remarks suggesting a sensitivity to the critical attitude of some members of the university college that might augur political interference with college affairs. At the present moment, a committee of enquiry is being set up by the government to review the facilities for higher education in Ghana. An outcome of this could be that political considerations will affect policy and control of the institutions of higher learning. In Nigeria, political ambition and regional interests have led Dr. Azikwe (formerly Prime Minister, Eastern Region, Nigeria) to press for the establishment of a separate university for Eastern Nigeria under American sponsorship, in contrast to University College, Ibadan, which was established under the auspices of the Inter-University Council for Higher Education Overseas. His original anti-British, or perhaps more correctly pro-American, attitude has, however, been modified and the project is now going forward under the joint auspices of Michigan State University and the University of London. Here we see local political interests bringing about an interesting experiment in joint Anglo-American sponsorship. Political interest has also been shown recently in Northern Nigeria where it is intended to establish a university for Northern Nigeria at Kano. How this proposal will fit in with the recommendations of the Ashby Committee at present reviewing the higher education needs of Nigeria for the next twenty years remains to be seen. What is clear is that political independence is likely to result in an emphasis on regional rather than on federal interests. Potentially the country is large enough for this to be of no great significance in the long run, but there may be difficulties in the initial stages. One of these, of course, will be financial. Another complication is likely to occur because political leadership in Northern Nigeria, which is Islamic, may look to the Sudan and possibly Egypt for assistance rather than to the United Kingdom or the United States. What is almost certainly true is that political influence will be against cooperation with the university institutions in Southern Nigeria.

In East Africa, federal or independent development of university resources is also likely to be influenced by political changes. At present, the University College of East Africa (Makerere, Uganda) serves Uganda, Kenya, and Tanganyika, and the Royal College of Arts, Science and Technology also serves all three territories. With the acceptance of the recommendations of the Lockwood Committee (1959), these institutions, together with a third university institution to be established in Tanganyika, will form a Federal University of East Africa. Political considerations may, however, make for difficulties in that the three territories are proceeding at different rates toward political independence, and Tanganyika, the territory least well equipped financially and educationally, will be the first to attain political independence. At present it has no institution of university pretensions.

Whereas the institutions in British or former British territories have had the full confidence of the local communities from their beginnings, this was not so in French Africa. For instance, in the early stages the Dakar Institute of Higher Studies (1950), now the University of Dakar, was regarded with suspicion as being an attempt to deprive the French African of the privilege of university education in Metropolitan France. These early suspicions were intensified by clashes between students sent to metropolitan universities and the supervisory and advisory bodies whose excessive parentalism, coupled with what was interpreted as stringent if not inadequate allowances, created a sense of discrimination that was resented by the African students and lent a degree of verisimilitude to anti-French agitation.

The development of higher education facilities in the Belgian Congo was initiated much later than in other parts of Africa. Lovanium University was opened in 1954 under the auspices of the University of Louvain. The State University of the Belgian Congo and Ruanda-Urundi was opened in 1956 under the direction of a Conseil d'Administration which includes in its membership the RECTEUR and representatives of the University as well as representatives of the Polytechnic Faculty of Mons and of the Institute of Agronomy and the School of Veterinary Medicine in Belgium. The consequences of political independence in the Congo for these institutions is difficult to foretell. There is no immediate prospect of their gaining autonomy but, at the same time, the anti-Belgian climate of opinion may make it impossible to continue development under direct Belgian patronage.

In all the territories expanded facilities for higher education are badly needed and there is not enough money to provide them. Up to the present, because the supply of persons qualified to benefit from higher education is limited, and because economic and industrial developments have not yet reached the stage where the shortage of persons with university or technological qualifications is serious, the need for these expanded facilities has been masked. The two territories where the needs are certain to be critical in the immediate future are the Belgian Congo and Tanganyika. In the former, political leadership, or rather failure to prepare Africans for it, may already have struck a near mortal blow to immediate prospects of expanding facilities; whereas in Tanganyika there is every hope that the political leaders will be able to obtain the support necessary for financing the development of higher education.

A feature of higher education which carries strong political overtones is the provision of scholarships for education overseas. In financial terms this often appears to be cheaper than making local provision, and in technological fields it is sometimes the only immediate possibility. But it is a policy that thwarts national prestige, and also delays the establishment of local teaching, research, and advisory services. The importance of the latter two aspects of institutions of higher education has not always been fully recognized by politicians anxious to be independent of foreign technical assistance.

Competition from interested parties outside Africa for influence in the newly independent territories has also introduced political considerations. In addition to the major ideological competition between Russia and the West, there has been competition between Western countries to obtain influence. In East Africa a scheme of scholarships for Africans to go to America has been sponsored by a group motivated by American anti-colonialism; this has been pursued without regard to local provisions. Unexpected problems, however, have made it more difficult than had first appeared for these efforts to be as fruitful as their sponsors hoped. One thing that needs to be kept in mind is that unfamilar qualifications are not always accepted locally. Where political independence has been attained, interpretation of qualifications is almost invariably in the hands of persons who obtained their qualifications under the former metropolitan regime, and they tend to show considerable, and sometimes excessive, conservatism in assessing "foreign" qualifications. Furthermore, persons likely to be under influences considered detrimental to the independence and authority of the newly established political power are not readily accepted for appointment to posts of influence.

Because so many factors affect the future provision of higher education, it is important that all resources, national and international, should be consolidated if the development of higher education in Africa is to proceed rapidly enough to meet African needs, to ensure the integrity of political independence, and to provide for the autonomy of the universities.

The curricula pursued in all the university and technological institutions are very closely related to those followed in the metropolitan or former metropolitan countries. There has been little, if any, political pressure on the academic aspects of the work of these institutions; even the lack of development of studies in African languages and culture has elicited little local criticism. This reflects a political drive to advance those features of Western education which are essential to economic and social material development, and it also reflects a lack of appreciation of the importance of African studies to social development in the fields of personal relations, administration, and government. Nowhere in Africa has there been any serious challenge to the accepted standards of qualification for admission to, and completion of, higher educational studies, though isolated voices have been raised suggesting that the Western standards are too demanding at this present stage of African development. On the other hand, the inclusion in the university institution of some nongraduate courses has not been regarded as detrimental to the general status of the institution by the general public, though this fear has been expressed by many of the university teachers.

In the field of technological studies, in former British territories, political independence has not been accompanied by any better appreciation of the relationship of technical requirements to technological ones than was shown by the preceding governments. Consequently there is at present an imbalance between the provision of facilities for technical and vocational training at the secondary level and for technological training at the higher level. It is unlikely that the significance of this will be clearly understood until manpower surveys are treated as an essential part of economic and industrial planning. In the Belgian Congo practically all the emphasis has been upon training technicians. The policy in French-speaking territories lies somewhere between British and Belgian practice.

Finance and control

The administration and financing of education is affected by the change from colonial to independent political status in a number of ways that call for comment. Prior to independence, the methods of administration and finance under the three major colonial powers differed. Under British authority responsibility for policy making and executive action was in the hands of the Director of Education of the territory. The Imperial government indicated broad lines of policy through advisory minutes and memoranda, but the "man-on-the-spot" was given paramount responsibility. With political independence, the Director of Education becomes the chief executive officer, the responsibility for policy being vested in a Minister of Education responsible to a legislature as a member of a cabinet or team of ministers. Not least of the consequences of this change is the direct political responsibility to the franchise. The extent to which education votes have been given a considerable, and, sometimes, a major place in budgets is a measure of the significance of this change. On occasions, the consequences have been less than fortunate. Ministers, lacking experience and not fully understanding the nature of their responsibilities, sometimes exercise their authority in a personal and arbitrary way. In Ghana there has been personal interference by a Minister in the admission of pupils to an individual school, and on one occasion an attempt was made to dictate what should be said at a university college refresher course. Recently in Western Region, Nigeria, the then Minister promulgated a directive concerning the content and layout of certain textbooks which was purely personal in taste and which was made in disregard of the advice of his professional advisers.

Another feature of change resultant upon political independence is the tendency to replace voluntary agency (mission) control and supervision by local and central government control. Related to this is the attempt to offload part of the financial burden from the central government to local authority budgets. This latter action has had little success, largely because assumptions about the readiness and capacity of the local authorities to carry the financial responsibilities had been mistaken. In this matter, local authorities, authorized by legislation, have been quite ineffective. Probably there was an error of judgment in assuming that local authorities in the United Kingdom pattern could be imitated in African societies.

In French and Belgian practice the administration has been much more centralized. Attempts to place responsibility for building schools upon local bodies in French Africa have proved in many instances to be penny wise and pound foolish. Because shoddy buildings were erected, maintenance costs rose very rapidly and an inordinate proportion of the recurrent grants for education had to be diverted to meet them. On the other hand, the policy of allowing local discretion to control the rate of expansion of primary education has on the whole proved effective. But the general pattern is toward centralization of administration and finance, as it is in Liberia, Ethiopia, Somaliland (Italian) and the French Community, and in the Belgian Congo.

It is difficult to arrive at valid comparisons of actual expenditures on education, derived as they are in various ways from local and central government sources. In addition there are the diminishing contributions in money and kind from the voluntary agencies, and the contributions being made from such outside sources as the Colonial Development and Welfare Fund (United Kingdom), the Investment Fund for Economic and Social Development—FIDES (France), the Fonds du Bien-Être Indigène (Belgian Congo), International Cooperation Administration—ICA (United States), and the United Nations and Specialised Agencies. But what is significant is that in every case political independence has resulted in vastly increased expenditures on education by the local governments.

Summary remarks

The movement toward political independence in Africa is accompanied by rapid expansion of primary education, relatively large expenditure on higher education, slower expansion of secondary education, and as yet inadequate improvement of training facilities for teachers. Politically there is a general recognition of the importance of education for economic and social development and the acceptance of the need to plan for it. But nowhere has the planning been sufficiently integrated with the rest of the economic and social planning. Ministerial responsibility for education has given impetus to educational development, but is sometimes marred through personal interpretation of authority by ministers, mainly from lack of experience. Despite the zest for educational expansion and the overwhelming financial burden it entails there has been as yet little imagination shown in reshaping education systems or in modifying the curricula. The value of the media of mass communication has not yet been sufficiently appreciated to have had an effect upon educational practice in proportion to their worth. The education of women and girls still lags behind that of men and boys and the social and economic consequences have yet to be recognized. Political independence has resulted in defections from education of the better-trained teachers in serious numbers with the result that dilution of professional standards is a threat in every newly independent territory. The growth of professional organizations promises the development of pressure groups of considerable power at national and international levels.

Problems of finance, content, and method are similar enough in character despite the diverse origins of the education systems in African countries to encourage regional and international cooperation and to offer scope for imaginative experiment.

It has been quite the order of the day here, for some years past, to discuss the subject of popular education. This is a subject which can no more be known without being treated comparatively, than anatomy can be known without being treated comparatively. . . . The notion of treating a matter of this kind as a matter of scientific study hardly occurs to anyone in this country, but almost everyone treats it as a matter which he can settle by the light of his own personal experience, and of what he calls his own practical good sense. Our rule of thumb has cost us dear already, and is probably destined to cost us dearer still.

—MATTHEW ARNOLD, *Schools and Universities on the Continent* (1868), pages 279–280.

References

United Nations, General Assembly:

Recent Developments in Technical and Vocational Training in the Non-Self-Governing Territories. A/AC.55/L.295. 1959.

Higher Education in Non-Self-Governing Territories. A/AC.35/L.302. 1959.

Illiteracy and Fundamental Education in Non-Self-Governing Territories. A/AC.35/L.303. 1959.

UNESCO: *Provisional Report of the Needs of Tropical Africa in the Field of Primary and Secondary Education.* Ed/Africa/2. 1960.

Phi Delta Kappan, Vol. XLI, No. 4, January 1960: "Africa, Its Educational Problems and Promises."

W. A. LEWIS, letter to the Editor of *The Economist,* January 10, 1959.

L. J. LEWIS, "Higher Education in the Oversea Territories 1948–1958," *British Journal of Educational Studies,* Vol. VIII, No. 1, November 1959.

1-4 French educational reform *

REFORM IN FRENCH EDUCATION HAS BECOME ALMOST A perennial topic, and one which, except in a very small circle, has long ceased to arouse any heat. That is not because reform is unnecessary, or because there are not hundreds of thousands who would welcome it, but because "hope deferred maketh the heart sick." Since the war so many plans have been worked out by so many groups and discussed in so many conferences that, when all this comes to nought—or nearly nought—enthusiasm inevitably turns to cynicism. It is, of course, the failure of successive postwar governments to put through the Chamber of Deputies any far reaching change or development that is to blame for this situation. When Western students of comparative education read recently, "French Educational Reforms: de Gaulle cuts short 13 years of argument," they could only rub their eyes and cry "Wonderful: may it prove to be so."

But we must now look back to see what changes were, and are, necessary. After the First World War a small group of keen pedagogues calling themselves *Les Compagnons de l'Université Nouvelle*, set to work to make secondary education of the academic kind, still mainly the preserve of those whose parents could

---

* Charles H. Dobinson, "French Educational Reform," *Comparative Education Review*, Vol. 3, No. 1 (June, 1959), 5–15.

Charles H. Dobinson

pay for it, available for all who could profit from it. After fifteen years they succeeded in getting a law passed which decreed that, from 1933, every class of eleven-year-old youngsters admitted to the *lycée* (selective secondary schools for the most able intellectually) should attend without any fees being paid by their parents. So by 1939, when war broke out, nearly all the boys and girls in the *lycées* were receiving free secondary education. But the curriculum was still almost entirely bookish; games, societies, and physical education had hardly any part; cramming was the order of the day; competition for marks and scholarships for higher education formed almost the sole motivation for the excessive memorization and secondhand disquisition on topics unsuited for immature minds; and buildings were as gloomy as barracks. So there was not really very much to show for twenty years of unremitting effort by the *Compagnons* and other reformers. It is true that in 1937 Jean Zay, a man of great intellectual power and discernment, had set on foot the *classes d'orientation.* These were intended to bring into secondary education, and particularly into the *lycées*, the concept of education fitted for the child, rather than that of compressing the child into the educational mold. But by 1939 the leaven had had little effect upon the lump.

The First World War, besides throwing up the *Compagnons* with their desire to reform the traditional secondary education had also had its effect upon technical education. In fact, the *Loi Astier* of 1919, promoted largely by discerning and farsighted groups from industry and commerce, is rightly known as "The Charter of Technical Education." This law made it obligatory for all the workers in a very great number of trades to have proper training, including theory, for which their employers must make proper provision or pay, upon a per capita basis, the *taxe d'apprentissage.* The employers were also compelled to release the young workers on various days of the week at such times as were necessary to enable them to attend the necessary classes in evening or in late afternoon.

The ill-fated Munich conference of 1938 also gave a fillip to technical education. When Neville Chamberlain and Eduard Daladier returned from Germany—the former quoting Shakespeare, "And so from out the nettle danger, pluck we this flower, safety"—and each set out to rearm his country rapidly. France was desperately short of young skilled workers. And so were started the apprenticeship Centres, too late to have any effect on rearmament but destined to play a great part in French postwar recovery.

Events swept on and from the autumn of 1939 to the summer of 1944 educational reform was a subject which was discussed only by members of the Resistance and others who were also planning for the France of the future. Particularly was this true after 1940, for the fall of France, or rather the surrender of France, was for millions of Frenchmen a matter of bitter shame. Just how strongly some of the workers in education felt about it is shown by the plans which, after 1942, began to be evolved by educational members of the Resistance. These culminated in the famous Conference in Algiers in 1943, after the occupation of North Africa by the Americans. At this important conference, presided over by M. Capitan, the following words (his) were read:

> "The defeat and the tyranny would not have been what they have been but for the faintheartedness, the default or the treason of the controlling groups in the army and the navy, in politics and finances, in industry and in commerce. Those who could claim to have come from the summit of our educational system are those whose cowardice has been the most scandalous."

From this damning indictment of the prewar education there followed this corollary.

> The renewed France will desire . . . to give her youth an education less exclusively intellectual. Without underestimating or neglecting the culture of the intelligence, France has learned, in the experiences of the war and the struggles of the Resistance, to give their full values to moral qualities and to qualities of character which have been lacking in many minds which are brilliant, but weak and corruptible. France will also desire that the practice of sports and of physical exercises shall produce a youth which is tougher and better balanced.

But toughness alone is not enough; these educators assembled at Algiers to blueprint a new and better system realized that social cohesiveness and social self-discipline stem from a highly developed social life inside a school community. So they desired to incorporate into the schools of the renewed France something of the system which had worked so well for generations in the schools on the other side of the English Channel. What they wrote was:

> One of the secrets of English education is the self-government exercised in the schools by the pupils themselves or by their representatives. They have thus acquired while young the sense of responsibility and discipline on a basis of consent, and this is one of the fundamentals of liberty.
>
> Youth movements, too, play a similar part but, above all, we value most the various forms of Scouting.

Here then, stated with clarity and conviction, are some of the principles which were to shape the educational system of the renewed France. How far had any of the objectives thus defined in 1943 been achieved by 1958?

After the Liberation of France in 1945 it was necessary to appoint an educational commission which could bring into the discussions men and women who had not been able during the occupation to find their way to Algiers. So arose the famous Langevin Commission, presided over by one of the most distinguished physicists that France has produced during the current century, Professor Paul Langevin.

Let us first consider some of the principles which this report laid down and then the plan of the system which the commission considered would satisfy these principles.

1. The principle of justice

All children, whatever their origin, social or racial, have equal rights to the maximum development that their personality permits. They should find no other limitation than their own aptitudes.

2. Raising the general standard of culture

The standards of culture should be raised less by methods of selection, which continually remove the most gifted and alienate them from the people, than by making culture more easily available to the less privileged groups.

3. Technical education

Manual tasks must receive more social esteem and perceptual education should not be considered of less value than conceptual.

4. Care of the individual

Legislation in a democracy should protect the weak, therefore legislation in a democracy should protect the children and should ensure that every child receives objective and individual study during his schooling.

5. The general culture of the nation

General culture enables a man to maintain liaison with other men outside his profession, to find interest in, and to appreciate the results of activities other than his own and to see his own in the perspective of the whole.

> In a democratic state, where every worker is also a full citizen, it is vital that specialization shall not be an obstacle to the comprehension of the vast problems of the world and that a broad and solid culture should liberate man from the narrow limitations of the technician.

Seeking to provide a scheme which should give expression to these principles, the members of the Langevin Commission produced a plan of reform about which a few explanatory notes are now necessary.

First, the legislated existence of publicly provided "schooling" for children between the ages of three and six is nothing new. The *école maternelle*, which provides kindergarten activities, basic training in hygiene and social response, dates from 1882, when a great educational Act was put through the Chamber of Deputies by Jules Ferry. Attendance at this age is, of course, on a purely voluntary basis.

From the age of six years schooling is compulsory and at present has its first selective break when children reach the age of eleven. Those children who do best in a selection examination are offered places in *lycées* and other highly academic secondary schools; the next group may be offered places in less academic *collèges modernes* or *cours complémentaires*, which may provide either general studies or industrial and commercial studies in a setting of general education. After other streams have been diverted, according to the provision of the locality, toward various forms of technical education, the remainder stay at school till the end of the school year in which they reach the age of fourteen. Before they leave school at fourteen the majority succeed in gaining the certificate of primary education, which signifies that they have reached a reasonable level of proficiency in arithmetic and the mother tongue. In the last two years of this schooling, too, in most primary schools which are large enough, there are courses which provide preliminary orientation toward the lesser skills for which one can train after having entered industry or commerce at the age of fourteen-plus. Some of these orientation courses are specially designed to give pupils a desire to enter the apprenticeship centers.

It is to be noted that under the Langevin plan firm decisions are not to be made at the age of eleven-plus. Instead, for all boys and girls the first cycle of schooling is to be followed by four years of the second cycle, known as that of *orientation*. It is argued that when a child is only eleven years of age the fairly firm setting of the course of his life's voyage toward this or that particular star in the firmament is premature. Educational reformers go so far as to say that even the boys and girls who are obviously highly intellectual and enter the leading *lycées* should, in their first two or three years, try their hand at a variety of studies and manual skills before selection is made of those which they will pursue to a great depth. They even argue that not all boys and girls of intellectual ability should necessarily study Latin from the age of eleven.

In terms of pure theory, then, there is much to be said for the Langevin plan of the *cycle d'orientation.* The real difficulty lies in the fact that to make this work properly a whole series of new buildings (every one of which would house the equivalent of a junior high school) is needed, and most of the existing secondary school buildings would have to be scrapped. So the people of an old country are prisoners of their history, not only through the ideas which, for better or worse, fetter them to their past, but also through the stones and the mortar that their forefathers sandwiched together.

In all events there is nothing unsound in the Langevin idea that between the ages of eleven and fifteen every child should be studied as an individual, his abilities and aptitudes discovered and recorded, his personality and tastes understood in the light of his home background, and his whole development so encouraged and interpreted that, at the end, he can be given guidance for his future which is likely to be soundly based. Perhaps, however, this guidance could be given at an earlier age than fifteen.

The plan then provides three groups of possibilities, each of these fanning out into an ever-widening range of diversifications.

We note first that a considerable proportion of the pupils in the French educational system is moving into the field of apprenticeship. This is a wider field than in the United Kingdom or the United States, partly because France is still a country with a strong agricultural basis and a widely dispersed population, partly because France still values the skilled independent artisan with his small business, and partly because, especially since the *Loi Astier* of 1919, almost every trade and skill has its own certificate which needs to be gained before the wage of a fully qualified worker in that field can be obtained. The old way of obtaining the qualification was to be apprenticed to an employer who would give practical training and encourage theoretical study at "night school."

The apprenticeship center, however, sets out to give a complete training to obtain the certificate of trade aptitude, and at the same time offers many elements of general education, in the space of three years of full-time study. A fairly full account of this is available elsewhere.[1] Here we can only express the opinion that the apprenticeship center

[1] C. H. Dobinson, *Technical Education for Adolescents* (London: Harrap & Co.,

is the most successful and worth-while development in low level technical education that has been widely established anywhere in the last century and that it has been largely responsible for the continued increase in French industrial productivity since the war. A center is neither a school in the normal sense, nor a factory, but a cross between the two, and only shortage of funds has prevented their developing more rapidly than they did in the first ten years after the war. The total number of students in the various forms of apprenticeship center, most of which are publicly provided, is in the region of a quarter of a million. There are, of course, many other forms of technical education at a slightly higher level, and altogether, of all pupils who are receiving any full-time form of what can be regarded as secondary education (including apprenticeship centers in this category), more than one-quarter are receiving some kind of technical education. This is a remarkable fact which is not widely known outside France. In this respect, at any rate, the "renewed" France has lived up to its resolutions of 1943.

The second group of pupils in the *cycle de determination* are shown moving into fields of technical and commercial education which take them to studies which are more advanced than in the apprenticeship centers. These schools include the *collèges techniques* and the *écoles nationales professionelles*, which give courses lasting as long as six years.

The third group—the smallest—continues academic education (which may, of course, be scientific and/or mathematical) at *lycées* and *collèges*. Most of these pupils, after competitive entry into one or other of the famous *Grandes Écoles* such as the *École Polytechnique*, or after the two years of concentrated "propedeutic" studies, will pursue studies at the very high level established in French universities.

Unfortunately the Langevin plan, excellent though it was, has never been implemented. One of the important reasons was that Langevin was a Communist and therefore his plan was condemned by many without any objective consideration. It is amusing that at this time, when the country is under a control which is nearing dictatorship—for General de Gaulle has more power than anyone since Napoleon III—the Langevin plan should at last come into its own. For what de Gaulle has in fact done in "cutting short 13 years of argument" is to put the existing school buildings and system, as far as may be done without

---

1951), and "The French Apprenticeship Centres," *Year Book of Education* (London and New York: Evans Bros., 1958).

incurring utterly ruinous expenditure, into the Langevin framework.

Let us note what reforms were made law in France on January 7, 1959. Here is an Act which takes effect immediately but which does not become binding upon pupils who are already in school but will bind all who enter their first school year after October 1, 1959. The most important point for them is that the school leaving age is raised to sixteen. This is admittedly two years lower than that proposed by Langevin, but it is fully halfway along the road.

Primary school for all will be along the same lines as today: obligatory from the age of six, and the first five years, with terminology reminiscent of Langevin, will be known as the *cycle élémentaire*.

After that, for everyone, the five-year cycle of orientation proposed by Langevin is telescoped into a two-year *cycle d'observation* in which the aptitudes, abilities, tastes, interests, and characteristics are studied prior to guidance into one of five main divisions of the third cycle.

For the least intellectual pupils there will be three years of education which, while based on general education, will be largely practical. There are four different possibilities under this head: (a) agriculture for boys, (b) agriculture with housecraft for girls, (c) rural crafts, and (d) urban work. In all these studies practical experience in agriculture or industry will be included.

For the next group, as indicated by intellectual performance and interests, there will be the existing apprenticeship centers which are to be renamed *collèges d'enseignement technique*. As has already been stated there are a wide range of different crafts that may be studied in the centers, including aspects of agriculture, winemaking, building, and so on, as well as all the main industrial skills.

Those whose interests are also technical but whose intellectual powers would warrant more mathematical and scientific content in their technical studies will be advised to enter the existing *collèges techniques* and *écoles nationales professionelles*, where they can obtain after four years of study the title *agent technique breveté*, after five years the title *technicien breveté*, and after six years the title *technicien supérieur breveté*. These forms of technical study are grouped under *l'enseignement technique*.

The group whose abilities are intellectual and nontechnical, but who are not suited for, or do not wish to undertake, the long years involved in schooling directed to the university, will be advised to enter the *cours complementaires généraux*, which are to be renamed *collèges d'enseignement général*. Here, as at present, there is a three-year course leading to an examination which will now carry the name *brevet d'enseignement général*. From these, as at present, the majority of recruits for the training colleges for primary teachers will be obtained. Others who obtain this *brevet* will enter municipal and industrial offices to provide personnel at an intermediate level of responsibility.

L'enseignement général long will, as at present, be reserved for the most gifted boys and girls. But within the *lycées* changes which have already begun to take place in the broadening of the curriculum will be accelerated. For instance, since the war one of the greatest achievements of the educational reformers has been the introduction of forms of the *baccalauréat* examination which break away from the traditional conceptions of intellectual study. Of these the most notable is perhaps the *baccalauréat technique* which, however, it must be admitted, is highly mathematical and would scarcely be called "technical" in many countries. Altogether there are seven different "lines" of work in the *lycée*, every one of which leads to a different *baccalauréat examination*. In the new developments great attention will be given to the strengthening of the new lines, especially the technical, and some *lycées* will be known as *lycées techniques*.

An astonishing achievement of General de Gaulle's reform—or perhaps only of M. Berthoin, who persuaded the Council of Ministers to accept these plans—is that the *baccalauréat* examination itself is to undergo some modification. The most remarkable achievement of all—if it ever has any effect—is the decision slightly to reduce the amount of study which *lycée* pupils have to endure every week. So that standards are not thereby lowered the long vacation is to be shortened. In theory, there are more weeks of work, but slightly less pressure in every week. The writer, knowing only too well what long hours of private study the highly competitive French educational system compels *lycée* pupils to put upon themselves, feels very skeptical about this proposed reform. He fears that before long it will merely mean more weeks of the tremendous intellectual pressure from which *lycée* pupils have suffered for too many generations, and which, as the reformers in Algiers stated in 1943, in many cases limits the full all-around development of the body and the personality.

This leads us on to consider the postwar attempts to reform the inner life of the *lycée* and the methods of teaching. For while one must acknowledge, with great enthusiasm, that General de Gaulle and M. Berthoin have succeeded in making a magnificent reform of the organizational framework of French education and that the resulting changes and development will be prodigious, we still have to deal with the intellectual conservatism of the French *lycée professeur*, a conservatism which may have been equalled by other groups of human society in various periods of human history, but which can never have been surpassed. Against this rock, waves of reform, of every size from Atlantic breakers to tidal waves set up by vast suboceanic cataclysms, have thundered and have been shattered. By and large, with exceptions which receive utterly disproportionate mention and homage, just because they are so few and therefore appear so novel, the lessons of the *lycée* are mainly either old-fashioned didacticism or, in the upper classes, university lectures slightly modified to suit a younger age group.

It was to alter this antiquated formalism, and to introduce into the *lycée* some of the social life and self-responsibility of English and American schools which the Algiers reformers praised, that the great experiment of the *classes nouvelles* was launched in 1945.

The administrative leader in this movement, who organized it from above, and whose wisdom and organizational skill made it possible, was M. Monod, head of the Department of Secondary Education in the Ministry of National Education. He was ably assisted by a group of brilliant, devoted, and farsighted educators of whom Madame E. Hatinguais, *Inspectrice Générale* and *Directrice* of the *Centre International d'Études Pédagogiques*, was the most outstanding. Formerly *directrice* of the *lycée* for girls at Algiers, which she made famous, and subsequently *directrice* of that most distinguished of all teachers' colleges for women—the *École Normale Supérieure de Jeunes Filles* at Sèvres—she brought to the task not only an educational insight and originality which has seldom been equalled, but also a wealth of successful educational experiment in education with youngsters from the age of eight to the age of twenty-four. Indeed, as the mother of two brilliant daughters, she was familiar, too, with the problems of the nursery where the bases of character are laid.

So at Sèvres there assembled in August 1945 the first 200 volunteer teachers of the *classes nouvelles*, those who were to be *chefs de groupe* and who, without any extra recognition, financial or otherwise, were assuming the burden of making a new approach to academic secondary education. It was to start in the bottom classes of the *lycées*, those containing the eleven-year-old new entrants.

There were many aims in this new education, but the first, which has prepared the way for the two-year *cycle d'observation* which General de Gaulle has now introduced, was to study the *child*. Instead of treating him, so to speak as just another client for a Turkish bath, who will be put through the series of processes precisely as were those who came before and those who come after, the child was to be given a wide range of activities—intellectual, artistic, and physical—and observed. Moreover, all the teachers would work as a small team, not exceeding five, in this observation. And every one of them would teach not just one subject to the class, but several subjects. Indeed, as far as possible—and it is remarkable how much is possible—lessons in the various subjects were to be correlated, and by weekly meetings of the teaching team not only could this be ensured, but discussions about the individual children could be made continuously fruitful.

New efforts were to be made—and were, successfully—to relate learning to life, and the study of the local environment, be it town or country, was allotted one or two teaching periods per week.

Every class—and the *classes nouvelles* were limited in size to twenty-five pupils—broke itself up into teams of four or five pupils, and instead of individual competition for marks there was group competition, which required cooperation within the group in the learning process. No one who has not seen such groups in action can appreciate how much this can add, not only to the fun of learning but to the *quality* of work produced. Moreover, of course, every pupil who helps another of his group is not only helping the teacher but is also helping to solidify his own understanding of what he explains to others.

The groups, too, took responsibility for various aspects of the class life and every class became without exaggeration, to some extent a small self-educating community and was able to receive and utilize a great deal of liberty. There is no doubt whatever that the methods of the *classes nouvelles* succeeded beyond expectation, but, of course, they demanded of the teachers far more work, far more time, and far more nervous energy in keeping up with the interests and enthusiasms of their pupils, than did the simple textbook, chalk, and talk lessons.

For every child a detailed *dossier scolaire* was kept, and there was continuous contact with the family. It is no wonder that in the years 1946–52 the writer met with many parents of children in *classes nouvelles* whose praise for the new methods was almost lyrical.

Year by year new groups of 200 teachers came to Sèvres and year by year the experiment crept further up the school til in many *lycées* there were four successive *classes nouvelles*. Naturally, however, as the classes moved nearer to the formal examination of the *baccalauréat* the methods had to approximate more and more to those which are demanded by the nature of the test.

It can, however, be said—for statistics prove it—that boys and girls who had the good fortune to have the new methods in some of their early years in the *lycée* performed at least as well as those who were subjected to the far less enjoyable traditional methods.

So the movement spread year by year til in 1952 there were nearly

1,000 classes nouvelles in secondary education. Then came, simultaneously, the retirement of M. Monod and the beginning of the pressure of the postwar birth rate on secondary schools. The new head of the Department of Secondary Education decided that excellent as were the achievements of the *classes nouvelles* the system could no longer support a large number of classes in which there were only 25 pupils, while many other classes were considerably larger. Accordingly he decided to close down most of the *classes nouvelles*, leaving a few to remain in *lycées pilotes*, which were to be regarded as experimental stations from which ideas could be taken by other *lycées* as opportunity might offer and as enthusiasm might justify.

It must not, however, be thought that the end of the widespread *classes nouvelles* meant in any way the end of the changes in classroom method. Rather a considerable number of the most successful and least expensive *classes nouvelles* schemes were, by Ministry ruling, incorporated into the work of *all* the lower classes of all the *lycées* and *collèges* of France. So the years of work by the group of one thousand *chefs d'equipe* were by no means wasted: they have left their mark on French secondary education for all time. And, moreover, in the *lycées pilotes* these same principles are giving rise to continuous experimentation and the development of new techniques to be made known generally as time goes on. Indeed, the *lycées pilotes* are continuing to do outstanding experimental work and particularly important is their contribution to the training of secondary school teachers in the regional centers.[2]

Incidentally we should note that this training is itself a postwar innovation, for before the Second World War it was thought that a university graduate, by virtue of his degree, already knew how to teach. Perhaps in the matter of reproducing the formal classroom technique he did already know how, but when the Algiers reformers of 1943 demanded that schools should affect character and personality a new dimension had to be added to the *lycée professeur*.

However, for an Englishman or an American the astonishing thing about the ending of the widespread *classes nouvelles* experiment was its suddenness. To us it seems incredible that by a single signature at the bottom of a short typewritten manuscript, which had been prepared without reference to a House of Commons or a House of Representatives, a great development which had taken seven or eight years could suddenly, and actually during the summer vacation of the schools, be brought to an end. Yet it was so, and some teachers who had been

---

[2] See *Comparative Education Review*, Vol. 2, No. 3, February 1950.

chefs d'equipe of *classes nouvelles* first learned that their "new" class would not exist in October when they read their newspaper while on holiday in August. Probably there could be no better way of destroying zeal for experiment, though nothing could have been further from the thought of those who had to make the decision.

Of course it is this same power of centralized authority to direct the educational system of the whole country which has made possible the de Gaulle reforms we have been applauding. But to a Scandinavian, an Englishman, or an American, accustomed as they are to a very large degree of local autonomy, in which groups of citizens and their representatives can have a considerable effect upon local educational policy, the centralized system is something to be avoided at almost all costs.

In the same way, reform of teaching methods is for us something which can never start at the top, but is a matter which rests with every individual teacher. New ideas, new experiments, are always being discussed and described, and courses to enable teachers to develop new skills and to improve their techniques are continually available, at low cost, for the teacher who chooses to attend. And in both the United Kingdom and the United States a large proportion of teachers attend such courses whether they are provided, as, in the United Kingdom by the Ministry, by Local Education Authorities, or by university institutes of education, or, as in the United States, mainly by the university schools of education.

In short, for us the reform of classroom teaching method is a continuous evolutionary process responding to changes in the nature and needs of society and to the inventions which can be utilized to make learning an easier and more successful part of human development.

For France changes take place more suddenly, perhaps more dramatically. But one aspect of French education is unlikely to change, whatever governments come and go, and that is the very high level of intellectual culture—literary, artistic, mathematical, and scientific—which is achieved by the most gifted young men and women of the nation. With an intellectual heritage which, through the Roman occupation, can be traced back almost without interruption to Greek thought, France is quite certain that to flower intellectually is to make the highest achievement of human life. As Aristotle put it:

> We ought not to follow the counsel of those who bid us think the thoughts befitting man's estate and not, mortals as we are, to be more proud than mortals should. What we have to do is to put on immortality, so far as we may, and to do all that we do with the view of living the life of the highest thing in us. Even if that part of us is small in bulk, yet in power and price it excels far beyond all the rest.

1-5 Comprehensive schools in England: their context*

An assessment and comparison of institutions of any type must accept two principles: to compare only things that are truly comparable; and to see them correctly in their context before evaluating them. To do this last thing it is necessary to recognise: (a) that the cherished values of one society are not always highly esteemed elsewhere; (b) that where there is agreement about values there may still be disagreement about priorities (either because of preference or because of shortage of funds, institutions, and personnel); and (c) that even where there is complete agreement about all these things there may still be legitimate disagreement about methods. In the case of comprehensive schools these ancient truisms need to be emphatically insisted on.

For the purposes of this article comprehensive schools are taken to be schools catering for a full ability range of children from the age of 11 or thereabouts until they reach the end of compulsory school attendance (15 now in England) or leave to take up work or further education at a later date. It goes without saying that if there is to be a genuinely full ability range there can be no selecting-in or selecting-out of children by means of examinations or school records. Ideally, to

* Edmund King, "Comprehensive Schools in England: Their Context," *Comparative Education Review*, Vol. 3, No. 2 (October, 1959), pp. 13–19.

Edmund King

the purists in comprehensiveness, there should not be selection by residence or parental choice either; but the only way of ensuring this state of affairs (if desired) would be to provide only one type of secondary school, to make it include an accurate cross-section of the whole community, and to eliminate any such variants as private or parochial schools or schools attached to teachers' colleges. Such comprehensiveness does not exist even in the communist countries. It would not be tolerated in the United States, and it would be tolerated still less in Britain.

Even if comprehensiveness were desired in a considerably modified form, it would not be possible in Britain on a large scale for many years to come because of the following difficulties: (a) the wide range of publicly provided secondary schools now in existence, mainly small by American standards, which offer education differentiated by "age, aptitude," etc.; (b) the unusually large number of fairly autonomous tax-supported schools (e.g. the parochial or "voluntary" schools which may have up to 95 per cent of their running costs met out of public funds; and many nondenominational schools of ancient foundation or experimental character, which have some public support); (c) the career power, social prestige, and academic excellence of many of the relatively small number of completely independent schools (including but not confined to the "Public Schools"); (d) the unreadiness of public opinion to accept the "comprehensive" principle; (e) the experimental and gradualist approach of those who do favor it; (f) a real shortage of funds, materials, and teachers; and (g) a genuine anxiety lest Britain's bread and butter, substantially earned by skill in a competitive world, be lost by failure to develop "intelligence" and professional expertise because of premature reliance on an experiment still in its early and uncertain stages in Britain.

These difficulties, partly real and material, and partly ideological and sociological but no less potent for that, must be accepted at face value before the story and the problems of Britain's comprehensive schools can be appreciated. Readers are referred to Chapter Four in this writer's *Other Schools and Ours* (Rinehart, New York, 1958) and to two articles by Professor G. Z. F. Bereday: "A comparative approach to social status in English education," contained in *Liberal Traditions in Education*, ed. Bereday (Harvard, 1958); and "Equal Opportunity" in the (English) *Journal of Education*, (February, 1958).[1] Professor Bereday's first essay, in this writer's opinion, overstates the case; but it bears a recognisable likeness. After facing up to these practical difficulties and the institutional and ideological obstacles, we can only be amazed that comprehensive schools have been established with such enthusiasm and success, and that the comprehensive principle is being widely extended to modify conventional-type schools in readiness for a comprehensive pattern in the future.

The Substitute for the Comprehensive Principle

It is well known that most of the completely comprehensive schools in England have been established under the jurisdiction of the London County Council. In Britain the counties, or the cities of status equivalent to counties, are the responsible education authorities. Under the general supervision of the (political) Minister of Education, as advised by the permanent (nonpolitical) staff of the Ministry of Education, the local education authorities have great autonomy. By January, 1959, the London County Council had established 23 very large comprehensive schools (some for boys, some for girls, some mixed); it had combined other types of school (grammar—academic and selective) with technical schools or with secondary modern schools in at least 25 other cases, and thus started the development of still more comprehensive schools. It had also blurred the outlines of the tripartite system, familiar from the 1944 Education Act, to such an extent that officials are reluctant to place many of the Council's schools firmly in one category, and hesitate to say how many comprehensive schools the Council has under its control. In other words, the experiment is continuing in full swing; and its repercussions in the amalgamation of schools, of courses, and of "types of mind" are so great that no one can say where they have reached or will end.

Before considering any single comprehensive school or the expanding process as seen in London, this picture of the ripples must be rounded off by taking note of some of their side-effects and more distant consequences. Partly because of the insufficiency of grammar school places available to children diagnosed as suitable for grammar school work or nearly so, but also partly because people refused to accept the "eleven plus" examination's diagnosis as fully reliable, many secondary modern schools have for years been preparing some of their children for the kind of academic examination which was once the closed preserve of the grammar school. Though secondary-modern children do not often have such highly educated teachers as do grammar-school pupils, and though they generally work under less favourable conditions, many of them are able to offer school subjects at the level of the General Certification of Education, and some of them are successful enough to pass on into the prestige-carrying "sixth form" of a grammar school. Thus they are, so to speak, in the vestibule of the universities and of the technical and commercial colleges which in England are most nearly comparable with the technical and professional courses of American universities. In addition, secondary modern schools increasingly offer general and "industrial arts" kinds of education that can lead to alternative certificates and further training opportunities, which in England matter very much as the emblems of above-elementary education. This may not be social justice or educational wisdom; but it is a partial effacement of the exclusiveness of the grammar school, and it prepares the way for developments of much greater consequence. The value of the process must be assessed in an English context.

One result of internal changes in the secondary modern school is that children stay on beyond the statutory age of compulsion of 15. In the better secondary modern schools about half the pupils stay on for an extra year, and in some cases the percentage is as high as 70 or 80. The Ministry of Education states that already the number of secondary-modern pupils staying on beyond the compulsory period has risen from 12,000 in 1948 to 38,000 in 1958. It is estimated that by 1965 the number of *17-years-olds* in any school will have doubled the present figure. When we recall that some 20 per cent of grammar school children (selected for "brightness" at 11) do not stay on until 16 or 17, we see that much of the increase is to be anticipated in the secondary modern school or in schools to which children have migrated after attendance at secondary modern schools. (There are not enough comprehensive or technical secondary schools to account for the difference.) It has also been noted that some of the children who shine late in the secondary modern school or its alternatives, often despite comparatively unfavourable conditions, are not those initially spotted as "near-grammar" types.

While 66 per cent of grammar-school children are now of "working-class" origin, those sons and daughters of middle-class families who may be considered unsuitable for grammar-school courses at the "eleven plus" examination suffer thus a certain academic and social relegation. The presence of these childern in the secondary modern school must clearly stimulate concern that the school be as enterprising and as humanistic as possible, and this it will generally contrive to be in the more favoured residential districts where the proportion of such children is likely to be highest. Moreover, many grammar schools and, indeed, "Public Schools" are rapidly making their programmes less bookish and more industry-oriented. This change is attributable in part to the dawning realisation that the country's future industrial progress will more fully recompense pupils who leave school with some academic and personal readiness for technological requirements; but it is also the result of direct pressure from industry. Firms dangle attractive "sandwich" courses and high-level apprenticeship schemes before those who leave grammar schools with the right qualifications or groupings of subjects. A £4,000,000 fund is being distributed by industry to the "Public Schools" to provide equipment and courses in science and technology. Some 65 per cent of boys and girls in the "sixth form" that crowns the grammar school are specialising in science. As secondary modern schools and technical schools also follow the same trend it becomes less justifiable to distinguish between the *content* of various types of secondary school than in the 1920's and 1930's, when the tripartite system was most influentially established.

All these developments, and others too numerous to mention, accumulate in the public consciousness a dim awareness (if no more) that from the point of view of *types of career* there is not so much to distinguish the various *types of school* as there used to be. Of course, there is much stratification still according to *levels of starting a career;* but that is another matter, which does not of itself affect readiness to see comprehensive or near-comprehensive schools established, especially for other people's children, and above all for the children of lower-income parents. Thus it comes about that administrators and politicians once opposed to comprehensive schools on ideological grounds are beginning to see that they are already partly here, that they are worth experimenting with as the possible solution for many pressing, practical problems. This "brass tacks" attitude may shock the purists; but it must be recorded as in keeping with: (a) the historical attitudes of British employers towards the establishment of public elementary schools in the nineteenth century, and of public secondary and university opportunities in this century; and (b) the whole pragmatic approach of the Anglo-Saxon tradition.

The Advance of the Comprehensive Principle

By small steps the comprehensive school, which in Britain has long been mistrusted as the cause of the "backwardness" of the United States and as the instrument of "the dictatorship of the proletariat" elsewhere, has been prepared for by the spasmodic march of recent historical events no less than by the revealed shortcomings of the 1944 Education Act. Its advance was aided further by a real shortage of highly qualified specialists in science and advanced academic subjects for grammar-school teaching.

Grammar schools are still comparatively small, and it is not easy to spread the available top-level staff to the best advantage among all the top-level children requiring them. The same goes for teachers with good industrial or commercial insight on the practical side. Therefore there develops a greater readiness for the grouping of schools to aid the fullest deployment of staff and interpenetration of subjects. The embarrassment of many grammar schools in relation to staffing is intensified in most secondary modern schools. In some of the better secondary modern schools in the more favoured suburbs of the London area it is becoming impossible to replace men teachers who resign by other men. In less favoured areas the situation is worse. (Teachers in all British schools get the same basic pay, and the same kinds of increments for qualifications, experience, and responsibility; so financial considerations alone are not the reason for this wastage from the secondary modern school in particular.) Qualifications and personality salable in industry or in grammar schools cannot be secured for modern schools. Staff shortages in subjects vital to the nation's economic well-being cannot be afforded; but combining schools in various near-comprehensive ways is likely to be tried as a remedy more readily than the obvious expedient of spending more money on salaries.

Alternative ways within the present school framework (such as sending pupils out for special instruction in adult technical colleges) seem at best a makeshift. More and more it is being realised that boys and girls are not being educated in school to the right level for industries to train further. There are shortages in recruitment of apprentices.[2] Apart from the apprenticeships, other forms of pre-professional training are being devised or contemplated in Britain as elsewhere to put into the schools somehow a respectable, latter-day equivalent of "life adjustment." [3]

Comprehensive Principle in Practice

Against this rather confused but cumulatively significant background, there is less surprise than might have been 10 years ago in discovering all kinds of experiments with all kinds of comprehensiveness in schools—especially comprehensiveness in curriculum but not excluding comprehensiveness of "types of mind." This is particularly tempting (as has already been said) where other people's children are concerned. At one time only the Labour Party advocated comprehensive schools, chiefly for egalitarian and social reasons, and Conservatives bitterly attacked them. It is a matter of record that a Conservative Minister of Education refused to approve some of the London County Council's comprehensive school schemes, which included the incorporation of an existing grammar school into the new institution. Those local authorities most inclined to set up comprehensive schools or prepare the way for them are predominantly Labour in complexion. Thus the comprehensive principle in Britain is for most opponents a nasty, socialist principle. But now the Conservative Party has officially stated that it will countenance experiments with more comprehensive schools. Some Conservative-dominated local authorities have been willing to establish a more or less common curriculum for all children between the ages of 11 and 13 or 14, followed by differentiation later.

A close approximation to comprehensive schools, which does not go the whole way, is the widespread adoption of "bilateral" schools, containing an enlarged grammar school "stream" of children, with other children pursuing pre-technical and pre-commercial general education of the type often found in secondary modern schools. Obviously, most such schools are much more catholic in their intake than grammar schools proper. A few of them are highly selective on academic grounds;[4] some of them take a "second cream" of the secondary modern schools at the age of 13; but most are by their very nature much more comprehensive in curriculum and "types" than the grammar school. In any case, a grammar-technical or other combined school must resemble the all-inclusive town schools of Scotland and the older secondary schools of Wales (taking in 40 per cent and more of a neighbourhood's children) rather than the more selective grammar schools of England, which in recent decades have creamed off only about 20 to 25 per cent. Parents and administrators (though comparatively few well-qualified teachers) are now ready to experiment with them.

Almost any kind of substitute for the "genuine" grammar school (even if assessed at the lowest possible level, as seen perhaps by an ignorant parent who is nevertheless laudably ambitious for his child) is better than no near-equivalent at all. One can discern the probable drift of this tendency in some rural districts of England (e.g. in Devon, Westmoreland, and the North Riding of Yorkshire) where small secondary schools which are comprehensive in all but name have long existed.[5] Willy-nilly, much present experimentation with so-called bilateral schools, and much expansion of curricula, must be a sort of return to an old-style "omnibus" country grammar school, except that such schools now charge no fees and take in all children.[6]

Another partial adoption of the comprehensive principle which has become very famous is that known as the Leicestershire experiment. In it, all children of two designated districts go to secondary modern schools (now called high schools) at the age of 11. They stay there either until the end of compulsory schooling or until they are transferred to another type of school for continued education. There is not a uniform curriculum, for children are allowed and encouraged to take subjects for which they seem suited. With a view to possible entry to the local grammar school at the age of 14, a three-year range of courses allows children in the high school to choose subjects like French, science, and Latin. At the age of 14, however, *all* children are offered the chance of entry to the grammar school. In one of the two districts (middle-class) 52 per cent chose the grammar school in 1958; in the other (working class, and enjoying industrial prosperity with high wages), nearly 40 per cent chose the grammar school. Obviously, a minority of these children were equal to the familiar, exactingly academic curriculum of the grammar school; therefore, more technical and prevocational subjects have been included. These can be offered in the General Certificate of Education examination, or its equivalent. To encourage this ambition, perhaps, all parents accepting the transfer of their children must promise to keep them at school until they are at least 16.

The Leicestershire experiment is being followed with great interest, everywhere. Other local authorities are considering similar plans. In Warwickshire, a populous county with a large industrial belt near Birmingham as well as typically rural areas, all the secondary modern schools which offer sound academic and pre-professional courses encouraging children to continue education after 15 are called "high schools." The Government's 1958 White Paper on Education suggests that other authorities might copy Warwickshire's example.

One of the most radical alterations proposed is that announced towards the end of 1958 in the county of Middlesex, which includes a large sector of the northern and western London suburbs. After political fluctuations during the past few years, Middlesex now has a Labour majority. The proposed scheme would make it the usual practice for all children in the country's primary schools to be transferred at the age of 11 to the nearest secondary school of any type. There, it is said, all types of children would be offered a full range of subjects according to aptitude and taste (including, no doubt, the taste of the parents). A press hand-out spoke of "grammar schools" (not comprehensive) for all. Bitter opposition has been voiced by parents, teachers, and many other observers—not all of them anti-socialists by any means. Apart from the demonstrable shortage of teachers and equipment, and other possible objections, critics forecast an accelerated exodus of teachers, a migration of parents to other areas, the withdrawal of children, a marvelous boom for private schools, and an educational disaster generally.

Rather than contemplate the unknown on such a cataclysmic scale it is better to look at some actual experiments with comprehensive schools which have been running long enough to reveal some of their special problems and opportunities. Turning aside from the external embarrassments of social structure, of institutional paraphernalia from another age, and of prejudice and politics, one can come to the evolving life and ethos of these very new schools—all postwar experiments. None of them can be properly described as a new creation, no matter how new their buildings or how eager their teachers. They must be housed in very real areas (often fairly poor) for the children of parents born and educated a generation ago, employing teachers of whom the same must be said. To a large extent comprehensive schools must still be described as peripheral to English education. Some of them are eager centres for a new gospel; some are perplexed and reluctant amalgams of still unassimilated groups of children and teachers; all are the victims of too much notice and propaganda. Yet it is interesting to see that, despite the remarkable autonomy permitted to English schools, they do appear to agree approximately on various principles and methods which promise to become generally viable and fruitful in an English context already in many ways prepared for them.[7]

References

[1] Also published in *Educational Forum,* January 1958, as "Equality, Equal Opportunity, and Comprehensive Schools in England."

[2] For example, in 1958 the London Master Builders' Association published a report on apprenticeship in the London region; it was stated that 2,000 apprentices a year could be absorbed in the industry, but that only about half that number came forward.

[3] For example, on 16 December 1958 the British Productivity Council called a nationwide meeting of industrialists, labor union leaders, and educators to discuss experiments in "productivity education" in secondary schools. At these, people from industry had helped in the education of selected pupils in their last school year in one school district (Burton). The Council expected the scheme to be greatly expanded [report in *Manchester Guardian,* 17 December, 1958].

[4] For instance the Arnold High School recently established in Nottingham, with Dr. J. H. Higginson as Headmaster.

[5] These can be read about in *Comprehensive Education*, by R. Pedley (Gollancz, London, 1956).

[6] A slowly growing number from homes which can afford increasingly heavy fees goes to prestige-conferring private schools. This leakage may be of great social importance in the circumstances of England, and it may directly affect a teacher's choice of employment.

[7] The sequel to this article "Comprehensive Schools in England: Their Prospects," will be published in the next issue of *Comparative Education Review*.

Introduction to

Contributors to section two:

Educational Policies Commission

William J. Platt

Dorothy Lee

Herbert Muller

Julian Huxley

Sri Aurobindo Ghose

The function of educat

section two: ion in a society

SECTION II

THAT EDUCATION SERVES VITAL PURPOSES SEEMS TO BE admitted by virtually everyone. What these purposes are supposed to be meets with much less agreement. Yet as we look back at the development of our educational system we become aware of immense progress in our conceptions of the broad purposes of education. The Educational Policies Commission statement made in 1937 on the function of education surveys in well nigh classical fashion the development of our national purposes for education. The first selection of this Section traces the historical development of our society's ideas about the purposes of schools.

The inescapable conclusion that education is a major factor in economic welfare must come to any student of education in underdeveloped countries. The readings in Section I have also demonstrated the connection between education and economic welfare in modern technological societies. In the second selection in this Section William J. Platt details the economic value of education.

One of the perplexing questions for many people in our culture and particularly for educators and other workers with youth is that of the relation between individual freedom or autonomy and the society's need for structure. Both anthropologists and psychologists have contributed to some resolution of the problem. The psychologists have pointed out the need for structure, for limits, if children are to be secure and if they are to be helped to test what reality is and must be. In Dorothy Lee's article, the author gives many examples of the variety of ways in which different cultures treat this problem. One of the contributions the anthropologist has made is to our conception of a pluralistic universe in which many kinds of behavior seem to succeed. At the same time this leads the educator to search for research bases for making wise selections among the various solutions for the problem of the individual in relation to his social group.

In discussing this problem in relation to the concept of an open society, Muller, in the third reading, points up how essential the development of inner controls by the individual must be to the preservation of an open society. Obviously the purposes of education derive from these considerations of societal and individual needs as well as from the societal expectations for knowledge and skills.

Huxley's paper on "Cultural Process and Evolution" develops the idea that "one moral system can be better than another" and appeals for "steps to be taken to ensure better cultural adaptation" by the application of "scientific method to the study of the central explanatory and interpretative elements of man's vision of destiny, with a view to the progressive replacements of mythical elements by scientifically based concepts tested against fact." It is apparent that, acknowledging the complex sources of men's behavior, still we are at the point when we could make choices as to behaviors to encourage, customs to discourage, practices to develop. The educational system can do no other than take note of these possibilities and to frame its purposes increasingly from the scientifically-based conclusions to which Huxley refers.

Aurobindo's essay on the philosophy of Indian education is certainly one of the most beautifully written discourses ever written about the education of children. Written in 1924, the essay invites comparison with the ideas expressed by Dewey during the same period. Their attitudes toward children's learning are very similar; the major distinction between Aurobindo and Dewey is the former's emphasis on the spiritual aspects of man and yet when Aurobindo says, "There is a strange idea prevalent that by merely teaching the dogmas of religion children can be made pious and moral. This is an European error, and its practice either leads to mechanical acceptance of a creed having no effect on the inner and little on the outer life, or it creates the fanatic, the pietist, the ritualist or the unctuous hypocrite," he was expressing the same conception of moral learning as Dewey.

The reader of Sections I and II will note how the purposes of education, though remaining broadly the same, shift from one society to another and from one historical period to another. The decisions that are in the making about education are constantly subject to revision in the light of new knowledge about human beings and new societal pressures. The teacher is necessarily an intense student of the factors important in making these new decisions.

See Section Bibliographies, page 361.

2-1 The founders of the republic exalted education as a national interest*

It is out of the historical development of American society that have come the ideas, aspirations, knowledge, and working rules which prevail today and set the task of education. There have been borrowings, of course. Beyond the founding of the Republic lies a vast background embracing the culture of antiquity, the Middle Ages, the Renaissance, and modern Europe. From this plenitude of resources American civilization has been enriched. But all that has been drawn from other times and places has been worked into the American heritage. Additional drafts may be made upon other nations in days to come. Research will bring new knowledge. Experiments may confirm new methods. Novel ideas may bid for favor. The spirit of inquiry and invention may be active. The aspirations of the living will be stirred by the eternal surge of the human heart. Even so, the past, distant and near, has given us our society, including all the material, intellectual, and moral manifestations with which education must work.

Its development falls into three broad periods

Judged by outstanding characteristics of policy and economy the history of this heritage in the United States falls into three general periods. The first extended from the establishment of the Republic to the advent of Jacksonian democracy. The second had a longer

---

* Educational Policies Commission, *The Unique Function of Education in American Democracy*, Washington, D.C.: National Education Association, 1937, 9–28.

reach—from the inauguration of Andrew Jackson in 1829 to the eve of the World War. The third covers the years since the coming of that cataclysm. To be sure, no sharp division separates these periods; the fixing of exact dates is an arbitrary action, and is accompanied by a warning against accepting them as more than conveniences. Nor were the features of the first age all destroyed in the second, or the features of the first and second in the third. There have been siftings and accumulations, borrowings and modifications, survivals and mergers, now incorporated in American society, the heritage with which we work today.

The republic was founded in an age of high tension

The independence of America was established by revolution and war, accompanied by inevitable concentration, storm, and stress. America had broken with the past in many respects and had founded government on a new base—social purpose as distinguished from the prescriptive rights of class. It was an infant republic in a world of warring monarchies. Its leaders were searching for ways and means of ensuring the perpetuity of government so conceived, developing natural resources, applying the technical arts, and realizing a better life for the free members of society.

Founders of the republic laid stress on the public interest

The founders of the American Republic were concerned with more than the material aspects of life—with more than the exploitation of natural resources, the pursuit of private interests, and the enrichment of individuals. They were public personages embued with a deep sense of social responsibility. They had staked their lives and their fortunes on independence and the security of the Republic. They had devoted time, energies, and talents to the public interest, waging war against a foreign foe and against greed and passions in their own midst. With justice does a biographer of Washington say: "Excluding his boyhood, there were but seven years of his life in which he was not engaged in the public service."

The early leaders did not subscribe to the economic theory that the pursuit of private gain would automatically bring about the establishment of independence, the creation of a constitution, or the security and prosperity of the American nation. In fact, during the Revolution they had seen gambling in goods and securities almost wreck their cause. After victory had been won they saw emphasis on personal and sectional interests threaten the Union with dissolution. They knew from bitter experience that devotion to the public good and self-denial in private matters were necessary to the achievement of great social ends. Having risked their all in the creation of a nation, the ablest among them gave unremitting attention to the study of public affairs and the methods calculated to preserve and improve the independent society which their labors had brought forth.

The idea of government by a fixed special interest was rejected

It is true that many extremists relied heavily upon the ancient weapon of statecraft—force—for the assurance of social order, and looked upon government as an instrument of private advantage. They would have entrenched great wealth in politics by the establishment of high property qualifications on voting and office-holding. They would have given life terms to Presidents and Senators, and restricted popular participation in public affairs to the smallest possible limits. They would have permanently established a class government—government by "the rich and well-born," and were largely indifferent to popular culture and education. But this faction, though influential, was challenged by events. The verdict of the majority finally ran against it. The verdict of history condemned it. In the course of years the government established by the founders of the Republic came to rest on a wide popular base; and with the passing of time that base was broadened by constitutional enactments and political practices.

The democratic idea was accepted

In fact there was in the United States no aristocracy buttressed by special privileges in public law to provide support for a monarchy or an oligarchy. In the long run the fate of government and society had to be entrusted to the wisdom and knowledge of a widening mass of people. Some Americans accepted that fate with a wry face, but made the best of it. Others greeted it as a fulfilment of the principles proclaimed in the Declaration of Independence, and as marking a humane departure from the despotisms of Europe. This document had asserted that all men are created equal, and endowed by their Creator with certain inalienable rights, including life, liberty, and the pursuit of happiness; that governments derive their just powers from the consent of the governed; and that the people have the right to alter or abolish any form of government which becomes destructive of these ends. Lifted up against the background of European societies founded on force and prescriptive privileges, these were revolutionary doctrines. The future was to decide whether any government so conceived and so dedicated could long endure.

Cultural responsibilities were imposed on government

Concerning the responsibilities of government in matters of economy and culture, leaders of the Republic had equally positive convictions. They did not conceive government as founded on sheer force and confined to the punishment of criminals. If doubts arise respecting this matter, they can be resolved by reading President Washington's first inaugural address and his first message to Congress. In assuming his duties he declared that the preeminence of free government must be "exemplified by all the attributes which can win the affections of its citizens and command the respect of the world." While recognizing the place of force in national defense and the maintenance of government, he commended to Congress "the advancement of agriculture, commerce, and manufactures by all proper means," and the promotion of science, literature, and education. In taking this broad view of statesmanship, Washington was profoundly moved by the challenge of the occasion, for he said: "The preservation of the sacred fire of liberty and the destiny of the republican model of government are justly considered, perhaps, as *deeply*, as *finally* staked on the experiment entrusted to the hands of the American people."

The vital relation of education to the social order was recognized

Having committed themselves to government by popular verdict, to a government with high social responsibilities, many founders of the American Republic turned to education as a guarantee that a government of this type would endure—not merely to political education narrowly adapted to the genius of American institutions, but to education in the arts, sciences, and letters, assuring a deeper foundation in civilization itself. If a contemporary, Samuel Blodget, is to be believed, the idea of establishing a national institution of learning was taken up with General Washington in 1775, while Revolutionary soldiers were quartered in buildings on the campus of Harvard College, and Washington then and there approved the idea.[1]

---

[1] Wesley, E. B. *Proposed: The University of the United States.* Minneapolis: University of Minnesota Press, 1936. 83 p.

American leaders turned to educational planning

However that may be, it is certain that shortly after independence was gained, many of the best minds in America began to draft comprehensive plans for systems of universal education, crowned by a national university. Among them was Dr. Benjamin Rush, physician, surgeon-general during the Revolutionary War, member of the Continental Congress, signer of the Declaration of Independence, and member of the Pennsylvania convention that ratified the Constitution. In 1786 he published an educational project, with the arresting title "Thoughts Upon the Mode of Education Proper in a Republic." A few years later the American Philosophical Society offered a prize for "the best system of liberal education and literary instruction, adapted to the genius of the Government of the United States; comprehending also a plan for instituting and conducting public schools in this country, on principles of the most extensive utility." The prize was divided between Samuel Knox and Samuel H. Smith. Other thinkers of the age, including Noah Webster, presented to the public large projects for the education of youth in a manner appropriate to American society and government.

Early educational plans were wide and deep in compass

This is no place to describe these plans or to smooth away their inconsistencies, but a summary of them shows that American ideas on education are the treasures of high statesmanship—not merely the theories of school administrators and teachers.[1] Taking numerous plans of the early Republic collectively, we may say that they were amazingly broad and comprehensive. They projected institutions of learning extending from the primary schools to a national university in charge of research, general instruction, and training for the public service. They dealt with education in its widest terms, as adapted to the nature of American society and government, and as serving the progressive development of individuals and society—not the one or the other exclusively—but both as inseparable. These schemes were not confined to the practical arts and subjects of utility in the conduct of government. They did emphasize, it is true, the practical and political arts; but they went beyond any narrow utilitarianism. They included pure science, letters, and all the arts deemed necessary for a rich, secure,

[1] Hansen, Allen O. *Liberalism and American Education in the Eighteenth Century*. New York: Macmillan Co., 1926. 317 p.

and enlightened civilization; and they recognized the truth that both government and economy rest upon wisdom, knowledge, and aspirations wider and deeper than the interests of immediate marketability.

The role of women in civilization was recognized

In seeking to enrich the moral and intellectual resources of society, some of the early educational planners gave attention to the role of women as makers and bearers of culture. They knew from impressive personal experience the part that women had taken in the war for independence—for instance, in keeping economy running, in furnishing war supplies, in sustaining and feeding the spirit of independence in newspapers, pamphlets, and plays, and in private councils. Leaders from General Washington down the line had recognized their services and paid open tribute to their part in the great drama.

It was no accident, then, that Noah Webster, perhaps the most indefatigable among the educational leaders, gave special consideration to the education of women. He believed that their influence in shaping the underlying ideals and policies of the nation was in many ways greater than that of men. Mothers gave to youth firm impressions of life's values and should be educated so that they would set youth in the republican way of life. Taking the cultural influence into full account, Webster insisted that the education of women "should therefore enable them to implant in the tender mind such sentiments of virtue, propriety, and dignity as are suited to the freedom of our government." For this reason he insisted that their education should not be confined to subjects usually taught in schools for girls, but should include science, history, geography, contemporary affairs, and all that then passed for the social studies. "In a system of education that should embrace every part of the community," he urged, "the female sex claims no inconsiderable part of our attention."

Freedom of inquiry was emphasized

As befitted the temper of the age, early educational planners insisted upon unlimited freedom of inquiry and exposition in institutions of learning. They cast off *a priori* notions of tradition and brought to the bar of critical examination "all things under the sun"—the works of nature, institutions of Church and State, the forms and distribution of property, the relations of property to government, the processes of government, the driving forces of social life, the family and its historic role, the maxims of industry and commerce, and international affairs. And they did this with insight, a wealth of learning and a firm grasp upon realities. For them, liberty of inquiry and exposition was not merely necessary to the working of popular institutions. It was indispensable to progress in every branch of human affairs. It was one of the noblest expressions of life among a free people. "What are the means of improving and establishing the Union of the States?" This was the question which Noah Webster encountered everywhere in his travels throughout the country in 1785. "Custom is the plague of wise men and the idol of fools!" he exclaimed. In this spirit, educational planners for the nation proposed to throw off denominational control of education, emphasized unhampered scientific research, and upheld the unfettered right of exposition, while cherishing a deep sense of social responsibility.

Education was deemed indispensable to popular government

The men who had set up the new government after the Revolution were, as a matter of course, especially concerned with political education, with the preparation of the people for self-government. The processes of democracy to which they were committed, explicitly or implicitly, embraced five essential elements: the right of citizens to propose measures and policies, the right to discuss freely all proposed policies and measures, the right to decide issues at the polls, the obligation to accept decisions duly made without resort to force, and the right to appraise, criticize, and amend decisions so made. The preservation of these processes of democracy was assured in part, the founders believed, by laws and institutions guaranteeing freedom of the press, discussion, and decision, but they knew that paper guarantees were not enough. Knowledge and a moral sense were required to sustain democratic processes and to make them constructive, rather than destructive. "In proportion as the structure of government gives force to public opinion," wrote Washington in his Farewell Address, "it is essential that public opinion should be enlightened." How? "Promote, then, as an object of primary importance, institutions for the general diffusion of knowledge."

Education was considered in the constitutional convention of 1787

In the convention that framed the Constitution, James Madison proposed that Congress be empowered "to establish a university," and Charles Pinckney urged a broader provision: "to establish seminaries for the promotion of literature and the arts and sciences." At a later time in the convention Madison and Pinckney joined in moving for the creation of a university. Upon their project Gouverneur Morris remarked: "It is not necessary. The exclusive power at the seat of government will reach the object." The motion was lost. No express provisions were made in the Constitution for the promotion of education, but leaders among the men who framed that document certainly believed that the power to perform this national service was positively implied. Even Jefferson, speaking later as a strict constructionist, declared that Congress could make appropriations of public lands for that purpose.

George Washington advocated national aids to education

That Washington regarded the fostering of education as an obligation of the Federal Government was made evident in his first annual address to Congress: "Nor am I less persuaded that you will agree with me in opinion that there is nothing which can better deserve your patronage than the promotion of science and literature. Knowledge is in every country the surest basis of public happiness. In one in which the measures of government receive their impressions so immediately from the sense of the community as in ours it is proportionably essential. To the security of a free constitution it contributes in various ways . . . Whether this desirable object will be best promoted by affording aids to seminaries of learning already established, by the institution of a national university, or by any other expedients will be well worthy of a place in the deliberations of the Legislature." In letters to his other colleagues, Washington also revealed his solicitude for education.

Washington took a broad view of education

And it was a broad interest. Although Washington, unlike Jefferson, had not enjoyed the privileges of a college education, and was a man of limited "book knowledge," he had a general and realistic view of education. Speaking of the proposed national university, he said: "I have greatly wished to see a plan adopted, by which the arts, science, and belles-lettres could be taught in their *fullest* extent, thereby embracing *all* the advantages of European tuition, with the means of acquiring the liberal knowledge, which is necessary to qualify our citizens for the exigencies of public as well as private life; and (which with me is a consideration of great magnitude) by assembling the youth from the different parts of this rising republic, contributing from their intercourse and interchange of information to the removal of prejudices, which might perhaps sometimes arise from local circumstances." So deeply impressed was he by the utility of such an institution that he left a part of his estate by will for the endowment of a university in the District of Columbia—a provision never acted upon by Congress.

Thomas Jefferson made education a primary interest

Although at odds with Washington on many points of policy and committed, while in the opposition, to a narrow construction of the Constitution, Thomas Jefferson was even more deeply and actively concerned with public education than the first President. As a biographer has truly said: "Jefferson was the first conspicuous advocate, in this country, of centralization in education, being a thorough believer in state aid to higher institutions of learning and free education in the common schools supported by local taxation. To him the schoolhouse was the fountain-head of happiness, prosperity, and good government, and education was 'a holy cause.'" A college graduate, a student of the classics, a leader in public affairs, interested in every branch of art, science, and letters, eager to make broad and deep the cultural foundations of democracy, Jefferson dedicated years of his life to the consideration and promotion of education in all its phases, from elementary instruction to advanced research in universities. He was, in many ways, the most highly cultivated man of his time, and, among the great directors of national affairs, he gave the most thought and personal attention to education.

His was no mere lip service. He sought to encompass education, to discover its possibilities, to give it an exalted and permanent position in public policy, and to make it enrich and serve the new society rising in America. It was characteristic of his concern that he omitted from the inscription which he prepared for his own tomb all mention of the high political offices he had held and included the fact that he was the founder of the University of Virginia.

Jefferson's plan included wide elementary education

Jefferson's plan of education for the state of Virginia embraced a scheme for elementary schools in every country, so placed that every householder would be within three miles of a school. On this base was to be erected district institutions of higher learning, so distributed that each student would be within a day's ride of a college. Crowning the structure was a university of the highest type dedicated to the freedom of the mind and unlimited research for truth. That sons of the poor might not be denied the privileges of education, Jefferson proposed that "the best genius" of each elementary school, if unable to pay his way, should be sent to the secondary school at public expense, and that the ablest in each secondary institution be maintained at the university free of cost. Thus the elements of learning were to be made available to all, and for the ablest boys, even those without financial resources, the pathway to the university was to be opened. Although the plan was never enacted into law, Jefferson saw clearly that the nation needed talent in public and private affairs, and education was to enable talent to flower.

Jefferson's educational objectives for lower schools were individual and social

In no single place did Jefferson summarize his philosophy of education, but the following passage from his writings indicates the nature of his thought respecting the ends to be attained:

"(1) To give to every citizen the information he needs for the transaction of his own business;

"(2) To enable him to calculate for himself, and to express and preserve his ideas, his contracts, and accounts, in writing;

"(3) To improve, by reading, his morals and faculties;

"(4) To understand his duties to his neighbors and country, and to discharge with competence the functions confided to him by either;

"(5) To know his rights; to exercise with order and justice those he retains; to choose with discretion the fiduciary of those he delegates; and to notice their conduct with diligence, with candor and judgment;

"(6) And, in general, to observe with intelligence and faithfulness all the social relations under which he shall be placed."

For his university Jefferson proclaimed untrammelled liberty of inquiry

As the motto for his University of Virginia, Jefferson chose the ancient saying: "And ye shall know the truth, and the truth shall make you free." In that spirit he stipulated complete freedom of inquiry and exposition for the professors, self-government for the faculty, and an honor system for the students. "I have sworn upon the altar of

God," he exclaimed, "eternal hostility against every form of tyranny over the mind of man."

In his university curriculum Jefferson emphasized the social and natural sciences

In laying out a program of university work, Jefferson placed emphasis on the social and natural sciences in a manner so comprehensive that his project may be still studied with advantage, and employed as a guide for educational thought. Its great purposes may be summarized in the language of a special student of Jeffersonian policies:

"(1) To form the statesmen, legislators, and judges, on whom public prosperity and individual happiness depend;

"(2) To expound the principles and structure of government, the laws which regulate the intercourse of nations, those formed municipally for our own government, and a sound spirit of legislation;

"(3) To harmonize and promote the interests of agriculture, manufactures, and commerce, and by well-informed views of political economy to give a free scope to the public industry;

"(4) To develop the reasoning faculties of our youth, enlarge their minds, cultivate their morals, and instill in them the precepts of virtue and order; and

"(5) To enlighten them with mathematical and physical sciences, which advance the arts, and administer to the health, the subsistence, and comforts of human life."

To Jefferson nothing human was alien; neither the thought of Virgil, nor the invention of a threshing machine. To preserve, advance, and disseminate knowledge in the improvement of individual well-being and social relations was, for Jefferson, a passion that endured to his last days.

Jefferson regarded education as a combined national and state interest

Despite his immediate concern with education in Virginia, Jefferson was also engrossed in education as a national interest. In his message of December 2, 1806, he suggested the appropriation of public funds "to the great purposes of the public education, roads, rivers, canals, and such other objects of public improvement as it may be thought proper to add to the constitutional enumeration of Federal powers." He was prepared to amend the Constitution, if necessary to promote education and economic welfare, but he recognized the fact that Congress already had some authority over these matters, including the power to dedicate public lands to "a national establishment of education." Again, in 1808, in his last message, Jefferson called upon Congress to consider the same theme. Thus even amid the turmoil of the Napoleonic wars, which violently disturbed the politics and economy of the United States, the President continued to urge upon Congress and the country an interest that lay close to his heart.

John Quincy Adams emulated the example of Washington

With the administration of John Quincy Adams, "the heroic period of the Revolution" drew to a close. In a strict sense Adams did not belong to it, but as a boy he had gone to Europe and assumed the duties of secretary to his father on a mission for the Republic then battling for existence. He was brought up in the Washington tradition and derived conceptions of policy from that source. Having started life as a Federalist and having transferred his allegiance to the Jeffersonian party, Adams found it possible to combine, in his thought, elements from the two systems of statesmanship. Unlike James Monroe, his immediate predecessor, Adams had no doubts about the constitutionality of the broad views entertained by Washington. With the exception of Jefferson, no President had been more deeply interested in natural science and its beneficent applications than John Quincy Adams. If he could have had his way, the nation's great endowment in natural resources would have been conserved and dedicated to internal improvements, the advancement of science, and the promotion of education. It was with extreme bitterness that he spoke of the "rapacity" with which politicians "fly at the public lands," engage in "pillage," and act as "enormous speculators and landjobbers."

Adams urged Congress to promote science, education, and the arts

Seeking to resist the pressure for the dissipation of the national resources, Adams urged upon Congress a broader social policy. "The great object of th; institution of civil government," he said in his first annual message, "is the improvement of the condition of those who are parties to the social compact, and no government, in whatever form constituted, can accomplish the lawful ends of its institution but in proportion as it improves the condition of those over whom it is established. Roads and canals, by multiplying and facilitating the communications and intercourse between distant regions and multitudes of men, are among the most important means of improvement. But moral, political, intellectual improvement are duties assigned by the Author of Our Existence to social no less than to individual man. For the fulfilment of those duties governments are invested with power, and to the attainment of the end—the progressive improvement of the condition of the governed—the exercise of delegated powers is a duty as sacred and indispensable as the usurpation of powers not granted is criminal and odious. Among the first, perhaps the very first, instrument for the improvement of the condition of men is knowledge, and to the acquisition of much of the knowledge adapted to the wants, the comforts, and enjoyments of human life public institutions and seminaries of learning are essential."

After laying down this controlling principle, Adams then urged the promotion of "scientific research and inquiry" in "geographical and astronomical science," the exploration of national territories and waters, the erection of an astronomical observatory "connected with the establishment of an university, or separate from it," the patronage of studies in the science of weights and measures, and the revision of the patent laws. Summarizing the powers of Congress, Adams indicated that they could be brought into action "by laws promoting the improvement of agriculture, commerce, and manufactures, the cultivation and encouragement of the mechanic and of the elegant arts, the advancement of literature, and the progress of the sciences, ornamental and profound."

If the language of these reflections and recommendations is somewhat stilted, there is no doubt respecting its thought and import. Adams had in mind a conception of the nation as a civilization and the use of its material, intellectual, and moral resources, under public auspices, in "the progressive improvement of the condition of the governed." The powers of the Federal Government he deemed ample for this purpose and refusal to use them, he thought, "would be treachery to the most sacred of trusts." "The spirit of improvement," he exclaimed, "is abroad upon the earth." Should the Federal Government fall behind state governments in "holding up the torch of human improvement to eyes that seek the light?"

But the times were not favorable for the promotion of plans for education

Admirable and promising as were many of these plans for education, the times were not propitious for bringing them to fruition. The great social and economic forces which were to call them into being some forty or fifty years after the adoption of the Constitution had not yet appeared. The population of America consisted of between three and four million persons, thinly scattered over a wide area. Rural civilization predominated. As late as 1820 less than five percent of the total population lived in the thirteen cities of 8,000 or over. Slow, crude means of transportation and communication resulted in isolation for most of the people. Collective action was extremely difficult. Moreover, the war for independence had exhausted the resources of the government and had left a war debt which threatened to keep them depleted over a period of years. The people were engrossed with political matters.

As a consequence of these adverse conditions, education declined to its lowest point since schools were founded by the colonists. The close of the period found local authority strongly entrenched in the administration of education. There was as yet no sign of that integration of small local schools into state school systems which came within the next fifty years. Although during the early national period the Federal Government began the policy of making land grants which forecast universal education, such grants are more accurately interpreted as a stimulus to the colonization of new territory than as a national policy whose primary purpose was to promote education. In general the National Government followed the policy of leaving the provision and administration of education to the states and local communities. Educational as well as national consciousness was yet to awaken, and it was not until some years after the second war with England that plans for popular education began to receive serious consideration; then, state plans, not national plans, were adopted as the schools passed from an administration predominantly local to an administration and control originating with the state.

Though temporarily rejected, the educational ideals of the founders remain basic for contemporary thought

It so happened, then, that the founders of the Republic did not live to see their ideals realized in the establishment of public institutions for education. For this outcome lack of popular interest, the opposition of private schools, and poverty of financial resources were partly responsible. Doubtless even more influential was the popular revolt against the broad conceptions of federal policy which they cherished. With the triumph of Andrew Jackson in 1828 the principles of the Federalist party, with which Washington was associated in spirit, and the principles of the Republican party, which Jefferson led, were repudiated in a surge of democracy that was suspicious of all government and soon fell under the dominance of the particularism known as states' rights. Events thus provided a new setting of ideas and interests for the period in which institutions of popular education were actually created and for educational thought itself. In other words, the age of concentration that marked the foundation of the Republic was followed by an age of diffusion, in which the security and perpetuity of the nation were largely taken for granted, despite the shadows of civil dissension. Yet, while the work of establishing institutions of public education fell principally to the states and communities, the Union organized by the founders was continued and furnished the institutional frame in which economy was being nationalized even while particularism seemed triumphant.

2-2 The economic value of education *

In this paper I propose to describe why economists are belatedly according education a prominence you knew it deserved all along. I want to show education is itself a growth industry and will continue to be. And with this background in the rudiments of the economics of education I want to do something that would seem to harmonize with the objectives of your workshop. I want to suggest a new arena for the battle against waste related to education. Waste is a handy charge for critics of schools and for status quo seekers. I hope to prove that armed with some simple weapons of economic understanding we can, and must, carry the battle to the real problems of economic waste related to education. Unless the battle is joined and won in that arena, our national values *will* be sterilized.

My first point probably needs little buttressing. It is that *economic growth of California and of the United States is essential to the achievement of national and free world aspirations.* The dimensions of this growth include not only increase in gross national product (GNP), but an equitable distribution of income, a high level of employment, a viable balance of payments, a meeting of national and international security obligations, an expanded assistance program to developing

---

* William J. Platt, "The Economic Value of Education," (Address to Conference of California Association of School Administrators, 1962).

William J. Platt

nations, and perhaps most importantly an opportunity for the individual citizen to widen his cultural and economic choices. The widening of these choices is, we believe, the path to individual dignity. All these good things come easier with a high GNP than with a low one, easier with growth than with stagnation. We, and every other nation that wants to preserve and extend its values, is "locked in" to growth.

Now where does education enter the growth process? The economy grows through investment. Investment increases the productivity of our people and of our plant and equipment. My second point, then, is that *education, along with research and development and the building of physical capital, is an investment.* The current investment in the United States is about $22 billion in formal education, $12 billion in research and development, $40–$70 billion in plant and equipment. Is this balanced, and is education getting its share?

So far as I know there is no big model that will tell how much should be invested in education versus research and development versus physical capital. But both analytic evidence and intuition suggest that returns from marginal investments would be highest for education. Compare the decision apparatus for the three forms of investment. In the United States hundreds of thousands of entrepreneurs are ever alert to opportunities for profit from additional investments in plant and equipment. And the capital goods industry, through its sales force, is urging those investments. Similarly, managements are looking for profitable investments in research and development. But it is not at all clear that there is an equally alert decision apparatus for education. Few of the policy makers in education acknowledge its investment nature, much less are they able to command additional resources when they do know that greater investments will profit society. Therefore, there's a strong presumption of structural underinvestment in education.

A number of recent economic studies are beginning to show the contribution to growth traceable to education. Becker [1] has studied the 1950 census to find the effect of educational level upon income. He found the following income differentials, based on the average income of an 8th grade graduate equalling 100: 4 years of elementary, an income of 79; high school diploma, an income of 124; college degree, an income of 181. The difference is certainly greater now than it was in 1950.

In measuring returns from education, Becker and other economists include as costs not only the private and public expenditures for education, but also foregone earnings. The latter are the earnings or income

[1] Becker, Gary S.,"Underinvestment in College Education," *The American Economic Review,* Vol. L(2), May 1960.

a person of 16 years of age or more might have expected to receive if he had been employed instead of going to school. Even with this added cost penalty, Becker found that education pays an 11% return on investment. This exceeds rates of return on physical wealth. It is further testimony to the attractiveness to the individual and to the community of creating more effective human capital.

An obvious complexity in measuring the payoff from schooling is the elapsed time between the investment in education and the realization of higher productivity from that investment. However, short lead-time demonstrations can occasionally be found. A dramatic illustration of the profitability of education (both to society and to the individual) occurs in the vocational rehabilitation program of the Department of Health, Education, and Welfare. Before rehabilitation training, 56,000 handicapped persons earned $15 million per year; after rehabilitation, they earned $102 million per year. The additional federal income taxes paid by the group in one year were alone more than the $8 million cost of the training program.[1]

Denison has looked at the national effects of education in his publication, "The Sources of Economic Growth in the United States and the Alternatives Before Us."[2] He demonstrates that much of our economic progress owes to increased investment in education. For example, he shows that if the 1960 labor force had been only as well educated as the 1950 labor force, our national production in 1960 would have been 10% lower than it was. At the end of his book, Denison lists a menu of choices available to increase the national growth rate from its average of about 3% per year to 4% per year, or one percentage point more. Prominent among available measures is to add 1-1½ years of schooling for everyone completing school between now and 1980, or "to make equivalent improvement in the quality of education." The United States needs to do both things—increase the average number of years of school completed *and* improve the effectiveness of education. We shall return to this point later.

The staff of the Joint Economic Committee of the Congress summarizes this point well in their report: "more adequate support for

---

[1] Office of Vocational Rehabilitation, Department of Health, Education, and Welfare, "The Disabled: The Rate of Vocational Rehabilitation in Improving the Economic Condition of Low Income Families," 86th Congress, 1st Session, Characteristics of the Low Income Population and Related Federal Programs, Government Printing Office, Washington, D.C., 1955, pp. 84–94.

[2] Denison, Edward F., "The Sources of Economic Growth in the United States and the Alternatives Before Us," Supplementary Paper #13, Committee for Economic Development, New York, 1962.

education is the single most important recommendation for strengthening our economy." [3]

At this point you may fear that I have made an education too valuable a property. Faraday was showing the statesman Gladstone through a laboratory. Gladstone asked, "What is the use of this new thing, electricity?" Faraday replied, "I suppose some day you may put a tax upon it." I suppose in the personal income tax we have done the same to education.

My foregoing preoccupation with the economic effect of education may seem to make me vulnerable to a charge of neglecting other equally important purposes of education. Some of these are the transmitting and enhancing of values, the instilling of civic responsibility, the encouragement of artistic creativity, the development of taste for enriching life. Fortunately, negligible conflict exists between these and economic goals of education, so I can and must, resist the temptation to stray from my assigned topic.

It may be helpful to look at countries beyond our borders, asking what role is education playing in the well-being of other societies? I have had some opportunity to do this in the last two years and find that the exercise helped to correct my cultural tunnel vision. My third point is that *comparative education shows dramatically the economic and social contribution of education.* Japan's century of development after the Meiji restoration owes greatly to a major investment in education. The Republic of the Philippines has surged into democratic independence and growth, largely by virtue of a broad base of education designed during the islands' association with the United States.

The deliberate use of a massive education program by the Communists in the Soviet Union and Communist China show that these regimes understand the investment nature of education.

What about newly developing countries? Those that have tried to look ahead at their education problems have found awesome gaps between their aspirations and their resources. At a conference in Ethiopia last year, 39 African countries tried to see what would be required for the following goal for education in 1980: universal primary, 23 percent of the appropriate age group enrolled in secondary, and 2 percent enrolled in high education. The Africans found that if they assumed an annual growth in national income rising from 4% to 6%, and if they further assumed a doubling of the percentage of national income de-

---

[3] Joint Economic Committee, *Staff Report on Employment, Growth, and Price Levels,* Washington, D.C., Superintendent of Documents, Government Printing Office, December 1959, p. 55.

voted to education, they would still be short of meeting the above program by as much as $1 billion per year.[4]

In newly developing countries there is thus what might be called an educational imperative. There people are demanding education as though it were a fundamental right, like malaria control, to which each person is entitled. But the tragedy is that economic realities allow less than half the children even a primary education in many countries of Africa, Asia and Latin America. Many of the countries are striving now to expand education. Increasingly it is a part of United States policy to assist in this most worthy movement.

What insights do we gain by looking at other countries having *advanced economies?* Western European countries have not had as universal an educational structure as the United States has. As they have chalked up remarkable economic growth in the last ten years, they have encountered shortages of talent, particularly managerial, technical, and highly skilled. And policymakers in those countries are beginning to make the correct diagnosis that *underinvestment in education* is the real limitation on further economic growth. They are setting about to double education investments during the next decade. Let this be early warning for us. The dynamics of our affluent technology and of our domestic and international obligations will catch up with our talent supply too. The enhancement and liberation of talent is the business of education. Let us be sure we do not too long postpone this step, as England may have. A British student of the economics of education, John Vaizey, ends his book, "Britain in the Sixties: Education for Tomorrow," as follows:

> "Britain is an inefficient, out-of-date, class-ridden society. It has in too many places an inefficient, out-of-date, class-ridden education system. If we want to change the society we have to change the education system. To do so will give us our best chance in the world of tomorrow." [5]

I need to develop one more concept of the economics of education: something three European economists call the "iron law of educational expenditures." [6] This is my fourth point. Their iron law simply

---

[4] Final Report, Conference of African States on the Development of Education in Africa, United Nations Economic Commission for Africa and United Nations Educational, Scientific and Cultural Organization, Addis Ababa, May 15–25, 1961.

[5] Vaizey, John, "Britain in the Sixties: Education for Tomorrow," Penguin Books, Ltd., 1962, p. 114.

[6] Svennilson, Ingvar, Friedrich Edding and Lionel Elvin, "Targets for Education

states that *educational expenditures grow faster than national output.* This iron law—that education will claim an increasing percentage of GNP—may be encouraging to us in the profession, since it tells us we're in a growth industry. It may be discouraging to us as taxpayers. It's not hard to understand why the law is valid. Some of the reasons may include:

1. The spreading educational imperative mentioned above.
2. The fact that enrollment increases with per capital income. Our college enrollment was 4% of the age group in 1904. In 1960 it was 38%.
3. The fact that teacher-to-pupil ratios improve with per capita income—educational quality improves with ability to pay.
4. The fact that education is both investment and consumption, being one of those delightful economic commodities in which we can be investing while we consume.
5. The fact that knowledge and technology accumulate geometrically, threatening to saturate us unless education is used to manage the accumulation.
6. Finally, because education pays off. It pays off in profits to the individual, in profits to the society, and, even more importantly, in human dignity.

The iron law operates in every country. Professor Schultz, former President of the American Economic Association, has found that in the United States the increase in educational investment has grown 4½ times as fast as GNP has increased.[7]

Let me isolate one of the growth segments in education—adult, or continuing education. What the individual and the society need increasingly is resilience in talent and skill. This means not just expertise, but retrainability and reeducability. That is what I mean by resilience. Only thus can the individual adapt flexibly to the dynamics of a technological age. Lifetime continuing education becomes essential. The Commencement exercise must now mean commencing further education!

The discussion up to this point has been homework. Now our class can start to apply some of the lore of the economics of education. Let's talk about waste. By one definition, the economists' objective is to

---

in Europe in 1970," Policy Conference on Economic Growth and Investment in Education, Washington, D.C., October 16–20, 1961, Organization for European Economic Co-operation, January 1962.

[7] Schultz, Theodore W., "Investment in Human Capital," *The American Economic Review*, Vol. LI, No. 1, March 1961.

help society prevent or minimize waste. Economizing in the economics sense is the art and science of allocating available resources so as best to satisfy wants. In other words, maximizing output per unit of input. Just as the clergy is against sin, the economist is against waste.

Let's enter our workshop here smarting (as some of us are) from attacks that there is great waste in education. The stereotype complaints are of frill courses (which often turn out to be whatever courses *my* children don't need); too many consultants (after all, the classroom teacher is certificated so why does she need all the superfluous experts for curriculum advice and in-service training); too high teachers' salaries (for young women who are going to get married in a couple of years anyway); excess playgrounds and landscaping. You are familiar with many other complaints. Now school administrators *do* need to have good answers for these critics. But what I would like to do is talk about much more serious wastes related to education. This is my fifth point. *These wastes can be grouped as wastes of (1) talent, (2) content and method, (3) organization, (4) the future, and (5) research opportunities.* Let me touch briefly on each.

1. Waste of talent

Each student hour in each year of school is a precious asset, potentially one that can unlock the talent of a Pasteur, or a Jefferson. Pasteur, incidentally, when asked what role luck had played in his discoveries, replied that it was a factor, "but chance favors the mind that is prepared." We trust our financial assets only to the banks and companies we believe to be competent and wise. Surely the nation's more valuable assets of young minds deserve even more care. To fail to liberate a single talent or intellect, to fail to educate to the maximum capacity all our future citizens is a waste greater than any of the stereotyped charges to which education is subjected.

Viewed from the vantage point of economics, an activity deserves additional resources until diminishing returns set in. In education this might mean that average expenditures per student should increase until we find that marginal utility, as measured perhaps by achievement or earning power, begins to be less than marginal input investment. The measurements we can make, particularly of earning power from additional years of general or specialized education, or of the same number of years of higher quality education, show just the opposite. They show increasing, instead of diminishing, returns. In other industries we would be guilty of waste if we operated in this portion of the input-output curve.

Dropouts are only one indicator of waste of talent. But they are easier to measure than the equally serious shortfalls of those in school remaining unchallenged. Each year in the United States, 60,000 to 100,-000 high school students in the top 30% of their class fail to go to college, primarily because of lack of funds. And about 60,000 students leave college for that reason.

One million students drop out before completing high school. This waste comes from a variety of reasons. If we allow individuals not to be educated to their capacities, we are condoning future shortfalls, if not blight, for the individual and for the community. By legislation passed in the current Congress, the U.S. is now getting under way a retraining effort for workers in industries and regions affected by economic dislocations. This effort already shows that resilience improves greatly with the number of years of previous schooling.

A waste of talent exists in part because we have not designed a good coupling between school and industry. Through cooperative efforts in placement, in vocational training facilities, in scholarships, and in curriculum materials we can give purpose to many students who now drift. In nearly all schools counseling and guidance activity is inadequate in size and in knowledge of career and educational opportunities. To perpetuate this condition is to be guilty of waste.

2. *Waste of content and method*

Modernized and proven content and method exist somewhere in the United States for almost every subject taught in every grade. But is every district using the best materials and methods? Is each district presenting, or pooling with other districts to present, in-service education to its faculty in modern mathematics and science? Is it applying what has already been demonstrated to be the strengths of programed instruction and of educational TV? Is it marshalling corrective resources whenever a poor reader is identified?

Recall that the economist Denison said we can increase the national growth rate by a whole percentage point merely by an improvement in the *quality of education.* By adopting proven reforms more widely in all districts this leverage on economic growth could be applied.

In industry the market place exercises an unseen hand (as Adam Smith called it) to encourage the diffusion of new and more productive techniques. Laggard entrepreneurs know that the profit statement is an unforgiving taskmaster. Education has no comparable discipline for each autonomous district to innovate improvements. The school administrator is the key to over-all progress in this realm.

3. Waste of organization

An elusive form of waste is the luxury of ineffective organization. Districts too small to be able to offer a good education somehow perpetuate themselves despite their subsidies and their shortfalls in developing talent. Unnecessary differences in the quality of education exist from district to district and from state to state. Waste here comes about because the location of potential talent is not correlated with the location of quality education. Latent talent may be anywhere—in poor as well as in rich districts.

Each year five million Americans move across state lines, and the movement within California is notorious. We cannot afford to balkanize our education with excessive differences in quality.

4. Waste of the future

By this I mean that in too many ways we are not looking ahead in education. For example, the human capital within education, like other forms of capital, must be maintained, replaced, and upgraded. And this poses particularly tough problems because of education's growth and the inexorable operation of the iron law of educational expenditures. Education is itself a consumer of talent, in competition with other employers of graduates. Future teachers must be attracted into education. They should be among our most talented and best trained because they must inspire others. Unfortunately the rewards we now give in the profession are not competitive with many other pursuits. Except where dedication dominates, those entering teaching are not the best equipped intellectually. Failure to regenerate education with the most talented and inspirational faculty is a long range waste. The teacher in the Soviet Union is accorded high prestige and high pay relative to other occupations. Ponder this disparity with the United States for the long run competition!

I have not even mentioned another growing requirement being placed on United States education. This is the assistance that developing countries need in the form of visiting teachers, peace corpsmen, and educational advisors. Educational capacities must be large enough for these requirements to be added to domestic demands.

We may expect a stepping up of foreign students going to school here. Over 50,000 foreign students are enrolled in our universities and colleges; a rapidly growing number of secondary level students is coming here. For all these international transactions in education we must provide more capacity and incentives to compete for high talent. Not to do so is waste.

5. Waste of research opportunities

Education is an underresearched industry. Many industries spend between 4 and 10 percent of total expenditures on research and development. The corresponding figure for education in the United States is about 1/10 of 1 percent.[8]

If we do not invest in research we fail to learn how to make education more effective. The industrial company without a research program is living on borrowed time. Let's help education avoid such a fate.

How does this discussion of waste relate to school administration? Very directly. Administrators have the center of initiative in public education. School administrators are managing a delicate and vital economic function—investment in human capital. This responsibility has economic and political overtones. Here is my sixth point. *You must educate your board and your community not just about district problems, but about education as an investment and as the means of transmitting and enhancing values and dedication.* You must keep your eye on the 1982 nation as well as today's nation. There is that kind of futurity in what we do in today's classroom. It is you who must warn your communities that when any proposal for higher quality education is defeated, the losers are not the proponents of the issue. The losers are the children and the nation.

Now that we have successfully traversed the Van Allen belt of economic inquiry, we have learned that education is an investment. It's a growth industry itself. Economics can furnish ample rationale for substantially greater investment in education. Other national imperatives lead to the same conclusion. President Kennedy said earlier this year in his message to Congress on education:

> "For education is both the foundation and the unifying force of our democratic way of life—it is the mainspring of our economic and social progress—it is the highest expression of achievement in our society, ennobling and enriching human life. In short, it is at the same time the most profitable investment society can make and the richest reward it can confer."

---

[8] Coombs, Philip H., "Technical Frontiers of Education," The Twenty-Seventh Annual Sir John Adams Lecture at the University of California, Los Angeles, delivered March 15, 1960.

2-3 *Individual autonomy and social structure**

Respect for individual integrity, for what we have called human dignity, has long been a tenet in American culture, and it is certainly no novel principle to anyone working in the area of interpersonal relations. However, in a heterogeneous society such as ours, and in an era of induced change and speeded tempo of living, it has been difficult to implement this tenet in the everyday details of living. We have to reconcile principles of conformity and individual initiative, group living and private freedom of choice, social regulation and personal autonomy. I believe that a study of other societies dealing with such issues in different circumstances can furnish us with insights which we can use in understanding our own situation. So I present here scattered material from a number of societies, ending with a brief sketch of the culture of the Navaho Indians, to show how the principle of personal autonomy is supported by the cultural framework.

In every society we find some organized social unit; but not everywhere does the social unit provide freedom to the individual or the opportunity for spontaneous functioning; nor do we find everywhere the value for sheer personal being of which I shall speak below. We often find a hierarchy where women or chil-

* Dorothy Lee, "Individual Autonomy and Social Structure," in Lee, Dorothy, *Freedom and Culture*, Englewood Cliffs, N.J.: Prentice-Hall, Inc., 1959, pp. 5-14.

Dorothy Lee

dren or the uninitiated or the commoners are accorded a minority status. In some societies we find what amounts to a dictatorship; in others, the group may demand such sacrifice of individual uniqueness as to make for totalitarianism. On the other hand, in some societies we encounter a conception of individual autonomy and democratic procedures which far outstrip anything we have practiced or even have conceived of as democracy. It is only the latter kind which concerns me here.

It is often difficult for us to decide exactly how much our principle of personal autonomy involves. We find ourselves asking questions such as: to what extent can we allow a child to make his own decisions, to speak and act for himself? And: at what point do we begin to allow him to do so? For example, obviously when the mother first takes her infant to the pediatrician, she has to speak for him. Exactly when does she begin to remain silent, waiting for him to understand and answer the doctor's questions and to express his own likes and opinions and conclusions? And to what extent can she do this, using up the time of her appointment, taking up the valuable time of a busy physician?

Many of us feel that to allow a child to decide for himself and to act according to his own wish, that is, to be permissive, is to show respect for the unique being of the child. Yet for many of the societies we know, it would be presumption for any person to "allow" another to take what is essentially his prerogative—the right to decide for himself. These people do not "permit" others. When their children, as for example the children of the Wintu Indians, ask "Can I?" they are asking for information on the rules of the structure; for instance, they may be seeking clarification about a religious taboo or a social custom. They are saying in effect, "Is it permissible for me to . . . ?" and not, "Do you allow me to . . . ?" These people do not "give" freedom to their children, because it is not theirs to give. If they do not impose an external time schedule on their infants, but feed them when they are hungry, and put them to bed when they are sleepy, they are not being "permissive"; they are showing their deep-seated respect for individual worth, and their awareness of the unique tempo of the individual.

Ethnographers have presented us with many incidents, apparently commonplace and trivial, which point out for us an amazingly thoroughgoing implementation of respect for personal quality. For instance, Marian Smith tells how, when she was visiting a Sikh household in British Columbia, she noticed that a small child, asked to entertain his baby brother, merely went up to the playpen and put in a toy truck. He did not show the baby how the truck worked, how he could make the wheels go round; he gave the truck silently. This amazed the visitor, since she knew that the Sikhs were people of great empathy and warmth, and with a great love for babies. She knew, also, that the child in question had approached the baby with friendliness and affection. Yet, under similar circumstances an American child would probably have told the baby what to look for. Then she remembered the personal autonomy of the Sikh, and realized that the boy was acting consistently with the cultural values; he was furnishing the baby with the raw material for experience, and leaving him to explore and discover for himself, without any attempt to influence him. He was expressing respect, not non-involvement.

Such respect for autonomy may appear extreme to us, yet it would be taken for granted in a number of the Indian tribes in this continent. For example, an anthropology student who was observing relations between parents and children was puzzled to see a baby with hair so long that it got in his eyes and seemed to cause him discomfort, though otherwise his mother treated him with care and affection. When she finally asked why the baby's hair had been left so long, the mother answered, "He has not asked to have it cut." The baby was about eighteen months old, and could barely talk; yet the mother would not take it upon herself to act for him without his request or consent.

These instances exemplify a belief so deep that it apparently permeates behavior and decisions, and operates without question or reflection or conscious plan. It is a belief so internalized as to be regarded as almost an organic ingredient of the personality. The individual, shown absolute respect from birth and valued as sheer being for his own uniqueness, apparently learns with every experience to have this same respect and value for others; he is "trained" to be constantly sensitive to the beginnings of others.

An instance of this "training" in sensitivity comes from the culture of the Chinese. American observers had noticed that Chinese babies had learned, by the time they were about six months old, to indicate that they wanted to micturate; yet they seemed to be treated very permissively, with no attempt at toilet training. A Chinese mother explained that there actually is such "training"; only it is the mother who "trains" herself. When the baby wants to urinate, his whole body participates in the preliminary process. The Chinese mother, holding the baby in her arms, learns to be sensitive to the minute details of this process, and to hold her baby away from herself at exactly the critical moment. Eventually, the infant learns to ask to be held out. The mother neither tries to control the baby, nor does she train the infant to control himself according to imposed standards. Instead, she sensitizes herself to his rhythm, and helps him to adopt social discipline with spontaneity, starting from his unique pattern. What is interesting here is that as an end result of this, the baby is "toilet-trained" at a very early age; but it has been an experience of spontaneity for him and his autonomy has remained inviolate, because his mother has had the sensitivity and the patience to "listen" to him.

Among the Wintu Indians of California, the principle of the inviolate integrity of the individual is basic to the very morphology of the language. Many of the verbs which express coercion in our language—such as to take a baby to (the shade), or to change the baby—are formed in such a way that they express a cooperative effort instead. For example, the Wintu would say, "I *went with* the baby," instead of, "I *took* the baby." And they say, "The chief *stood with* the people," which they have to translate into English as, "The chief ruled the people." They never say, and in fact they cannot say, as we do, "I have a sister," or a "son," or "husband." Instead, they say, "I am sistered," or "I live with my sister." To *live with* is the usual way in which they express what we call possession, and they use this term for everything that they respect, so that a man will be said to live with his bow and arrows. In our society, when we try to express respect for individual uniqueness, we have to do it in so many words, and even then we have to grapple with an uncooperative language. This is why we have to resort to terms which actually defeat our ends; terms such as *permissiveness*, or phrases such as *to give freedom to the child*. In Wintu, every interpersonal reference is couched in grammar which rests on the principle of individual integrity. Yet, for this people, the emphasis on personal inviolability did not mean that the individual was an isolate. There was such pervasive empathy among them that this, too, was expressed in the grammatical forms; if a boy was sick, the father used a special form of the verb phrase *to be sick*, and thus said, "I-am-sick-in-respect-of-my-son."

A corollary of the principle of individual integrity is that no personal orders can be given or taken without a violation of personal autonomy; we have been familiar with this corollary, particularly in rural areas where the farmer and his wife had "help" but not "servants." In a society such as that of Upper Burma before it was much affected by Western administration, there were no agricultural laborers nor household help at all. In the monasteries, where novices performed menial tasks, the monks did not give orders. Instead, the work was structured throughout the day; and all that the monk said to get the work done was, "Do what is lawful," reminding the novice to act according to the cultural tenet, not ordering him.

This last illustration introduces a further principle: that of structure. Many people in our society have been apprehensive of the implications of personal autonomy, because they have felt that it is apt to lead to lawlessness and chaos. Yet actually it is in connection with the highest personal autonomy that we often find the most intricately developed structure; and it is this structure that makes autonomy possible in a group situation. For example, the Burmese novices could proceed without receiving orders only because the structure clearly indicated what could and could not be done and at what time of the day or month or year.

Margaret Mead and Gregory Bateson have described this combination of autonomy and structure for the Balinese. These people have an exceedingly complex calendrical system, consisting of a permutation of ten weeks of differing lengths; and this system, in combination with an intricately patterned spacial and status system, furnishes the structure according to which an individual behaves. For instance, according to the specific combination of "weeks" on which his birthday falls, and according to his status, an individual has to participate in a special way at a particular temple festival. No one imposes this tribute upon him; and no one asks for his contribution. However, because of the enormous amount of detail involved in the precision of the structure, there are officials known as reminders, who merely remind the people of the exact character of the pending festival. Each person then proceeds to act according to his peculiar position in the temporal structure, acting autonomously, finding guidance in the structure.

When the specific aspects of the structure are not clear, the people in such societies can turn to authority for clarification. And here we often find, as with the Burmese or the Navaho Indians, that the authority of the headman or the chief or the leader is in many ways like the authority of the dictionary, or of Einstein. There is no hint of coercion or command here; the people go to the leader with faith, as we go to a reference book, and the leader answers according to his greater knowledge, or clarifies an obscure point, or amplifies according to his greater experience and wisdom. He does not say: You must do this, because I order you to. Yet, he does use the *must* or its equivalent; he says, so to speak: As I see it, this is what must be done. In a sense, it is like the recipe which says: You must not open the oven door for ten minutes after you put the cake in. No housewife, preparing a cake and going to the cookbook for guidance, feels that her personal integrity is violated by this interdiction. Once she is committed to the cake-making, she finds the recipe, the structure, enabling and guiding; she finds it freeing, not restricting.

If permissiveness at times leads to lawlessness and chaos, and even to immobilization instead of the freedom to be and to act, this happens usually in those cases where "permission" goes from person to person, in a structural vacuum. It happens when the structure is by-passed through the dictatorial permissiveness of the person who takes it upon himself to allow, and by implication to forbid, another person. In the societies which were mentioned above, where we find absolute valuing of unique being, what often takes the form of permissiveness in our society exists as the freedom to be, and to find actualization; and it is found within a clearly delineated structure.

Such is the society of the Navaho Indians of Arizona and New Mexico. How long this picture will last, we cannot predict. The mineral resources of their land are now being developed, and rapid change is being introduced. What I say here draws on the autobiographies of Navaho men, as well as on recent ethnographies.

In these accounts, we find a tightly knit group, depending on mutual responsibility among all its members, a precisely structured universe, and a great respect for individual autonomy and integrity. We find people who maintain an inviolable privacy while living as a family in a one-room house, sharing work and responsibility to such an extent that even a child of six will contribute his share of mutton to the family meal. The family unit is so closely knit that, if a child of five is ill or absent, the family suffers because there is a gap in the cooperative effort; and when a man goes hunting, he can get nothing unless his wife cooperates at home by observing the necessary taboos. The well-being of a Navaho, his health and the health of all his undertakings, depend on the maintenance of harmony with nature. All being is both good and evil; and by walking carefully according to a highly structured map of procedure, within a detailed framework of "do's," and "don'ts," the Navaho can keep the proper balance of good and evil in his life, and thus find health and harmony. The rules according to which he lives originate in the structure, and come to him as guidance from the parents, not as commands.

Within this structured universe and tightly knit society, the Navaho lives in personal autonomy. Adults and children are valued for their sheer being, just because they *are*. There is no urge toward achievement; no one has to strive for success. In fact, neither is there reward for success, nor is success held out as a reward for hard work. Wealth may be the result of hard work and skill, but obviously it is also the blatant result of lack of generosity, lack of responsibility for one's relatives, perhaps even of malicious witchcraft. No good Navaho becomes and remains "wealthy" in our terms.

Hard work is valued in itself, as a personal quality which combines the ability to withstand hardship with the paramount sense of responsibility for the work of the group. Even a young child will be trained to see to it that the whole flock of sheep is safe before he takes shelter during a blizzard. This means a systematic program in developing hardihood. He is waked up at daybreak in winter, so that he may run for miles; and in summer, he runs in the hot sun of noontime. Presently, he intensifies this program by his own decision, perhaps putting sand in his moccasins to make the running more rigorous; that is, he relates himself to this discipline with spontaneity. Children learn responsibility by being given indispensable household tasks; in addition, they are given sheep of their own from the time they are about five. They are responsible for the care and welfare of these animals; thus, they acquire a further opportunity at responsible participation. Now they can take their turn at supplying the meat for the family meal, and they can contribute mutton when this is needed for ceremonials, or to entertain visitors.

Most of all, an individual has to learn to walk safely through life, maintaining his harmony with the universe. This involves learning to observe a large number of taboos and procedures, which are aspects of every act: to learn, for example, what is to be done with the left hand, which direction to have his hogan face, what is to be started in a sunwise direction, or to be taken from the east side of a tree; what to avoid touching, or saying, or looking at. All this could be seen as inhibiting, or negative, or as interfering with the individual; but to the Navaho it is guidance in the acquisition of an essential skill—the freedom to act and to be. The intricate set of regulations is like a map which affords freedom to proceed to a man lost in the jungle.

In Navaho autobiographies we often find the phrase, "I followed the advice of my parents," but rarely, "I obeyed my parents." The good Navaho does not command his child; and a mother who is aggressive toward her children, who "talks rough" to them, is strongly criticized. In teaching her children the tremendous number of taboos they have to learn for their well-being, the good Navaho mother does not say: I will punish you if you do thus-and-thus; but: Such-and-such an unpleasant thing will happen to you. The mother is guiding the child; and if the child takes a wrong turn, if he breaks a taboo, he is not "guilty." He has not committed a sin against the mother and is not in need of forgiveness. He has made a mistake which he must set right.

This attitude is basic to all Navaho relatedness, so that here man is not burdened with guilt, and does not feel apologetic toward human or divine beings. He is neither grateful nor abject to his gods. As a matter of fact, he must never humble himself before them, since the process of healing, of the recovery of harmony with the universe, involves identification with the appropriate god, who would be slighted if the patient humiliated himself. This means that the Navaho has—and indeed must have—as much respect and value for himself as for others; in fact, this is the Navaho version of the principle that we have discovered so recently in our society: that we cannot accept and respect others until we learn to accept and respect ourselves.

In what I have said, I have made no distinction between adults and children, as the Navaho do not differentiate between the two in the respect they show for personal autonomy. There is no minority status for children. For example, a good Navaho will not take it upon himself to speak for another, whether for adult or child. A man, asked by a white what his wife thinks on a certain subject, is likely to answer, "I don't know, I haven't asked her." In the same way, a father, asked to sell his child's bow and arrow, will refer the request to a five-year-old boy, and abide by the child's decision not to sell, even though he knows the child is badly in need of the clothing that can be bought with the price of the toy. A woman, asked whether a certain baby could talk, said "Yes"; and when the ethnographer was puzzled by the "meaningless" sounds the baby was making, she explained that the baby could talk, but she could not understand what the baby said. All that she had the right to do was to speak for herself, to say that she could not understand. She would not presume to speak for the child, and to say—as I think we would have said—that the child was making meaningless sounds.

So the individual remains inviolate. No one coerces another among the Navaho. Traditionally, parents do not force their children to do what they unequivocally do not want to do, such as going to school or to the hospital; children are not coerced even "for their own good." As the mother of two unschooled children put it, "I listen to my children, and I have to take their word." There is no political coercion, and all leadership is traditionally incidental. A man finds himself in a position of leadership when the people seek him out because of the high degree of his inner development; because of his wisdom, his knowledge, his assumption of responsibility, his physical skill and hardihood, the wealth which he is ready to use to help his relatives. Men do not seek leadership; and white employers have found that the Navaho are reluctant to become foremen, however able they may be, and in spite of the higher pay involved. It is "fundamentally indecent" according to Clyde Kluckhohn, "for a single individual to presume to make decisions for the group," and therefore not even a leader will make decisions for others, or give orders to others.

For the Navaho mother, personal autonomy means that her child has the freedom to make his own mistakes, to suffer pain or grief or joy and learn from experience. And the child has his freedom because the mother has faith in him. This does not mean that she has high expectations of him, but that she trusts him. She knows that he is a mingling of good and evil; she knows that life is unpredictable, and that a mistake may bring disaster. But she is willing to refrain from interfering with her child as he explores, as he takes his steps in life. When the baby starts walking, the mother does not see to it that he is out of reach of the fire, and that all the sharp knives have been put away. The child gets burned a little, and the mother helps him learn from this experience that he has to be careful of fire, he has a small accident, and the mother helps him understand and deal with that particular danger. By taking a chance on her child, the mother teaches him to be ready to meet and deal with danger, instead of warning him away from danger.

This trust means that the child has freedom to move, to act, to undertake responsibility. It means that the child is given significant tasks in the household. A psychiatrist visiting a Navaho family wrote in her diary: "After supper the girl (ten years old) went to water the horses, and the boy (five years old) to take the little flock back to some older members of the family who lived in a hogan a quarter of a mile away." No mention is made here of orders given, nor of any checking on the mother's part to see that the job was done.

Coexistence of Autonomy and Limits

If the societies I have mentioned here present an enviable consistency in the expression of the principle of individual integrity, it is well to keep in mind that there may be no special virtue in this; at the time these societies were studied, they enjoyed great social homogeneity, and were relatively unchanging over time. This means that the children could learn the adult role at home by gradually sharing the life of the father or mother—as a matter of course, expecting and wanting to live the life of the parents, and to hold the same values and principles. However, the fact remains that consistency was there; that the principle was upheld by the various aspects of the culture, even by the very grammar of the language, as among the Wintu.

The practices I have presented here are not for us to copy, but rather food for thought, the basis for new insights. I have tried to show that law and limits and personal autonomy can coexist effectively, that spontaneity is not necessarily killed by group responsibility, that respect for individual integrity is not an end to be achieved by specific means, but that it can exist only if it is supported by deep conviction and by the entire way of life.

References

DYK, WALTER, RECORDER. *Son of Old Man Hat. A Navaho Autobiography.* New York: Harcourt, Brace and World, Inc., 1938.

KLUCKHOHN, CLYDE and DOROTHEA LEIGHTON. *The Navaho.* Cambridge: Harvard University Press, 1946.

LEIGHTON, DOROTHEA and CLYDE KLUCKHOHN. *Children of the People.* Cambridge: Harvard University Press, 1947.

REICHARD, GLADYS A. *Prayer, The Compulsive Word.* Monographs of the American Ethnological Society. J. J. Augustin, New York, 1944.

2-4 The open society*

WHAT, THEN, IS THE MEANING OF HISTORY? THE ANSWER presumably should come at the end of this work, where conclusions belong. My conclusions were in fact modified during the course of my studies, and will be restated at the end. Yet it would be idle to pretend that we are now about to embark on a voyage of exploration, with no idea of our destination. My answer has been implicit in all that I have written so far, and will determine the content of the chapters that follow. It amounts to a basic assumption, a premise that should be laid face up on the table. Briefly, my answer is at once a negation and an affirmation. History has no meaning, in the sense of a clear pattern of determinate plot; but it is not simply meaningless or pointless. It has no certain meaning because man is free to give it various possible meanings.

His freedom is sharply limited, of course. Man has to choose within the conditions imposed by his biological structure, his natural environment, and his cultural heritage. He cannot do whatever he has a mind to, and at that his mind has been largely made up by his ancestors. For such reasons he is always prone to believe that history somehow makes itself, in spite of his efforts, by the automatic operation of natural laws or

---

* Herbert J. Muller, *The Uses of the Past.* New York: Oxford University Press, Inc., 1952, pp. 69–71.

Herbert J. Muller

God's will. Still, at any moment he has a wide range of choices and is willy-nilly making more history, discovering the meanings of his past and determining the meanings of his future. The most significant 'facts' he has to face are of man's own making. Marxism, for all its theoretical determinism, is the clearest illustration of how history is made by men's beliefs about what has happened, what is happening, and what should happen.

This insistence on human freedom is not simply cheering. It means that we have to keep making history, instead of leaning on it, and that we can never count on a final solution. It means the constant possibility of foolish or even fatal choices. Yet the dignity of man lies precisely in this power to choose his destiny. We may therefore welcome the conclusion that we cannot foretell the future, even apart from the possibility that it may not bear knowing. Uncertainty is not only the plainest condition of human life but the necessary condition of freedom, of aspiration, of conscience—of all human idealism.

It is the business of the future to be dangerous, Whitehead remarked; and we can always trust it to keep on the job. I again stress the uncertainties, however, because the dangers are always intensified by the pretensions to absolute certainty or finality. These are the ultimate source of corruption, the reason why the best becomes the worst and crusaders for heaven make a hell on earth. And none is more insidious than the principle of historical predestination. Knowing in advance how history is going to turn out, men climb on the bandwagon, ride the wave of the future.[1] They can then indulge any policy, from supine resignation to ruthless violence. So the Communists can justify the most barbarous behavior: like hangmen, they are merely executing 'the verdict of history.' They corrupt morality at its very base by implying that it is man's duty to fight for the inevitable, or that historic might makes right. Even in self-sacrifice they are profoundly irresponsible. Our business as rational beings is not to argue for what is going to be but to strive for what ought to be, in the consciousness that it will never be all we would like it to be.

Among the possible 'meanings' of history—to restate my premises in these terms—the most significant is the growth of this power of self-determination, or freedom to make history. I assume that for interpreting the past and choosing a future we must begin with a full acknowl-

[1] James Burnham is especially agile in the performance of this feat. In the name of hard-boiled realism, he has so far ridden at least three waves—the Marxist revolution, the managerial revolution, and the imperial destiny of America. Presumably he has a weather eye open for the next wave; but meanwhile he still tends to deride visionary idealists who are more intrested in making history than in predicting it.

edgment of the claims of reason: a humble reason that makes no claim to finality or metaphysical certitude, because such claims cannot be rationally substantiated, and that recognizes its finiteness and fallibility; a proud reason that nevertheless maintains its authority as the final judge of all claims to truth, insisting that its tested knowledge is no less real and reliable because it is not a knowledge of ultimate reality, and that only by a further exercise of reason can its limitations and its fallacies be clearly discerned. We are not forced to choose between reason and faith in the conventional sense—we may choose between more or less reasonable faiths. The ideal of rationality in turn requires the ideal of freedom, the right to be an individual. A rational person is not merely one who has good habits or right principles, but one who knows what he believes and assumes the intellectual and moral responsibilities of his beliefs; and first he must be free to think for himself, make up his own mind. Although non-rational behavior may exhibit admirable qualities, such as the loyalty, fortitude, and daring found in barbarians, or even in the animal world, these qualities are not wholly admirable, or trustworthy, unless they are conscious, responsible choices. The only possible virtue in being a civilized man instead of a barbarian, an ignoramus, or a moron is in being a free, responsible individual with a mind of one's own.

The best society, accordingly, is that which is most conducive to the growth of such persons. It is what Karl Popper has called the 'open society.' It is an adventurous society that has broken with the universal, prehistoric custom of regarding ancient customs as magical or sacred, that views its institutions as man-made for human purposes and examines their suitability for these purposes, that welcomes variety and change instead of enforcing rigid conformity, and that accordingly provides its members with personal opportunities and responsibilities beyond mere obedience. It is Athens as opposed to Sparta.

Today it is us; and thereby hangs our tale. Because we have made the farthest advance toward the open society we are likely to feel more impotent than men have ever felt before. The novel idea of progress, or simply of 'opportunity,' has been so deeply engrained in our everyday thought and feeling that we are incapable of passive acceptance and endurance; in a crisis we take for granted the possibility and the need of 'doing something about it.' Having accumulated a vast deal of sociological and historical knowledge, we are also more aware of the difficulty of doing anything about it, and are more critical of the simple faiths that once made it easier for men to do or die for God, king, and country. We bear the cross of consciousness. In a fuller consciousness the burden may be eased—and this is the reason for the chapters that follow. Our adventure in freedom is so recent that what appear to be our death rattles may be growing pains. But in any event the pains are unavoidable. For a society as for an individual, the hardest problems begin with freedom. Today the future of the open society is wide open, to triumphs or to disasters of a magnitude hitherto undreamed of.

2-5 *Cultural process and evolution*[*]

YOU HAVE INVITED ME, A BIOLOGIST, TO GIVE MY VIEWS about the central subject matter of cultural anthropology, and indeed of human history. If you ask a representative of one branch of science to express his views on the main subject matter of another, you cannot expect more than the fruits of his immediate reactions to a new landscape of fact and idea. This is all I can offer—a series of obiter dicta, doubtless colored by my biological knowledge and ideas. However, they will at least show how your subject looks to an outsider; the attitude will help to arouse opposition and stimulate discussion, and may perhaps serve as a broad background against which individual contributions may appear in a better perspective.

As I see it, culture in the anthropological sense is neither an entity nor a principle: it can only be treated as a type of process. It is not just the sum or even the organization of all "artefacts, socifacts, and mentifacts," but constitutes a self-reproducing and self-varying process whereby the pattern of human activities is transmitted and transformed in the course of time.

As organisms are what evolve in the biological phase of evolution, so cultures are what evolve in its

---

[*] Julian S. Huxley, "Cultural Process and Evolution," in Anne Roe and George Gaylord Simpson, *Behavior and Evolution,* New Haven: Yale University Press, 1958, pp. 437–454.

Julian S. Huxley

psychosocial or human phase. To put the matter baldly, biological species, with their bodies and their physiological functions, confront the environment with organized systems of self-reproducing matter and its products: the human species does so with organized systems of self-reproducing mind and its products, superimposed on the constituent biological organisms.

In general, cultures are not so highly organized nor so specifically adapted as organisms. Indeed, in the present state of our knowledge, a culture is best envisaged merely as a system of human activities and products which happens to survive and be transmitted and so to possess continuity in time. Cultures will accordingly always be in some degree "adapted" in the narrow sense of being suitably related to their immediate environment. However, since the rate of cultural change can sometimes be rapid, and since a cultural group can unconsciously or deliberately alter its environment, the concept of adaptation as applied to cultures must include a suitable relation to change, both to changes in themselves and to changes in their environment.

It should be noted that this dual concept of adaptation—adaptation to long-term survival as well as to immediate success—has recently been found necessary in biology also.[1] Thus certain types of genetic system permit accurate, immediate adaptation; but they do so at the expense of reserve variability, so that environmental changes (as of climate) may cause their extinction. For continuing success, a compromise has to be reached between the immediate advantages, conferred by inbreeding, of accurate adaptation to the present environment, and the long-term advantages, conferred by outcrossing, of extra variability (and therefore less accurate present adaptation) as a reserve against possible future environmental change. On a still more extended time scale, extreme specialization will also reduce potential variation; so that specialized products of one biological type are likely to be extinguished in competition with the products of a biologically higher type (as happened with most groups of reptiles in favor of mammals in the late Mesozoic).

Cultures, too, though not so highly organized or so fully integrated as higher organisms (as is obvious when one looks at, say, American or British culture today), do of course show some degree of organization or pattern. Cultural organization too necessarily stands in some relation with social organization.[2] However, the relation need

[1] See e.g. C. D. Darlington, *The Evolution of Genetic Systems,* Cambridge, England, 1947.

[2] I am using social organization in the broad sense, to include political organization.

not be either close or exact. Thus in classical times the Greeks shared a common culture but were socially organized in the form of separate and often competing or conflicting city-states. A similar situation exists in modern Europe, with the existence of competing or conflicting nation-states within a single cultural framework. In other cases, as with ancient Egypt, the boundaries of the culture and the social organization are essentially coterminous; even then, however, cultural and social organization cannot be equated.

Cultures, like organic types, also show differentiation or diversification, usually on a geographical basis. Thus, to take an obvious case, European culture (or civilization—for from the broad anthropological point of view one can only define civilization as culture at a certain high level of technological and social organization) is differentiated into main subcultures, such as Latin, Germanic (Nordic), and Slavic, and these again into subsectors, such as French, Italian, Portuguese, and Spanish within the Latin subculture. Here again the cultural and social boundaries need not coincide: the obvious example is that of Switzerland, in which Latin (French) and Germanic (German) subcultures (as well as others) coexist.

To return to our central topic, I would suggest that the adaptiveness of cultures is best considered as a problem in relatedness, and that the essential relation is the relation between the form and pattern of the culture and what I may, perhaps provocatively, call the group's current vision of destiny. Under this head I would include the current knowledge, ideas, assumptions, and beliefs, often unconscious or only partially conscious, concerning human nature as embodied in the particular group, the nature of the environment, and the relations between the two. It is often, but I believe falsely, stated that cultures are *determined* by their environment—climate, geography, fauna and flora, and resources. It is of course true that they are *related* to the environment, but the relation is not a simple one. It is conditioned by the knowledge which men have about the environment, by the skills which they have developed for coping with it, and by their ideas and attitudes concerning it and themselves.

This applies even to the exploitative aspects of culture, the human activities concerned with getting a living from the environment. In Arabia the same environment which conditioned the development of a nomad culture in the pretechnological Semitic population is now beginning to support a culture based on the exploitation of oil resources, which in previous periods were unsuspected and even if they had been known could not have been utilized for want of technical skill. Similarly, the technical skills of horse training and horse breeding, when introduced by Europeans to the North American continent, completely transformed the culture of the Plains Indians.

Perhaps the most striking examples are those like North America and Australia, where the same environment has provided the basis for cultures at radically different levels of knowledge, skill, and organization. The cultural contrast is most extreme in Australia; but it should be remembered that the high level of white culture could never have been established there without the introduction of domestic animals and plants, of technological skills and their products, and of ideas and attitudes, from other regions. All such examples, of course, emphasize the great importance of culture contact and cultural diffusion in the genesis, development, and transformation of cultures during the process of cultural evolution.

The suggestion that cultures are essentially related to the current vision of human destiny can now be amplified. The most important factor in progressive long-term cultural evolution appears to be knowledge or, to use a more general term, awareness. In this, two elements are involved. One is the quantitative amount and accuracy of factual knowledge, and of its application in the form of skills and technology; the second is the way in which knowledge and awareness are organized, whether in explicit concepts and ideas, in esthetic and ritual expressions, or in conscious or unconscious beliefs, assumptions, attitudes, and general approach. I would emphasize that any over-all progressive trend in cultural evolution can only be detected when the process is looked at on the largest possible time scale. On smaller time scales what is detected is recurrence, as by Toynbee and Spengler, or limited advance or specialization, as in histories covering limited areas for limited periods.

The basic difference between man and other organisms is that human experience can be cumulative over the generations. This clearly applies primarily in the sphere of knowledge, its organization and its practical applications; but increased and better organized knowledge will eventually affect social structure, political organization, attitudes, belief systems, and modes of expression. We must, however, remember that social, political, and ideological organization, once established, can in their turn affect the central process of accumulating and organizing knowledge: the general change-resisting properties of ancient Egyptian civilization, and the ideological opposition of the Church of Rome to scientific advance in many fields, are examples.

From the evolutionary point of view, the most important characteristics of a culture concern cultural stability (self-reproduction) and cultural change (self-transformation). Some degree of stability is of course necessary, and some degree of change is probably inevitable.

But, broadly speaking, cultures can be classified into two main types: those which promote stability and resist change, and those which encourage or at least permit change. And this difference is associated with different views or assumptions about destiny. Thus most primitive cultures are adapted simply to securing their own continuance in conditions which are assumed to remain constant.

In general, savage societies accept the continuance of their environment and of their methods of making a living from it; and the rituals (*rites de passage*, hunting or agricultural magic, etc.) and the ethicosocial systems (taboos, kinship and marriage systems, etc.) are designed to give cohesion and continuity to the cultural group. High civilizations may continue to be stability-centered—e.g. ancient Egypt, or historical China with its ancestor worship and reliance on tradition. At the other extreme we have that modern phenomenon: cultures focused on the idea of transforming themselves and the environment, and relying on science and the scientific method, which itself is consciously based on the idea of increasing the amount and improving the organization of knowledge.

There are of course a number of intermediate cases. Sometimes the idea of change becomes operative in one department of life, for instance in nations which become obsessed with the idea of increasing their size or their power by military conquest, though they may be stability-centered in other ways, e.g. in their religion or ideology: ancient Assyria provides a crude example, and the classical Roman Empire a more elaborate one. In the politico-religious sphere, Islamic expansion resulted in a conscious and explosive transformation, but since then socially and intellectually Islam has been stability-promoting and tradition-ridden, resistant to change. Or the idea of intellectual and artistic discovery may become powerful, as in classical Greece. In this case, freedom and change were consciously sought in the ideological sphere but (owing to various peculiarities of Greek culture) not emphasized in technology and the application of scientific knowledge.

In other cases, notably in the French and Russian Revolutions, what may be called the millenary notion of change has been operative: the idea that a violent revolutionary change could and would initiate a new, better, and definitive stable system. This has always proved deceptive, for the simple reason that the process of change, whether in the biological or the psychosocial sphere, does not operate in this way. Though revolutionary periods may occur in which change is particularly rapid and old systems are largely destroyed, evolutionary change is always a dialectic process, in which stability, even if reached, is reached slowly and gradually. Furthermore, man's cultural evolution is so near its beginning that it is now quite impossible to envisage the possibilities before it, and especially to envisage any definitive stable state.

There is also the frequent phenomenon of what has been picturesquely (though not very correctly) called cultural fossilization. This often occurs when culturally important ideas or attitudes become embodied in an organized institutionalized system: the cultural inertia of such a system, together with the powerful vested interests which it creates, will usually promote resistance to social and cultural change. Obvious examples are the institution of absolute monarchy based on the concept of Divine Right, and that of the Roman Catholic Church based on the authoritarian assumptions of revelation and dogmatic certitude; but the phenomenon has been widespread in all periods and places. The fundamental cleavage is between the assumption of continuing stability, leading to backward-looking cultures based on tradition, and that of possible change, especially change for the better, including quantitative change in knowledge and qualitative change in ideas, leading to factual discovery and ideological revaluation and so to technological and social transformation.

When we envisage the matter of cultural adaptedness in the broadest possible way, we see that the basic problem is that of adapting cultural systems to the facts of the evolutionary process in all its sectors, including the progressive realization of new and desirable possibilities. Regarded in this light, the development of change-promoting cultural systems is seen as itself an increasingly adaptive and progressive evolutionary trend. Various steps in this trend can then be recognized. There was first the discontinuous or sporadic appearance of change-promoting elements in various cultures, the most notable being the already mentioned rise of the spirit of free inquiry in classical Greece.

Continuity of the trend has only become apparent since the transition between the Middle Ages and the Renaissance in the 15th century. It began with the idea of geographical discovery, which was soon complemented by that of historical discovery, or if you prefer, the rediscovery of ancient knowledge. Then came the idea of scientific discovery, in the 16th century largely confined to mathematics and astronomy, but soon extended to other branches of "natural knowledge." In the 17th century, thanks in the first instance to Bacon, the idea of scientific discovery was generalized in the concept of scientific method. This was a truly revolutionary event, leading to the supersession, in field after field of study, of backward-looking tradition by the idea of forward-looking attitudes and research. The former inevitably and sometimes consciously resisted change; the latter inevitably facilitated and sometimes deliberately encouraged it.

Rapid cultural change, especially if also progressive, usually stems from the discoveries or achievements of exceptional individuals, but will not operate effectively except in a group receptive to the notion of change and technically and professionally equipped to apply the new discoveries and ideas. As Kroeber has shown, the effective manifestation of the gifts of exceptional individuals is elicited by the cultural environment. The effective application of their achievements is then made possible through the activities of less exceptional individuals in the cultural group. For rapid progress, both an adequate supply of exceptional individuals and also an appropriate culture and an adequately educated community are necessary. It should be stressed, however, that the role of the individual in evolution has increased in importance, not only in the passage from biological to cultural evolution but also in that from stability-promoting to change-promoting cultures.

The promotion of change need not imply the abandonment of the ideal of stability, but it does imply the replacement of a static concept of stability with a dynamic one: the ideas of stability and change tend to become combined in the ideal of integrated process—the moving equilibrium of an ordered transformation. This is the eventual step; in earlier stages the ideal of a stably integrated but directional process was lacking, and change, at least change in certain aspects of a culture, might be regarded as desirable per se, and little attention paid to its direction or to its effects on other aspects.

Before this eventual step could be taken, the fact of evolution had to be discovered. With this, the change-promoting method of science revealed the fact that nature itself was not, as had been previously assumed, a static mechanism but a dynamic process, a process of orderly or at least comprehensible self-transformation. In the heady intoxication generated by this discovery, together with the spectacular results of the practical application of scientific knowledge, a misconceived and oversimplified idea of the change-promoting process arose: the myth of universal and inevitable progress was born.

It remained to clarify and extend the concept of evolution, and to apply scientific method to the study of man, including his values and his history. This has brought us to a fresh critical point. We now are beginning to see the whole of reality as a unitary process of evolution (though comprising three distinct sectors or phases), and man as the agency by means of which that process is becoming self-conscious and could become consciously purposeful. Evolutionary progress, both in the biological and the human sector, is now seen as a fact, but as occurring only rarely and by no means inevitably: from being a myth, it is becoming a subject for scientific study. From a slightly different angle, we may say that cultural evolution, i.e evolution in the psychosocial phase, can now be seen as an extension of biological evolution, but with its own peculiarities of method and results, and "progress" and "advance" can be profitably redefined as processes leading to greater realization of desirable possibilities.

As our analysis of the evolutionary process in general, and of evolutionary progress in particular, becomes more accurate, as our knowledge of them becomes fuller, and as our application of that knowledge grows more efficient, a new and decisive increase in the adaptedness of culture will have been taken. Human culture will be not merely purposefully but also adaptively change-promoting: the type of change which it sets itself to achieve will become increasingly adjusted to the realities of the actual process, including both its limitations and its possibilities. Man's vision of his destiny will become more closely adjusted to the facts of destiny; and the direction in which he consciously steers will become increasingly "right"—in other words, will have more long-range adaptedness. This statement is not, as some may think, uncritically optimistic. I believe it to be a reasonable extrapolation from past human history. In any case, it is optimistic only in the long run: any such process will take a long time, and will be subject to many temporary and local setbacks. But pessimism is the result of incomplete knowledge or of too short a view: any general or long-run pessimism is contradicted by the facts of evolutionary progress in the past.

So far, I have only been considering what may be called directional adaptedness: the better adaptation of cultures to the process of cultural change, so as to permit that change to be as progressive as possible. It now remains to consider diversificational adaptedness: the adaptation of different cultures or subcultures to local conditions, including of course their history, traditions, achievements, and existing organization, as well as the conditions of their physical and biological environment, resulting in greater variety in cultural evolution.

With the increase of communications, population pressure, economic interdependence, and interpenetration and culture contacts of all sorts, the maintenance of satisfactory cultural diversity is becoming increasingly urgent as a practical problem: with the obvious and inevitable trend toward world unity in all spheres, it will speedily pose itself as a basic theoretical problem. Just as the basic theoretical problem in the sphere of directional adaptedness is the reconciliation of stability with change, and their synthesis in a moving but integrated equilibrium, so in that of diversificational adaptedness the basic theoretical problem is the reconciliation of uniformity with diversity, and their synthesis in a system of variety-in-unity. This appears to me as one of the most important fields for cultural anthropologists and social scientists to explore at the present time. Here I can merely give a few examples to illustrate its nature and its importance.

In general, when cultures differing in level of scientific and technological advance come into contact, the less advanced are more affected. But the result differs widely in different cases. Sometimes the less advanced culture simply disappears, as has happened with that of the Australian aborigines over much of Australia, and seems destined to happen to many tribal cultures in Africa. Sometimes it persists in modified and partial form as a subordinate factor in an invading culture, as with the pre-Columbian elements in much of Latin America; or elements of it persist subterraneously in the basement, so to speak, of the new culture, as with witchcraft and magic in medieval Europe or with voodoo and similar practices in the West Indies today; or it may persist, though with considerable transformation, as an overt but minor factor in the new culture, as with the Maoris in New Zealand. Or it may be eroded or even degraded by the infiltration of cheap, mass-produced goods, as in too many Asian areas today; or by that of new but imperfectly assimilated ideas, as too often when missionaries impose Christianity on primitive peoples. In this last case, new and alarming ideological systems may arise, as with various of the nominally Christian sects in black Africa.

It is an empirical fact that primitive cultures react in very different ways to contact with more advanced cultures. Some are exceedingly fragile and go to pieces under the impact; others are tough and are capable of assimilating suitable new elements while preserving their basic identity and continuity and their essential values. Here is an important field for urgent study.

Sometimes the preservation of less advanced cultures has depended on historical and geographical accident. Thus the barbaric but highly organized cultural systems of the kingdoms of West Africa were saved from destruction at the hands of Moslem (Fulani) invaders from the north by the tsetse flies of the forest zone, which killed the horses on which Fulani military success depended. In general terms, the problem that now faces the world in this sphere is how to ensure that the contact between more developed and less developed cultures (especially as regards technological and industrial techniques but also in regard to political, social, and religious ideas) should have the maximum of desirable effects and especially the minimum of undesirable ones. Or the problem can be formulated in a more restricted way: how desirable elements of advanced scientific and technological culture may penetrate into "underdeveloped" areas without destroying what is good and desirable in the recipient cultures. The usual tendency is for cheap, mass-produced goods from outside (and, after industrialization, from inside) to cause the decay of craftsmanship and the creative arts; for population increase consequent on improved death control to disrupt the social and economic system; for industrialization to create a depressed urban proletariat cut off from local cultural tradition; and for the overready adoption of ideas and idea systems from advanced cultures (e.g. democracy, Christianity, Communism, self-determination, etc.), leading to meaningless slogans, unworkable political systems, nationalist touchiness, and so on. Ideas and idea systems can rarely be imported and maintained intact, and in point of fact usually become more or less seriously distorted and degraded in an alien and unprepared cultural environment, resulting in an undesirable hybrid culture.

When racial (ethnic) differences as well as differences in cultural level are involved within a single political area, the problem may become highly complex. Thus in South Africa the drawing off of male Bantu labor, notably for the mines, is causing a radical deterioration of the social setup in the reserves, while at the same time it is creating a detribalized Bantu proletariat in the cities. And the coexistence of a dominant white minority with a subordinate Bantu majority, with all the fears, conflicts, and cultural clashes that it involves, has led to the formulation of the unworkable and theoretically undesirable cultural principle of racial *apartheid*, and to a potentially explosive political situation.

When the two racial-cultural groups reproduce at markedly different rates, further difficulties arise. Thus in Fiji the immigrant Indian population not only has work habits, cultural background, and attitudes to education quite different from those of the native Fijians, but is multiplying so much faster that it will shortly be in the majority [as this book goes to press, already is]. It is indeed clear that attitudes toward family planning and population control are becoming important elements in the world's cultural setup.

The problem may be illustrated with reference to two cultures with which I have a slight personal acquaintance. India is a large and powerful but in many respects underdeveloped independent state which has deliberately embarked on the task of modernizing itself, not only scientifically, technologically, and industrially but also socially (e.g. in regard to the untouchables and the depressed classes and the large tribal elements in the population) and politically (e.g. in regard to constitution, political democracy, and administration). Modernization has to be superposed on a traditional culture, inevitably dependent on agriculture, and involving such important elements as caste and the village system; pervasive non-doctrinal and nonecclesiastical religion ranging up to great spiritual heights from the depths of essentially magic and sometimes barbaric rituals, rigid taboos and a kaleidoscopic polytheism, and including veneration both for cattle and for holy poverty and meditation; a newborn nationalism of a very particular kind; and various legacies of Gandhi's influence, such as a belief in non-violence and satyagraha, in the superiority of hand over machine production, in the desirability of prohibition and the undesirability of birth control. It has to be carried out in an environment whose agricultural resources have been impoverished by erosion, deforestation, and bad methods of cultivation, and with a population which is largely undernourished, already excessive, and still rapidly increasing. The picture is further complicated by the existence of strong and often mutually hostile religious minorities, by considerable ethnic differences, and by great linguistic diversity.

Among the resultant practical problems I may mention the following: How to increase the well-being, the competence, and the productivity of the villager while maintaining his satisfactions and without undermining the stability of the village system. How to introduce scientific ideas and methods without either destroying the entire framework of traditional beliefs and practice or introducing a grave cleavage of thought between different sections of the population. Conversely, how to do away with the bad effects of what are essentially superstitions such as belief in the sanctity of cattle, or in the merit of suttee, without damaging the general spiritual framework of Indian life, or provoking violent reactions. In the most general terms, the problem is how to induce the common man and woman to want and to work for desirable change in a desirable way. I am sure that this can be accomplished; but it will not always be easy. On one hand, there is a massive inertia and resistance to change; on the other there is a dawning awareness, even among remote illiterate villagers, that science is somehow making possible a freer life and a greater well-being. But this awareness is still mainly on the mythical level: the limitations in the way of quick scientific application, the need for slow, rational advance in place of magical or millenary wish fulfillment, are not yet apparent. Here as elsewhere the proper organization of public awareness is a prerequisite for desirable change, and right education is an essential key to progress. Truly desirable change can never be wholly imposed from outside; it must be essentially a self-generating process.

Then there is the problem of how to reconcile the potent new idea of democratic equality with the facts of biological and social inequality and the inevitable limitations of opportunity. Here the distortion of the idea of democracy has introduced new difficulties. For instance it is perfectly obvious that there are now many too many college and university students in India. Many are destined to fail; there are not nearly enough positions for the remainder; and meanwhile professors and lecturers are grossly overworked and the standards of teaching and research are being depressed. But any suggestion that colleges and universities should restrict their intake of students is met by the statement that this is impossible because it would not be "democratic."

Finally there are the problems of national unity and of international integration. In both these fields an exaggerated nationalism and an understandable but unfortunate reaction against anything British are creating difficulties. English is the only language that has ever been shared by all the different regions of India; and it is the language which is far and away the most able to help India to advance in all international fields, notably in science and learning. Yet because of the prevalent nationalist spirit it has been decreed that Hindi, though normally spoken only by a minority of the population, shall become India's official language; and, though it lacks many scientific terms and though its adoption will make interchange of scientific and other ideas more difficult, it has been decreed that it shall become the medium of instruction even at the highest educational level. Recently there has even been a recommendation that an Indian national calendar should supersede the Gregorian calendar, which would introduce still further difficulties. These last examples show how important it is, from the standpoint of cultural adaptedness, to distinguish between the sectors where uniformity is desirable and those where variety is desirable.

My other example is Bali. This differs from India in many ways, notably in being a small, dependent portion of a definitely underdeveloped state and in being inhabited by a homogeneous cultural minority (Hindu instead of Moslem like the rest of Indonesia). It is probably unique in that, with insignificant exceptions, the entire population engages in and finds satisfaction from creative activity of some sort or another—music, dance, drama, celebrations of various sorts, decoration, carving, painting; even the normal heavy tasks of agricultural labor are clothed with cultural satisfactions, in the shape of communal rituals of various kinds.

The resultant "cultural democracy" is obviously something very vital and very desirable. Meanwhile, however, Bali is already being exposed to a flood of cheap and often esthetically nasty mass-produced goods; health leaves much to be desired; and in many fields educational standards are low. The Indonesian Government is taking measures to improve health and is introducing education of essentially Western type (with Western uniforms for the children); and it has permitted the entry of Christian missionaries (there is even a Roman Catholic bishop in Bali). Bali is not at the moment overpopulated. But as health measures succeed the death rate will drop; and unless birth control is not merely permitted but encouraged, population will soon outrun food supply. Then population pressure will result in increased pressure toward technical efficiency and industrialization.

In Bali the major conflict is a straightforward one between two desirable ends—the maintenance of a creative cultural democracy on the one hand, and on the other better health and greater intellectual and scientific enlightenment. Desirable ends may have certain undesirable consequences—e.g. overpopulation as the result of improved health; and the situation is further complicated by the intrusion of alien elements under the cloak of freedom—mass-produced industrial products under that of freedom of trade, missionaries under that of freedom of belief. If the Balinese come to feel that their creative activities are in any sense inferior or stand in the way of the better health and education that they rightly desire, the resultant change will be a retrograde step in cultural evolution. Here again it is apparent that compromise is necessary, but the precise nature of the most desirable type of compromise must be determined in relation to local circumstances. Unfortunately speed is also necessary; changes of various sorts are already rapid, and if not corrected may quite unbalance the entire culture. In such a situation, it is eminently desirable to consult real experts—those who have studied and thought deeply about similar problems elsewhere. They will undoubtedly make mistakes, but their mistakes will certainly not be as serious as those made by local politicians in a hurry.

It would be possible to prolong this disquisition to almost any length. There are obviously many interesting points which I have not discussed. There is the long-term nonadaptedness of certain cultural trends—some (like unchecked militarist expansion or addiction to the idea of world dominance) being manifestly in the long run self-defeating; others, like a belief in one's own intrinsic racial superiority, manifestly untrue; still others, like overexploitation of resources, self-limiting. There is the notion of ideas as transmissible, self-reproducible cultural templates; the question whether such ideas are most effective in the recipient when fully conscious or when largely subconscious, when fully rational or with the pill of rationality covered with an emotional or esthetic coating; and how and under what conditions they may be distorted in the process of translation into action by the recipients. There is the problem whether certain primitive cultures, such as that of the Congo pygmies, admirably adapted to their original conditions but obviously destined to disappear if brought into free and full contact with modern civilization, should be preserved intact as living cultural specimens for their own good and for the interest of the rest of mankind; and there is of course the greatest purely cultural problem of our time, of how to cope with the politico-ideological conflict between organized Communism and the Western world—whether by war, hot or cold, by competitive coexistence, or by some attempt at cooperative synthesis. But the limits of my competence and of my and your energy and time make such discussion impossible here.

I will close by summing up my main argument from a rather different angle. In the past half century there has been much talk, chiefly originating from cultural anthropologists, of the relativity of morals, which has often been construed to mean that no type of morality is or can be better than another; much talk too, chiefly originating from psychoanalysts and psychiatrists, but reinforced from the camp of dogmatic religion and obscurantist philosophy, of the nonrational bases of human behavior, which has often been construed to mean the supremacy of the irrational, the bankruptcy of reason, and the inadequacy of science, and has indeed led to a widespread revolt against reason and a glorification of unreason. Even among professional biologists, who ought to know better, the thesis has been proclaimed that no organism can properly be called higher or lower than another, because all, by the fact of their existence and survival, are "equally adapted." And historians have asserted that there is not, or even cannot be, any such thing as progress in human affairs.

These unfortunate assertions turn out to be quite erroneous when considered *sub specie evolutionis*. Adaptation is not merely the capacity to survive, nor is it merely to the immediate present. It also covers adaptation to change; and when change is so rapid and drastic as it can be in the psychosocial sector, adaptation to change and to the direction of change may become of overriding importance.

As regards *higher* and *lower* in the biological sector, for one thing it is obvious to inspection that some organic types have a higher (more complex, more efficient, and more integrated) organization than others; and for another, paleontology and comparative anatomy have demonstrated that the proof of the pudding has been in the eating—the acquisition of higher organization in this sense has in fact conferred evolutionary success, the more highly organized types having become more abundant and dominant at the expense of less highly organized types. Similarly progress, when adequately defined, is seen as a fact of evolution, both in the biological and the human sector. And finally, when for *relativity* we substitute *adaptation*, in the proper sense of appropriate relatedness on all levels, we at once realize that one moral system can be "better" than another. And a morality which is adapted to a tribal community emerging from ignorance in a sparsely populated world will not be adaptative in a large industrialized community based on vastly increased knowledge in a densely populated world.

Since in the long run the decisive element in a culture appears to be the predominant "vision of destiny," better cultural adaptation connotes a more adequate relation between the formulation of that vision and the facts of the situation, including both the static and directional elements in it, both the short-term events and the long-term trends, both the actualities and the possibilities of the external environment and of human nature. This being so, cultural adaptation, like biological adaptation, will always involve a compromise between many conflicting or competing advantages. Again like long-term biological adaptation, it will tend in the long run to produce organized pattern systems of greater integration and better equilibrium. Further, we must never forget the many fundamental differences between organisms and cultures, between evolution on the biological and on the psychosocial level. Besides the totally new methods of transmission available in the psychosocial sector, including culture contact and idea diffusion, and the totally new types of result involving convergence toward unity instead of only divergence toward variety, there is the fact that the average and especially the maximum, speed of cultural evolution show a marked acceleration during their course, as against their general uniformity in biological evolution; and that in recent times cultural evolution has proceeded at speeds many hundreds of times greater than anything seen in the biological phase. This means that the emphasis in modern cultures must shift from maintenance and stability to progress and change, and that backward-looking visions of destiny must be replaced by forward-looking ones. Here again, education is needed, to ensure that these ideas enter the general awareness of the human species.

There is also the fact (often overlooked or played down owing to the overintellectualization of most philosophers and educators and learned men in general) that in all man's creative activities, including the construction of "visions of destiny," imagination and intuition are as essential as logic and reason. And there is the further fact that if knowledge is lacking on which to build a coherent and satisfying vision, imagination will almost universally be called on to provide mythical[3] explanations and interpretative extrapolations of actuality; and that these imaginative formulations may then canalize and condition the whole culture.

It follows that one of the most important steps to be taken to ensure better cultural adaptation is the application of scientific method to the study of the central explanatory and interpretative elements in man's vision of destiny, with a view to the progressive replacement of mythical elements by scientifically based concepts tested against fact. Note, however, that I do not say *scientific* but *scientifically based* concepts. The analytic and rational concepts that are effective in the natural sciences are inadequate by themselves for constructing a useful "vision of destiny," whose supporting framework must always include values. For this, the scientific and rational basis must be compounded with imagination, emotion, and aspiration. This is another way of saying that cultural adaptation involves adaptation both to the external facts of physical and biological nature and to the internal facts of human nature —including value judgments and their results. Furthermore, facts in this context must be taken to include our knowledge of future possibility (and limitation) as well as present actuality.

In a few final words, I must try to relate my topic to the more general field of behavior and evolution proposed for this symposium. There are two points I would like to make. The first is that in man behavior has been largely internalized and subjectivized, in the form of concepts and intellectual ideas, memories and imaginative creations. From an evolutionary point of view, human thought and indeed all higher mental processes can be regarded as latent or potential action— internal behavior. My second point is that culture, in the anthropological sense, is an organ of human behavior. A culture consists partly of overt acts of behavior such as rituals, partly of the concrete results of overt behavior in the shape of material artefacts, partly of potential behavior in the shape of assumptions, ideas, values, and other mentifacts, or of various combination of these. Thus in the perspective of evolution culture is seen as an organ of behavior of human groups, and potentially as the organ of behavior of the entire human species. Through human culture, behavior has reached a supraorganismal level.

---

[3] I am of course using "mythical" in the same sort of broad sense as Cassirer does.

2-6 A system of national education*

The Human Mind

THE TRUE BASIS OF EDUCATION IS THE STUDY OF THE human mind, infant, adolescent and adult. Any system of education founded on theories of academic perfection, which ignores the instrument of study, is more likely to hamper and impair intellectual growth than to produce a perfect and perfectly equipped mind. For the educationist has to do, not with dead material like the artist or sculptor, but with an infinitely subtle and sensitive organism. He cannot shape an educational masterpiece out of human wood or stone; he has to work in the elusive substance of mind and respect the limits imposed by the fragile human body.

There can be no doubt that the current educational system of Europe is a great advance on many of the methods of antiquity, but its defects are also palpable. It is based on an insufficient knowledge of human psychology, and it is only safeguarded in Europe from disastrous results by the refusal of the ordinary student to subject himself to the processes it involves, his habit of studying only so much as he must to avoid punishment or to pass an immediate test, his resort to active habits and vigorous physical exercise. In India the disastrous effects of the system on body, mind and character are only too apparent. The first problem in a

* Sri Aurobindo Ghose, *A System of National Education.* Calcutta, India: Arya Publishing House, 1948.

Sri Aurobindo Ghose

national system of education is to give an education as comprehensive as the European and more thorough, without the evils of strain and cramming. This can only be done by studying the instruments of knowledge and finding a system of teaching which shall be natural, easy and effective. It is only by strengthening and sharpening these instruments to their utmost capacity that they can be made effective for the increased work which modern conditions require. The muscles of the mind must be thoroughly trained by simple and easy means; then, and not till then, great feats of intellectual strength can be required of them.

The first principle of true teaching is that nothing can be taught. The teacher is not an instructor or task-master, he is a helper and a guide. His business is to suggest and not to impose. He does not actually train the pupil's mind, he only shows him how to perfect his instruments of knowledge and helps and encourages him in the process. He does not impart knowledge to him, he shows him how to acquire knowledge for himself. He does not call forth the knowledge that is within; he only shows him where it lies and how it can be habituated to rise to the surface. The distinction that reserves this principle for the teaching of adolescent and adult minds and denies its application to the child, is a conservative and unintelligent doctrine. Child or man, boy or girl, there is only one sound principle of good teaching. Difference of age only serves to diminish or increase the amount of help and guidance necessary; it does not change its nature.

The second principle is that the mind has to be consulted in its own growth. The idea of hammering the child into the shape desired by the parent or teacher is a barbarous and ignorant superstition. It is he himself who must be induced to expand in accordance with his own nature. There can be no greater error than for the parent to arrange beforehand that his son shall develop particular qualities, capacities, ideas, virtues, or be prepared for a prearranged career. To force the nature to abandon its own *dharma* is to do it permanent harm, mutilate its growth and deface its perfection. It is a selfish tyranny over a human soul and a wound to the nation, which loses the benefit of the best that a man could have given it and is forced to accept instead something imperfect and artificial, second-rate, perfunctory and common. Every one has in him something divine, something his own, a chance of perfection and strength in however small a sphere which God offers him to take or refuse. The task is to find it, develop it and use it. The chief aim of education should be to help the growing soul to draw out that in itself which is best and make it perfect for a noble use.

The third principle of education is to work from the near to the far, from that which is to that which shall be. The basis of a man's nature is almost always, in addition to his soul's past, his heredity, his surroundings, his nationality, his country, the soil from which he draws sustenance, the air which he breathes, the sights, sounds, habits to which he is accustomed. They mould him not the less powerfully because insensibly, and from that then we must begin. We must not take up the nature by the roots from the earth in which it must grow or surround the mind with images and ideas of a life which is alien to that in which it must physically move. If anything has to be brought in from outside, it must be offered, not forced on the mind. A free and natural growth is the condition of genuine development. There are souls which naturally revolt from their surroundings and seem to belong to another age and clime. Let them be free to follow their bent; but the majority languish, become empty, become artificial, if artificially moulded into an alien form. It is God's arrangement that they should belong to a paticular nation, age, society, that they should be children of the past, possessors of the present, creators of the future. The past is our foundation, the present our material, the future our aim and summit. Each must have its due and natural place in a national system of education.

The Powers of the Mind

The instrument of the educationist is the mind or *antaḥkaraṇa*, which consists of four layers. The reservoir of past mental impressions, the *citta* or storehouse of memory, which must be distinguished from the specific act of memory, is the foundation on which all the other layers stand. All experience lies within us as passive or potential memory; active memory selects and takes what it requires from that storehouse. But the active memory is like a man searching among a great mass of locked-up material; sometimes he cannot find what he wants; often in his rapid search he stumbles across many things for which he has no immediate need; often too he blunders and thinks he has found the real thing when it is something else, irrelevant if not valueless, on which he has laid his hand. The passive memory or *citta* needs no training, it is automatic and naturally sufficient to its task; there is not the slightest object of knowledge coming within its field which is not secured, placed and faultlessly preserved in that admirable receptacle. It is the active memory, a higher but less perfectly developed function, which is in need of improvement.

The second layer is the mind proper or *manas*, the sixth sense of our Indian psychology, in which all the others are gathered up. The function of the mind is to receive the images of things translated into sight, sound, smell, taste and touch, the five senses and translate these again into thought-sensations. It receives also images of its own direct grasping and forms them into mental impressions. These sensations and impressions are the material of thought, not thought itself; but it is exceedingly important that thought should work on sufficient and perfect material. It is, therefore, the first business of the educationist to develop in the child the right use of the six senses; to see that they are not stunted or injured by disuse, but trained by the child himself under the teacher's direction to that perfect accuracy and keen subtle sensitiveness of which they are capable. In addition, whatever assistance can be gained by the organs of action, should be thoroughly employed. The hand, for instance, should be trained to reproduce what the eye sees and the mind senses. The speech should be trained to a perfect expression of the knowledge which the whole *antaḥkaraṇa* possesses.

The third layer is the intellect or *buddhi*, which is the real instrument of thought and that which orders and disposes of the knowledge acquired by the other parts of the machine. For the purpose of the educationist this is infinitely the most important of the three I have named. The intellect is an organ composed of several groups of functions, divisible into two important classes, the functions and faculties of the right hand, the functions and faculties of the left hand. The faculties of the right hand are comprehensive, creative and synthetic, the faculties of the left hand critical and analytic. To the right hand belong judgment, imagination, memory, observation; to the left hand comparison and reasoning. The critical faculties distinguish, compare, classify, generalise, deduce, infer, conclude; they are the component parts of the logical reason. The right-hand faculties comprehend, command, judge in their own right, grasp, hold and manipulate. The right-hand mind is the master of the knowledge, the left-hand its servant. The left-hand touches only the body of knowledge, the right-hand penetrates its soul. The left-hand limits itself to ascertained truth, the right-hand grasps that which is still elusive or unascertained. Both are essential to the completeness of the human reason. These important functions of the machine have all to be raised to their highest and finest working-power, if the education of the child is not to be imperfect and one-sided.

There is a fourth layer of faculty which, not as yet entirely developed in man, is attaining gradually to a wider development and more perfect evolution. The powers peculiar to this highest stratum of knowledge are chiefly known to us from the phenomena of genius,—sovereign discernment, intuitive perception of truth, plenary inspiration of speech, direct vision of knowledge to an extent often amounting to revelation, making a man a prophet of truth. These powers are rare in their higher development, though many possess them imperfectly or by flashes. They are still greatly distrusted by the critical reason of mankind because of the admixture of error, caprice and a biassed imagination which obstructs and distorts their perfect workings. Yet it is clear that humanity could not have advanced to its present stage if it had not been for the help of these faculties, and it is a question with which educationists have not yet grappled, what is to be done with this mighty and baffling element, the element of genius in the pupil. The mere instructor does his best to discourage and stifle genius, the more liberal teacher welcomes it. Faculties so important to humanity cannot be left out of our consideration. It is foolish to neglect them. Their imperfect development must be perfected, the admixture of error, caprice and biassed fancifulness must be carefully and wisely removed. But the teacher cannot do it; he would eradicate the good corn as well as the tares if he interfered. Here, as in all educational operations, he can only put the growing soul into the way of its own perfection.

The Moral Nature

In the economy of man the mental nature rests upon the moral, and the education of the intellect divorced from the perfection of the moral and emotional nature is injurious to human progress. Yet, while it is easy to arrange some kind of curriculum or syllabus which will do well enough for the training of the mind, it has not yet been found possible to provide under modern conditions a suitable moral training for the school and college. The attempt to make boys moral and religious by the teaching of moral and religious text-books is a vanity and a delusion, precisely because the heart is not the mind and to instruct the mind does not necessarily improve the heart. It would be an error to say that it has no effect. It throws certain seeds of thought into the *antaḥkaraṇa* and, if these thoughts become habitual, they influence the conduct. But the danger of moral text-books is that they make the thinking of high things mechanical and artificial, and whatever is mechanical and artificial is inoperative for good.

There are three things which are of the utmost importance in dealing with a man's moral nature, the emotions, the *saṁskāras* or formed habits and associations, and the *svabhāva* or nature. The only way for him to train himself morally is to habituate himself to the right emotions, the noblest associations, the best mental, emotional and physical habits and the following out in right action of the fundamental impulses of his essential nature. You can impose a certain discipline on children, dress them into a certain mould, lash them into a desired path, but unless you can get their hearts and natures on your side, the conformity to this imposed rule becomes a hypocritical and heartless, a conventional, often a cowardly compliance. This is what is done in Europe, and it leads to that remarkable phenomenon known as the sowing of wild oats as soon as the yoke of discipline at school and at home is removed, and to the social hypocrisy which is so large a feature of European life. Only what the man admires and accepts, becomes part of himself; the rest is a mask. He conforms to the discipline of society as he conformed to the moral routine of home and school, but considers himself at liberty to guide his real life, inner and private, according to his own likings and passions. On the other hand, to neglect moral and religious education altogether is to corrupt the race. The notorious moral corruption in our young men previous to the saving touch of the Swadeshi movement was the direct result of the purely mental instruction given to them under the English system of education. The adoption of the English system under an Indian disguise in institutions like the Central Hindu College is likely to lead to the European result. That it is better than nothing, is all that can be said for it.

As in the education of the mind, so in the education of the heart, the best way is to put the child into the right road to his own perfection and encourage him to follow it, watching, suggesting, helping, but not interfering. The one excellent element in the English boarding school is that the master at his best stands there as a moral guide and example, leaving the boys largely to influence and help each other in following the path silently shown to them. But the method practised is crude and marred by the excess of outer discipline, for which the pupils have no respect except that of fear and the exiguity of the inner assistance. The little good that is done is outweighed by much evil. The old Indian system of the *Guru* commanding by his knowledge and sanctity the implicit obedience, perfect admiration, reverent emulation of the student was a far superior method of moral discipline. It is impossible to restore that ancient system; but it is not impossible to substitute the wise friend, guide and helper for the hired instructor or the benevolent policeman which is all that the European system usually makes of the pedagogue.

The first rule of moral training is to suggest and invite, not command or impose. The best method of suggestion is by personal example, daily converse and the books read from day to day. These books should contain, for the younger student, the lofty examples of the past given, not as moral lessons, but as things of supreme human interest, and, for the elder student, the great thoughts of great souls, the passages of literature which set fire to the highest emotions and prompt the highest ideals and aspirations, the records of history and biography which exemplify the living of those great thoughts, noble emotions and aspiring ideals. This is a kind of good company, *satsaṅga*, which can seldom fail to have effect so long as sententious sermonising is avoided, and becomes of the highest effect if the personal life of the teacher is itself moulded by the great things he places before his pupils. It cannot, however, have full force unless the young life is given an opportunity, within its limited sphere, of embodying in action the moral impulses which rise within it. The thirst of knowledge, the self-devotion, the purity, the renunciation of the Brahmin,—the courage, ardour, honour, nobility, chivalry, patriotism of the Kshatriya,—the beneficence, skill, industry, generous enterprise and large open-handedness of the Vaisya, —the self-effacement and loving service of the Sudra,—these are the qualities of the Aryan. They constitute the moral temper we desire in our young men, in the whole nation. But how can we get them if we do not give opportunities to the young to train themselves in the Aryan tradition, to form by the practice and familiarity of childhood and boyhood the stuff of which their adult lives must be made?

Every boy should, therefore, be given practical opportunity as well as intellectual encouragement to develop all that is best in the nature. If he has bad qualities, bad habits, bad *saṁskāras*, whether of mind or body, he should not be treated harshly as a delinquent, but encouraged to get rid of them by the Rajayogic method of *saṁyama*, rejection and substitution. He should be encouraged to think of them, not as sins or offences, but as symptoms of a curable disease, alterable by a steady and sustained effort of the will,—falsehood being rejected whenever it rises into the mind and replaced by truth, fear by courage, selfishness by sacrifice and renunciation, malice by love. Great care will have to be taken that unformed virtues are not rejected as faults. The wildness and recklessness of many young natures are only the overflowings of an excessive strength, greatness and nobility. They should be purified, not discouraged.

I have spoken of morality; it is necessary to speak a word of religious teaching. There is a strange idea prevalent that by merely teaching the dogmas of religion children can be made pious and moral. This is an European error, and its practice either leads to mechanical acceptance of a creed having no effect on the inner and little on the outer life, or it creates the fanatic, the pietist, the ritualist or the unctuous hypocrite. Religion has to be lived, not learned as a creed. The singular compromise made in the so-called National Education of Bengal making the teaching of religious beliefs compulsory, but forbidding the practice of *anuṣṭhāna* or religious exercise, is a sample of the ignorant confusion which distracts men's minds on this subject. The prohibition is a sop to secularism declared or concealed. No religious teaching is of any value unless it is lived, and the use of various kinds of *sādhanā*, spiritual self-training and exercise is the only effective preparation for religious living. The ritual of prayer, homage, ceremony is craved for by many minds as an essential preparation and, if not made an end in itself, is a great help to spiritual progress; if it is withheld, some other form of meditation, devotion or religious duty must be put in its place. Otherwise, religious teaching is of little use and would almost be better ungiven.

But whether distinct teaching in any form of religion is imparted or not, the essence of religion, to live for God, for humanity, for country, for others and for oneself in these, must be made the ideal in every school which calls itself national. It is this spirit of Hinduism pervading our schools which—far more than the teaching of Indian subjects, the use of Indian methods or formal instruction in Hindu beliefs and Hindu scriptures—should be the essense of Nationalism in our schools distinguishing them from all others.

Simultaneous and Successive Teaching

A very remarkable feature of modern training which has been subjected in India to a *reductio ad absurdum* is the practice of teaching by snippets. A subject is taught a little at a time, in conjunction with a host of others, with the result that what might be well learnt in a single year is badly learned in seven and the boy goes out ill-equipped, served with imperfect parcels of knowledge, master of none of the great departments of human knowledge. The system of education adopted by the National Council, an amphibious and twy-natured creation, attempts to heighten this practice of teaching by snippets at the bottom and the middle and suddenly change it to a grandiose specialism at the top. This is to base the triangle on its apex and hope that it will stand.

The old system was to teach one or two subjects well and thoroughly and then proceed to others, and certainly it was a more rational system than the modern. If it did not impart so much varied information, it built up a deeper, nobler and more real culture. Much of the shallowness, discursive lightness and fickle mutability of the average modern mind is due to the vicious principle of teaching by snippets. The one defect that can be alleged against the old system was that the subject earliest learned might fade from the mind of the student while he was mastering his later studies. But the excellent training given to the memory by the ancients obviated the incidence of this defect. In the future education we need not bind ourselves either by the ancient or the modern system, but select only the most perfect and rapid means of mastering knowledge.

In defense of the modern system it is alleged that the attention of children is easily tired and cannot be subjected to the strain of long application to a single subject. The frequent change of subject gives rest to the mind. The question naturally arises: are the children of modern times then so different from the ancients, and, if so, have we not made them so by discouraging prolonged concentration? A very young child cannot, indeed, apply himself; but a very young child is unfit for school teaching of any kind. A child of seven or eight, and that is the earliest permissible age for the commencement of any regular kind of study, is capable of a good deal of concentration if he is interested. Interest is, after all, the basis of concentration. We make his lessons supremely uninteresting and repellent to the child, a harsh compulsion the basis of teaching and then complain of his restless inattention! The substitution of a natural self-education by the child for the present unnatural system will remove this objection of inability. A child, like a man, if he is interested, much prefers to get to the end of his subject rather than leave it unfinished. To lead him on step by step, interesting and absorbing him in each as it comes, until he has mastered his subject is the true art of teaching.

The first attention of the teacher must be given to the medium and the instruments, and, until these are perfected, to multiply subjects of regular instruction is to waste time and energy. When the mental instruments are sufficiently developed to acquire a language easily and swiftly, that is the time to introduce him to many languages, not when he can only partially understand what he is taught and masters it laboriously and imperfectly. Moreover, one who has mastered his own language, has one very necessary facility for mastering another. With the linguistic faculty unsatisfactorily developed in one's own tongue, to master others is impossible. To study science with the faculties of observation, judgment, reasoning and comparison only slightly developed is to undertake a useless and thankless labour. So it is with all other subjects.

The mother-tongue is the proper medium of education and therefore the first energies of the child should be directed to the thorough mastering of the medium. Almost every child has an imagination, an instinct for words, a dramatic faculty, a wealth of idea and fancy. These should be interested in the literature and history of the nation. Instead of stupid and dry spelling and reading books, looked on as a dreary and ungrateful task, he should be introduced by rapidly progressive stages to the most interesting parts of his own literature and the life around him and behind him, and they should be put before him in such a way as to attract and appeal to the qualities of which I have spoken. All other study at this period should be devoted to the perfection of the mental functions and the moral character. A foundation should be laid at this time for the study of history, science, philosophy, art, but not in an obtrusive and formal manner. Every child is a lover of interesting narrative, a hero-worshipper and a patriot. Appeal to these qualities in him and through them let him master without knowing it the living and human parts of his nation's history. Every child is an inquirer, an investigator, analyser, a merciless anatomist. Appeal to those qualities in him and let him acquire without knowing it the right temper and the necessary fundamental knowledge of the scientist. Every child has an insatiable intellectual curiosity and turn for metaphysical enquiry. Use it to draw him on slowly to an understanding of the world and himself. Every child has the gift of imitation and a touch of imaginative power. Use it to give him the groundwork of the faculty of the artist.

It is by allowing Nature to work that we get the benefit of the gifts she has bestowed on us. Humanity in its education of children has chosen to thwart and hamper her processes and, by so doing, has done much to thwart and hamper the rapidity of its onward march. Happily, saner ideas are now beginning to prevail. But the way has not yet been found. The past hangs about our necks with all its prejudices and errors and will not leave us; it enters into our most radical attempts to return to the guidance of the all-wise Mother. We must have the courage to take up clearer knowledge and apply it fearlessly in the interests of posterity. Teaching by snippets must be relegated to the lumberroom of dead sorrows. The first work is to interest the child in life, work and knowledge, to develop his instruments of knowledge with the utmost thoroughness, to give him mastery of the medium he must use. Afterwards, the rapidity with which he will learn will make up for any delay in taking up regular studies, and it will be found that, where now he learns a few things badly, then he will learn many things thoroughly well.

The Training of the Senses

There are six senses which minister to knowledge, sight, hearing, smell, touch and taste, mind, and all of these except the last look outward and gather the material of thought from outside through the physical nerves and their end-organs, eye, ear, nose, skin, palate. The perfection of the senses as ministers to thought must be one of the first cares of the teacher. The two things that are needed of the senses are accuracy and sensitiveness. We must first understand what are the obstacles to the accuracy and sensitiveness of the senses, in order that we may take the best steps to remove them. The cause of imperfection must be understood by those who desire to bring about perfection.

The senses depend for their accuracy and sensitiveness on the unobstructed activity of the nerves which are the channels of their information and the passive acceptance of the mind which is the recipient. In themselves the organs do their work perfectly. The eye gives the right form, the ear the correct sound, the palate the right taste, the skin the right touch, the nose the right smell. This can easily be understood if we study the action of the eye as a crucial example. A correct image is reproduced automatically on the retina, if there is any error in appreciating it, it is not the fault of the organ, but of something else.

The fault may be with the nerve currents. The nerves are nothing but channels, they have no power in themselves to alter the information given by the organs. But a channel may be obstructed and the obstruction may interfere either with the fullness or the accuracy of the information, not as it reaches the organ where it is necessarily and automatically perfect, but as it reaches the mind. The only exception is in case of a physical defect in the organ as an instrument. That is not a matter for the educationist, but for the physician.

If the obstruction is such as to stop the information reaching the mind at all, the result is an insufficient sensitiveness of the senses. The defects of sight, hearing, smell, touch, taste, anaesthesia in its various degrees, are curable when not the effect of physical injury or defect in the organ itself. The obstructions can be removed and the sensitiveness remedied by the purification of the nerve system. The remedy is a simple one which is now becoming more and more popular in Europe for different reasons and objects, the regulation of the breathing. This process inevitably restores the perfect and unobstructed activity of the channels and, if well and thoroughly done, leads to a high activity of the senses. The process is called in Yogic discipline *nāḍi-śuddhi* or nerve-purification.

The obstruction in the channel may be such as not absolutely to stop in however small a degree, but to distort the information. A familiar instance of this is the effect of fear or alarm on the sense action. The startled horse takes the sack on the road for a dangerous living thing, the startled man takes a rope for a snake, a waving curtain for a ghostly form. All distortions due to actions in the nervous system can be traced to some kind of emotional disturbance acting in the nerve channels. The only remedy for them is the habit of calm, the habitual steadiness of the nerves. This also can be brought about by *nāḍi-śuddhi* or nerve-purification, which quiets the system, gives a deliberate calmness to all the internal processes and prepares the purification of the mind.

If the nerve channels are quiet and clear, the only possible disturbance of the information is from or through the mind. Now the *manas* or sixth sense is in itself a channel like the nerves, a channel for communication with the *buddhi* or brain-force. Disturbance may happen either from above or from below. The information outside is first photographed on the end organ, then reproduced at the other end of the nerve system in the *citta* or passive memory. All the images of sight, sound, smell, touch and taste are deposited there and the *manas* reports them to the *buddhi*. The *manas* is both a sense organ and a channel. As a sense organ it is as automatically perfect as the others, as a channel it is subject to disturbance resulting either in obstruction or distortion.

As a sense organ the mind receives direct thought impressions from outside and from within. These impressions are in themselves perfectly correct, but in their report to the intellect they may either not reach the intellect at all or may reach it so distorted as to make a false or partially false impression. The disturbance may affect the impression which attends the information of eye, ear, nose, skin or palate, but it is very slightly powerful here. In its effect on the direct impressions of the mind, it is extremely powerful and the chief source of error. The mnd takes direct impressions primarily of thought, but also of form, sound, indeed of all the things for which it usually prefers to depend on the sense organs. The full development of this sensitiveness of the mind is called in our Yogic discipline *sūkṣmadṛṣṭi* or subtle reception of images. Telepathy, clairvoyance, clairaudience, presentiment, thought-reading, character-reading and many other modern discoveries are very ancient powers of the mind which have been left undeveloped, and they all belong to the *manas*. The development of the sixth sense has never formed part of human training. In a future age it will undoubtedly take a place in the necessary preliminary training of the human instrument. Meanwhile there is no reason why the mind should not be trained to give a correct report to the intellect so that our thought may start with absolutely correct if not with full impressions.

The first obstacle, the nervous emotional, we may suppose to be removed by the purification of the nervous system. The second obstacle is that of the emotions themselves warping the impression as it comes. Love may do this, hatred may do this, any emotion or desire according to its power and intensity may distort the impression as it travels. This difficulty can only be removed by the discipline of the emotions, the purifying of the moral habits. This is a part of moral training and its consideration may be postponed for the moment. The next difficulty is the interference of previous associations formed or ingrained in the *citta* or passive memory. We have a habitual way of looking at things and the conservative inertia in our nature disposes us to give every new experience the shape and semblance of those to which we are accustomed. It is only more developed minds which can receive first impressions without an unconscious bias against the novelty of novel experience. For instance, if we get a true impression of what is happening—and we habitually act on such impressions true or false—if it differs from what we are accustomed to expect, the old association meets it in the *citta* and sends a changed report to the intellect in which either the new impression is overlaid and concealed by the old or mingled with it. To go farther into this subject would be to involve ourselves too deeply into the details of psychology. This typical instance will suffice. To get rid of this obstacle is impossible without *citta-śuddhi* or purification of the mental and moral habits formed in the *citta*. This is a preliminary process of Yoga and was effected in our ancient system by various means, but would be considered out of place in a modern system of education.

It is clear, therefore, that unless we revert to our old Indian system in some of its principles, we must be content to allow this source of disturbance to remain. A really national system of education would not allow itself to be controlled by European ideas in this all-important matter. And there is a process so simple and momentous that it can easily be made a part of our system.

It consists in bringing about passivity of the restless flood of thought sensations rising of its own momentum from the passive memory independent of our will and control. This passivity liberates the intellect from the siege of old associations and false impressions. It gives it power to select only what is wanted from the storehouse of the passive memory, automatically brings about the habit of getting right impressions and enables the intellect to dictate to the *citta* what *saṁskāras* or associations shall be formed or rejected. This is the real office of the intellect,—to discriminate, choose, select, arrange. But so long as there is not *citta-śuddhi*, instead of doing this office perfectly, it itself remains imperfect and corrupt and adds to the confusion in the mind channel by false judgment, false imagination, false memory, false observation, false comparison, contrast and analogy, false deduction, induction and inference. The purification of the *citta* is essential for the liberation, purification and perfect action of the intellect.

Sense-Improvement by Practice

Another cause of the inefficiency of the senses as gatherers of knowledge, is insufficient use. We do not observe sufficiently or with sufficient attention and closeness and a sight, sound, smell, even touch or taste knocks in vain at the door for admission. This *tāmasic* inertia of the receiving instruments is no doubt due to the inattention of the *buddhi*, and therefore its consideration may seem to come properly under the training of the functions of the intellect, but it is more convenient, though less psychologically correct, to notice it here. The student ought to be accustomed to catch the sights, sounds, etc., around him, distinguish them, mark their nature, properties and sources and fix them in the *citta* so that they may be always ready to respond when called for by the memory.

It is a fact which has been proved by minute experiments that the faculty of observation is very imperfectly developed in men, merely from want of care in the use of the sense and the memory. Give twelve men the task of recording from memory something they all saw two hours ago and the accounts will all vary from each other and from the actual occurrence. To get rid of this imperfection will go a long way towards the removal of error. It can be done by training the senses to do their work perfectly, which they will do readily enough if they know the *buddhi* requires it of them, and giving sufficient attention to put the facts in their right place and order in the memory.

Attention is a factor in knowledge, the importance of which has been always recognised. Attention is the first condition of right memory and of accuracy. To attend to what he is doing is the first element of discipline required of the student, and, as I have suggested, this can easily be secured if the object of attention is made interesting. This attention to a single thing is called concentration. One truth is, however, sometimes overlooked; that concentration on several things at a time is often indispensable. When people talk of concentration, they imply centring the mind on one thing at a time; but it is quite possible to develop the power of double concentration, triple concentration, multiple concentration. When a given incident is happening, it may be made up of several simultaneous happenings or a set of simultaneous circumstances, a sight, a sound, a touch or several sights, sounds, touches occurring at the same moment or in the same short space of time. The tendency of the mind is to fasten on one and mark others vaguely, many not at all or, if compelled to attend to all, to be distracted and mark none perfectly. Yet this can be remedied and the attention equally distributed over a set of circumstances in such a way as to observe and remember each perfectly. It is merely a matter of *abhyāsa* or steady natural practice.

It is also very desirable that the hand should be capable of coming to the help of the eye in dealing with the multitudinous objects of its activity so as to ensure accuracy. This is of a use so obvious and imperatively needed, that it need not be dwelt on at length. The practice of imitation by the hand of the thing seen is of use both in detecting the lapses and inaccuracies of the mind, in noticing the objects of sense and in registering accurately what has been seen. Imitation by the hand ensures accuracy of observation. This is one of the first uses of drawing, and it is sufficient in itself to make the teaching of this subject a necessary part of the training of the organs.

The Training of the Mental Faculties

The first qualities of the mind that have to be developed are those which can be grouped under observation. We notice some things, ignore others. Even of what we notice, we observe very little. A general perception of an object is what we all usually carry away from a cursory half-attentive glance. A closer attention fixes its place, form, nature as distinct from its surroundings. Full concentration of the faculty of observation gives us all the knowledge that the three chief senses can gather about the object, or if we touch or taste, we may gather all that the five senses can tell of its nature and properties. Those who make use of the sixth sense, the poet, the painter, the Yogin, can also gather much that is hidden from the ordinary observer. The scientist by investigation ascertains other facts open to a minuter observation. These are the components of the faculty of observation, and it is obvious that its basis is attention, which may be only close or close and minute.

We may gather much even from a passing glance at an object, if we have the habit of concentrating the attention and the habit of *sāttvic* receptivity. The first thing the teacher has to do is to accustom the pupil to concentrate attention.

We may take the instance of a flower. Instead of looking casually at it and getting a casual impression of scent, form and colour, he should be encouraged to know the flower—to fix in his mind the exact shade, the peculiar glow, the precise intensity of the scent, the beauty of curve and design in the form. His touch should assure itself of the texture and its peculiarities. Next, the flower should be taken to pieces and its structure examined with the same carefulness of observation. All this should be done not as a task, but as an object of interest by skilfully arranged questions suited to the learner which will draw him on to observe and investigate one thing after the other until he has almost unconsciously mastered the whole.

Memory and judgment are the next qualities that will be called upon, and they should be encouraged in the same unconscious way. The student should not be made to repeat the same lesson over again in order to remember it. That is a mechanical, burdensome and unintelligent way of training the memory. A similar but different flower should be put in the hands and he should be encouraged to note it with the same care, but with the avowed object of noting the similarities and differences. By this practice daily repeated the memory will naturally be trained. Not only so, but the mental centres of comparison and contrast will be developed. The learner will begin to observe as a habit the similarities of things and their differences. The teacher should take every care to encourage the perfect growth of this faculty and habit. At the same time, the laws of species and genus will begin to dawn on the mind and, by a skilful following and leading of the young developing mind, the scientific habit, the scientific attitude and the fundamental facts of scientific knowledge may in a very short time be made part of its permanent equipment. The observation and comparison of flowers, leaves, plants, trees will lay the foundations of botanical knowledge without loading the mind with names and that dry set acquisition of informations which is the beginning of cramming and detested by the healthy human mind when it is fresh from nature and unspoiled by unnatural habits. In the same way by the observation of the stars, astronomy, by the observation of earth, stones, etc., geology, by the observation of insects and animals, entomology and zoology may be founded. A little later chemistry may be started by interesting observation of experiments without any formal teaching or heaping on the mind of formulas and book knowledge. There is no scientific subject the perfect and natural mastery of which cannot be prepared in early childhood by this training of the faculties to observe, compare, remember and judge various classes of objects. It can be done easily and attended with a supreme and absorbing interest in the mind of the student. Once the taste is created, the boy can be trusted to follow it up with all the enthusiasm of youth in his leisure hours. This will prevent the necessity at a later age of teaching him everything in class.

The judgment will naturally be trained along with the other faculties. At every step the boy will have to decide what is the right idea, measurement, appreciation of colour, sound, scent, etc., and what is the wrong. Often the judgments and distinctions made will have to be exceedingly subtle and delicate. At first many errors will be made, but the learner should be taught to trust his judgment without being attached to its results. It will be found that the judgment will soon begin to respond to the calls made on it, clear itself of all errors and begin to judge correctly and minutely. The best way is to accustom the boy to compare his judgments with those of others. When he is wrong, it should at first be pointed out to him how far he was right and why he went wrong; afterwards he should be encouraged to note these things for himself. Every time he is right, his attention should be prominently and encouragingly called to it so that he may get confidence.

While engaged in comparing and contrasting, another centre is certain to develop, the centre of analogy. The learner will inevitably draw analogies and argue from like to like. He should be encouraged to use this faculty while noticing its limitations and errors. In this way he will be trained to form the habit of correct analogy which is an indispensable aid in the acquisition of knowledge.

The one faculty we have omitted, apart from the faculty of direct reasoning, is Imagination. This is a most important and indispensable instrument. It may be divided into three functions, the forming of mental images, the power of creating thoughts, images and imitations or new combinations of existing thoughts and images, the appreciation of the soul in things, beauty, charm, greatness, hidden suggestiveness, the emotion and spiritual life that pervades the world. This is in every way as important as the training of the faculties which observe and compare outward things. But that demands a separate and fuller treatment.

The mental faculties should first be exercised on things, afterwards on words and ideas. Our dealings with language are much too prefunctory and the absence of a fine sense for words impoverishes the intellect and limits the fineness and truth of its operation. The mind should be accustomed first to notice the word thoroughly, its form, sound and sense; then to compare the form with other similar forms in the points of similarity and difference, thus forming the foundation of the grammatical sense; then to distinguish between the fine shades of sense of similar words and the formation and rhythm of different sentences, thus forming the formation of the literary and the syntactical faculties. All this should be done informally, drawing on the curiosity and interest, avoiding set teaching and memorising of rules. The true knowledge takes its base on things, *arthas*, and only when it has mastered the thing, proceeds to formalise its information.

The Training of the Logical Faculty

The training of the logical reason must necessarily follow the training of the faculties which collect the material on which the logical reason must work. Not only so but the mind must have some development of the faculty of dealing with words before it can deal successfully with ideas. The question is, once this preliminary work is done, what is the best way of teaching the boy to think correctly from premises. For the logical reason cannot proceed without premises. It either infers from facts to a conclusion, or from previously formed conclusions to a fresh one, or from one fact to another. It either induces, deduces or simply infers. I see the sunrise day after day, I conclude or induce that it rises as a law daily after a varying interval of darkness. I have already ascertained that wherever there is smoke, there is fire. I have induced that general rule from an observation of facts. I deduce that in a particular case of smoke there is a fire behind. I infer that a man must have lit it from the improbability of any other cause under the particular circumstances. I cannot deduce it because fire is not always created by human kindling; it may be volcanic or caused by a stroke of lightning or the sparks from some kind of friction in the neighbourhood.

There are three elements necessary to correct reasoning: first, the correctness of the facts or conclusions I start from, secondly, the completeness as well as the accuracy of the data I start from, thirdly, the elimination of other possible or impossible conclusons from the same facts. The fallibility of the logical reason is due partly to avoidable negligence and looseness in securing these conditions, partly to the difficulty of getting all the facts correct, still more to the difficulty of getting all the facts complete, most of all, to the extreme difficulty of eliminating all possble conclusions except the one which happens to be right. No fact is supposed to be more perfectly established than the universality of the Law of Gravitation as an imperative rule, yet a single new fact inconsistent with it would upset this supposed universality. And such facts exist. Nevertheless by care and keenness the fallibility may be reduced to its minimum.

The usual practice is to train the logical reason by teaching the science of Logic. This is an instance of the prevalent error by which book knowledge of a thing is made the object of the study instead of the thing itself. The experience of reasoning and its errors should be given to the mind and it should be taught to observe how these work for itself; it should proceed from the example to the rule and from the accumulating harmony of rules to the formal science of the subject, not from the formal science to the rule, and from the rule to the example.

The first step is to make the young mind interest itself in drawing inferences from the facts, tracing cause and effect. It should then be led on to notice its successes and its failures and the reason of the success and of the failure; the incorrectness of the fact started from, the haste in drawing conclusions from insufficient facts, the carelessness in accepting a conclusion which is improbable, little supported by the data or open to doubt, the indolence or prejudice which does not wish to consider other possible explanations or conclusions. In this way the mind can be trained to reason as correctly as the fallibility of human logic will allow, minimising the chances of error. This study of formal logic should be postponed to a later time when it can easily be mastered in a very brief period, since it will be only the systematizing of an art perfectly well-known to the student.

Introduction to

Contributors to section three:

Jacob W. Getzels and Philip W. Jackson

Gordon Allport

J. P. Guilford

Lawrence S. Kubie

James S. Coleman

David McClelland, et al.

Martha Wolfenstein

Contributions of the be

section three: the behavioral sciences SECTION III

THE SCIENCES THAT CONCERN THEMSELVES WITH PEOPLE and their institutions provide a fair amount of the essential scientific basis for educational decisions. At the same time many educational problems are better researched by educators. Nevertheless, as the educational process deals with the young who respond to their own internal pressures, to parental pressures, and to the pressure of their society and its times and peculiarities, psychology, sociology, anthropology and political science, to name a few, have a great deal to insist upon.

The nature of the research process leads inadvertently, but inevitably, to an enthusiastic partisanship on the part of the individual researcher. The nature of the findings in behavioral science research leads, however, to probabilistic results which can be, and sometimes are, refuted later by another man in another place or in another time. This is as it should be; for out of this balancing and counterbalancing process a gradual and increasingly impressive body of tested knowledge about people and the way they grow, learn and live has been accumulating.

Sometimes, though, educators have been led down the primrose path by the adherents of a particular research trend. This seems to happen when a particular set of findings or conceptualizations are seductive in their clarity but turn out to be only partly right or when the blindness of a particular era prevents the obvious from being seen. In the paper by Jacob W. Getzels and Philip W. Jackson, "Varieties of Giftedness in Children" (This is the introduction to their very interesting book, *Creativity and Intelligence*) the sobering history of the concept of I.Q. is reviewed. The ignored attempts of some early researchers to insist on other kinds of giftedness are instructive and perhaps premonitory.

At the present time a like amount of pressure seems to be coming from a small but vigorous group of lay people who are concerned about children grasping the "fundamentals"; this lay pressure finds natural support and comfort from the professional adherents of the reinforcement theory of learning, who would insist that most (some psychologists say all) learning is accomplished by establishing association bonds between one thing and another. (Correct bonds are rewarded and thus "stamped in," and incorrect bonds are thought, of course, to be dropped out because of punishment.) Scientific testing of this theory, like earlier I.Q. research, is comparatively easy. The concerns of citizens and vigorous professional partisans have culminated in the economic adventure of the teaching machine. Elsewhere in this volume Jerome Bruner discusses the educative and learning issues of the teaching machine dispassionately. Within this section one of the wise and mediating deans of American psychology, Gordon Allport, considers the varieties of learning theories and the difficulties of each.

The whole notion of creativity, which by definition involves the production of the novel, the original and the unmemorized, immediately gives trouble to a theory which would emphasize the primacy or regency of association bonds. Although the problems of designing creativity research are difficult, the work of J. P. Guilford represents one important attack on the aspects of "divergent" thinking as opposed to the rote memory, "convergent thinking." Guilford addresses himself to educators in his paper, "Factors That Aid and Hinder Creativity."

For many a decade educators have known that the motivational level of some of the children all the time, and all the children some of the time, is an undependable and skittish ally of the instructor in the process of learning. Descriptively and simply the case has been stated by saying that the whole child comes to school. Psychoanalysis was the first discipline to insist that a description of a whole person necessarily includes unconscious processes as well. Lawrence S. Kubie, a latter day psychoanalyst, has concerned himself with a symbiosis that he feels has existed between the educational process and an unconscious universal neurosis. In "Education for Preconscious Freedom and Its Relation to Creativity and to the Process of Maturation" he questions whether present educational methods free children for effective functioning and maturity or whether they reinforce obsessive dawdling, intergenerational conflict, sibling rivalries and neurotic submissiveness. Kubie focuses his dissatisfaction on the educational system as the most important institution having to do with the young, but it is evident that it is with society that he finds his quarrel. Many another, less knowledgeable and less pleasant, critic has done the same.

James S. Coleman investigated the value preferences of boys and girls in fourteen different high schools and reported his findings in *The Adolescent Society*. His paper, "Adolescence and Secondary Education in Modern Society," is taken from that book. Being dismayed with the discrepancies among the value preferences of the various high schools he studied (irrespective of their individual predominant social class orientation) Coleman questions whether educators are entirely clear as to the value implications that the reward atmosphere of high schools may be conveying to adolescents. He discusses the meaning and ramifications of competition. Similar questions could be raised for elementary schools.

Earlier in this volume the educational and acculturation choices of a number of different societies was presented in the section on comparative education. McClelland, Sturr, Knapp and Wendt's paper on "Obligations to Self and Society in the United States and Germany," does not comment on education, *per se*, but is concerned with the balance between "egocentricism" and "sociocentricism." They define "egocentricism" as the individual's inevitable and necessary committment and responsibility to himself whereas "sociocentricism" is defined as the individual's commitment and responsiveness to the demands of others and society. The nature of the balance between obligations to self and obligations to society is necessarily arbitrated by the educational and child rearing practices of successive generations within each society. The American ethic and the German ethic in this regard are investigated by McClelland and his associate, and their findings raise immediately a number of provocative questions in regard to educational choice and the ensuing character development which a society may value. The role of formal education in evoking and rewarding a society's preferred values is obvious.

The socialization matrix of the young would be incomplete without the inclusion of the pervasive influence and effects of the family, as an agent, for itself and for society on the developing child. The paper, "French Parents Take Their Children To The Park," has been chosen for this purpose. The author, Martha Wolfenstein, describes sensitively and delightfully the Parisian child's interrelation with his parents, his siblings, and his playmates while engaged in a typical French recreation. She further contrasts these observations with her own extensive observations of the behavior of American children in similar situations. The overall affect is to call attention again to the differing behavioral consequences of educational procedures whether practiced by a formal teacher or an informal teacher, a parent.

See Section Bibliographies, page 361.

3-1 Varieties of giftedness in children*

ANY SYSTEMATIC CONSIDERATION OF GIFTEDNESS IN CHILDREN must begin with reference, however brief, to the monumental studies by the late Lewis M. Terman.[1] Prior to his work—and to some extent even since, for stereotypes die hard—the gifted student was portrayed as an unattractive, bespectacled, badly co-ordinated, if not altogether anemic child, who was an outcast among both other children and adults. Terman's studies contradicted all this. The gifted student was found to be healthier than the average, more attractive personally, better co-ordinated, and in general to be enjoying a richer and fuller life.

To those interested in studying giftedness in children, Terman left a research model that was both simple and powerful. Briefly stated, here is the basis of Terman's procedure. He entered the schools of a particular area—in his case, California—and, applying group or individual intelligence tests, selected children in the top 1 or 2 or 3 per cent in IQ. Calling these children "gifted," he proceeded to pose the question: What

* Getzels, Jacob W., and Philip W. Jackson. *Creativity and Intellect*, New York, John Wiley & Sons, Inc., 1962, pp. 1–8.

[1] L. M. Terman *et al.*, *Genetic Studies of Genius*, Vol. I, *Mental*

Jacob W. Getzels
and
Philip W. Jackson

other qualities are associated with this exceptional intellectual ability ("exceptional intellectual ability" being of course defined by the high IQ)? It was not long before other investigators were applying this model to other populations—invariably using the IQ metric, relating it to other qualities, and finding essentially what Terman had found. Information about the child with a high IQ accumulated rapidly.

Some efforts have been made to collect and summarize the overall findings, to take inventory, as it were, of what we have been up to in these studies of gifted children. Typical is a 1954 symposium whose participants included Terman himself, his associate Melita Oden, Margaret Mead, Ruth Strang, Paul Witty, and others who have done significant work in this area.[2] The task of the symposium was to bring us up to date—some 30 years after Terman's first publications—on what was known about the gifted student. The most striking conclusion from the collection of papers is that the things that could be said with certainty in 1954 about the gifted child did not differ substantially from Terman's earliest findings. Although each paper is excellent in its own right, together they reflect a slackening of progress in our understanding of giftedness in children. Many of the statements made tentatively by Terman in 1925 could be made with greater conviction, and the importance of this should not be minimized. Yet by and large, further conceptual development and fundamental knowledge seems not to have been forthcoming. The crucial problem, for us, became "why?"

It seemed that the primary block to further work lay in epitomizing giftedness in children within the one concept of intelligence as represented by the IQ metric. In most studies, the word "gifted" was synonymous with "high IQ," and the term "gifted child" was for all intents and purposes only a shorthand way of saying "child with a high IQ." A child who did not have a high IQ, no matter how accomplished in other respects, was not considered "gifted." Al-

---

and Physical Traits of a Thousand Gifted Children, Stanford: Stanford University Press, 1925; Catharine M. Cox *et al.*, *Genetic Studies of Genius*, Vol. II, *The Early Mental Traits of Three Hundred Geniuses*, Stanford: Stanford University Press, 1926; Barbara S. Burks, Dortha W. Jensen, and L. M. Terman, *Genetic Studies of Genius*, Vol. III, *The Promise of Youth*, Stanford: Stanford University Press, 1930; L. M. Terman and Melita Oden, *Genetic Studies of Genius*, Vol. IV, *The Gifted Child Grows Up*, Stanford: Stanford University Press, 1947; L. M. Terman and Melita Oden, *Genetic Studies of Genius*, Vol. V, *The Gifted Group at Mid-Life*, Stanford: Stanford University Press, 1959.

[2] Ruth Strang (Chairman) A symposium—the gifted child, *J. Teach. Educ.*, 1954, 5, pp. 210–232.

though this psychometric definition has great heuristic value, it is not without at least three severe limitations.

First, it suggests that the common intelligence test supplies all, or at least a sufficiently broad range, of known cognitive abilities. It thus discourages the observation of other types of cognitive functioning. On the contrary, the items on the typical intelligence test seemed to us to represent a rather narrow band of intellectual tasks, relying chiefly on those requiring in Guilford's terms "convergent thinking" and neglecting those requiring "divergent thinking." [3] To do well on the typical intelligence test, the subject must be able to recall and to recognize, perhaps even to solve; he need not necessarily be able to invent or innovate.

Second, although the correlation between the IQ and learning is positive—and we ought to say at once that we recognize the IQ as probably the best single measure we have—it nevertheless rarely accounts for more than one-quarter of the variance in such crucial factors as school achievement and academic performance. The student with a higher IQ who is doing poorly in school and the student with a lower IQ who is doing well appear too often for the IQ to stand as the only predictive measure of intellectual ability or as the sole criterion of giftedness. Moreover, it is commonly observed that many children who are very high in intelligence as measured by IQ are not concomitantly high in such other intellectual functions as creativity, and many children who are very high in creativity are not concomitantly high in intelligence as measured by IQ.

And third, the IQ metric has been peculiarly immune to advances in our understanding of thinking and behavior. Despite significant transformations in our theories of cognition, learning, and problem solving, the conceptual base of the intelligence test has remained unaltered. The soundness of a new intelligence test is often measured by the degree of its correlation with an old intelligence test, that is, the new test must measure the same mental processes as the old test. This procedure effectively perpetuates the original conception of intelligence and guards it from serious theoretical and empirical scrutiny.

These considerations, among others, led us to wonder whether the slackening of progress in the understanding of gifted children might not be due to the too-heavy reliance on the concept of intelligence as reflected in the intelligence test. Are there not other

---

[3] J. P. Guilford *et al.,* A factor-analytic study of creative thinking II: administration of tests and analysis of results, *Reports from the Psychology Laboratory,* Los Angeles: University of Southern California, 1952, No. 8.

intellectual qualities—qualities not presently sampled by the intelligence test—that are also representative of giftedness? Is not creativity just such a quality? The assumption of most studies of giftedness is that intelligence and creativity are so highly correlated that the highly intelligent student is also the highly creative student. Is the assumption tenable?

That creativity and intelligence might not be closely related was suggested in psychological literature even before the intelligence test as we now know it had been developed. As early as 1898, Dearborn studied the imaginative responses of Harvard students and faculty to a series of inkblots.[4] In discussing his results, he commented that two of the poorest records were made by "students of decidedly 'intellectual type.'" Several years later Colvin[5] studied "inventiveness" in the English compositions of grade-school children. Two of his scoring categories were "logical power" and "spontaneity," the one referring to organizational ability and the other to imaginative ability. Colvin concluded, "If we further study the . . . results we will see that for both boys and girls . . . logical power varies largely with the extent of the composition, but does not seem to accompany any particular element of spontaneity. . . ."[6] In 1906 Colvin and Meyer[7] repeated the original study with the same results. "Logical power shows no pronounced relation to any type of imagination except the visual," they reiterated. In 1916, to give one other instance of these early investigations, Laura Chassel[8] studied a number of different tests, ranging from tests of word building and coding to those requiring unusual and original responses to novel situations. The former tasks were quite similar to those included in many present tests of intelligence, the latter quite similar to many present tests of "divergent thinking" or creativity. Chassel found that performance on the IQ tasks bore relatively little relation to performance on the creativity tasks.

By 1920 the intelligence test in its standard form was very much with us. It had been used in military selection, and was being widely applied to all sorts of decisions involving children. Terman's own studies were under way. From the beginning, effectiveness of the IQ

[4] G. V. Dearborn, A study of imagination, *Amer. J. Psychol.*, 1898, 5(9), pp. 183–190.

[5] S. S. Colvin, Invention versus form in English composition: an indicative study, *Pedagog. Semin.*, 1902, 9, pp. 393–421.

[6] *Ibid.* p. 411.

[7] S. S. Colvin and I. F. Meyer, Imaginative elements in the written work of school children, *Pedagog. Semin.*, 1906, 13, p. 91.

[8] Laura M. Chassell, Tests for originality, *J. Educ. Psychol.* 1916, 7, pp. 317–328.

as a comprehensive measure of cognitive functioning was challenged by a number of people. R. M. Simpson, writing for the *American Journal of Psychology* in 1922, had this to say:

> Tests devised to ascertain either native intelligence or acquired knowledge are certainly valuable to an employer . . . [However] there are no elements in them to extract from the mind of the individual his powers of creative productivity and his tendencies toward originality. If his creative ability is expressed in many of these tests, the methods of scoring have failed to take it into consideration. It is evident that we need tests designed to give us more direct and dependable information upon this essential element of progress—creative imagination.[9]

He went on to develop a number of tests of creativity and to try them out on several samples of school children. He concluded that such "creative tests" should be given as a supplement to tests of general intelligence if we wished to obtain "a more accurate statement of the worth of the individual." [10]

These early statements of belief and tentative empirical observations were followed in due course by more direct studies comparing performance on tests of imagination or originality and tests of intelligence. In 1930 Elizabeth Andrews [11] developed three tests of imagination (e.g. originality of reactions to visual stimuli), and administered them to a sample of pre-school children. The correlation coefficients between the children's intelligence test scores and their scores on the three tests of imagination were .15, .02, and .03. In 1931 McCloy and Meier [12] administered to seventy-nine school children a test of "re-creative imagination," requiring the subjects to respond to the symbolism in abstract paintings, and correlated the quality of their responses with their IQ scores. The correlation was .22. Sporadically through the years other correlational studies produced the same results. For example, in 1946 Welch [13] administered to forty-eight college students a test requiring the reconstruction of ideas into new and original patterns, and correlated the originality of

---

[9] R. M. Simpson, Creative imagination, *Amer. J. Psychol.*, 1922, 33, pp. 234–35.

[10] *Ibid.*, p. 243.

[11] Elizabeth G. Andrews, The development of imagination in the pre-school child, *University of Iowa Studies in Character*, 1930, 3(4).

[12] W. McCloy and N. C. Meier, Re-creative imagination, *Psychol. Monogr.*, 1931, 51(5), pp. 103–116.

[13] L. Welch, Recombination of ideas in creative thinking, *J. Appl. Psychol.*, 1946, 30, pp. 638–643.

their responses with their performance on the Wonderlic Intelligence Test. The correlation was .27. The casual observation by Dearborn in 1898 had become a commonplace research finding—giftedness in intelligence and giftedness in creativity were by no means synonymous.

Despite this the intelligence test remained essentially the same, emphasizing learning ability and school achievement, and neglecting creative ability. And for all intents and purposes—surely in the school situation—the intelligence test score was most often presumed to be a comprehensive representation of the child's intellectual capacity, both of his mind *and* imagination, as it were. The crucial question as to whether creative ability might not of itself be related to school achievement was simply never raised. This question aside, Stephenson's statement of the significant issue between intelligence tests and creativity in his *Testing School Children* is well worth noting.

> All well-made Intelligence Tests are exercises in 'objective' thinking, and it is far from true that the most intelligent person writes the best poetry. How to distinguish between creative and merely intelligent work is the crucial matter, and I am not likely to succeed in a description of the difference, except perhaps to say that the one is characterized by cognitive complexity, and the other by its 'pregnancy with newly expressed emotions.'[14]

We may conclude this very abbreviated and illustrative summary of relevant research and comment by citing several excerpts from J. P. Guilford's 1950 presidential address to the American Psychological Association. The observations are not only "official" but seem to us very well taken.

> Examination of the content of intelligence tests reveals very little that is of an obviously creative nature. . . .
>
> Many believe that creative talent is to be accounted for in terms of high intelligence or IQ. This conception is not only inadequate but has been largely responsible for the lack of progress in the understanding of creative people. . . .
>
> If the correlations between intelligence test scores and many types of creative performance are only moderate or low, and I predict that such correlations will be found, it is because the primary abilities represented in those tests are not all important for creative behavior. It is also because some of the primary abilities important for creative behavior are not represented in the test at all. . . . In other words,

[14] W. Stephenson, *Testing School Children,* London: Longmans, Green and Co., 1949, p. 64.

we must look well beyond the boundaries of the IQ if we are to fathom the domain of creativity.[15]

Our argument then is this. Giftedness in children has more frequently been defined as a score on an intelligence test, and especially the study of the so-called gifted child has been equated with the study of the single IQ variable. Involved in this definition of giftedness are several types of confusion, if not of outright error. First, there is the limitation of the single metric itself, which not only restricts our perspective of the more general phenomenon, but places on the one concept a greater theoretical and predictive burden than it was intended to carry. For all practical purposes, the term "gifted child" has become synonymous with the expression "child with a high IQ," thus blinding us to other forms of excellence. And second, within the universe of intellectual functions themselves, we have most often behaved as if the intelligence test represented an adequate sampling of all mental abilities and cognitive processes. Despite the already substantial and increasing literature regarding the intellectual functions closely allied to creativity,[16] we still treat the latter concept

---

[15] J. P. Guilford, Creativity, *Amer. Psychologist,* 1950, 5, pp. 444–454.

[16] There has been a surge of interest in research on creativity since 1950. One indication of this rising interest may be found in the number of articles appearing under the heading "creativity" or "creativeness" in the *Psychological Abstracts.* In all, 240 such articles are listed between 1927 and 1959. Of this total, the first 20 per cent appeared during the first 13 years, the most recent 20 per cent in only the last 2 years. Another indication is the number of symposia and anthologies devoted recently to this topic. Among these are:

Anderson, H. H. (Ed.), *Creativity and Its Cultivation,* New York: Harper and Brothers, 1959.

Ghiselin, B. (Ed.), *The Creative Process,* New York: *Memoir Books,* 1955.

Smith, P. (Ed.), *Creativity: An Examination of the Creative Process,* New York: Hastings House, 1959.

Taylor, C. W. (Ed.), *The 1955 University of Utah Research Conference on the Identification of Creative Scientific Talent,* Salt Lake City: University of Utah Press, 1956; *The Second (1957) University of Utah Research Conference on the Identification of Creative Scientific Talent,* Salt Lake City: University of Utah Press, 1958; *The Third (1959) University of Utah Research Conference on the Identification of Creative Scientific Talent,* Salt Lake City: University of Utah Press, 1959.

Torrance, E. P. (Ed.), *Creativity: Proceedings of the Second Minnesota Conference on Gifted Children,* Minneapolis: Center for Continuation Study, University of Minnesota, 1960.

Recent empirical studies may roughly be divided into two major types: those using creative persons (e.g. artists and scientists) as subjects, and those concerned chiefly with creative abilities in other groups. Examples of the first type may be found in:

Barron, F. and G. S. Welsh, Asiatic perception as a possible factor in

as applicable only to performance in one or more of the arts to the exclusion of other types of achievement requiring inventiveness, originality, and perfection. The term "creative child," in becoming synonymous with the expression "child with artistic talents," has limited our attempts to identify and foster cognitive abilities related to creative functioning in areas other than the arts.

Despite its longevity there is after all nothing inevitable about the use of IQ in defining giftedness. Indeed we might argue that in many ways this definition is only a historical accident—a consequence of the fact that early inquiries in the field had as their con-

---

personality style: its measurement by a figure preference test, *J. Personality*, 1952, 33, pp. 199–203.

Bloom, R S., Report of creativity research at the University of Chicago. In C. W. Taylor (Ed.), *The 1955 University of Utah Research Conference on the Identification of Creative Scientific Talent*, Salt Lake City: University of Utah Press, 1956, pp. 122–46.

Cattell R. B. and J. E. Drevdahl, A comparison of the personality profile (16 P.F.) of eminent researchers with that of eminent teachers and administrators and of the general population, *Brit. J. Psychol.*, 1955, 46, pp. 242–61.

MacKinnon, D. W., Identifying and developing creativity. A paper presented at the Conference on Selection and Educational Differentiation, sponsored by the Field Service Center for the Study of Higher Education, University of California, Berkeley, May 25–27, 1959. Mimeo.

Munsterberg, Elizabeth and P. H. Mussen, The personality structure of art students, *J. Personality*, 1953, 21, pp. 457–66.

Roe, Anne, A study of imagery in research scientists, *J. Personality*, 1951, 19, pp. 459–70.

Stein, M. I. and B. Meer, Perceptual organization in a study of creativity, *J. Psychol.*, 1954, 37, pp. 39–43.

Examples of the second type may be found in:

Barron, F., The disposition toward originality, *J. abnorm. soc. Psychol.*, 1955, 51, pp. 478–485.

Drevdahl, J. E., Factors of importance for creativity, *J. clin. Psychol.*, 1956, 12, pp. 21–26.

Flanagan, J. C., The definition and measurement of ingenuity. In C. W. Taylor (Ed.), *The Second (1957) University of Utah Research Conference on the Identification of Creative Scientific Talent*, Salt Lake City: University of Utah Press, 1958, pp. 109–18.

Guilford, J. P., N. W. Kettner, and P. R. Christensen, A factor-analytic study across the domains of reasoning, creativity, and evaluation I: hypotheses and description of tests, *Reports from the Psychology Laboratory*, University of Southern California, 1954.

Lowenfeld, V., *Creative and Mental Growth*, New York: Macmillan, 1957.

Torrance, E. P., Explorations in creative thinking in the early school years, VIII, IQ and creativity in school achievement, Minneapolis: Bureau of Educational Research, University of Minnesota, 1959. Mimeo.

For an extensive bibliography containing summaries of both empirical and theoretical work in the area of creativity see:

Stein, M. I. and Shirley J. Heinze, *Creativity and the Individual: Summaries of Selected Literature in Psychology and Psychiatry*, Glencoe, Ill.: The Free Press, 1960.

text the classroom and its attendant concern with academic abilities and achievement. If we were to move the focus of inquiry from the classroom setting, we might identify cognitive qualities defining giftedness for other situations just as the IQ did in the classroom. Should we change only the original criteria of learning, we might change the cognitive qualities defining giftedness even in the classroom. For example, if we recognize that learning involves the production of novelty as well as the remembrance of course content—*discovering* as well as *recalling*—measures of creativity as well as IQ become appropriate defining characteristics of giftedness.

Thurstone put the issue as follows.

> To be extremely intelligent is not the same as to be gifted in creative work. This may be taken as a hypothesis.
>
> It is a common observation in the universities that those students who have high intelligence, judged by available criteria, are not necessarily the ones who produce the most original ideas. All of us probably know a few men who are both creative and highly intelligent, but this combination is not the rule.
>
> The confusion between intelligence and creative talent is common. For example, Quiz Kids are often referred to as geniuses. They would undoubtedly score high in memory functions, including incidental memory and rote memory. But it is doubtful whether they are also fluent in producing original ideas.[17]

Nor is there anything inevitable about limiting the concept of giftedness to cognitive excellence alone, however defined. Although the question may be largely a semantic one, there is no doubt that many desirable qualities exist beyond those with an exclusively intellectual focus. Are there not some social qualities—say, moral character or psychological adjustment—which also might lead us to call an individual gifted, and might perhaps be reflected in superior school performance, to say nothing of excellence in other areas such as public service? Surely the study of such qualities might well be an adjunct to any general and systematic examination of giftedness.

---

[17] L. L. Thurstone, Creative talent, In L. L. Thurstone (Ed.), *Applications of Psychology*, New York: Harper and Brothers, 1952, p. 20.

3-2 Principles of learning *

INHERITANCE, AS WE HAVE SEEN, EXERTS A UNIVERSAL INfluence in shaping personality—particularly in the regions of physique, basic abilities, and temperament. And yet, considering the course of development as a whole, we are tempted to say that *learning* is a factor of still greater importance. Perhaps it is unprofitable to estimate the proportions in this way. A florist never asks "how much" of his prize chrysanthemum is due to seed and "how much" to soil and cultivation. Be that as it may, it is clearly a fact that compared with all other organisms, man is extremely modifiable. The raw materials he inherits can be molded in a vast number of ways.

Think for a moment of how many *kinds* of learning take place in the course of life. We learn to walk, talk, and dance; to drive automobiles, swim, and play the piano; to spell, write, and read; we memorize facts, phone numbers, and poems. We learn what to eat, what to fear, what to shun, and what objects to desire sexually. We acquire morals, values, and interests. We come to embrace religions, beliefs, ideologies. We develop preferences, prejudices, and manners. We learn new concepts, meanings, and conformities; also

---

* Gordon W. Allport, Principles of Learning in *Pattern and Growth in Personality*. New York: Holt, Rinehart and Winston, Inc., 1961, pp. 83–109.

Gordon W. Allport

foreign languages. We learn new motives, ambitions, and hopes. We learn signs, cues, and symbols. Gradually we acquire our own traits and trends of personality, and evolve a guiding personal conscience and a more or less comprehensive philosophy of life. We even learn how to learn.

Before undertaking to review some of the main principles of learning, two important statements must be made.

1. The array of things learned is so vast that we ought not to expect any simple theory of learning to suffice. No problem in psychology has inspired so much experimental research as learning. Much has been discovered. Yet if we were to criticize the output to date we should say that current theories tend to be one-sided and narrow. They lack the sweep required to embrace the many forms of learning that occur.

2. Theories of learning (like much else in psychology) rest on the investigator's conception of the *nature of man*. In other words, every learning theorist is a philosopher, though he may not know it. To put the matter more concretely, psychologists who investigate (and theorize about) learning start with some preconceived view of the nature of human motivation. This issue (*the philosophy of motivation*) is so important that we must now examine it directly, and return again to the problem in Chapters 9 and 10.

Contrasting Views of Motivation

From the window of a farmhouse I see an old barn, weathered, disintegrating, and unable to repair itself, gradually collapsing. Beside the barn are sturdy, ever-expanding growths of bamboo, raspberry bushes, and wild cherry. They are marching over the hayfield and at the same time competing with each other for the rich earth and for space to expand.

Inanimate nature obeys the second law of thermodynamics. Lifeless matter decreases in its degree of organization, becoming more and more random, run-down. *Entropy* the process is called. Rocks erode, the sun loses its heat, barns collapse.

By contrast life is inherently synthetic. From substances both organic and inorganic it manufactures new organic compounds of bewildering variety. The key of the process is *organization*, the opposite of entropic disorganization. The organizing capacity of life is not confined to its chemical syntheses. Organisms *adapt*, *reproduce*, *invent*, and *grow* in a manner unknown to inanimate nature. This creativity is more marked among animals than among plants, and most marked of all among human beings. Whatever else personality may be, it is the crowning example of the principle of expanding organization. It is an open and growing system.

Philosophers of science are perplexed by this double channeling in nature. As soon as an organism dies its body starts immediately to disintegrate under the impact of weather and bacteria, which it successfully resisted and turned to its own use during life. The living person continually synthesizes foodstuffs, oxygen, bacterial action, past experience, present needs, and images of the future. By so doing he not only survives as an independent being but develops and grows in such a way as to become ever more characteristic of what he is. The bamboo and the wild cherry are stubbornly fulfilling the destiny of their kind. Human personality is doing more: it is advancing toward the fulfillment of plans and hopes. *Self-actualization* is the term often employed. Philosophers of science call this aspect of growth *teleological*, meaning that it is marked by an advance toward goals.

At the same time all manner of mechanical determinants act on living organisms. If we scorch our hand in a flame the resulting burn is mechanically caused, though the process of self-repair that immediately sets in is not. Like inanimate nature, living beings are subject to the effects of heat, moisture, gravity, and (most sensitively) radiation; yet our organizing powers are normally such as to preserve us from their fatal effects. We invent air conditioning, build shelters, elevators, and discover antidotes to poisons.

In philosophical terms we must allow for both *mechanical determinism* and *teleology*. One student of the subject, after examining the evidence, concludes "Nothing more remains but to admit that the riddle surpasses us and to conclude that the contrast of mechanism with teleology is the very foundation of the order of nature, which must ever be regarded from two complementary points of view." [1]

At the same time—and here we are gradually approaching the problem of motivation—philosophers and scientists are restive in the face of such contradictory principles. Is it not possible, they ask, to find one common type of law? They wish to achieve a "unity of science" rather than two separate kinds of science, or two violently contrasting sets of principles for any one life-science to handle.

Now the earliest triumphs of science dealt only with inanimate nature. Even today natural science is far out in front of the life-sciences, including the science of personality. It is easy, therefore, to understand why the concept of mechanical determinism is popular. And it is easy

[1] L. J. Henderson, *The order of nature* (Cambridge, Mass.: Harvard Univ. Press, 1917), p. 209.

to understand why many psychologists think that personality theory would do well to confine itself to conceptions *as mechanical as possible*.

Thus—and now we come at last to motivation—research in and theory of personality, especially in America, have evolved various sets of quasi-mechanical concepts. We name them *quasi*, for they are not wholly mechanical. No psychologist can completely fit human conduct to measures of centimeters-grams-seconds; nor to the functions found in biochemistry, in electronics, and in "thinking machines," although attempts of this order are often made.

Quasi-mechanical theories try so far as possible to discover simple *pushes* capable of explaining human conduct. They try to empty the organism of inner teleological forces (such as instincts, attitudes, intentions, purposes). This type of "empty organism" approach we call stimulus-response psychology. *S* (stimulus) and *R* (response) are on the outer fringes of the person. As such they seem free from teleological flavor.

The Quasi-mechanical View

Most of the research supporting the S-R approach comes from work with animals, chiefly rats. Rats to be sure, like any living creature, display organization, but they are relatively simple animals, and one hopes that by studying them, instead of human beings, one may discover how alleged teleology can be reduced to a more mechanical type of causation. The argument proceeds essentially as follows.

Drive

Suppose one's stomach is empty: it sags, and thus creates a "deficit stimulus" which impels the organism to make restless movements. The fact that hunger is also caused by chemical deficiencies in the blood stream complicates but does not alter the essential picture. A drive—any drive—is defined as a "tissue change" that sets up nervous activity until the equilibrium of the tissue is restored. Hunger and thirst, oxygen lack, and a craving for sugar or salt are examples of "deficit" stimulation. Other drives, such as urination, defecation, and perhaps fatigue and sexual cravings may be viewed as "excess" stimulations arising from the pressure of waste or secretions within the body. Since a great deal that a person does is clearly impelled by these and other "tissue changes" we must admit that we have here a simple and compelling beginning for a theory of motivation. Let it be noted that in order to keep as close as possible to mechanical causation we are not here speaking of "instincts." With a few exceptions, drives at the start of life seem to lead only to random, restless, or mechanically reflex action. The newborn infant, to be sure, seems to suck automatically, to breathe freely (after the first slap), and to eliminate automatically. But none of this activity is as "purposive" as instincts are usually thought to be. That is to say, there are no clearly set goals such as would exist if we assumed an instinct of mating, of self-preservation, of escape, or of gregariousness.

Tension-reduction

Pursuing the quasi-mechanical view one step further, S-R psychologists seek a law that will define the over-all operation of drive. Since all drives clearly arise from some disequilibrium in tissues (excess or deficit stimulation) it seems clear to these psychologists that drive motivation is always a process of reducing tension. And if man, like all other animals, has no essential motives other than drives, it follows that *all motivation is a pressure toward tension-reduction.*

If you ask how all motivation can result in drive-reduction, the answer is that *learning* (to which we shall soon turn) is responsible. Learning provides us with habitual strategies that relieve our tensions. Learning also accounts for the fact that not all our motives seem to be based on primitive tissue needs. Thus if you say that one of your main motives in life is to make your aged parents comfortable, the explanation is given that this motive is simply a learned and complex extension of your earlier desire for food. If you say that you are intent on learning a profession, again the motive is explained in terms of satisfying food, sex, fatigue, or other drives.

The theory of tension-reduction has interesting historical antecedents. In ancient Greece the Epicureans held that all man does in life is to try to *avoid pain* (tension). If we are wise we try to diminish our desires so as to have a minimum of tension to reduce. Some philosophers stated the matter in a more cheerful way, saying that tension-reduction brings pleasure, and therefore all man's motives are to be summed up as *pleasure-seeking*. Throughout the centuries philosophers and psychologists have insisted, as did Jeremy Bentham, that "pain and pleasure are our sovereign masters." The view is called *psychological hedonism.*

The modern S-R psychologist does not speak of pleasure and pain, simply because these are words describing conscious states; and the S-R psychologist feels that a good mechanical theory ought not use the language of "mind." There is no "mind" in mechanical process: hence "tension-reduction" is the preferred term for modern hedonism.

Some psychologists, less extreme in their views, are worried about so simple a formula. They point out that the quickest way to reduce tension is to commit suicide. Yet most people try to stay alive at all costs, thus maintaining and increasing their desires. To live at all is to have tension. Kluckhohn and Murray suggest a compromise. Men do not really seek a tensionless state, but rather seek the *process* of reducing tension. We like the activity involved in solving our problems, in seeking rest, in eating, in sexual pursuit, in working—because though not tensionless, such activities lead us away from want and strain.[2]

Homeostasis

Another favored, and related, conception is borrowed from physiology. The capacity of the body to keep its chemical composition, its temperature, its state of health at a proper level is intricate and awe-inspiring. Some psychologists, borrowing the concept, say that homeostasis is also the basic law of human motivation. We tend to persist in being what we are in a "steady state." We maintain the tonus and tensions necessary to life. We desire balance, equilibrium, preservation of our being.[3] This picture of motivation is obviously somewhat more teleological than tension-reduction. Life has a tendency to preserve itself and repair itself; it is not merely something goaded by excess or deficit stimulation. Yet homeostasis is a stay-put conception. It is static, unprogressive, allowing inadequately for either change or growth. The picture is one of a semi-closed system, not of a system fully open to the world, capable of expanding and becoming more than it is.[4]

---

[2] C. Kluckhohn, H. A. Murray, and D. M. Schneider, *Personality in nature, society, and culture* (Rev. ed.; New York: Knopf, 1953), p. 36.

[3] R. Stagner, Homeostasis as a unifying concept in personality theory, *Psychol. Rev.*, 1951, 58, 5–17.

[4] For a fuller discussion and criticism of homeostasis see G. W. Allport, The open system in personality theory. In *Personality and social encounter* (Boston: Beacon, 1960), Chap. 3. See also Chapter 22 of the present volume.

Recent studies of the "reticular activating system" in the brain stem of mammals indicate that there is a nervous mechanism to maintain continuous, spontaneous activity during the waking state. The organism cannot help being active; it need not wait to be goaded by stimuli nor to re-establish a disturbed equilibrium. The waking organism is always "on the go." See M. Arnold, *Emotion and personality* (New York: Columbia Univ. Press, 1960), I, 223.

Critique of Quasi-mechanical Motivation

Opponents of these views say that they account for only a small part of the desires, aspirations, hopes, and yearnings of the human person. They say it is impossible to reduce elaborate adult motives to a drive-basis. Drives exist, yes, and for the most part they do tend to push the organism to seek relief from tension. But they are only the primitive, and animallike, part of human motivation. They have a basic protective function, making for safety but not for growth and development.

This criticism is explicitly developed by Maslow, who distinguishes between safety motivation and growth motivation in both children and adults. Safety comes first. Before he can grow in a psychological sense the child must have reached a stage where he can trust his parents and his environment to provide the basic satisfactions of nourishment, comfort, safety. If he does not successfully pass this stage he grows up as an anxious, apprehensive person who is always fixated on the satisfaction of his immediate drives. In mental hospitals (but also in ordinary life) we meet people who seem to have no capacity for growth but are centered entirely on their vegetative life—on the satisfaction of their segmental (drive) cravings.

On the other hand, a child who has a basic relation of trust with his environment is a child who reaches out to the world in wonder and interest. He is literally delighted with all that he finds: shells on the beach, stories he hears, new skills that he acquires. He is free from fear, free from constant protective needs, entering greedily into the process of becoming.[5]

The healthy child and adult are continually building up tensions, in the form of new interests, and are going way beyond the basic, safety level of homeostasis. New experiences, which most of us crave, cannot be put in terms of tension-reduction, nor can our desire to acquire knowledge for its own sake, to create works of beauty and usefulness, nor to give and receive love, for love involves all manner of responsibilities and strains. Nor can the sense of duty—doing the best one can throughout one's life—be logically reduced to drive psychology. The history of the Arctic explorer, Roald Amundsen, shows us the difficulty of basing a theory of motivation wholly upon drives or homeostasis.

[5] A. H. Maslow, *Motivation and personality* (New York: Harper, 1954).

In his autobiography he tells how from the age of fifteen he had one dominant passion—to become a polar explorer. The obstacles seemed insurmountable, but the interest and striving persisted. When he experienced success he did not relax with tensions reduced. He raised his level of aspiration to accord with his commitment. Having sailed the Northwest Passage, he embarked on the painful project that led to the discovery of the South Pole. Having discovered the South Pole, he planned for years, against extreme discouragement, to fly over the North Pole, a task he finally accomplished. His commitment never wavered until in the end he lost his life attempting to rescue a less gifted explorer, Nobile, from death in the Arctic. Not only did he maintain one style of life without ceasing, but this central motive enabled him to resist many temptations to diminish segmental tensions created by fatigue, hunger, ridicule, and danger.[6]

Quasi-mechanical views give us a picture of goads, pushes, drives. What is conspicuously missing is the forward or future thrust that seems always to mark mature motivation.

In spite of these severe criticisms we must accept the importance of drives as motivating factors throughout life. Klineberg rightly calls them "absolutely dependable motives"—found in all men and in all cultures.[7] Although drives cannot account for all later motivation, they are with us all our life, and in infancy they completely dominate the motivational scene.

Drives, then, form the *starting point* for our theory of development. Not only are they themselves quasi-mechanical in nature; they are, especially in early life, acted upon (modified and controlled) by quasi-mechanical principles of learning.

Quasi-mechanical Factors in Learning

Learning is the modification of psychological characteristics resulting from experience. The quasi-mechanical theorist, as we have said, starts with drives. His next step is to look for an explanation of the way drives change during lifetime, so far as they do, and of the way movements become more expert so that the drives may be satisfied.

At once the mechanical model runs into some difficulty. Why an organism should learn at all is a problem. Inanimate nature doesn't

[6] Drawn from R. Amundsen, *My life as an explorer* (New York: Doubleday, 1928).

[7] O. Klineberg, *Social psychology* (Rev. ed.; New York: Holt, Rinehart and Winston, 1954).

learn, nor does it have drives. Snow is blown into drifts and ice will crack rocks, but the forces of change are wholly external and there is no organization of their effects into a continuing system. Hence even a mechanical theory of personality must make the assumption that life-processes are, after all, not wholly mechanical.

So far as they go, several quasi-mechanical principles are acceptable and important. We shall review these briefly.

Registration of traces and imprinting

A mechanical theory, like any theory, must assume that the nervous tissue is capable of retaining some faint copy of the original experience. All impressions linger—some a short time (such as the after-image in the eye), some all one's life long (such as an intense emotional shock, due to accident, illness, or bereavement). In fact, it is safe to assume that nothing that impresses the nervous tissue at all is ever totally lost. Some trace is left that makes later excitation by a similar stimulus more probable. And even when individual experiences are gradually fused into habits and attitudes, so that no one single memory predominates, still the result of the imprint is there.

Some recent research suggests that *first* imprinting may be of major importance. A baby gosling, for example, may follow any object that first meets its eye after hatching. Usually the object is the mother goose, but if the object happens to be a human being, then the human form is what the gosling will follow.[8]

Whether anything quite so primitive occurs in the learning of human infants we cannot say. It is conceivable that the infant's mother, as well as other features of its environment, becomes imprinted in such a way that the baby early comes to "identify" with the mother, and also comes to regard its familiar environment as a safe and desirable frame of life. It may also be that at certain "critical phases" the child becomes susceptible to new forms of imprinting.

For the present, we can only suggest that the first and basic law of learning is that impressions remain in some form as nervous traces. As imprinting continues, the result is a richer and richer store of material to be organized and utilized. The process by which impres-

---

[8] K. Z. Lorenz, Comparative behaviourology. *Proc. of WHO Study Group on Psychological Development of the Child* (J. M. Tanner and B. Inhelder, Eds.; New York: Int. Univ. Press, 1957), I, 108–131. Also, for an introduction to modern "ethology," see K. Lorenz, *King Solomon's ring* (New York: Crowell, 1952).

sions are absorbed into existing systems of experience is called *assimilation.*

Conditioning

The burned child avoids the flame. This familiar proverb sums up the principle of conditioning. The flicker of a flame at first attracts the infant, but once he is burned, the sight of the flame will cause avoidance. The law of the conditioned reflex may be stated as follows: Whenever a stimulus has a motor outlet, any stimulus occurring simultaneously will tend to acquire the same motor outlet; after sufficient repetition (sometimes one occasion is enough) the second stimulus alone will suffice to produce a discharge in that motor outlet. Withdrawal from intense heat is an unconditioned (inborn) reflex; withdrawal from the *sight* of the flame is a conditioned reflex.

A bold S-R psychologist might say that conditioning is the only (or almost the only) principle of learning that we need. Drive plus conditioning, he might argue, accounts for all of personality. We give an example of how the combination might work.

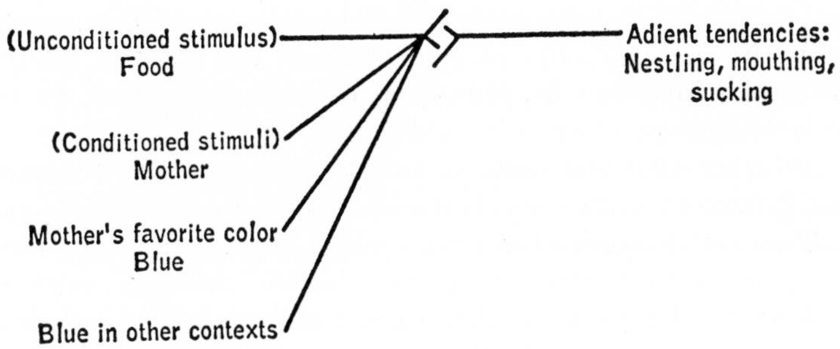

FIGURE 3-1. development of a taste through conditioning

Suppose that a woman decorates her room in blue, is fond of blue dresses, plants many blue flowers in her garden. She has a strong general preference for blue. The developmental story in terms of conditioning might be told as in Figure 3-1. Originally food caused approaching (adient) response. This is an inborn, unconditioned reflex. The mother is a "stimulus occurring simultaneously"; so by the law the mother arouses approaching behavior (i.e., acquires the same "motor outlet" as did the food). In due time other things associated with the mother (e.g., her preference for blue) become second-order conditionings. The mother is perhaps now dead, but blue in any context still causes our hypothetical lady to "approach." Some such history of conditioning could be invoked to explain an adult's liking for pictures, vocations, churches, foods, races of people, philosophical or moral doctrines.

Although the law has considerable validity, it applies most clearly to animals and infants. Adults make trouble for it by selecting, rejecting, avoiding, or assisting the conditioning process according to their own desires and by following other, perhaps contradictory, principles of learning. No one is at the mercy of all the host of possible stimuli that might theoretically condition an ongoing drive-response. For example, the mother in our illustration might always have worn eyeglasses, but this feature has acquired no conditioning power.

A variant of the conditioning doctrine should have special mention. *Reintegration* tells us that some small part of an original experience, now occurring, can reactivate the whole original experience. The photograph of a friend can arouse all manner of memories and sentiments. The smell of a certain flower can cause us to relive a whole chapter of our childhood. A college student, who behaves as an adult away from home, is uncomfortable in his parents' presence, for they were a part of his childhood, and in their presence he feels forced back into his juvenile role. Here, we note, the emphasis is on a part-whole relationship, whereas in simple conditioning, the linkage is seen as stimulus-stimulus relationship. But the basic principle is the same.[9]

Stimulus generalization

A year-old baby may have learned the word "daddy," and may cause mild embarrassment by calling every adult male by this name. Of course he has some very special responses for his own father, but his store of words is small at this age—perhaps five or six. Hence he uses them overtime. At eighteen months one child called his toy dog "toodle-oo" but he also called the wart on an old lady's face "toodle-oo." Speaking pseudo-mechanically we may say that the stimulus to a response becomes generalized; many different objects are

[9] Aristotle first noted the associative link between parts and wholes (subordinates reactive superordinates). Later the principle became the major law of learning in the writings of Sir William Hamilton and H. L. Hollingworth. Recently it has been used as the chief explanatory principle in a book on personality theory: R. W. Leeper and P. Madison, *Toward understanding human personalities* (New York: Appleton-Century-Crofts, 1959).

treated as if they were one. A child frightened by a dog may shy away from cats, rabbits, hens, and animals in general. A cruel farm-hand locked a small boy in a room with a fox. The boy was terrified. In later years he forgot (repressed) the incident, but for a long time he was seized with uncontrollable alarm if the doors of the room he was in were closed. His claustrophobia was cured only when the original memory was recovered and put in perspective with the aid of a psychiatrist.

Adults, too, behave according to stimulus generalization. We learn that toadstools are poisonous, and so we avoid all fungi in the woods, including edible mushrooms. We know that weeds are not good to eat (a false bit of "knowledge") and so avoid them all, even those that are nourishing. We may once have had an unpleasant experience with a Chinese, or a Jew, or a Negro. On the basis of this slender evidence we may acquire prejudice against a whole ethnic group.

Correct stimulus-generalization is a good thing. We could not possibly live if we had to learn a separate adjustment to every book, flower, food, person—to every possible stimulus in our life-space. But *incorrect* categorizing (treating too coarse a group of stimuli as alike) is responsible for race prejudice, for false classifications, and for most errors of reasoning.

Reinforcement

Figure 3-1 shows that classical conditioning is entirely a principle of *afferent* modification, that is to say, it deals only with the extension of cues or stimuli that come to evoke a given response.

But how about the response itself? The lady whose passion for blue is indicated in the diagram does not as an adult mouth, suck, or nestle when blue bobs up in her horizon. Rather, she buys clothing, papers her room, gazes with rapture at the sky—all to express her love of blue. How does she come to make these adaptive, adult acts?

The principle of *reinforcement* (formerly called the law of effect) says, in brief, that in the beginning an infant's drives cause it to make all sorts of wiggly and audible responses (random movements). Now, in time, some of his actions or cries are "rewarded." Thus, if he reaches correctly for his nursing bottle he can get it to his mouth and satisfy the hunger drive. This correct (adaptive) act is thus "reinforced." Success stamps it in (hedonists would say "pleasure" stamps it in).

Let us continue the illustration. Reaching for the bottle proves to be more often rewarded than merely whining or crying. Later, going to the refrigerator for the carton of milk is "stamped in" as a successful way to satisfy the drive. Also, the child learns that asking politely is good strategy—usually more successful than demanding. Later still he discovers that in most human relationships a tactful approach pays off. The diplomat learns that flowery and indirect language usually accomplishes more for his purposes than do rougher tactics. And so it goes: we learn those ways of acting that successfully reduce tension.

Here obviously is an intriguing law of immensely wide applicability. It is so widely useful that we find "reinforcement" hailed as the primary, if not the sole, law of learning. Since it "explains" efferent modification (changing actions) it can be used together with conditioning (afferent modification) to make a whole system of S-R learning theory.[10]

There are many weaknesses as well as merits in this formulation. Certainly we learn to make the "right" movements in talking, riding a bicycle, selling merchandise, on the basis of reward. But the theory does not explain why we so often change or vary a previously successful response and take risks. A man who generally wins at chess when he uses the king's pawn opening will nevertheless try new and novel gambits. According to the strict law of reinforcement he should not do so. In his well-known poem "If," Rudyard Kipling speaks of success and failure as "twin impostors." His point is that true maturity leads us to do things for reasons that are not mechanically enslaved to the principle of reward and punishment.

Frequency, primacy, and recency

Before we leave the listing of quasi-mechanical principles we should mention three additional familiar principles. *Frequency* tells us that "practice makes perfect"—the oftener any connection is made, the stronger it becomes. *Primacy* tells us that, other things being equal, the first in a series of impressions is likely to be powerful (cf. imprinting). We recall the first line of a poem or a hymn much better than later lines. Our early childhood experiences are often indelibly impressed upon us. The principle of *recency*, though opposite to primacy, seems also to hold broadly. We recall this morning's breakfast better than a breakfast we ate a week ago. These are all useful principles though we find many exceptions to them.

[10] The work of Clark Hull and of the so-called Yale School of learning theory is of this order.

Comment

Already we see that learning is a complex subject—and our account is by no means complete. While we do not want to multiply principles needlessly, we shall be doomed to failure if we rest the case of personality development solely on the quasi-mechanical principles here described. They have a true but limited utility.

It is important to note that none of these quasi-mechanical principles makes any use whatever of an "active intellect." Rather, they refer to properties of the nervous system that are supposed to come into play automatically when properly goaded. They overlook such factors as a person's deliberate intent to learn, his effort, his striving, and his ability to perceive the fitness or appropriateness of an act for his purposes. There are no planning and no guiding self-image to steer and intensify the learning. Such factors are not allowed for, and yet they are of prime importance in the learning process.

But before turning to these additional principles of learning let us depict the consequences of learning (any form of learning) for the structure of personality.

Differentiation and Integration

The course of nature, said Goethe, is to divide what is united, and to unite what is divided. He was expressing well the two aspects of all growth. The process of development may be viewed in part as the progressive *differentiation* of structure and of behavior; and in part as the progressive *integration* of behavior and structure.

Differentiation

Lewin points out that the child, to a greater extent than the adult, is a dynamical unity. The infant acts first with its whole body and only gradually acquires the ability to execute part actions.[11] At first the child is capable only of mass movement, gross retractions or outreaching, or else random twisting and squirming of the whole body. Gradually from this amorphous matrix finer activities emerge. Vocal habits, reaching, handedness become differentiated; later, working,

---

[11] K. Lewin, Environmental forces in child behavior and development. In C. C. Murchison (Ed.), *Handbook of child psychology* (1st ed.; Worcester, Mass.: Clark Univ. Press, 1931), Chap. 4.

spending, saving, collecting, and skills and interests of all sorts emerge from the original global whole. We may represent this progressive differentiation of regions after the manner of Lewin in Figure 3-2. The boundaries between the functional systems are weak in infancy (if one drive is aroused the child is aroused "all over"); likewise the barrier between the child and his environment is less firm, leaving him a prey to all manner of environmental stimuli that later in life he will be able to disregard. The weakness of this barrier prevents the development

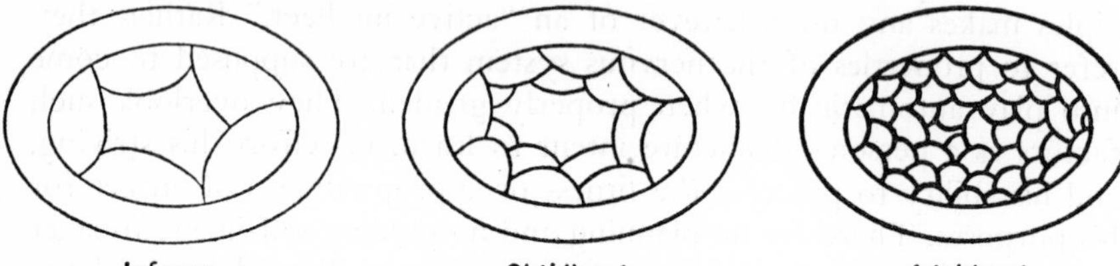

FIGURE 3-2. differentiation of functional systems

of sharp self-consciousness in the first year or two of life. The young child cannot distinguish himself from his surroundings.

A good example of differentiation comes from the infant's emotional life. At birth it is impossible to distinguish different systems of emotion; there is only a diffuse distress-excitement. By the end of the first year, as Figure 3-3 shows, the child still has far fewer emotional systems than does an adult, but he does express differentially anger, fear, distress, delight, and affection.

Although the principle of differentiation is especially clear in early childhood, much of the progressive change in later life shows the same course. All knowledge can be viewed as a matter of making finer and finer distinctions. We first approach the subject of psychology, let us say, and find it a great confused blur. The process of learning the subject is one of breaking it up into constituent topics, laws, concepts, theories. The child who first tries to "make a boat" is all thumbs; he simply cannot execute the necessary separate movements to handle saw, hammer, and nails. The later precision of the boat builder, the surgeon, the pianist, involves finer and ever-finer differentiations.

In part differentiation is explained by *maturation.* Maturation means ripening without learning. It is clear that the nervous capacities of the child are not complete: his brain is not fully equipped with a myelin sheath. His glandular development is incomplete. Not until puberty is there maturation of the sexual glands. We see maturation when certain motor coordinations appear: creeping, walking, climbing, babbling, laughing—none of which is possible at birth. Some authors (McDougall, for example) say that some "instincts" mature late (mating, parenthood, collecting); but the difficulty with this theory is that the child has already learned so much pertaining to these activities that we cannot assume an "instinct" is involved at all.

Differentiation is also explained by all the laws of learning we have discussed and shall discuss. It is not a separate principle of learning, but rather an over-all product of many processes of development. The same is true of integration.

Integration

The significance of the concept of integration is best understood by referring to the cell theory in biology. The initial fact is that the human body contains trillions of cells, over nine billion of which are

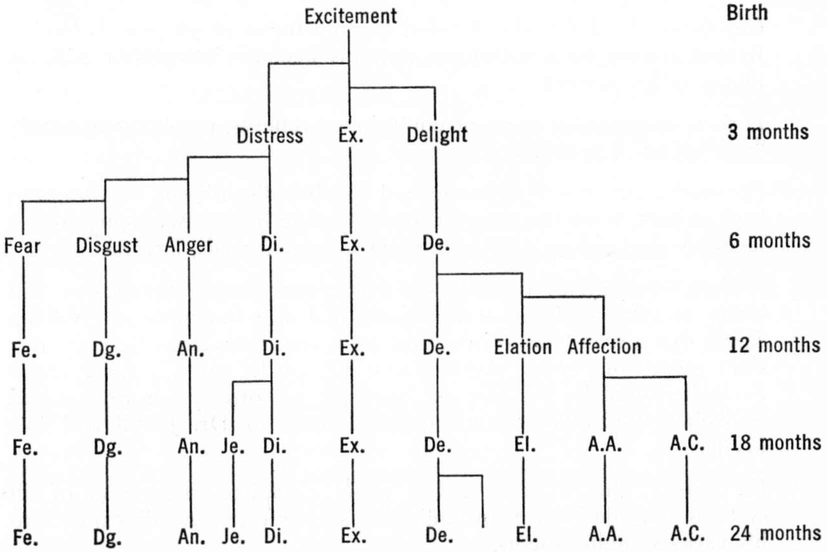

KEY: A.A. = affection for adults. A.C. = affection for children. An. = anger. De. = delight. Dg. = disgust. Di. = distress. E. = elation. Ex. = excitement. Fe. = fear. Je. = jealousy. Jo. = joy (from K. M. B. Bridges, Emotional development in early infancy, *Child Development*, 932, 3, 340).

FIGURE 3-3. differentiation of infant's emotional life

found in the brain. Somehow out of this astronomic array of single bits a relatively unified personality is constructed. Separate nerve cells function together in such a way as to lose their independence. From the many there emerges the one; the motto of integration is *e pluribus unum.* We hasten to add that personality is never completely unified, but the trend of integration is toward this goal.

Integration suggests a hierarchical organization of personality. The simplest possible integration would be of two nerve cells (one sensory and one motor) functioning together as a simple reflex arc. Whether or not there are any reflexes involving as few as two neurones is not known. C. S. Sherrington, the physiologist who above all others is responsible for the concept of integration, regards this limiting case of integration as a "convenient though improbable abstraction." Similarly, at the opposite extreme, the completely integrated personality is also a convenient though improbable abstraction. But between these limiting cases there is ample room for the operation of actual integration. In ascending order we might distinguish a hierarchy of integrative levels as follows:

> *Conditioned reflexes,* the simplest learned forms of adaptive behavior. Responsiveness to a substitute stimulus becomes integrated with an innate reflex system.
>
> *Habits,* integrated systems of conditioned reflexes, involving especially "reinforced" responses.
>
> *Personal traits,* more dynamic and flexible dispositions, resulting, at least in part, from the integration of specific habits. Belonging to this level are dispositions called sentiments, values, needs, interests.
>
> "*Selves,*" systems of traits that are coherent among themselves, but likely to vary in different situations. (Cf. the statement of William James that a man "has as many different social selves as there are distinct *groups* of persons about whose opinion he cares.") An extreme example would be the case of "multiple personality" as represented in Robert Louis Stevenson's fictional story of Dr. Jekyll and Mr. Hyde.
>
> *Personality,* the progressive but never complete integration of all systems that deal with an individual's characteristic adjustments to his various environments.

The integrative theory of personality can be suggested, somewhat imperfectly, in the diagram in Figure 3-4.

We should not speak of the infant as well integrated, in spite of the totality of his response. Through differentiation he must first learn specific and skilled adjustments, separate words, single conditioned responses. Later he can "put together" what he has learned into his own preferred patterns of adjustment, forming characteristic habits and traits, and later still dispositions to play certain roles in certain surroundings (called in the diagram "Selves").

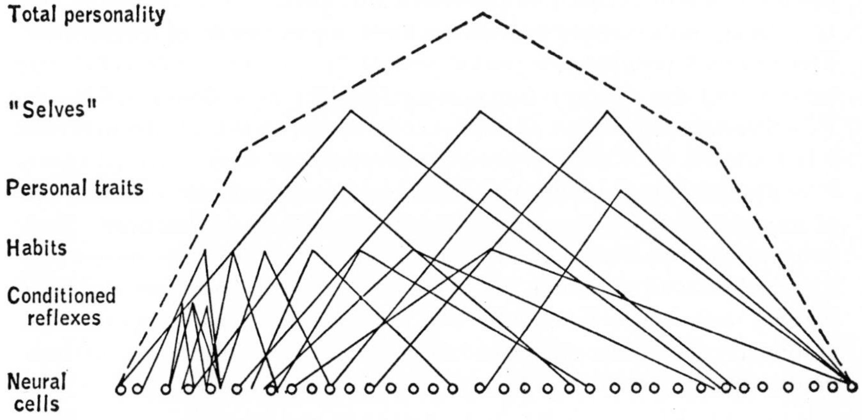

FIGURE 3-4. schematic representation of integration

We do not imply that older people have achieved perfect, or even extensive integration. Although unity is an ideal, still in actual life an adult is to some extent a mere bundle of conditioned reflexes, habits, traits, "selves" that often war with one another. Relative to the infant, however, the adult shows broader systems of integration. An infant is a homogeneous biological system, but an adult is more of a psychologically differentiated and integrated system.

Cognitive (Organizational) Learning

Integration and differentiation are the consequences of intricate learning processes. While such quasi-mechanical principles as conditioning and reinforcement may account for some learning, they do not account fully for the strikingly rich changes which experience produces in the growth of personality. The elementary principles we have described offer little more than a starting point—and are more applicable to animal and infant learning than to adult human learning. As Razran has said, the quasi-mechanical processes apply to the "unknowing" level of learning.[12] They leave out the role of conscious weighing, understanding, intention, and ego-relevance.

We have already called attention to the diversity of things that must be learned by the developing personality, including skills, knowledge, attitudes, interests, traits, hopes and fears, hates and loves, a sense of humor, a conscience, culture.[13] It is not likely that any single theory of learning will suffice. And so we continue our task of listing additional needed principles.

Learning sets

Consider two young children, Harry and Joe, each three years of age. Harry's parents are irascible and unpredictable. Sometimes they punish him severely, reject him, and frighten him. At other times they shower him with affection, give him gifts and pats on the head. Harry never knows where he stands. The very same act that brings reward at one time brings punishment at another. His only hope is to be constantly on guard, to distrust his parents in general, and learn by small cues whether they are in an accepting or a rejecting mood. Even if he tries to learn what specific acts he must avoid, he can never be sure, since he is treated so inconsistently. This style of child training, we have good reason to believe, creates a frightened, distrustful, suspicious outlook on life. It leads, among other things, to ethnic prejudice, for Harry's "learning set" is broadly generalized to distrust all human beings, especially those who are unfamiliar to him.[14] Young Harry will probably become anti-Jewish, anti-Negro, anti-most-everything.

Joe, by contrast, has parents who are affectionate and entirely consistent in their rewards and punishments. Even when they punish him they do not withdraw their love. He knows that however badly he may behave he is accepted. He grows up therefore with a basic trust. He generalizes from his experience at home. People are assumed to be decent and trustworthy. He develops no social alarm, no generalized hostility, no prejudice.

We use this example to show how certain broad postures of learning may influence the whole course of development. Trust and

---

[12] G. Razran, Conditioning and perception, *Psychol. Rev.*, 1955, **62**, 83–95.

[13] Cf. also J. J. Gibson, The implications of learning theory for social psychology. In J. G. Miller (Ed.), *Experiments in Social Process* (New York: McGraw-Hill Book Co., Inc., 1950), Chap. 8.

[14] For a fuller discussion of the two styles of child training described here see D. P. Ausubel, Ego-development and the learning process, *Child Develpm.*, 1949, **20**, 173–190.

distrust are basic attitudes affecting the child's learning about human relationships.

Many additional learning sets could be identified. One child develops early hostility toward mathematics. He cannot and will not learn it, and his schoolwork is adversely affected for this reason. Another child early forms a strongly favorable set toward a medical career. Throughout his youth, indeed throughout his life, he absorbs greedily all medical knowledge that comes his way. He may be obtuse to art, hobbies, and religion, but not to medical matters. In this area of learning he is a sponge.

Besides such long-range sets there are short-range intentions to learn. Quasi-mechanical theories fail to recognize that very little conditioning or rewarding is effective after *infancy* unless the child or adult *wants* to learn. Even repeated experiences are unlikely to register unless one desires them to. You may look up a given phone number fifty times in the directory and still not remember it; but if you put your mind to the task of memorizing it—then it sticks.

Insight

To introduce this important principle we take a few elementary instances from early life.

> A little girl of thirteen months, not yet able to walk, had a habit of pulling herself to a standing position by the kitchen range and turning on the gas. Because of the danger the mother sharply slapped the offending hand every time, hard enough to cause crying. Now the quasi-mechanical principles of conditioning and reinforcement would say that the child would soon learn to withdraw from the tempting gas cock. Not at all! The baby persisted in the misdemeanor. What she did learn, however, was to hold out her hand to be slapped after each transgression.

In this case the child saw some vague connection between her misdeed and the slap. She put two and two together, but not with the result intended by the mother. (Of course in many cases the conditioning slap works as intended—but not always.)

Another simple example, this one from the parents' diary of little Andrew:

> *9 months.* A. watches intently father smoking his pipe. When father offers A. the pipe (properly cleaned), A. puts the stem into his mouth and *blows* vigorously.

According to quasi-mechanical principles Andrew should have *sucked* the stem (as he would a nipple or pacifier). But Andrew was trying to imitate the father by blowing out the smoke. He was deliberately attempting to re-create the situation *as understood* by him. He could not, of course, know that smoking required sucking as well as blowing. Again from Andrew's history:

> *14 months.* A. always objects to having his nose wiped; but he takes handkerchief out of his mother's apron pocket, puts it to his own nose and snuffles.
>
> *20 months.* The doctor gave A. discomfort by depressing his tongue with a spatula while examining his throat, causing A. to cry, squirm, and reject the object. Fifteen minutes later, left to himself, A. picks up the spatula and puts it down his throat just as the doctor had done.

In these instances we see Andrew deliberately reinstating situations that caused annoyance and pain. According to the principles of reinforcement and conditioning he should not have done so. Here we see at work a desire to comprehend, to reproduce a structure of events that has been previously experienced. Andrew was trying to execute a *meaningful* act.

Insight has been defined as the process of forming a mental structure that corresponds to some outside structure in nature. When we suddenly see how the parts of a Chinese puzzle fit together, we have insight. It has sometimes been labeled as the "ah ha" type of learning.

Our last three examples have dealt with insightful imitation. We do not imply that all imitation illustrates learning by insight. There are cases where quasi-mechanical principles apply. Thus a child of two may laugh when he hears adults laugh but without knowing the reason. This is clearly a simple conditioned response type of imitation. Or a younger child may learn that by doing as his older brother does he finds many rewards (the hidden candy, the kiss from the home-coming daddy), and so by reinforcement he develops a "set to imitate." [15] On the other hand, some imitation is not due to conditioning or reinforcement but is deliberate copying of others' acts in order to solve problems; it is insightful, not blind. Our conclusion is that "imitation" is not itself a separate principle of learning, but is a mirroring type of behavior, different forms of which reflect different kinds of learning.[16]

---

[15] Cf. N. E. Miller and J. Dollard, *Social learning and imitation* (New Haven, Conn.: Yale Univ. Press, 1941).

[16] For a fuller analysis of the forms of imitation see G. W. Allport, Historical background of modern social psychology. In G. Lindzey (Ed.), *Handbook of Social Psychology* (Cambridge, Mass.: Addison-Wesley, 1954), Chap. 1.

Identification

A special form of imitation is emotional identification. A child of nine asks his father, "Daddy, what are *we?*" Are we, he is asking, Republicans, Democrats, Presbyterians, Methodists, Scotch-Irish, American Yankee? Every child regards himself as automatically belonging to the same group as his parents. He is identifying with his parents, and under this broad, emotionally toned, learning set he acquires many of his attitudes, values, and forms of reasoning. Freud held that identification is almost the only principle of learning that we need in order to explain the development of personality. While much that we do, think, say, and feel is affected by identification, we cannot place as much weight on this factor as does Freud.

Identification works in subtle ways. A young boy's imagination is fired by the exploits of a baseball hero. This hero is a kind of ego-ideal for the lad. He would like to have the prowess and status and adult prerogatives of his hero. In his fantasies he may feel that he is this hero. Under this broad learning set, he is therefore attentive to every detail: to his hero's manner of speech, to the neckties he wears, to his posture and gait. All these and other tokens of prowess the boy imitates. He cannot have the whole of his hero's status but he will take what parts he can.

Subsidiation

Much learning seems to be chiefly a matter of rounding out, of filling in some incomplete structure. In Bartlett's terms, we are almost always making an "effort after meaning." Learning is a matter of completing what is incomplete. Gestalt psychologists speak of "closure tendency." Jung refers to "the constellating power of a complex." Thorndike maintains that "belongingness" is a central principle of learning. Whatever term we use (and here I suggest that *subsidiation* expresses the idea fairly well) we call attention to the active, organizing property of all cognition. We are saying in effect that thought-processes to some extent contain their own motivation: they insist on forming firmer structures, on completing unfinished business, on putting bits and pieces of experiences into systems of meaning. We shall assume the existence of the principle of subsidiation as we now discuss our final set of learning principles.

Participation (Biographical Learning)

Attention and intent to learn. To common sense nothing is more obvious than the fact that learning requires concentration, effort, sustained attention, or absorbing interest. If these conditions are present in sufficient degree we can learn almost anything. If they are not present, very little learning takes place, and this little is called "incidental learning." According to a theory developed by Köhler and Wallach, when attention is concentrated on an object, the underlying electronic cortical process will be intensified.[17] Such intensification leads to clear perception and to retention.

Attention is so obviously required for learning that we might venture as the first and most important law that the individual will learn what he is "set" to learn, "set" being considered as participation through the centering of attention, effort, or interest on the acquisition of skills or knowledge.

Levels of participation

We may distinguish two levels of attention and concentration. The first of these we may call *task-involvement*, meaning that the individual is actively doing something about the object of his attention.

A classic experiment by Gates on learning at school shows that children may learn twice as much if they spend more time in reciting than in passive study.[18] The present author asked several hundred college students to recall some memory of their grammar school days. The great majority recalled a recitation, game, or event in which they themselves were actively participating. Few reported incidents where they were passive, such, for example, as merely listening, seeing, reading. Razran shows that the establishment of so simple a form of learning as the conditioned reflex is speeded up if the subject himself *does* something in the experiment (such as turning the switch that starts the conditioning buzzer).[19]

Summing up such evidence as this, and adding new evidence of

---

[17] W. Köhler and H. Wallach, Figural after-effects. *Proc. Amer. Phil. Soc.*, 1944, **88,** 269–357.

[18] A. I. Gates, Recitation as a factor in memorizing, *Arch. Psychol.*, 1917, **6,** No. 40.

[19] G. Razran, Attitudinal control of human conditioning, *J. Psychol.*, 1936, **2,** 327–337. Also, The dominance-contiguity theory of the acquisition of classical conditioning, *Psychol. Bull.*, 1957, **54,** 1–46.

their own, Haggard and Rose formulate the *law of participation:* "When an individual takes an active role in a learning situation (a) he tends to acquire the response-to-be-learned more rapidly, and (b) this response tends to be more stably formed, than when he remains passive." [20]

Why does such task-involved *doing* bring about more rapid and more stable learning? In doing, there is a more complete neurophysiological involvement. Passivity means that there is *impression* on the nervous system, but no *expression;* sensory and cortical nerves are involved but few motor nerves and muscles. The whole sensorimotor circuit is required for building firm traces and systematized habits. (This, of course, is the reason why the project and laboratory methods of teaching are usually to be preferred over the lecture method.) Croce, the Italian philosopher, insists that unless we engage in some form of *expression* we cannot know. Sometimes a student will say to his teacher, "Well, I know the answer, but I cannot express it." Croce would say, "Sorry, my lad, but unless you can express it, you don't know it."

But there is a still deeper level of participation which we may call *ego-involvement.* Two children may participate equally in taking piano lessons or in studying geography; that is to say, they spend an equal amount of time at the task, make the same movements, and give a superficially similar performance. They are task-involved to the same extent. But they may not be equally "ego-involved." The participation of one child may be at the circumference of his personality, so to say; of the other, at its center. To one child the activity is important; to the other it is not.

We are obviously speaking now of *interest.* In this chapter we have encountered various principles that claim to be "the most important" law of learning; but the case for interest is strongest of all. Interest is participation with the deepest levels of motivation.

Personal relevance

The point is so important that we venture to restate it. After the age of infancy, we encounter partially formed interest systems. These systems distinguish the central and "warm" portions of personality from portions that are on the rim of one's being. The child is developing a sense of "self" and his interests fit into the self-system. An

[20] E. A. Haggard and R. J. Rose, Some effects of mental set and active participation on the conditioning of the auto-kinetic phenomenon, *J. Exper. Psychol.*, 1944, **34,** 45–59.

eight-year-old boy who finds himself interested in moths and butterflies will absorb much relevant knowledge, and for the time being learn less from his schoolroom tasks. A teen-age girl learns more about cinema and TV stars than about her high school history. We learn most from ego-involved experiences; they have more personal relevance and therefore more staying power. Borrowing a term from Razran, we may call this process of acquisition "biographical learning." [21] Whatever is ego-relevant is absorbed and retained.

Comment

For convenience we have separated our descriptions of learning principles to an unwarranted degree. We should try to think of them as operating simultaneously—difficult though it is to do so. Perhaps in animal learning it is possible to demonstrate pure conditioning and reinforcement. But in human learning, such an effort is doomed to failure. To explain how a person develops an interest in surgery, a liberal political outlook, a prejudice, or a religious sentiment certainly requires many, if not all, principles of learning working in concert.

Summary

How personality develops is basically a problem in the psychology of learning. But our theory of learning is tied to our view of the nature of man. Specifically, if we think of man as a thing, pushed and pulled by external forces (or even "half think" of him in this way) we seek for quasi-mechanical principles of learning. We embrace a stimulus-response view that puts as much emphasis as possible on simple physiological forces (drives) and on elementary processes of nerve tissue. As a result we try to explain the development of personality largely in terms of traces, conditioning, reintegration, stimulus generalization, reinforcement, frequency, primacy, and recency. These are all valid principles—up to a point. They seem by and large more applicable to the learning process as we find it in animals and in infants than in the more advanced stages of personality development.

It is helpful to view the growing individual as progressing in both differentiation and integration. Learning brings about both types of structural change, and leads to an organization marked by the articulation of finer systems (differentiation) and by the hierarchical

[21] G. Razran, Conditioning and perception. See note 12.

arrangements of these systems within the total personality (integration).

In order to account for these systems we need principles of learning that are "cognitive" as well as S-R in type. Among these principles we discover the signal importance of learning sets, of insight, of identification (and other forms of imitation), and finally of subsidiation.

In general, however, S-R principles seem too external to the growing life, and cognitive principles seem (for the most part) too intellectualistic. We need to place additional emphasis on the fact that participation is basic to learning. Participation may occur at the simple level of attentiveness; at the level of motor doing (task-involvement); and at the most significant level of all—ego-involvement and personal relevance.

The issue we have raised has to do with the problem of *organization.* Whatever else personality may be, it has the properties of a system (wherein all parts are mutually related). Quasi-mechanical views of learning stress fragmentary acquisition. They do not allow adequately for coherence and self-relevance. Hence we must accept additional principles to account more fully for pattern and organization within the total personality system.

3-3 Factors that aid and hinder creativity *

In the part of our current "zeitgeist" pertaining to psychology and education, no word has had a more dramatic rise in popularity than "creativity." After generally ignoring the subject, psychologists have come to realize their backwardness in knowledge of this subject. Employers have been asking for more inventive scientists, engineers, and managers. Special courses on how to think creatively have been springing up by the score. Special institutes are being held on the subject. Teachers and educators are asking how they can make courses more stimulating and how they can arouse more productive thinking on the part of students.

The interest is international, as well it might be. The whole world faces two very critical problems—how to feed its exploding population and how to keep the peace. It has been estimated that in the next 20 years we shall need three times the number of scientists and engineers we now have, and they shall have to exercise all the ingenuity of which they are capable. We are reminded by the scriptures, however, that man does not live by bread alone. There is, I think, a very

---

* J. P. Guilford, "Factors That Aid and Hinder Creativity," *Teachers College Record*, Vol. 63, No. 5 (February, 1962), pp. 380–392.

Adapted from an address presented at the Creative Education Institute at San Jose State College, June 21, 1961.

J. P. Guilford

noticeable surgence of interest in the arts in all their forms. We wish to walk in beauty as well as in peace, freedom, and dignity. There is also good reason to desire increased creativity to achieve aesthetic goals.

Investigation of Creativity

My topic suggests that I give most consideration to the abilities and other traits of individuals that make some of them creative and some not. Knowing these traits should help us to recognize which persons are likely to have the potentialities of becoming creatively productive. The same knowledge should help us in taking steps that should increase creative output in ourselves and in others, and other steps that may remove obstacles in the way of creative productivity. Our primary concern, then, will be the basic facts concerning the nature of creative thinking and of the more creative persons, with reference to the application of this information.

Serious investigation of creativity by psychologists began only in recent years. For centuries the common idea had been that only the exceedingly rare person is genuinely creative and that creativity is a divine gift. As such, it was not to be investigated, or at best, there was little hope of understanding it. Even after Darwin came upon the scene, when creativity came to be regarded as some kind of rare, hereditary blessing, there was still little incentive to attempt to understand it because there was thought to be little that one could do about it. In addition to being very rare, the highly creative person's behavior is sometimes eccentric. This has sometimes branded him as being abnormal and even pathological. Mental pathology was similarly avoided as a subject of study by scientific investigators for a long time.

Creativity became an object of scientific study primarily because of the general interest in individual differences. This approach recognizes that individuals differ psychologically in traits or attributes that can be conceived as continua or dimensions—that there can be varying degrees of a quality possessed by different individuals. This concept was eventually applied to creativity, but in serious ways only about a dozen years ago. This new way of looking at the matter permitted us to think that not only a few peculiarly gifted persons but individuals in general possess some degree of the same creative trait or traits.

This conception has opened the door to many kinds of research. We need no longer study creativity by catching the rare persons who are recognized as having creativity to high degree; a multitude of subjects is now available to investigators. We can discover the various aspects of the phenomenon called "creativity." We can find out the conditions under which creative performance occurs or does not occur.

As in the case of all psychological characteristics that make up personality, we may be forced to recognize that heredity establishes limits of development for an individual. But there is considerable faith among educators that rarely does an individual realize full development in any respect and that there is generally considerable room for improvement. This faith should also be applied to the creative aspects of personality.

Basic Traits and Creativity

There are a number of approaches to the investigation of the traits or characteristics in which creative individuals are most likely to excel. Some investigators appear to regard the phenomenon of creativity as a single dimension of personality. It is my view that the creative disposition is made up of many components and that its composition depends upon where you find it. Practically all investigators recognize that there are many potentially contributing conditions.

When the problem is approached from the standpoint of individual differences, the most natural scientific technique to apply is that of factor analysis. This is the approach that my associates and I have taken almost exclusively in the Aptitudes Project at the University of Southern California.

According to our original hypotheses (7), we expected to find the more creative individuals to think with greater fluency, with more flexibility, and with greater originality. The tests designed to measure fluency present very simple tasks, and the quantity of output determines the scores. When told to produce a list of items of information of a certain kind, how many responses can the examinee give in a limited time? Quality does not count, but, of course, the responses must be appropriate.

Flexibility in thinking means a *change* of some kind—a change in the meaning, interpretation, or use of something, a change in understanding of the task, a change of strategy in doing the task, or a change in direction of thinking, which may mean a new interpretation of the goal.

There has been some debate concerning the meaning of "originality." In our research and in that of others, originality means the production of unusual, far-fetched, remote, or clever responses. But there are some who say that an idea is not original or novel unless no human being has ever thought of it earlier. This conception is worthless to the scientist because there is no way of knowing that an idea has never existed before. It is somewhat better to say that a novel idea is a new one so far as the particular individual who has it is concerned. But unless we know the individual's past history of thinking, we cannot be sure of meeting this criterion either.

Fortunately, we can resort to empirical signs of novelty in terms of the statistical infrequency of a response among members of a certain population that is culturally relatively homogeneous. This gives us some workable operations for applying the criterion of unusualness. The index of unusualness can therefore be purely objective. As for the far-fetched or remote associations and the clever responses, we have as yet no way to avoid some degree of subjectivity of judgment in assessing test performance to obtain an index of originality.

Another somewhat popular criterion of an original idea is that it is socially useful. Those who deal with practical affairs may be appropriately concerned about this aspect of produced ideas. But such a criterion involves us in values in a way that science cannot deal with directly; hence, the criterion of social usefulness can be quickly dismissed by the psychologist. This does not mean that as a person he is unconcerned about social usefulness. It does mean that as a scientist he cannot afford to be so concerned and so restricted.

Fluency Factors

We shall now give closer attention to the various factors of fluency, flexibility, and originality. It turns out that in verbal tests alone there are three differentiated fluency factors (*9*). Ideational fluency has to do with the rate of generation of a quantity of ideas. The idea produced may be as simple as a single word, as complex as the title for a picture or a story, or as phrases and short sentences that convey unitary thoughts. In a test, we may ask the examinee to list all the things he can think of that are solid, flexible, and colored. He may respond with *cloth*, *leaf*, *rose petal*, *hair*, *skin*, *leather*, and so on. Any response that fulfills the specifications accepted and counts toward the total score. In other tests, we may ask the examinee to list the consequences of a certain action or event, the various uses of an object, or some appropriate titles for a given story. In all such tests, there are strict time limits.

It is easy to see where an operation such as that in tests of ideational fluency fit into problem solving of many kinds. Perhaps a problem situation, when interpreted in a certain way, calls for an object with a certain set of specifications in order to solve it. Once these specifications are realized, the person who can list pertinent possibilities most rapidly could, other things being equal, solve the problem most quickly.

Many a problem calls for a running through of the likely possibilities during the earlier stage of interpreting or structuring it as well as during the stage of finding solutions. This process also probably depends in some degree upon ideational fluency. Of course it is not necessary to run through *all* the logical possibilities in solving a problem. One can ignore the less promising ones. This point will be touched upon later.

Another kind of fluency is called "associational fluency." It pertains to the completion of relationships, in distinction from the factor of ideational fluency, which involves giving ideas that fit a class. As a test of associational fluency, we may ask the examinee to list all the words he can think of that mean the opposite, or nearly the opposite, of the word "good." He may respond with *bad*, *poor*, *sinful*, *defective*, *awful*, *terrible*, and so on. This ability is most obviously of use to the creative writer, who wants to find quickly a variety of verbal expressions without having to resort to a thesaurus.

The factor of associational fluency may have more general utility—for example, whenever we apply thinking by analogy as our strategy in solving problems. Thinking of a correlate is the completion of an anology. Many solutions to new problems are achieved by the practice of thinking by analogy. The success of certain kinds of engineers in their work has been predicted to a small extent by means of a test of associational fluency as found by Saunders (*21*, 1956).

A third kind of fluency is called "expressional fluency." It has to do with the facile construction of sentences. We ask the examinee to write as many four-word sentences as he can, all different, with no word used more than once. We may give the initial letters of the four words, the same four being specified for each sentence—for example, "W_____ c_____ e_____ n_____." To this task, he may reply "We can eat nuts." "Willie comes every night," "Wholesome carrots elevate nations," "Weary cats evade nothing," and so on. You will probably not be surprised when I tell you that in a ninth-grade sample, the girls obtained a higher mean score than the boys.

We do not know yet how much generality to attach to this factor, whether it is limited to tasks such as the writing of sentences or whether it is so broad as to pertain to organizing ideas into systems.

If it is as broad as the latter suggestion, it should be of considerable consequence, perhaps in something as important as the trial-and-error development of a scientific theory. The factor has been found significantly related to ratings by psychologists of the creative performances of military officers.[1]

Flexibility Factors

One type of flexibility we first recognized as "spontaneous flexibility" because the tests that measure it do not even suggest that the examinee be flexible (*5*). Without his knowing it, he can make a good score if he varies his *kinds* of responses. If we tell the examinee to list all the uses he can think of for a common brick, the total number of uses listed is a good score for his status on the factor of ideational fluency. But we also score his performance in terms of the number of times he changes *category* of uses. For example, the person who responds with *build a house*, *build a school*, *build a factory*, etc., does not change his class of uses. Another person who responds with *make a paper weight*, *drive a nail*, *make baseball bases*, *throw at a cat*, *grind up for red powder*, *make a tombstone for a bird*, etc., changes class with each new response. He shows much more flexibility.

The person who makes a low spontaneous-flexibility score is rigid in the sense that he perseverates within one or a very few classes. As there are several kinds of flexibility in thinking, so there are several kinds of rigidity. When someone tells you that a certain person is rigid, beware of overgeneralization of the term. We do not find in normal (nonpathological) people a very general trait of rigidity vs. flexibility. We find several. This does not say that there are no individuals who are rigid in just about every respect, but the general rule is that they may be rigid in some respects and not in others, at least so far as thinking is concerned.

A new hypothesis may be considered in connection with the factor of spontaneous flexibility. Some advisers on how to think creatively suggest that in starting to solve a new problem, we keep our thinking at a rather high level of abstraction. We think of it first in very general terms. Thus, the person who goes from class to class in the Brick Uses test is operating within the frame of reference of a much broader class within which there are subclasses. A higher level of

[1] From an unpublished study conducted jointly by the Aptitudes Project at the University of Southern California and the Institute for Personality Assessment and Research, University of California, Berkeley.

abstraction may mean thinking in terms of broader classes. This has the effect of broadening the scope of the scanning process in searching for information. Going from one class to another in the Brick Uses test also means considering all the properties of a brick—its weight, its color, its texture, and so on. These are abstractions all lying within the class of the total nature of a brick. This is reminiscent of a stock method of practicing creative thinking, a method known as "attribute listing" and advocated by Crawford (*3*).

A second kind of flexibility has been called "*adaptive* flexibility" for the reason that in tests in which it was first found, the examinee, to succeed, must make changes of some kind—changes in interpretation of the task, in approach or strategy, or in possible solutions. Our current interpretation of the factor of originality is that it is adaptive flexibility in dealing with verbal information.

We have a kind of test, called Plot Titles, in which the examinee is told a very short story and that he is to suggest as many appropriate titles for the story as he can. One of the stories is about a wife who is unable to speak until a specialist performs the appropriate surgery. Then her husband is driven to distraction by her incessant talking until another surgeon eliminates his hearing, when peace is restored in the family.

The number of commonplace titles given to the story may be used as a score for ideational fluency. Such titles include,

A man and his wife
Never satisfied
Medicine triumphs
A man's decisions
Talking and hearing

The number of responses rated as "clever" serves as a score for originality. Such titles are exemplified by

The deaf man and the dumb woman
Happiness through deafness
Operation—peace of mind
Yack, yack, hack

Several other types of tests serve to indicate individual differences in the factor of originality.

Elaboration

In the course of our investigations of abilities involved in planning (*1*), we found another kind of ability we have called "elaboration." In one test, given the bare outlines of a plan, the examinee is asked to produce the detailed steps needed to make the plan work. The more details he adds, the better is his score. We believe that the unique feature of this ability is that in tests for it, one item of information leads to another as a kind of extension or completion. In more technical language, we say that the examinee is producing a *variety of implications.*

It was eventually recognized that the abilities of fluency, flexibility (including originality), and elaboration are similar in that the tests of them call for a variety of answers. There is no right or fully determined answer in connection with the information given in the item. There are now parallel tests in which each item *does* have one right answer because it is fully determined by the information given or because there is one conventionally accepted answer. A distinction has therefore been made between *divergent* thinking and *convergent* thinking to represent the two classes of abilities. The abilities of which I have been speaking thus far belong in the divergent-thinking category. Because the individual has to generate his answer or answers, starting from given information, in both categories of abilities, we speak of divergent-*production* factors vs. convergent-*production* factors, respectively.

Quantity vs. Quality

Several questions arise concerning the relationship of quantity and quality of production. One debated and investigated hypothesis is that "quantity breeds quality." This hypothesis holds that if a person produces a greater total number of ideas, he also produces a greater number of high-quality ideas in a limited time. Another view is that a mental set for quantity is inefficient because if a person spends his time producing a lot of low-quality responses, he cannot produce so many good ones.

There is another aspect of this controversy. When a person is set to give "good" answers, he is applying judgment or evaluation as he goes along. On the one hand, it is believed that an evaluative or critical attitude is generally inhibiting to the flow of ideas, good and poor alike. On the other hand, it is believed that the application of evaluation as one proceeds has a selective effect, holding back the low-quality responses and letting the high-quality responses come through.

The well-known brainstorming technique, attributed to Alex Osborn (*18*) and employed by many others, conforms to the first of these two schools of thought. One of its chief claimed virtues is that the separation of production and evaluation—in other words, suspended judgment—is better procedure. As originally applied, of course, brainstorming has other features, which include thinking in small groups rather than thinking by individuals in seclusion.

The experimental results bearing upon the issue of suspended judgment are somewhat mixed. Meadow *et al.* (*16*) report that with suspended judgment, the production of "good" answers was a little more than doubled. The problems were to suggest unusual uses for a wire coat hanger and for a broom. The criteria for "good" responses were "unique" and "useful."

In our Aptitudes Project (*2*), we gave the Plot Titles test with and without the specific instruction to give clever titles. It was expected that the instruction for clever titles would entail more evaluation. The effects of this instruction were shown by a reduction in the number of low-quality responses, an increase in the number of high-quality responses, and a higher average rating of degree of cleverness.

Hyman (*13*) found that his subjects generated 68% more responses under quantity instructions, but that this increase in "good" responses, where "good" meant uncommon and of "high quality," failed to keep pace with the total output. Hyman is probably right when he concludes that quantity may breed quality for some types of problems but not for others. It is also probably true that the *kind* of evaluative attitude applied by the thinker has much to do with the quantity and quality of responses he produces.

Divergent thinking is a matter of scanning one's stored information to find answers to satisfy a special search model. Evaluation comes into the picture in determining whether or not the produced information fits the search model. Relaxed evaluation would permit a broadening of the base of the search, whereas an evaluative attitude with some degree of strictness should narrow the search. In doing so, however, it may lead more efficiently to good answers. This should depend upon the clarity and accuracy of the search model. If the thinker has a good search model, the application of evaluation while he thinks should be helpful.

But if evaluation is of a more vague kind, such as that involving a fear of being unconventional, a fear of thinking socially unacceptable thoughts, or a fear of being wrong, it should be definitely better to suspend judgments based on such criteria. Evaluation incident to an overly strong desire for a quick solution would also be handicapping. But evaluation for the sake of efficient scanning, where there is good strategy in the scanning process, should be beneficial.

Hyman (*13*) has found that a general critical attitude can have rather broad transfer effects in solving problems. A group of engineers, in Hyman's experiment, read some previously given solutions to a certain practical problem under the instruction to list all the good points that they could see in those solutions. A second group was instructed to list all the faults they could see in the same solutions. Later, in solving the same problem and in solving a new one, the uncritical readers suggested solutions of their own that were rated higher on the average than those of the critical group. Thus, very general critical attitudes must be taken into account.

Group vs. Individual Thinking

The question of group thinking vs. individual thinking has received a great deal of attention. The virtue claimed for group thinking in brainstorming is that one person stimulates another. In support of this hypothesis, Osborn (*19*) reports that about a third of the ideas produced in group brainstorming are of the "hitchhiking" type. In such a case, one person's idea is based upon another person's idea.

There are results which do not support his hypothesis, however. Taylor *et al* (*23*) found a larger number of unrepeated ideas produced by individuals working alone than by those working in groups, where both kinds of thinkers were working under the condition of suspended judgment. Taylor points out that the group condition may have the effect of channeling thinking in similar directions, reducing the variety and therefore the quantity of unrepeated ideas.

Perhaps neither the group nor the isolation condition is best under all circumstances or for all individuals. It is quite possible that both can be applied to advantage. The preference of the thinker should have something to do with the choice of condition. A great deal is made of the point that the highly creative person is an independent thinker and that his creation may be a highly personal thing. Torrance (*21*, 1959) found that the more highly creative child (as indicated by his test scores) in a small group often works by himself or is somehow induced by the others to do so.

Whatever the outcome of brainstorming sessions in particular instances, experiments show that courses on creative thinking that are heavily weighted with brainstorming exercises seem to leave the students with beneficial results, and these results have some degree of permanence (*15*, *20*). How much of the improvement to attribute to the brainstorming technique and to which aspects of it the improvement should be attributed are open questions.

Context of Creation

From the discussion thus far, one may conclude that creative performances are to be identified psychologically as a small number of divergent-production operations. Two different qualifications must be introduced. One exception is that two of the factors that we in the Aptitudes Project regarded from the first as being pertinent to creative thinking fall outside the divergent-production group. The other exception is that I have not yet told the whole story regarding the divergent-production factors. I shall make good on the latter omission first.

I have repeatedly stated that the tests on the factors thus far described are *verbal* tests. They pertain to verbally stated information. There are other kinds of information, and the question comes up whether the same person is usually equally creative in handling different kinds of information, material, or content. From our analytical results, we can say that it can happen, but we should rarely expect the same person to be equally capable of creativity in science, in the arts, mathematics, administration, and musical composition. Highly creative individuals in many of these different areas may have outstanding qualities in common, but psychological study indicates that they also have some marked differences.

In the area of divergent-production abilities alone, we find that individuals may be uneven in handling verbal vs. concrete vs. symbolic material. Symbolic material is the kind with which the mathematician deals—numbers and letters. Fluency, flexibility, and elaboration in dealing with concrete (perceived) material are probably of greater importance to the inventor of gadgets, the painter, and the composer, whereas the same kinds of abilities for dealing with verbal material or content are more important for the creative writer and the scientist. In other words, there are parallel abilities for dealing with concrete (or figural) material, symbolic material, and verbally meaningful (or semantic) material.

One of our earlier hypotheses (7) was that the unusually creative person has a high degree of sensitivity to problems. One person notices something wrong or in need of improvement, whereas another fails to observe defects, deficiencies, or errors. The observation of imperfections starts the creative person on his way to creative production. The observation of inadequacy of solutions also keeps the creative thinker at work on his problem (*17*).

Factor analysis has consistently upheld this hypothesis by finding an ability common to a variety of tests calling for the noticing of defects and deficiencies in such things as common household appliances, social customs, or in solutions to problems. Such an ability, however, seems to fit better in the general category of evaluative factors than it does in that of divergent production.

Not being satisfied with things as they are is a matter of evaluation. We hear a great deal about the "divine discontent" of the creative person. It is said that Thomas A. Edison frequently admonished his workers with the comment, "There must be a better way. Go and find it." The uncreative, in contrast, are often willing to settle for half-way measures and tolerably successful solutions to problems.

Another of our initial hypotheses was that many an invention or new idea is the revision of something that is already known. But the revision is not an obvious one. It takes quite a change in the meaning, interpretation, or use of an object to achieve such an innovation. One of our tests, designed for such an ability, asks which of five objects or their parts could be most reasonably adapted to be used to start a fire when there are available the following items: a fountain pen, an onion, a pocket watch, a light bulb, and a bowling ball. The accepted answer is "pocket watch," since the cover of the watch face could be used as a condensing lens. Since this and other such tests call for one best answer, this factor falls logically in the convergent-production category. The feature that makes a contribution to creativity is that a *transformation* must occur; objects must be redefined. Individuals who are clever at improvising seem to show this kind of ability.

There are other abilities outside the divergent-production category that make some contribution to creative performances in their own ways. We have seen that one of the evaluative abilities—sensitivity to problems—has a function in getting the creative thinker started.

Other evaluative abilities should have their uses, whether judgment is suspended or not, in determining whether the products of thinking are good, useful, suitable, adequate, or desirable. If the creator is to finish his job, he will eventually appraise his product, and he will revise it if he feels that revision is called for.

Cognition and Memory

Thus far I have spoken of three major categories of intellectual factors—abilities of divergent production, convergent production, and evaluation. There are two other major categories—cognitive abilities and memory abilities—all distinguished from those in the first-mentioned categories and from each other. Cognitive abilities have to do with discovery, recognition, or comprehension of information in various forms. Memory abilities have to do with storage or retention of information.

Many people, including some teachers, have for some reason disparaged memory and memory abilities. Some of them, who emphasize the importance of thinking, seem wrongly to believe that good thinking and good memory are incompatible qualities, perhaps even negatively correlated. Actually, good memory contributes to good thinking.

It is not a good, well-stocked memory, as such, that is bad, for even the most creative people have given due credit to stored information. It is the way in which storage is achieved and organized that makes the difference between the graduate who is sometimes described as "merely a walking encyclopedia" and the graduate who has a usable and fruitful fund of information. Memory abilities thus make their indirect but important contribution to creative performance.

The question often arises concerning the relation of creativity to intelligence. In connection with this question, the usual conception of "intelligence" is that which is measured by such tests as the Stanford Binet, the Wechsler scales, or the California Test of Mental Maturity.

In discussing abilities related to creativity, I have referred to them as intellectual factors. It is very doubtful whether these abilities, particularly those in the divergent-production category, are represented to any appreciable degree in standard IQ tests. IQ tests were designed to predict success in school learning, particularly in reading, arithmetic, and the subject-matter or informational courses. But we now know that there are many other kinds of intellectual abilities.

Studies of groups of research scientists and engineers (*22*) show that such groups have high average scores on IQ tests. They would need to have higher-than-average IQs to have passed all their academic hurdles, most of them including the PhD. But only a fraction of these are outstanding for creative performance. But within groups of scientists and engineers, the correlation found between IQ-test scores and creative performance is usually rather low. This is due in part to the restriction of range of IQ within such groups. The evidence seems to indicate that although the qualities in traditional IQ intelligence may be of some help to the creative scientist or engineer, they are by no means sufficient.

The low correlation between creativity and IQ is also found at younger age groups. In high school students, Getzels and Jackson (*21*, 1959) found that if the highest 20% of the subjects on IQ were selected as "gifted," 70% of those who stood in the highest 20% in terms of divergent-thinking tests would have been missed. Torrance (*21*, 1959) has reported a similar finding in the elementary grades. In both instances, it was reported that the teachers knew their high-IQ students better and liked them better. The high-creative without high IQs were often regarded as nuisances, and they were somewhat estranged from other students. Those with both high IQ *and* high creativity were recognized as having unusual but sound ideas, to be good in planning and improvising, and effective in getting attention (*21*, 1959).[2]

Non-aptitude Traits

The assessment of traits of temperament, interest, and attitude in connection with creativity has been approached in various ways. One approach has been to find the most outstanding creative individuals in different professional groups, such as architects, writers, and scientists, and to assess them quite thoroughly by methods that are available. If a creative group differs systematically from the general population or, better, some group outside the profession but matched with it for age, sex, and educational level, it is concluded that this creative group stands apart or is distinguished by the personality trait or traits in question.

There are obvious dangers in drawing conclusions from studies

[2] For systematic treatments of a unified theory of intelligence see references (*8*, *11*).

of this kind, unless an appropriate control group has been used. When it is found that creative architects, scientists, mathematicians, and writers alike tend to score highest on theoretical and esthetic interest on the Allport-Vernon-Lindzey *Study of Values*, this may occur just because any high-IQ group would do the same (*14*). When it is found that the creative males tend to score relatively in the direction of femininity on the masculinity-femininity scale of the *Minnesota Multiphasic Personality Inventory* scale, we remember that Terman and Miles (*24*) found that as members of the two sexes are more intelligent and better educated, they respond more alike to test items on masculinity vs. femininity. Nor should it be surprising that the creative groups just mentioned should tend to score high on the Strong *Vocational Interest Blank* scales for architect, psychologist, and author-journalist.

A somewhat better approach is to obtain two samples from the same profession, composed of highly creative and less creative individuals, respectively. The groups can then be compared with respect to various assessed qualities. Sometimes the groups are distinguished on the basis of judgments by their teachers (*4, 12*). In still other studies, subjects of mixed occupations but similar in IQ and educational level have been tested with measures of creative aptitude and of non-aptitude traits (*10*).

Non-aptitude Differences

We have had to recognize that creative occupational groups share parallel but different exceptional abilities. We should expect the various groups to show some non-aptitude qualities in common and also to show some differences. One difference, for example, has been noted between creative students of art and of science. The more creative art student has been reported to be more of an observer than a participant in what is going on (*12*). The more creative science student is reported to be more of a participant than the less creative student (*6*). Such observations should prevent our generalizing conclusions obtained from one creative group to all other creative groups.

There are many ways in which creative people of many groups are alike, however. There is general agreement that the highly creative person, particularly the original person, is self-confident. Which comes first, originality or self-confidence? It is a little like the old hen-and-the-egg problem. Probably, it works both ways: Originality yields success and hence self-confidence, and self-confidence leads the individual to attempt to solve problems where others would give up. In some instances, self-confidence goes over into conceit, as we have all been aware. Sometimes this is fed by the adulations of admirers. Sometimes it may suggest an underlying hypersensitivity to criticism.

Along with self-confidence, there is usually self-assurance or social boldness. The creative person is especially confident about his own judgment and his own evaluations of his work. He is often described as an independent thinker, which includes having an independent set of values. If he thinks his product is good, he discounts the criticisms of others and may disparage their judgments.

Not only is he more or less independent of other people's judgments, he may be self-sufficient in that he can take people or he can let them alone. He is likely to find ideas more important than people, though he is not necessarily a social recluse. These qualities do not add to his popularity with others, so he is in danger of becoming estranged from his parents, his teachers, and his peers. Contributing to this state of affairs also is a lack of mutual understanding. The creative child and his associates may need special counseling to help smooth over some roughness in interpersonal relationships. This can be done without curbing development along creative lines.

We have found that young men who stand high in one or more kinds of fluency are likely to be somewhat impulsive, cheerful, and relaxed. Those who score high in tests of originality tend to have strong esthetic interests, and they like to indulge in divergent thinking. They do not feel much need for meticulousness or for discipline. Somewhat surprisingly, they show no particular dislike for conventional or socially approved behavior, nor do they show signs of neuroticism.

One of the striking traits found by Getzels and Jackson (*21*, 1959) among high school students who stand high in divergent-thinking tests is a strong sense of humor. This is shown particularly in the kinds of stories they tell in response to pictures. For example, one picture showed a young man working at his desk at six-thirty in the morning. A bright but less creative student wrote the following kind of story: "This young man is very ambitious to get ahead. He comes early every morning to impress his boss so he will be promoted." A more creative student told the following kind of story: "This picture is the office of a firm that manufactures breakfast cereals. It has just found a formula to produce a new kind of cereal that will bend, sag, and sway. The man is a private eye employed by a rival firm to obtain the formula. He thinks he has found it and copies it.

It turns out to be the wrong formula, and the competitor's factory blows up."

Such stories usually involve some novel twist or transformation, such as the expression regarding the cereal that will "bend, sag, and sway." Many stories derive their humor from such a source. The person who makes up such stories is exhibiting verbal or semantic transformations, which is a sign that he has a fair degree of the factor of originality. Since this is a semantic ability, and since Getzels and Jackson's tests were verbal, we may well question whether the affiliation of humor and the ability to produce transformations extends to other kinds of content, figural or symbolic. It is probably true, however, that creative painters, composers, and mathematicians also experience a certain amount of enjoyment, if not amusement, in playfulness with their own kinds of materials.

Final Suggestions

Although the temperament and motivational qualities can help us somewhat in identifying potentially creative people, no one of them is a dependable sign, nor would all of them collectively be sufficient. Neither do these qualities help us very much in understanding the nature of the creative processes. On the whole, we have less chance of changing individuals with respect to these qualities in order to increase their creativity, except for changing certain attitudes.

Our chief hope, then, of either identifying the more creative persons or enhancing their creative performances lies with the aptitude factors. If we regard the intellectual factors as distinct but somewhat generalized thinking skills, this statement seems more reasonable. We develop skills by practicing them. The question, then, is one of what kinds of practice can best be applied and under what conditions.

An understanding of the nature of the skills is one of the most important steps either for the teacher or the student. When we know what kind of skill is to be developed, we have a more clearly defined goal toward which to work. Torrance (*21*, 1959) reports that even after 20 minutes of instruction on the nature of divergent-thinking processes, grade-school children showed a clearly observable improvement in performing tasks of this type.

Although special courses on creative thinking have proved beneficial, our whole educational system can be of greater help by giving more attention to this subject. There is abundant opportunity to teach almost any subject in ways that call for productive thinking rather than rote memory. Even the multiplication tables can be taught in ways that give the pupil insight into properties of the number system.

In some experimental courses at the University of Illinois in which mathematics is taught from the lower grades on by what is called a "discovery" method, instead of telling the child the axioms and other principles of mathematics, the teacher lets him discover them for himself by exposing him to appropriate examples. Also at the University of Illinois, science is being taught to children by a discovery method. Some natural phenomenon is demonstrated without explanations to the class, perhaps in motion-picture form. From then on, it is a matter of the students' asking questions, with minimum information being given by the teacher, until the student develops his own satisfactory hypothesis.

Education in this country has unfortunately been too much dominated by the learning theory based upon the stimulus-response model of Thorndike, Hull, and Skinner. People, after all, are not rats (with a few exceptions), and they are not pigeons (with similar exceptions). Let us make full use of the human brains that have been granted to us. Let us apply a psychology that recognizes the full range of human intellectual qualities. We must make more complete use of our most precious national resource—the intellectual abilities of our people, including their creative potentialities.

References

1. Berger, R. M., Guilford, J. P. & Christensen, P. R. A factor-analytic study of planning abilities. *Psychol. Monogr.*, 1957, 71, (Whole No. 435).
2. Christensen, P. R., Guilford, J. P., & Wilson, R. C. Relations of creative responses to working time and instructions. *J. Exp. Psychol.*, 1957, *53*, 82–88.
3. Crawford, R. P. *Techniques of Creative Thinking*. New York: Hawthorne Books, 1952.
4. Drevdahl, J. E. Factors of importance for creativity. *J. Clin. Psychol.*, 1956, *12*, 21–26.
5. Frick, J. W., Guilford, J. P., Christensen, P. R., & Merrifield, P. R. A factor-analytic study of flexibility in thinking. *Educ. Psychol. Measmt.*, 1959, *19*, 469–496.
6. Garwood, D. S. Some personality factors related to creativity in young scientists. Unpublished doctoral dissertation, Claremont Graduate School, 1961.

7. Guilford, J. P. Creativity. *Amer. Psychologist,* 1950, *5,* 444–454.

8. Guilford, J. P. Three faces of intellect. *Amer. Psychologist,* 1959, *14,* 469–479.

9. Guilford, J. P., & Christensen, P. R. A factor-analytic study of verbal fluency. *Rep. Psychol. Lab.,* No. 17. Los Angeles: Univer. Southern California, 1957.

10. Guilford, J. P., Christensen, P. R., Frick, J. W., & Merrifield, P. R. The relations of creative-thinking aptitudes to non-aptitude personality traits. *Rep. Psychol. Lab.,* No. 20. Los Angeles: Univer. Southern California, 1957.

11. Guilford, J. P., & Merrifield, P. R. The structure of intellect model: its uses and implications. *Rep. Psychol. Lab.,* No. 24. Los Angeles: Univer. Southern California, 1960.

12. Hammer, E. F. *Creativity.* New York: Random House, 1961.

13. Hyman, H. *Some Experiments in Creativity.* New York: General Electric, Relations Services, 1960.

14. MacKinnon, D. What do we mean by talent and how do we use it? In *The Search for Talent.* New York: College Entrance Board, 1960.

15. Meadow, A., & Parnes, S. J. Evaluation of training in creative problem solving. *J. Appl. Psychol.,* 1959, *43,* 189–194.

16. Meadow, A., Parnes, S. J., & Reese, H. Influence of brainstorming instructions and problem sequence on a creative problem solving test. *J. Appl. Psychol.,* 1959, *43,* 413–416.

17. Merrifield, P. R., Guilford, J. P., Christensen, P. R., & Frick, J. W. A factor-analytical study of problem-solving abilities. *Rep. Psychol. Lab.,* No. 22. Los Angeles: Univer. Southern California, 1960.

18. Osborn, A. F. *Applied Imagination.* New York: Scribner's, 1953.

19. Osborn, A. F. *Development of Creative Education.* Buffalo, N.Y.: Creative Education Foundation, 1961.

20. Parnes, S. J. & Meadow, A. Evaluation of persistence of effects produced by a creative problem solving course. *Psychol. Reports,* 1960, 7, 357–361.

21. Taylor, C. W. (Ed.) *Research Conference on the Identification of Creative Scientific Talent.* Salt Lake City, Utah: Univer. of Utah Press, 1956, 1958, 1959.

22. Taylor, D. W. Thinking and creativity. *Ann. N.Y. Acad. Sci.,* 1960, *91,* 108–127.

23. Taylor, D. W., Berry, P. C., & Block, C. H. Does group participation when using brainstorming facilitate or inhibit creative thinking? *Admin. Sci. Quart.,* 1958, *3,* 23–47.

24. Terman, L. M., & Miles, Catherine C. *Sex and personality.* New York: McGraw-Hill, 1936.

3-4 Education for preconscious freedom and its relation to creativity and the process of maturation*

Introduction

I MUST INTRODUCE THIS CHAPTER BY SAYING THAT IT may be heavy going and possibly bad-tempered. This is because I am impatient with educators and psychiatrists, with scientists and artists, with all of us in fact, and always for the same thing: namely, for our complacency, for our failure to demand higher goals, and for the ineptitude with which we fail to turn criticism of education into the experimental search for new ways.

My central thesis will be that we do not need to be taught to *think:* indeed that this is something that cannot be taught. Thinking processes actually are automatic, swift, and spontaneous when allowed to proceed undisturbed by other influences. Therefore, what we need is to be educated in how not to interfere with the inherent capacity of the human mind to think. We need also to be helped to acquire the tools of communication: i.e., how to read and listen to words, how to speak and write them. Yet even this is

---

* "Education for Preconscious Freedom and its Relation to Creativity and to the Process of Maturation", in Lawrence S. Kubie, *Neurotic Distortion of the Creative Process,* Lawrence, Kansas: University of Kansas Press, 1958, pp. 104–136.

Lawrence S. Kubie

only one component in the complex art of communication: since here again the more imperative need is to learn how not to let unconscious needs and conflicts and affects and defenses distort the work of the fully educated eye and ear and tongue and hand, lest these unconscious forces alter what we perceive in the act of apperceiving, and alter in the very act of communicating that which we have set out to communicate.

My point is that education will continue to perpetrate a fraud on culture until it accepts the full implications of the fact that the free creative velocity of our thinking apparatus is continually being braked and driven off course by the play of unconscious forces. Educational procedures which fail to recognize this end up by increasing the interference from latent and unrecognized neurotic forces.

Let me give a few random examples of the failure of education, as we know it, to deal adequately with this intricate problem. Each of these examples will be drawn from youngsters of superior endowments and achievements. Examples of more diffuse distortion and blocking will come later.

(1) A brilliant lad in mid-adolescence, always an eager student, always priding himself on getting his work in on time, finds himself unable even to start, much less to complete, a theme on the history of the Oedipus myth. Instead, he becomes quite uncharacteristically depressed and surly and irritable with every fresh start. Finally the paralysis begins to invade other areas of work. Even his unusually imaginative and friendly teacher is unable to help. Nor does this teacher seem to realize how atypical of the student's usual relaxed adjustment is his behavior at this time. An older relative, used "to listening with the third ear," finally persuades the boy to tell him the basic Oedipal tale. He notes that the lad tells it flawlessly, except that (as happens so often in recounting a dream) he omits two critical points: to wit, that the king that Oedipus murders was his father, and that the queen he marries was his mother. Can any educational system educate when teachers are too naïve to realize the dynamic significance of such myths in human life, and therefore too naïve to be alert to the unconscious meanings of this youngster's blocked state?

(2) Consider also the interplay of forces which surrounded first the imprisonment and then the release of another child, as he made his transition from day school to boarding school. This devoted youngster of thirteen had always been "a good boy" and a good student, a good little citizen in a conventional but thoughtful day school. For many reasons having to do with the complex nature of his relationship to his home, when he went to boarding school he felt lost, be-

wildered, frightened, and confused, both in class and out. He dropped swiftly from the top to the bottom of his class. In that same unhappy year he took leave of childhood in another sense by growing ten inches to become the tallest in his class. His voice changed. He became hairy. He was the only boy who had to shave daily. He felt "like a stupid lout." He had his first wet-dreams and his first struggles with masturbation.

His father, noting what had happened, wanted to build a bridge for him from school to home. He thought imaginatively in terms of a symbol of transportation, which led him to do something which would be frowned upon by most pedagogues. As the boy and his father wandered around the Auto Show together admiring a "sports" model, he offered the boy the car if he could climb back to somewhere near the top of the class where he belonged.

I shall not try to enter into or describe the underlying problems, but shall limit myself to pointing out that the gift relieved the lad of his paralyzing sense of guilt and loss. Without effort the boy could again read and listen and understand and recall. Within two months he had made an effortless leap to the top three in a large class in one of our most difficult preparatory schools.

This was, of course, a fortunate stroke in the dark. It left many things unresolved. I describe this not as an example to be followed universally, but to illustrate certain other points. Through his unusually sensitive, intuitive rapport with his son, this father was able to make a gesture which unlocked the boy's spontaneous use of his own latent abilities. In this particular situation, had the school handled the problem with punitive or disciplinary techniques it would have driven the boy deeper into guilt and depression, with consequences which might have paralyzed him in his subsequent academic career both in school and college. This is an example of the importance of developing techniques by which we can explore such situations fully enough to be able to tell when to depend upon the distribution of rewards and punishments and even sometimes a symbolic bribe. The argument is certainly not to be taken as a universal defense of bribery, punishment, or rewards, but as an example of the need for flexibility and precision. However, this will flow from a deeper knowledge of what is going on than is available to us under ordinary educational circumstances. Any effort to implement the theoretical solution encounters many practical problems of personnel and training. This, however, is another story.

(3) A brilliant young girl in early adolescence developed a passionate interest in Greek sculpture, costumes, culture, political or-

ganization, and literature. Then suddenly her interest evaporated. She stopped all studying, and from being a leader in her class dropped to the bottom. On investigation it gradually came to light that what had captured this youngster's interest in Greek civilization was the fact that the men and women seemed to dress alike. This meant to her that they *were* alike; that this had been a world in which the difference between herself and her brother, a difference against which she was rebelling, did not exist. A chance remark from her teacher about the homosexual implications of this culture had exploded this fantasy, and had plunged the girl into a depression in which she felt enraged, cheated, and resentful. It was this disillusionment which had initiated her unwitting sit-down strike.

(4) A little boy of seven became in essence a cartographer. Not only did he take great joy in the most painstaking and meticulous execution of maps, but he also memorized time-tables of train services all over the world. He became the class spokesman in all matters that had to do with things geographical. Geography led to history, history to politics, politics to the law. There, unfortunately, he tumbled into an illness which had many serious schizophrenic features. It was not an irreversible illness, however; and in the course of time and as the result of long searching treatment, the meaning of his early interests came to light. He had lost his mother in a foreign land when he was four. Then shortly before he was seven he was taken on a trip, and during his absence his nurse died on a visit to her home in Scotland. In each instance death had been described to him as "going away"; and the youngster's heart was caught up in an unconscious fantasy of finding again the two women whom he had loved and lost. (I have seen the same kind of response more than once as a reaction to the early death of a parent who was far away at the time.)

(5) Another lad at an early age became a radio expert in a modern school. He built many radios, but he never played them. An obsessive preoccupation with electricity carried him through school and college and into graduate training in mathematical and nuclear physics. Then came a catastrophic breakdown when he found that mathematical thinking was touching off violent erotic excitement, often culminating in orgasm. Illness brought him to treatment. Treatment led back to earlier sources of his illness, *which were identical with the original roots of his interest in radio.* This had started with a panic at the sound of a telephone bell, a panic which in turn was related to many highly charged early problems, the nature of which I need not discuss here, beyond saying that the radio meant keeping in touch with his absent father to protect himself against certain fears

which were generated by his mother's overstimulation of erotic fantasies and needs.

(6) Let me give one other illustration. A gay, eager, and extremely intelligent youngster, always the leader in her class, went through a long series of special interests: American Indians, Vikings, writing, painting, the modern dance, piano, economics, and several others. This had begun with Indians and Vikings. She wrote stories about Indian and Viking boys. She painted their pictures. She dressed up to look like them. She acted their roles in the little plays which she wrote. Later she danced them. It turned out that in all of these "interests" she was acting out in varied forms her fantasies of being made over in her older brother's image. In the end, however, since every activity left her unaltered, and since everything that she attempted failed to work the magical change which she was seeking, she ran through such a long series of inconstant interests and in spite of exceptional endowments ended up stalled and inert and indifferent.

Culture and Education

The indices of failure. It has long been known that in early years children have an extraordinarily inventive imagination, transposing experience freely among the various sensory modalities, using delightful and original figures of speech and allegory. Thus a little boy of five had a drawing and a name for each day in the week. One was "stars and marrow," another was "black slide," a third was a "red stove," etc. This is the natural mode of the symbolic language of childhood; and, as I pointed out in an earlier article it is rooted equally in the internal experiences of the body and the concurrent experiences of external percepts. Another little boy is a poet as he sits on his potty and passes wind and then says, "There's the whistle; now the train will come along." What happens to this poet's gift under the stultifying impact of that which we call our educational system? Lois Murphy has amassed evidence of this culturally imposed sterilization of the spontaneous creativity of childhood in her studies of the art of childhood.

Let me rephrase this ancient problem by asking what happens to the free play of preconscious functions in the course of conventional education?

My unhappy conviction is that much of the learning which has traditionally been looked upon as an essential attribute of the educated man has no necessary relevance either to creativity or to maturity, and that instead many ingredients in the process by which men become learned tend actively to obstruct them both. It seems that it is not learning or the learning process which matures men; it is maturity, however won, which makes it possible for learning to become creative.

I must warn that I am not going to suggest remedies for this state of affairs, nor detail any preventive measures. I will limit myself to an attempt to point out that there is in fact a state of illness in the educational body. The physician is so accustomed to being in this position that he is surprised when it arouses popular indignation. The doctor knows that for many years he may be able only to recognize that something is wrong, slowly adding to this the ability to define its nature. These two steps constitute the process of diagnosis; and he takes it for granted that they may precede even by generations the moment when increasing knowledge will enable him to contribute to prevention or therapy. In the history of medical science there have been only a few exceptional instances in which successful treatment or prevention has preceded diagnosis.

Social phenomena are even more complex than physiological ills, since in social problems physiological, economic, social, psychological, and developmental variables are concurrently operative. Nevertheless, people become unjustifiably angry if anyone points out that something is wrong in politics, economics, social organization, the family, or education, unless the prophet of doom simultaneously offers a remedy. It is to forestall this misplaced indignation that I emphasize at the outset that I will offer no easy solutions to the problems I will describe. Since educators and people generally must first acknowledge that something is amiss before they will begin the search for remedies, I will be content if I am able to convince even a few that there is something quite basically wrong with our approach to education, and if I can define what is wrong in terms of the crippling influence on the creative process of much of what occurs in school. Only at the end will I suggest a few directions in which it is reasonable to seek for corrective or preventive techniques. This is as far as I will presume to go; but I hope that experienced educators, with their more intimate knowledge of the details of educational procedures, may be able to offer more definitive remedies. Indeed, some educators and certain special schools have long since begun to attack the problems described. But I must leave this to them. My function is to challenge, not to offer panaceas.

The premises from which I start are not happy ones. Yet they are not pessimistic either, since they carry the implication that if we face these problems fearlessly we can solve them, and that if we solve them we will open a new era in human culture. Let me then state these premises:

(1) The great cultural processes of human society, including art and literature, science, education in general, the humanities and religion, have three essential missions—namely: to enable human nature itself to change; to enable each generation to transmit to the next whatever wisdom it has gained about living; to free the enormous untapped creative potential which is latent in varying degrees in the preconscious processes of everyone. It is my belief that in all three respects all of our great cultural efforts have failed.

Our knowledge of the external world and our ability to represent the world as it is or as we would like it to be has grown enormously, but our ability to meet wisely the challenge of how to be human beings has not developed equally. Everyone acknowledges this intellectually; yet no one has accepted the full implications which this failure entails for education. The Art and Science of being a Human Being is still an assignment for which the Human Race is inadequately prepared.

The failure of education to make it possible for Man to change is due to a specific component in human nature: to wit, that psychological rigidity which is the most basic and most universal expression of the neurotic process—far more universal than are those more obvious quirks which comprise the clinical neuroses. Indeed, this neurotogenic rigidity is so universal that it is popularly accepted as normal even among many psychiatrists and analysts, as though the mere fact that everybody is rigid in one or more aspects of his personality meant that rigidity is normal. Cavities in the teeth are not normal merely because everybody has cavities. Nor is a cold normal because everybody catches cold. Actually, this psychological rigidity, which is a manifestation of the masked but universal neurotic ingredient in human nature, constitutes the major challenge not only to education but to any general forward movement on the part of human culture.

(2) Since all that I will say is predicated upon what I regard as this basic failure of human culture, I must enumerate the indices of this failure, even if in doing so I repeat part of what I have already said:

First there is the universality of the neurotic process itself, in every culture about which we know anything. From one society to another there are minor variations in the forms in which the neurotic process manifests itself. Yet the universality of its essence is attested by its appearance in these varied forms among peoples from all cultures.

Second, there is the basic failure of the race as a whole, plus the failure of men as individuals, to evolve and change psychologically.

Third, there is the failure of traditional methods of imparting that wisdom about living which would be manifest in socially creative and individually fulfilling lives of work and play and love. We dare not pretend to ourselves that we have solved this problem. Thus we know what kinds of behavioral conventions tend to conserve any association of men in a livable society. We call these ethical principles. Yet we cannot claim that we know how to perpetuate and inculcate such ethical principles, or how to seat them firmly in the saddle in human affairs. Instead we know that out of unsavory soil some people grow up to be ethical, while others become unethical from equivalently favored circumstances. The son of a criminal may become a minister: and the son of a minister, a criminal. Or if we take marriage as another example, the progeny from happy marriages may make unhappy unions, and vice versa: just as happens in the careers of the sons of "great" men or of failures. Clearly there are basic gaps in our knowledge of how to transmit the fruits of experience from one generation to the next. The consequence is that in forms which change only in details, country after country and generation after generation repeat the errors of their predecessors.

The cumulative significance of these interdependent manifestations of the failure of culture is to place at the heart of our problem the universal masked neurotic components in "normal" human nature. Therefore, we must ask ourselves whether the educational process as we know it increases or decreases in the student the incidence and the sway of hidden neurotic forces in human life.

Education and the neurotic process

It is often said that one could not get through school at all without a neurosis of some degree and kind. The neurosis which is implied here is the "compulsive work drive." Yet compulsive drives are not a separate clinical entity; since there is a compulsive nucleus in all manifestations of the neurotic process. Furthermore, even if this has been true in the past (which has certainly seemed to be the case for graduate professional schools), it need not always be our fate. But it is with the defects of the present that we must concern ourselves, if we are to reach a better future. Therefore it is this unhappy symbiosis between education and the ubiquitous neurotic process that we must consider.

Obviously, every man is a pupil for many years before he attains the state of being an adult with more or less independent fields of activity. Just as we carry over into adult life the distortions which arise in the nursery, so we carry into our adult years the stresses and strains of our educational adolescence: i.e., the years during which we struggle to acquire knowledge, craftsmanship, technique, and discrimination. Whether he becomes an artist, a scientist, a professional man, a postman, a plumber, or a salesman, the adult bears the imprint of the child. The unconscious projection of the years of childhood onto the screen of adult years limits our capacity to mature by anchoring us to the past. Therefore, the educator who is interested in making education serve the process of maturity must study the ways in which such projections from the past influence four elements in education, i.e.:

1. the *setting* in which we impart education;

2. the *methods* by which we teach and learn;

3. the *data* which we try to impart;

4. the *symbolic process.*

(1) The setting of education: and its influence on the neurotic process

The schoolroom and the school as a whole confront the child with surrogate parents and siblings. If we were naïvely optimistic we might expect that schools would long since have seized on this as an opportunity to explore each child's responses both to parental authority and to sibling rivalry, so as to help him to understand himself in these basic relationships and thus to achieve a capacity for mature self-direction. Instead, in most schools the structure of school "society" is such as to allow the child merely to relive blindly the buried hates and loves and fears and rivalries which had their origins at home—sacrificing understanding to some limited degree of blind "self-mastery." Schooling tends rather to accentuate whatever automatic patterns of child-to-adult and child-to-child relationship each child has brought to his school years, and not to change them. The schoolroom as we know it tends neither to balance nor to neutralize these conflict-laden feelings, nor to render them less fixed and rigid by bringing them within the reach of conscious selection, direction, and control. Self-control as taught is limited to a control of the secondary consequence of these conflicts, never directed at their inner sources. The exceptions to this are rare. At best, most schools today constitute a pragmatic test of the extent to which a student as he comes to them can either accept or reject or modify or exercise authority.

One could choose at random a number of illustrations of the consequences of this. First among them is the child who in his struggle with authority becomes an obsessional dawdler. This may begin in the nursery in dawdling about eating, excreting, washing, dressing, or undressing. Such a toddler grows up to be an obsessional dawdler about play, chores, and studies. As we have said, the school patterns of young lives do not arise *de novo*, but carry the imprint of a nursery prehistory which antedated schooling. One phase merges into the next. Consequently, unless these earlier neurotic deviations have been effectively resolved in the home before the youngster reaches school, they will invade and warp his later approach to study of all kinds.

Yet the school does nothing to give the child either insight into them or freedom from them. Instead it usually increases this paralyzing tendency, so that the same patterns will persist to plague the lifework of potentially brilliant and creative adults. It is in this way that the deviations of each untreated phase are accentuated in later phases, and gather new and increasingly costly secondary consequences. One can trace this story in many lives.

For some the only escape from this prison is to turn away from all formal and informal education, rejecting any guidance from the past, and from those products of Man's experience which are embodied in "rules" or "principles." This is a not infrequent source of the undisciplined, chaotic, and rebellious pseudo-creativity which characterizes the early work of many young artists, writers, musicians, and scientists. As children many of them had been paralyzed by the obsessional dawdling which is a carry-over from nursery years. In the effort to escape, they grow up to accept unwittingly the tyranny of an internal "*Führer*" of which they are unaware. They are seduced by the illusory freedom of a blind reaction against all external authority. Yet because the road to freedom is never found by submitting to irresponsible authority (whether this authority is internal or external), inevitably they pay for this in the stereotyped and repetitive quality of their work. Such creativity wears only a mask of freedom. All too often their continued enslavement becomes manifest in a crippling work-block, and in years of total unproductivity which may engulf and paralyze even great creative artists. (Cf., for instance, Sterba, 73, De Voto, 11.)

At the opposite pole from the obsessional dawdler is the compulsive rusher, the youngster who has to plunge headlong from one half-finished task to another, afraid to tarry long enough to complete anything lest he be overtaken by some nameless fate, some dreaded exposure. These two oppositely paced obligatory patterns may alternate in the same individual, and may arise out of almost identical neurotic soil, that is to say, out of essentially identical unconscious conflicts. Yet in later life these will have dramatically different secondary and tertiary consequences. The relevant and disconcerting point is that both of these opposing neurotic patterns tend to be reinforced and not lessened by the pressures of our formal educational processes.

Consider also the influence of the educational setting on another pair of neurotic mechanisms. The "bad" student explodes in automatic defiance, with the repression of all latent compliant impulses. In the so-called "good" student, whose "goodness" may be equally automatic, the same struggle is often buried in neurotic submissiveness, with the repression of all latent rebellion. This is one of several reasons why every analyst has a category of patients who can best be called "Campus Heroes," i.e., men and women who have done extraordinarily well through school and college on the basis of a neurotic submissiveness, which ultimately explodes in their forties and fifties under the pressure of unresolved underlying problems.

Such clinical experiences as these challenge us to ask whether there is any better way to conduct the educational process, which will free it on the one hand from the subtle distortions of neurotic submissiveness with its unimaginative conformity, and on the other from unconscious rebellion with its pseudo-originality; and also from the diffuse blocking which can be a manifestation of unconscious sabotage and of other neurotogenic inhibitory constellations.

The accepted settings of education reinforce still other neurotogenic sequences. For instance, the classroom perpetuates on every level the struggle within each generation, as well as between child and adult. This happens because most schools still exploit competitively the hostilities and the sibling rivalries which arise automatically in every nursery. Almost never are these resolved or illuminated in the classroom with insight, grace, or compassion. Consequently a competitive rivalry occurs which can overstimulate one student and overinhibit another. I have seen this happen with disastrous consequences to two pairs of identical twins. In each of these one of the pair was overstimulated and the other overinhibited by reliving in the schoolroom the sibling situation at home. Here again are destructive forms in which the classroom can constitute a screen upon which the bitter, hidden residues of earlier years can be projected into the child's present and the adult's future. This is one of the prices our culture pays for the failure of schools to use the classroom as an opportunity to resolve these corroding conflicts.

In considering how to deal with these difficult and ubiquitous problems we do not need to conjure up a Utopian School in which no nursery battles would be re-enacted. As a guiding principle we need only remember that the immediate and the remote effects of these internal and external sources of conflict upon each child and adult will depend *not* upon the fact that these struggles occur, but upon the level on which they are waged, i.e., whether this level is preponderantly conscious, preconscious, or unconscious. Therefore we can justly challenge our schools to see what they can do to make sure that these battles will be fought out on conscious and preconscious levels. With this reasonable and attainable goal in mind, they could use the classroom replications of infancy as an opportunity to develop in each child at least that degree of self-knowledge which would be sufficient to free him from passive submission to the tyranny of his ancient and submerged patterns. It would seem to be an essential ingredient of any truly educational experience to enable each child to face in himself those painful conflicts from which he shrinks but which shape his character. Instead, it has been the traditionally accepted role of the school to impose even stronger taboos on self-knowledge than are generated at home, thus reinforcing and reproducing in the classroom the very limitations on self-awareness which characterize our adult culture. Thus what passes for Education strengthens that all-too-human tendency to shrink from the facing of painful facts, which the child brings to school from his nursery.

Neither traditional disciplinary education nor progressive education has solved the technical problems which this goal involves; although progressive education has launched a courageous if sometimes blind struggle towards their solution. Disciplinary techniques alone, even when seemingly "successful," give the child a sense that he must control something, but fail to make clear what there is inside to control or redirect. Especially in its early years, "progressive" education encouraged the child to act out his problems, but failed to realize that acting-out will not alone bring any increase in self-understanding or in self-mastery. Indeed, like blind discipline, blind acting-out can distort and block insight; as we see in the psychopath. This fallacy was manifested in the misapplication to education of a procedure which is valid in therapy, but even there only under certain circumstances.

It was not strange that in its early stages progressive education should have made this mistake. This error has long been abandoned; but without finding what to put in its place. About this I will presently make a few tentative suggestions.

(2) *The influence of the techniques of education on the neurotic process*

We must next ask ourselves how often traditional teaching methods distort the education even of highly gifted youngsters, (a) blocking these youngsters by intensifying the activity of inhibiting neurotic forces, or (b) overdriving them by masked neurotic obsessions and compulsions. In other words, does the educative process, even at its current best, tend to reinforce the neurotic process? I believe that it has precisely this effect, and primarily through the misuse of the techniques of repetitive drill.

In the tangled interweaving of the processes of learning and the neurotic process, repetition plays a major role. By imperceptible gradations, the repetitive drills of the learning process shade over into the automatic involuntary repetitions of the neurosis. But whenever repetition becomes automatic and obligatory, it constitutes the kernel of the neurotic process itself. Unhappily this is precisely what often occurs in education, with the consequence that an intensification of the neurotic process through repetitive drill mars our educational system from primary grades through professional and graduate levels.

This neurotic distortion of repetitive drill in the learning process can frustrate the practice of the athlete, of the musician, of the student of languages, of mathematics, of history, of the young scientist, indeed of any effort to memorize or master anything. As a consequence of this contamination of the learning process by neurotic automaticity, repetitive drill makes imperfect at least as frequently (and probably far more frequently) than it makes perfect. It grinds in error and makes more "bad habits" than good. If this were not true, practice would turn all of us into virtuosi, champion athletes, and TV quiz experts.

These facts are observable every day in every home and every school. Limitless repetition without the guidance of insight is not merely self-defeating; it does deeper damage by hampering spontaneous, "intuitive," i.e., preconscious functions. There is considerable evidence that the freer is the learning process from neurotic distortion, and the less obstructed it is by counter-processes which are rooted in unconscious conflicts (i.e., the more "normal" it is), the less repetition is needed. Nevertheless in the acquisition of any skills, whether manipulative, symbolic, or instinctive, the teacher continues to place major emphasis on repetitive drill.

The most efficient learning is essentially effortless and almost instantaneous. This is that *preconscious* learning, to which the closest analogy is the automatic and almost photographic or phonographic hypermnesia of hypnosis. For example, under hypnosis enormous amounts of material can be recorded effortlessly, almost as on a photographic plate. Here drill and repetition play no role; and their introduction would actually interfere with automatic recording. This is true whether the learning process is predominantly visual, auditory, manipulative, or kinesthetic, although there may be differences in inherent endowments in this respect. In general, however, the degree to which learning depends upon repetitive drill is a measure of the degree to which guilt, anxiety, anger, and repression, whether conscious or unconscious, are blocking the assimilative component of education. Thus dependence on drill is actually a measure of the failure of at least one important ingredient in the educational process, while reflecting the influence of the educator's anxiety as well. The result is to increase the entanglement of preconscious functions in a thicket of unconscious guilt, terror, rage, and conflict. An illuminating contrast is provided by the "idiot-savant," a person of limited mentality who functions so nearly free of conflict as to be able to record preconsciously as though under hypnosis, and thus is able to produce extraordinary feats of memory, of lightning calculation, etc. Occasionally one encounters a man or child whose preconscious learning processes, through some happy accident, operate freely. He learns effortlessly. To the consternation and anger of his classmate he wins highest grades in a heavy schedule without studying. Yet because he has done this with Seven League Boots, and at the speed of all preconscious processes and without laboring through the intermediate steps, he is unable to explain to anyone else how he has done it. Nor can he teach. Similarly the great virtuosi and the greatest athletes are rarely the great teachers.

(3) The influence of unconscious projection on the materials to be mastered in the educative process

There is another technical aspect of education which points up its interrelation with the neurotic process. The learning process is a continuous two-way interchange. It has acquisitive elements insofar as it involves the assimilation of new data. Yet at the same time every new thing that we attempt to assimilate becomes a target for projections, comparable to the projections which are demonstrated in the Rorschach Test, the Thematic Apperception Test, the Zondi tests, etc. William James characterized this many years ago when he said that every Perception requires a prior Apperceptive act: i.e., the integration of the data of the perceptual process into a mass of previously acquired data which he called the "apperceptive mass." Freud restated this when he said that every Cognition implies a process of Recognition.

Whenever the eager student undertakes to master a new discipline, its special data are at first amorphous and structureless. Each new discipline is like a cinema screen onto which each student projects representations of his own unresolved unconscious problems. In this way we first distort what we attempt to learn, and then learn what we have distorted. Everything that we study undergoes this double process and acquires multiple significance: (a) There is the process of perceiving and of apperceiving new facts and new combinations of facts, leading to new concepts. (b) Paralleling this, we continuously project onto this material distillates of our own unconscious psychological processes. This occurs whether we are studying literature, the arts, music, languages, or mathematics, the sciences, history, philosophy —anything. Through such projections onto the subject matter of various disciplines, as we master them the disciplines themselves are converted into complex, challenging thematic apperceptive devices.

Presumably, this process of projection must play a major role among the several forces which determine a man's choice of his occupation or of fields for study and research. Vocational choices have never been studied from this angle. Yet this type of distortion, which plagues the educational process, can itself be made the object of research by techniques which are available to us, but which have never been used for this purpose. This, however, is not the occasion for a discussion of details of research into the educative process.

(4) *Symbolic distortions*

A further difficulty in educational procedures which is related to these projective experiences arises through the neurotic distortion of the symbolic process itself. Of this the most obvious and universal manifestation is the dream; but in subtler form the same thing occurs in learning. The symbolic process always represents a condensation of conscious, preconscious, and unconscious symbolic values. In elementary learning quite as much as in the higher levels of research, there can be a subtle and unnoticed shift from the conscious import of anything to its unconscious connotations. In turn this can initiate blindly compulsive workdrives in unprofitable directions. One encounters this repeatedly in the lives of scientists, artists, and writers. Alternatively it may set up equally blind resistances to the processes of learning, resistances which may be either selective or all-inclusive. It is in this way that the symbolic process can become an obstacle to the learning process instead of its chief tool.

Thus, at every level of education from the kindergarten to postgraduate study, educational procedures become intricate networks of normal and neurotic mechanisms. Moreover, because as we have seen, traditional techniques of teaching employ mechanisms similar to those which dominate the neurotic process, education itself involves a subtle trend towards neurotic distortion, the correction of which demands a continuous use of clinically appropriate preventive devices. People talk glibly of neuroses as a kind of mal-education and of psychotherapy as a process of learning. Both statements are oversimplifications, slighting and overlooking among other considerations the basic fact that conventional educational techniques exploit and depend upon some of the essential ingredients of the neurotic process. The consequence is that one cannot dissociate an unsparing study of how to improve the learning processes from the understanding and control of neurotic mechanisms. Therapy and learning constitute together a joint field for research in education and psychiatry. Therefore, education and therapy are complementary and inseparable.

From all of these considerations we are forced to conclude that there is a continuous conflict and not a happy synergy between erudition and maturity. This conflict begins in the primary grades but continues unabated to and through the highest echelons of postgraduate education.

Erudition without wisdom or maturity

I have never been able to regard seriously any partisan arguments that the study of any particular aspect of man's folly-ridden history will determine whether the scholar ends up with mature wisdom or with the pseudo-erudition of an idiot-savant. The conflict between education as we have known it and maturity as we can envisage it depends upon something more profound than whether we master the history of an art-form called painting or of an art-form called science. There is no educator who does not know scholars who lack the least quality of human maturity and wisdom, yet who are true masters of their own fields, whether this field is the humanities, art, music, philosophy, religion, law, science, the history of ideas or the languages by which men communicate ideas. The absent-minded professor may be a stereotype, a burlesque, and an exaggeration; but he symbolizes a remoteness from wisdom and maturity which demonstrates that there is no degree of learning about the phenomenology of the outer world or about the histories of *other* lands, *other* peoples, and *other* men's lives, which in and of itself brings wisdom. The absent-minded professor, whatever his field, is the living proof that the scholarly humanist is not necessarily wiser by virtue of his special knowledge than is the technical scientist, or vice versa. Indeed nowadays we are all technicians. The measure of our wisdom about living is not determined by the breadth of our knowledge, or by the sharpness of the focus of our specialization.

If only as a contrast, it might shed some light on the elusive relationship between formal education and maturation to consider what happens to medical students during the course of their medical education. All close observers agree that it has a remarkable impact on many, if not on all. Furthermore, this critical change seems to start not when the students are studying books or dissecting corpses or working in laboratories, but when they are brought into contact with the sufferings of patients. This is a moment which forces them to accept some measure of responsibility for human suffering other than their own. For each student this is an experience which precipitates a powerful if masked internal struggle among conflicting impulses. Shall he or shall he not be his brother's keeper? Shall he cling to the unrecognized prerogative of childhood to shut out the suffering of others or even secretly to exult in it? Or shall he yield to those simultaneous, powerful, internal and external pressures which medical tradition brings to bear on him, to force a confrontation with human needs other than his own? Will this extricate him from the cocoon of his childhood to identify with others through ministering to them?

This may give us a clue to another basic defect in our entire educational process. Perhaps above anything else the adolescent needs not only to be exposed to human suffering, but also to be given responsibility to play a role in ministering to it. At present the educational years cultivate in each student a maximal concentration on himself. One can conjure up many methods by which this problem might at least be explored.

The difficulty is intensified by the fact that the increasing duration of education competes with the equally essential needs of young men and women for experience and responsibility. We know that the essence of maturity can come only through the insight which arises out of the interaction between living, blundering, and studying and dissecting our blunders. Neither living without self-study, nor study without living is enough. We sometimes forget that the founders of the Republic lived and also often died young—and that in their moment of national greatness many were only in their thirties. Yet this is precisely where the rub is; because the increasing duration of the process of formal education tends to incarcerate the student for many decades in an adolescence of limited responsibility in which he lives on a dole, thus obstructing the very processes of maturation for which we are striving. The effort to educate fully may take so many years that it can make unattainable the very development at which it aims. The persistent immaturity of the perpetual student is a familiar phenomenon on every campus; and when any training program lasts too long, independent spirits tend to drop out along the way, until only the docile, the submissive, and the uncreative survive the full indoctrination. We face this problem in all forms of education. How to achieve the fullest degree of intellectual preparation without emotional stunting challenges us to find ways in which without limiting education we can facilitate those aspects of emotional maturity which emanate only from the direct experience of living and from carrying a sobering responsibility for others.

I take it for granted that our educational processes must continue to last longer and longer. This means, however, that unless the student is exposed concurrently to maturing experiences, he will continue to end up as an erudite adolescent. The mere passage of time makes maturity possible, but never guarantees it. Without the challenge of independent responsibility (personal, professional, and/or clinical), the duration of training tends to limit the emotional maturation which is a vital component in the equipment of anyone who hopes to achieve wisdom.

Precisely here is where the educational system, the neurotic process, and the emotional demands of the creative impulse come into a three-way collision. For reasons which I have tried to indicate, the imperious creative impulse frequently arises in a young man or woman who is rebelling against all external authority, yet who has unwittingly remained enslaved to his own unconscious. He brooks no external interference: but also will not welcome any well-meant efforts on the part of others to help him to become free from the internal slave-driver about whose existence he is both unconscious and paradoxically defensive. Therefore he rejects not only formal educational responsibility but also any depths of self-understanding. Thus he turns his back on both types of potentially maturing experience to which the human spirit can be exposed. He will not wait humbly for the wisdom that can be won only at the "autopsy table," i.e., through the study of his own errors, which is the only path we know to self-knowledge in depth. His rebellious spirit may instead seize upon his own particular field of art or music or literature or science, to use it as a vehicle for aggressive expression of his own neurosis.

As with all Priesthoods this is to him a "calling" of sorts; and like all "callings" it feeds on the fantasy that he can create out of revelation. In one field the revelations are absolute truths from a Deity. In another they arise out of some secret wellspring of Absolutes from within. Out of this unconscious arrogance has grown the unspoken Dogma that ignorance in the creative artist should be cultivated as a positive advantage, so as to leave him unencumbered by reality. Yet curiously enough, as with all such notions, it contains a minute grain of truth.

One obvious implication runs through everything I have said, namely, that if education is to become a matter not only of the mind but of the spirit, and that if it is ever to facilitate the maturing process instead of limiting and distorting it, then it must deal with the universal, masked, neurotic ingredient in human nature. Clearly this will require an unsparing reappraisal of all traditional educational goals and methods. This leads me to my final argument.

The Role of Self-Knowledge

These are grave facts to be pondered gravely by every educator. You will understand why I began by stating that I have no easy solutions. Nevertheless as I draw to a close I will urge that one thing is an essential ingredient in any solution. This is self-knowledge in depth.

Thus far my ruminations have merely led me up to the brink of this critical question: namely, what is the effective value of knowledge of externals in the absence of equally deep personal insight? Can there be wisdom, even about the objective world around us (considering how many distorting fantasies we project onto this outer world) in the absence of wisdom about the inner world from which these projections arise? It is my conviction that education without self-knowledge can never mean wisdom or maturity; and that self-knowledge in depth is a process which like education itself is never complete. It is a point on a continuous and never-ending journey. It is always relative, and never absolute. It is a process which must go on throughout life, if at all; and like the fight for external freedom, it demands eternal vigilance and continuous struggle. This is because in every one of us, from the beginning of life until its end active forces are at work which tend repeatedly to confuse and obscure our images of ourselves. Therefore, that well-known average man who lacks self-knowledge in depth, looks out upon the world through glasses which are discolored by the quality of his own unconscious self-image. Without self-knowledge in depth we can have dreams, but no art. We can have the neurotic raw material of literature but not mature literature. We can have no adults, but only aging children who are armed with words and paint and clay and atomic weapons, none of which they understand. And the greater the role in the educational process which is played by unconscious components of symbolic thinking, the wider must be this ancient and dishonorable gap between erudition and wisdom. It is this gap which makes a mockery of the more pretentious claims of art, of science, of education, and of religion. If self-knowledge has been the forgotten man of our educational system, and indeed of human culture in general, then we are forced to the conclusion that up to now it has been possible for men in general to be only erudite rather than wise. Wisdom when it has graced any one of us has come not by design but as a happy accident. This challenges us to have the courage to face this failure of education as we have always known it, with a determination to do something effective about it.

I would not like this argument to be misunderstood or exaggerated. Self-knowledge is not all there is to wisdom and maturity; but it is an essential ingredient which makes maturity at least possible. Yet it is the one ingredient which is almost totally neglected. This lack is both an index and a cause of the immaturity of our culture.

Summary and Suggestions

If I now summarize these reflections, what do we find? We find ourselves confronted with a whole series of difficult paradoxes and dilemmas, and with no simple indication of how to reconcile or solve them. The amount of data which every educated man must master is enormous already and is constantly increasing. Yet if we hold him at the student level too long, the process of emotional maturation which is so essential an ingredient of education is in danger of being stunted. And as more and more must be learned, the danger of stunting will increase unless we can find a way to make over the life of the student, so that in itself it will become a maturing experience.

Here again the use of what we have learned through psychoanalysis from these exaggerations of the normal which we call abnormal will play a critical role. Even if we do not already possess the techniques by which to implement fully the knowledge we have gained, we can at least formulate our goals. Education must include opportunities to undo some of those subtle restrictions of the human spirit which arise as a result of the ubiquitous if masked influence of both the neurotic and the schizophrenic processes in every culture known to man. Furthermore, in our society many active forces obstruct any effort to apply even the imperfect and incomplete knowledge which we now possess. Entrenched special interests oppose change, because they are threatened by change. Therefore, progress will not come just from sitting back and hoping, or from studying. It will come only as a reward for an uncompromising defense of the creative value of doubt, and from an unsparingly critical re-examination of every educational premise. When we meet the currently popular and all too easy assumption that the humanities will solve these problems, we should remind the optimist that the humanities have never served us that well in the past. The crucial question is not whether one should study science or the humanities, but what can be done to convert the years of the student's life into a maturing experience. Either the basic structure of that life must be altered; or else periods of study must be interspersed with periods devoted to other types of experiences; or techniques of group psychotherapy must be adapted to the educational scene to supplement formal education in the service of greater maturity. Or all of these must be tried.

The emotional and intellectual maturity which the returning veteran brought to his studies after World War II, the subtle birth of a larval maturity in the medical student as he first experiences the suffering of others and participates in its alleviation, what we have learned about the imprisoning of the human spirit by the neurotic process—these lead us in the direction in which we must seek solutions to these fundamental problems of how education can enable the human spirit to grow and change. We cannot be wise yet remain immature. Maturity requires the capacity to change, to become different, to react in varied and unanticipated ways. All of these words describe different facets of this same human need: and none of it is attainable as long as the human spirit remains imprisoned in its masked neuroses. This is the ultimate challenge to the value of any educational process in any culture.

3-5 *Adolescence and secondary education in modern society* *

WE HAVE DOCUMENTED THE CHARACTER OF THE ADOLESCENT society in ten high schools. These schools do not represent the whole United States, but they cover a wide range of living conditions—from farm to city to suburb; from working class to executive class. Most important, they include segments of American society likely to be representative of the future, especially in the affluent suburb of Executive Heights.

The results of this research are disturbing to one concerned with the ability of an open society to raise its children today and in the future. This was once a task largely carried out within the family or in local places of work, a task with which the larger society had little need to concern itself. But the rationalization of society more and more inhibits the "natural" processes, by separating the adolescent off into institutions of his own, and insulating him from adults' work and adults' perspective. The adolescent remains in these institutions, treated as a child, for a longer and longer period, while he gains social sophistication earlier and earlier. If there was one most striking difference between the adolescents of Marketville or Farmdale and those of Executive Heights, it was the greater social sophistication of the latter. They were more nearly

* James S. Coleman, "Adolescence and Secondary Education in Modern Society," in *The Adolescent Society*, Glencoe, Illinois: Free Press of Glencoe, 1961, pp. 311–329.

James S. Coleman

teenagers, less children; their own peers were of more importance to them, and their parents of less importance. Yet most of them would be forced to remain in school, as children, longer than their small-town counterparts.

As our society moves more and more away from the era of farm and small town, the family has less chance to train its adolescents—not only in their occupation, but in all areas of life. It was once true that the major interaction between a father and son were in the father's activities—helping with his work, or in jobs around the house. In these activities, the boy learned adult work and adult responsibilities. Now the major interactions must be in the *son's* activities—Little League baseball, Boy Scouts, and play activities of various sorts. The father's participation brings him into the son's world; but the son gets no chance to move into the father's world. (Every teacher knows the distinction between the teacher who becomes popular with students by coming down to their level, and the teacher who gains his popularity—or at least respect—by bringing them up to his level. The first type of teacher has lost his potential for influence, for he has tacitly agreed to become like them, rather than the reverse.)

The adolescent lives more and more in a society of his own, he finds the family a less and less satisfying psychological home.[1] As a consequence, the home has less and less ability to mold him.

One strategy to solve this problem is to bring the adolescents back into the home; to reduce the pervasiveness of the adolescent society, and return to a state in which each boy and girl responds principally to parents' demands. This strategy should be seriously considered, for if successful, it would make a society's task of educating its adolescents far simpler. But it is well to recognize the kind of effort it would require. For example, families must reduce their mobility, both geographic and social. Such mobility rips a child from the community which provides, along with his family, a psychological home. A move from one neighborhood to another insures that the adolescent will not know personally any adults other than his parents, adults to whom he might turn for advice and aid.

If such a strengthening of the home and weakening of the adolescent community is to occur, families must exert many other efforts

[1] One important reason for the latter has been the radical shift in family structure. A family of husband, wife, and children, geographically mobile, has no existence for a child apart from its particular members. In contrast, the three-generation stable family of the past was a unit with an existence over and above its particular members. If one member died or left, the family went on. It had continuity through generations, and a physical location. Now, if husband or wife is gone, the family is truly disrupted for the child.

as well as that of staying in one place. Parents in modern middle class suburbia must forego the social patterns to which they have become accustomed. Their social engagements must cease being the evening parties and cocktail parties which include adults alone; they must have association with other families *as families*, including all members of the family. A few recent developments, such as boating and similar leisure pursuits, facilitate this, but most developments, such as the removal of man's work to a bureaucracy which is physically far from the family, and the increasing removal of the woman from the home into the labor market, discourage such family association. Family institutions and "occasions" must be consciously developed, so that the life within the family has a richness and attractiveness to the adolescent. Further, the family must reinstitute more authoritarian control, keeping the implements of adult pleasures out of its children's hands: cars, expensive dress, commercial entertainment. If this is not done, the economic affluence of the adolescent, whether gained through family money or his own after-school job, gives him independence from the family, and the ability to carry out activities autonomously with his peers.

The family must be prepared, if it is to regenerate itself to take over the adolescent, to deal with his early social sophistication. Mass media, and an ever-increasing range of personal experiences, gives an adolescent social sophistication at an early age, making him unfit for the obedient role of the child in the family.

It should also not be overlooked that, even if such a strategy were extremely successful, it would have serious disadvantages: a child's success in society would depend more on his parents' position in it than is presently true. If his parents were criminals, he would learn their habits, their attitudes, their techniques, just as surely as he would if his parents were law-abiding citizens. Equality of opportunity, which becomes ever greater with the weakening of family power, would hardly be possible.

Thus the strategy of strengthening the family to draw the adolescent back into it faces serious problems, as well as some questions about its desirability. It is a strategy which an individual family may carry out successfully, and one toward which the exhortations of ministers, family counselors, and social psychiatrists can be devoted. It seems particularly unpromising, however, as a solution for the society itself, in designing its educational system, and its programs for adolescents.

The other possible strategy is just the reverse of this: to take the adolescent society as given, and then *use* it to further the ends of adolescent education. Rather than bringing the father back to play with his son, this strategy would recognize that society has changed, and attempt to improve those institutions designed to educate the adolescent toward adulthood. In order to do this, one must know how adolescent societies function, and beyond that, how their directions may be changed. The first of these tasks has been the aim of this book. It is the second to which a few comments will be directed now.

The two major effects of the adolescent social system to which these remarks will be directed are upon the amount and direction of *energy* or *effort* that it induces in its members; and its *psychological effects* upon them. (These two effects correspond roughly to the areas examined in chapters IX and VIII respectively.) The means through which the adolescent society has these effects is primarily the rewards and punishments it dispenses among its members. These rewards and punishments include popularity, respect, acceptance into a crowd, praise, awe, support and aid, on the one hand, or isolation, ridicule, exclusion from a crowd, disdain, discouragement, disrespect. As in the larger society, these rewards and punishments, coming from others who are important to a person, exert a powerful influence on his subsequent efforts, and can have a powerful effect upon his psychological equanimity.

These rewards and punishments dispensed by the adolescent society to its members are largely incorporated in the status system. The adolescent society has little material rewards to dispense, so that its system of rewards is reflected almost directly in the distribution of status. This is the reason for our focus on the status system among adolescents throughout this book—because this status system shows the pattern of rewards and punishments dispensed by the adolescent society.

Several attributes of a status system have been examined here, all of them important to our inquiry:

a) the *content* of those activities which are rewarded and those which are punished. This content varied somewhat from one school to another, but in all cases athletics was extremely important for the boys, and social success with boys was extremely important for girls. Scholastic success received differing amounts of rewards, and sometimes punishments, in the different schools.

b) the degree of *ascriptiveness* of a system: whether status was awarded because of who a person *is*, or because of what he *does*. The schools differ sharply in the importance of family background for the status system, with family background generally being more important in schools which have a high component of upper-middle-class children. In such systems, where social acceptance depends upon a person's fixed attributes rather than what he *does*, there are many people whose efforts are dampened completely, since these efforts can gain them nothing.

c) the *range* of activities rewarded. In some schools, such as Green Junction, a single activity (e.g., football) completely dominates the status system. In others, like Marketville, a boy can be *either* a scholar or an athlete, and receive the rewards of his peers. In still other schools, like Maple Grove and Executive Heights, the range of rewarded activities is just as narrow as in Green Junction, but the rewarded "activity" includes a combination of elements: a boy must be an athlete *and* a reasonably good student *and* have social sophistication *and* have enough money to dress well and meet social expenses. The system is no more pluralistic than that of Green Junction in the activities it rewards; it is the special combination called the "all-around boy" that is rewarded.[2]

How then can the status systems among adolescents be changed? There have been many clues throughout the preceding chapters, and it will be the intent of the succeeding sections to examine the implications of these clues.

The Opportunity for Responsible Action

One of the most important recent changes in adolescents has been their increasing social sophistication. They are no longer content to sit and be taught. It is Executive Heights, not Farmdale, where the "brilliant student" image is most shunned by girls; it is Executive Heights where the boys are uninterested in the quiet, conforming, studious girl, obedient to teachers' and parents' demands. Modern adolescents are not content with a passive role. They exhibit this discontent by their involvement in positive activities, activities which they can call their *own:* athletics, school newspapers, drama clubs, social affairs and dates. But classroom activities are hardly of this sort. They are prescribed "exercises," "assignments," "tests," to be done and

[2] There are numerous important variations in status systems which remain unexamined. For example, there has been no examination of the question of whether all students in school award status on the same bases, or whether these bases differ from group to group. Is the school broken down into relatively separate status systems, or does it have a single, all-encompassing one?

handed in at a teacher's command.[3] They require not creativity but conformity, not originality and devotion, but attention and obedience. Because they are exercises prescribed for all, they do not allow the opportunity for passionate devotion, such as some teen-agers show to popular music, cars, or athletics. Compare, for example, the diversity among students in time spent watching television with their homogeneity in time spent on homework. Television apparently "captures" some adolescents and pulls them further and further, while homework captures no one, but remains compressed toward an average level. Jacques Barzun, discussing the schoolwork carried out by students, notes this lack of passionate devotion:

> No, it is at best industry, a virtue not to be despised, but lacking the essential element of work, which is passion. It is passion in work and for work that gives it its dramatic quality, that makes the outcome a possession of the worker, that becomes habit-forming and indeed obsessional. Of all the deprivations that modern life imposes on intellectual man, the abandonment of work is the cruellest, for all other occupations kill time and drain the spirit, whereas work fills both, and in the doing satisfies at once love and aggression. That is the sense in which work is "fun," with an irresistible appeal to man's love of difficulty conquered.[4]

Barzun writes of college students, where the problem exists as it does in high schools. In college as well as in high school, the opportunity for passionate devotion to scholarly work is nearly absent. The structure of education puts both a floor and a ceiling upon scholarly effort, and prevents scholarship from truly competing for an adolescent's energy.[5]

In part, the floor and the ceiling are established by the prescribed "assignments," in part by the norms of the adolescent community against excessive effort. Not only do these "exercises" seldom provide the opportunity for passionate devotion by a boy or girl; when they do so, his efforts are purely individual, and contribute nothing to the

---

[3] I do not mean to suggest that all schoolwork is of this sort. Some teachers are able to devise projects involving positive, responsible, creative action of the sort I suggest below. However, these are sporadic cases, dependent on the special abilities of a teacher. The problem is to build a structure of education in which the ordinary teacher can easily develop such activity.

[4] Jacques Barzun, *The House of Intellect* (New York: Harper & Row, Publishers, 1959), p. 125.

[5] For a discussion of education and the competition for energy, see James S. Coleman, "The Competition for Adolescent Energies," *Phi Delta Kappan,* 1961.

adolescent community as a whole. Instead, they make matters more difficult for others, who must work harder to keep up with this "curve-raiser." The norms of the adolescent community, damping down such excessive effort, are merely a response to this situation.

Another consequence of the passive, reactive role into which adolescents are cast is its encouragement of irresponsibility. If a group is given no authority to make decisions and take action on its own, the leaders need show no responsibility to the larger institution. Lack of authority carries with it lack of responsibility; demands for obedience generate disobedience as well. But when a person or group carries the authority for his own action, he carries responsibility for it. In politics, splinter parties which are never in power often show little responsibility to the political system; a party in power cannot show such irresponsibility. In an industrial plant, a group of workers that has no voice in decisions affecting it is purely irresponsible; a stable union with a role in decision-making is responsible. An adolescent society is no different from these.

In the history of education in America, this fact is exemplified well. One of the major avenues for positive action, for passionate devotion to a task in high schools and colleges, is in athletic contests. However, colleges and high schools did not always have such contests. Their introduction had a great impact upon discipline problems in school. As one pair of authors notes, "The early history of American colleges, before the advent of organized sports, is full of student violence, directed at each other, at the faculty, the institution, and the townies." [6] Organized athletics provided an avenue for positive action of the student body as a unit, and this action carried its own discipline with it. It is likely that without organized athletics, some of the high schools in this research would show violence and rebellion of the sort described above. In other schools, there are enough different extracurricular avenues to capture this energy. But in none of the schools is this possibility for positive, responsible action built into the purely scholarly activities—except in isolated examples, like debate teams.

The present research, and more particularly this chapter, cannot lay out a concrete plan for a structure of education which answers this problem. The above paragraphs state the problem, and the comments below indicate possible means of partial solution.

---

[6] Burton R. Clark and Martin Trow, "Determinants of College Student Subculture," in *The Study of College Peer Groups*, Theodore Newcomb, ed., 1961. See also Richard Hofstadter, "Part One: The Development of Higher Education in America," in R. Hofstadter and C. Hardy, *The Development and Scope of Higher Education in the United States* (New York: Columbia University Press, 1952).

Competition

Competition in schools has always had an ambiguous position. It has always been explicitly utilized as a motivating device in scholastic activities through the use of grades. It has at times been utilized in other ways, such as spelling bees, debates, and other contests. Yet some educational theory, particularly that of recent years, has emphasized the psychological ill effects which competition, and the resultant invidious comparison, can bring about. Thus the movement in education in the 1930's, 40's, and 50's has been away from scholastic competition, toward a minimization of differences in achievement. At the same time, the attempt to do away with grades has never met with success, and even in the recent anti-competition climate of public education, the use of I.Q. tests has come to be greater than ever.[7]

The attempt to do away with competition as a motivating device in schools is based on three important misconceptions, as follows:

a. There is a failure to recognize that the fundamental competition among children, adults, or anyone, is a competition for respect and recognition from others around them. In different systems, different achievements will bring this respect and recognition. The removal of scholastic achievement as a basis of comparison does not *lessen* the amount of competition among adolescents; it only *shifts* the arena from academic matters to non-academic ones. There is nothing so awesome as the competition between two girls for the attention of a boy; there is nothing so cruel as the world of a girl who's been rejected by a crowd she aspires to. Thus the psychological ill effects of competition are fully as present in a school where there are no grades and no possible comparison of scholastic achievement, as in a school where such criteria are in full view. There are no fewer psychological effects of competition in Green Junction than in Marketville, no fewer in Executive Heights than in Midcity. It is only the *bases* of competition which are different.

b. Learning never takes place without a challenge, that is, a dis-

---

[7] It can probably be easily shown that I.Q. and achievement tests in school serve primarily two purposes, and have increased in use as these two purposes have become more important: as classification devices, for allocating students to classes grouped by achievement level, and as protective devices, to give the teacher an objective standard to justify to parents the poor performance of a child. For example, Executive Heights, in which these needs are greatest, administered a multitude of standardized tests to parents; Farmdale, where these needs are least great, administered almost none.

crepancy between a desired state and one's existing state. A "satisfied" person does not learn, as the similarity of this word to the concept of "satiation" in learning theory suggests. The remarkable strides of young children derive in large part from the wide discrepancy between their present state and an ability to cope with the social world.

Competition is a major means by which such a challenge occurs. Competition against nature, against other persons, against other groups constitute attempts to overcome obstacles. If such competition is removed and no other challenge is substituted, then learning will not take place at all. Because of this, most attempts to do away with competition in schools through a removal of grades have failed, because no substitute challenge was provided. There has been much talk of substituting cooperation for competition, with little recognition that cooperation is not a substitute for competition as a motivating device. It is a tribute to the inconsistency of American ideology that Americans can extol "free competition" as the only device for generating economic enterprise, and at the same time deplore the existence of competition in the classroom, attempting to replace it by communal cooperative efforts.

c. In pointing to the psychological ill effects of the invidious comparisons produced by differential achievement, there is usually a failure to realize that these invidious comparisons are not due to competition itself, but to the *structure* of competition. A person is psychologically hurt when he fails *relative to those around him.* Thus when he fails relative to his friends, when they progress and he stays behind, his psychological equilibrium must be upset. Or when he succeeds while his friends fail, the relation between him and his friends is eroded. Interpersonal competition and the resulting distinctions it creates between potential friends, undercuts bonds between people.[8]

---

[8] This is evidenced in numerous arenas of life. Two examples of research illustrate this well. In the American Army during World War II, the morale of different army units was studied. It was found that Military Police noncommissioned officers had greater satisfaction with the promotion system than did Air Force noncommissioned officers, although their rate of promotion was less. Further investigation indicated that the faster rate of promotion created invidious comparisons among the Air Force officers, and left them dissatisfied. Where almost no one was promoted, in the Military Police, then everyone was doing as well as those around him, and there was satisfaction with the system. See S. A. Stouffer, *et al., The American Soldier,* Vol. 1 (Princeton: Princeton University Press, 1949), pp. 250–254.

A study of the system of ranks and levels among sales clerks in department stores shows the proliferation of minute gradations, each level with its own title.

However, such erosion of interpersonal ties stems not from competition, but from the *interpersonal* structure of scholastic competition. When a boy or girl is competing, not merely for himself, but as a representative of others who surround him, then they support his efforts, acclaim his successes, console his failures. His psychological environment is supportive rather than antagonistic, is at one with his efforts rather than opposed to them. It matters little that there are others, members of other social communities, who oppose him and would discourage his efforts, for those who are important to him give support to his efforts.

Another element in the structure of competition also shapes its psychological consequences. This is the source of the reward. If the win or loss depends upon subjective judgment of a "judge," then there can be maneuvering for position, claims of unfairness, attempts to gain favor of the judge, conformity to the judge's (i.e., teacher's) wishes rather than an all-out attack on the problem, and numerous other degrading activities. Yet when the win or loss stems truly from the activity at hand, as in a footrace, a game of football, or a game of chess, no such subjective judgment occurs. Thus the degrading activities so familiar in the classroom (where teacher is judge and student is competitor for a grade) are absent in other competitions where the race itself decides the winner.

In sum, then, the criticism of scholastic competition in education has been misplaced on several counts. And while this criticism developed, competition of the kind whose effects are most deleterious continued unabated in schools, both in the scholastic arena and in the social arena. It has continued in the scholastic arena simply because educators have found no alternative to it as an energizing device—just as economic systems, including those in Communist countries, have found no substitute for it. The proposals below do not attempt to do away with scholastic competition, but even to increase it in some areas (thus draining off the abscess of purely social competition, with its ill effects). The proposals are aimed at the *structure* within which competition takes place.

The study shows how these gradations and frequent tiny promotions undercut the development of strong communal relations among the clerks, and reduce the possibility of collective bargaining or union formation. See Carl Dreyfuss, "Prestige Grading: A Mechanism of Control," in R. K. Merton et al., *Reader in Bureaucracy* (Glencoe: Free Press, 1952), pp. 258–264.

Interscholastic Competition and the Channeling of Effort

One approach is made obvious by the dominant role of interscholastic athletics in the schools studied here. It is evident in the chapters above that it is the interscholastic structure of athletic competition that directs so much energy toward athletics. It is evident also that part of the reason for less ascriptiveness in the boys' status system is the lack of anything for girls comparable to interscholastic athletics.

Similarly, it is possible to substitute interscholastic (and intramural) competition in scholastic matters for the interpersonal competition for grades which presently exists. Such a substitution would require a revision of the notion that each student's achievement must be continually evaluated or "graded" in every subject. It would instead make such evaluations infrequent or absent, and subsidiary to contests and games, both within the school (between subgroups) and between schools.

Such a change from interpersonal to intergroup competition would also make it necessary to create, with considerable inventiveness, the vehicles for competition, intellectual games, problems, group and individual science projects, and other activities. Yet there are some examples which show that it can be done: debate teams, music contests, drama contests, science fairs (though science fairs as now conducted lack one crucial element, for they are ordinarily competitions between individuals, and not competitions between schools, thus lacking the group reinforcement which would go along with "winning for the school"). There are, in one place and another, math tournaments, speaking contests, and other examples of interscholastic competition.

In other places, one can find the bases from which to develop new kinds of scholastic competition. For example, Rand Corporation sociologists have developed "political gaming," in which teams represent policymakers in various countries. An international situation is set up, the policy-making teams respond to it and to one another's moves (under the supervision of referees), and a game is pursued in earnest. It is not too difficult to see how this, and modifications of it to include legislative politics, union-management bargaining, and other such situations, could be brought to the high school level and used in interscholastic competition. (Rand reports that an experiment in political gaming at MIT induced such interest among the student players and spectators that for weeks afterwards they avidly followed international news events, to see how their moves corresponded with actual policies as they developed.)

As another example, business executives are now being trained in a few companies by "management games," in which hypothetical situations are set up requiring teams of executives to make decisions and take the consequences. Electronic computers provide the hypothetical situation, and teams of executives "play games" in which each team is a firm in competition with the other. With effort and ingenuity, such games could be adapted to training in high school, not only in business economics, but in other areas.

A similar example is a political game recently devised at Johns Hopkins University in conjunction with the 1960 election. A sample of voters was interviewed to determine their attitudes toward various issues. Then processes by which these attitudes could affect vote intentions were programmed on an electronic computer. A class was divided into two sets of campaign strategists (a "Nixon team" and a "Kennedy team") and each team made campaign decisions in an attempt to influence the electorate. These decisions were fed into the computer, which gave back preliminary vote intentions. New decisions were made, and their consequences assessed. After a fixed number of decisions, the campaign was ended, and the candidate with most votes was the winner. In one use of this game, the class learned far more about election processes than in previous courses using ordinary techniques. In part, they taught each other, through their meetings and discussions of strategy. In part they were taught by the results of their previous decisions, as manifested in the effect on the electorate.

There are many examples in high schools which show something about the effects interscholastic competitions might have. When I was attending a small-town school in Ohio, a slight, unprepossessing senior boy placed among the first ten in a state-wide physics competition. From that day, the senior boy—and physics as well—enjoyed a prestige and a prominence neither would have otherwise had. Rather than ridicule or indifference, his efforts were treated with respect and encouragement—for he was bringing glory to the school.

It is true that many of the examples and experiments mentioned above have had far less effect in bringing informal social rewards, encouragement, and respect to participants than the present analysis would suggest. The reason is clear, however: such social rewards from the student body as a whole are only forthcoming in response to something the individual or team has done for *them,* such as bringing glory to the school by winning over another school. If the activity, whether it be debate or math competition or basketball, receives no publicity, no recognition in the newspapers and by the community generally, then its winning will have brought little glory to the school, and will bring little encouragement to the participants. If it does receive recognition, it will encourage not only the participants, but those on the sidelines as well. In many high schools, boys not on the basketball team shoot baskets at noontime; every football team has its "Monday-morning quarterbacks"; a chess game has its kibitzers. In such ways, the energies of even the non-participants turn toward the game activity.

Sporadic and infrequent cases of interscholastic competition in nonathletic activities, with no attention to promotional activity, have little effect. However, if there were systematically organized games, tournaments, and meets in all activities ranging from mathematics and English through home economics and industrial arts to basketball and football, and if promotional skills were used, the resulting public interest and student interest in these activities would undoubtedly increase sharply. Suppose such a set of activities culminated in a "scholastic fair," which like a state fair included the most diverse exhibits, projects, competitions, and tournaments, not between individuals, but between *schools*. I suspect that the impact upon student motivation would be remarkably great—an impact due to the fact that the informal social rewards from community and fellow-students would reinforce rather than conflict with achievement.

These are simply examples of what might be done to change the structure of rewards in high schools—to shift from interpersonal competition, with its conflict-producing effects, to intergroup competition, in which group rewards reinforce achievement. More important than these examples, however, is the general principle—that motivations may be sharply altered by altering the structure of rewards, and more particularly that among adolescents, it is crucial to use the informal group rewards to reinforce the aims of education rather than to impede them.

Contests, Games, and the Absence of Judges

Even when games and contests are interpersonal, rather than interscholastic, they constitute an important difference from the present structure of competition in the classroom. For another deleterious consequence of competition as it exists in the classroom is the prevalence of subjective judgment to decide a student's success. Teachers are forced, by the system which exists, to be judges as well as teachers. Much of the rebellion and the conformity, the alienation and the subservience of students can be traced to this role of the teacher. A system which eliminates these judgments would restore the role of teacher *as* teacher, remove from the teacher the onus of sorting and grading students, and allow a boy or girl to see far more clearly the relation between his work and his resulting success. This is the virtue of contests and games which provide their own criterion of success. In the games described above, the outcome of the game provides the success or failure; no intermediate judgment of a teacher is necessary. To be sure, it is difficult to devise such games in certain areas (e.g., creative writing); but it is not impossible. And even in such areas, the existence of contests (such as debates) makes more explicit the criteria of success, so that attempts to influence the teacher (or judge) can have far less effect.

In general, games and contests, with their explicit (and usually intrinsic) criteria of success remove the ill effects of a teacher's subjective judgment. No longer do the rewards go to the quiet little girl in the front row who makes no trouble for the teacher and is always ready with the "right" answer; the rewards are directly linked to achievement.

Two recent researches are relevant in illustrating the difference between these two kinds of competition. John Holland has studied creativity of National Merit Scholarship winners. He found that among the winners, there was no correlation between scores on tests of creativity and grades received in school. On the other hand, there was a correlation between creativity scores and success in various contests of skill during high school; winning music, speech, art, writing, or science contests, writing something which was published, etc. Those students who had *won* in some such contests of skill were not generally students with the highest grades, but were students with a high potential for creativity. Further, the creative students showed such personal traits as independence, intellectuality, low sociability, while those with high grades showed perseverance, sociability, responsibility, and were rated high on "citizenship" by teachers.[9]

In another study, Getzels and Jackson compared two groups of students: those high in scores on creativity tests, but not especially high in scores on I.Q. tests; and those high in I.Q., but not especially high in scores on creativity tests. Although the two groups were nearly

---

[9] John L. Holland, "Creative and Academic Performance among Talented Adolescents," submitted for publication to *Journal of Educational Psychology*.

identical in their performance on standardized achievement tests, they differed sharply in other respects: the highly creative were far less interested in conforming to the teacher's demands, were far more imaginative, more given to humor, more wide-ranging in their interests. The personal traits they preferred for themselves were negatively correlated with those they felt teachers preferred, while the personal traits preferred by the high I.Q. studies were highly correlated with those they felt teachers preferred. Correspondingly, the teachers in fact preferred the high I.Q. students to the highly creative ones.[10]

The results of these two studies suggest that the teacher's role as judge tends to inhibit creativity, and to systematically underselect creativity. This could hardly be otherwise, for teachers must also be disciplinarians, and their judgments must reward conformity as well as achievement. Creativity can be troublesome to a teacher confronted with classroom discipline. When the outcome is intrinsic to the competition, however, the pure achievement, unadulterated with conformity, is rewarded. At the same time, the contest provides its own discipline for the highly creative, who must organize their energies to succeed, and cannot get by with uncoordinated flashes of brilliance or with mere verbal adroitness.

Games have also a peculiar motivating quality, quite apart from the above considerations. This perhaps derives from the close connection they provide between action and outcome. A player sees the consequence of his moves, and is immediately able to test them against a criterion: the moves of the opponent. An economist has this to say about games and motivation:

> Most human motives tend on scrutiny to assimilate themselves to the game spirit. It is little matter, if any, what we set ourselves to do; it is imperative to have some objective in view, and we seize upon and set up for ourselves objectives more or less at random—getting an education, acquiring skill at some art, making money, or what-not. But once having set ourselves to achieve some goal it becomes an absolute value, weaving itself into and absorbing life itself. It is just as in a game where the concrete objective—capturing our opponents' pieces, carrying a ball across a mark, or whatever it may be—is a matter of accident, but to achieve it is for the moment the end and aim of being.[11]

---

[10] J. W. Getzels and P. W. Jackson, "The Study of Giftedness: A Multidimensional Approach," in *The Gifted Student*, Cooperative Research Monograph No. 2, U.S. Department of Health, Education, and Welfare (Washington: United States Government Printing Office, 1960), pp. 1–18.

[11] Frank H. Knight, *Risk, Uncertainty and Profit* (Boston: Houghton Mifflin, 1948), p. 53.

Unfortunately, the game spirit induced by the present structure of competition in high schools is often a game between students and teachers, the students devising strategies (individual and collective) to reduce the effort necessary for a grade, and the teacher devising strategies to increase this effort.

Competition among Schools for Students

Competition as a motivating device may be used in other ways as well. Almost all high schools in almost all cities serve a single district, and all the students in that district attend that school. Because of this, the school is never induced to attract "customers" by competing in the marketplace of students. There is no such marketplace. As a consequence, a principal's rewards are all for holding the school together, for keeping it running without upsetting the equilibrium, except in special cases when outside forces press for addition or modification of courses. There is no mechanism built into the system itself for change and improvement.

The effect of competition on such a state of affairs can be illustrated by the recent history of certain colleges in the United States. Before World War II, the admissions policies of Harvard, Yale, and Princeton Colleges were heavily weighted toward wealth and position. These were schools for the sons of the business elite in the East, most of whom had attended private preparatory schools. They were too expensive for other boys, and an old graduate's son was given special preference. Since the war, however, a sharp change has occurred in the student composition in these colleges. This occurred first at Harvard, with the introduction of broad scholarship funds, and has occurred more recently at the other colleges. The composition of these student bodies has moved sharply in the direction of public-school scholarship boys.

The consequence of this change has been a sharp shift in the social climate of these colleges. They were once dominated by the "gentleman's C," and all that went with it. Today there are still adherents of this standard, but they are in a minority. The climate of these colleges has shifted from one approximating that which exists today in Executive Heights High School to a climate in which scholastic achievement is a valued accomplishment.[12] The change has been

---

[12] However, because the structure of competition is interpersonal, the student's psychological environment is not supportive, but antagonistic. The atmosphere is one of intense and sometimes bitter interpersonal competition for grades.

largely wrought by the change in admissions policies. The schools are now competing for talented boys, not merely accepting their old grads' sons.

This example serves to show how the climate of certain colleges has changed as a result of competition for students. A similar change is occurring in colleges throughout the country, colleges which once attracted only a local audience, but are now competing for a national one. This competition is fraught with more uncertainties about admission, both for the colleges and the applicants. But for those colleges which are entering the national market, this competition has sharp effects on their social climates.[13]

To be sure, competition *per se* does not bring these effects; the content upon which the competition is based is important as well. But so long as that content includes a large academic component (and in high schools this is partially assured by the increasingly important goal of college admission), then it will shift the social climate of the school in an academic direction.

Such competition is not unknown among high schools, though it is infrequent. There are now, and have been in the past, schools in large cities which accepted only students who qualified by an examination: Townsend Harris and others in New York, Walnut Hills in Cincinnati. But the examples are few, and usually limited to a single school in a city. If all high schools in a city were forced to compete for students, then we might expect surprising changes.[14]

The major point is that school administrators have been deprived of the competitive market as a mechanism for sharpening and improving their products. The structure of schools today militates against change, for every school administrator sees his job as keeping the system in some kind of equilibrium, and keeps a protection against elements which might "rock the boat." If the community desires continual change and improvement in its schools, it must build in a mechanism for such change.[15]

[13] For a discussion of the changes in some schools, see L. Bloomgarden, "Our Changing Elite Colleges," *Commentary*, February, 1960, *29*, pp. 150–154.

[14] David Riesman has proposed the formation of public boarding schools for other effects which the free selection of a school might bring about: the chance for a student to find others who shared his interests, and focus his energies. See his *Constraint and Variety in American Education*, Introduction to Anchor Edition (Garden City: Doubleday, 1957).

[15] The example of competition among colleges shows that a perfect mechanism for such change in colleges is a national scholarship policy, in which the scholarships are *not* allocated to specific colleges, but for which the colleges must compete. A slight variant of this has already occurred with the National Merit Scholarships, for some colleges have begun to seek out near-winners with scholarship offers.

Competition for Salary by Teachers

Teachers have characteristically been paid according to seniority. However, there has been some use, and wide discussion, of merit pay increases. Yet the problems which such a salary scale introduces are great, for the evaluation of a teacher is difficult. The principal's evaluation of teachers is based on subjective and debatable criteria even more than is the teachers' allocation of grades. Merit pay raises in such a situation of ambiguous criteria of merit provide a perfect context for charges of favoritism and unfairness. Furthermore, teachers are hardly known outside their own school, so there is no market mechanism to give them bargaining power and to provide a measure of their value. For one type of teacher in the school, however, merit is far easier to assess, and there does exist a market mechanism for adjusting his value. This is the athletic coach (and in places where debate or music contests are prominent in schools, the debate or music coach as well). The existence of interscholastic competition allows his abilities to be known outside his own school, and the success of his teams provides the criterion. To be sure, there is more to a good coach than providing winning teams; but the coach, like the athlete, has the possibility of becoming known outside the school, and having his talents appraised, while the teacher, as the student, remains in seclusion, his abilities and deficiencies hidden by the walls of the classroom. It is no coincidence that coaches' pay in many schools is so much higher than that of teachers. The structure of activities makes the coach able to bargain for his salary, while the teacher, caught inside the classroom, must wait for his pay increase until national attention becomes focused on the plight of the schoolteacher.

Special Tasks of Education in Modern Society

Let us go back some time, to an earlier way of life. A child at one time had little more to learn than to cope with his physical environment. He needed to learn to draw back when he touched a hot substance; to watch out for moving objects. He needed no school to learn these things, other than the school of hard knocks. Neither did he need a school to learn how to survive, for he learned at the hand of his father to hunt or to till the soil. But when men came to depend on others at far distances, a boy needed to learn to read and write;

and when money came into existence, he needed to learn to count and calculate. He needed to know these things simply in order to survive in this new environment, for the environment involved relations-at-a-distance, and the skills for such relations were not learned by first-hand experience. Thus schools became necessary to inculcate these skills: the three R's of reading, 'riting, and 'rithmetic.

But this change in society to relations-at-a-distance has been succeeded by another, equally important in its implications for education. It might well be termed relations-with-large-institutions. No longer are a man's essential relations mostly with other men; they are often with large institutions or organizations: big government, big manufacturers, big employers, big unions, mass entertainment, and mass persuasion through advertising. Credit financing has become the basis of economic activity, for the consumer as well as the businessman.

Yet a boy or girl has no experience, either in his daily life or in his school classes, with this impersonal world of large institutions. Growing up as a young adult, he has no way of extrapolating his past (which involves only relations with other *people*) into the future, where he is tiny compared to the large entities which surround him. He often does not even know of those agencies designed to help him out of trouble, or to give him advice. So what can he do, except learn by bitter experience?

The recent development of games of strategy using electronic computers provides an answer to this question. Games can be devised in which a boy or girl would face decisions like those he will face in later life, and then feel the consequences of these decisions as they develop. A computer game is possible which is simply the reverse of the management game discussed earlier. The computer would make the many demands upon a consumer's budget, and the student would make decisions as a hypothetical householder. After a hypothetical twenty-year period, the unwary consumer at age 40 would find himself with a new car but a double mortgage on his house and no money to send his children to college.

Games of this type, a game of "careers," in which a boy or girl must weave his or her way through the occupational structure, political games, legislative games, collective bargaining games, and others would provide the adolescent with practice in dealing with those large institutions which make up his environment as an adult. Such games would not be difficult to devise; they would be little more than existing parlor games like Monopoly, Careers, and others, made immensely more realistic and detailed.

The general idea, then, is this: a boy or girl growing up never has a chance to "practice" with many of the difficult problems which will face him as an adult, because these are not interpersonal problems. They are problems involving a more impersonal and more powerful environment—the large institutions with which he must cope if he is to survive in this complex society. Computer games can be used in schools as they have already been used in management training, to provide this practice—to condition him to the world he will face.

A Concluding Note

When problems in education convulsively come to the attention of the public and the government, the responses are simple and direct. If only teachers are paid more, if only school buildings are better, if only laboratory equipment is better, the schools will be all right. But it simply is not so. Besides the examples in this research, there are many others: the survey mentioned earlier of 10th graders in all Connecticut schools showed no relation between achievement and per-pupil expenditure, when intelligence was held constant; a study of the productivity of scientists among American colleges showed that the schools with highest productivity were not the high-cost colleges, but others which had some intangible quality, though they spent less money in educating students.[16]

Like the *nouveau riche*, a newly rich society looks to the simple solutions which can be purchased with money. But neither the status problems of the *nouveau riche* nor the educational problems of a newly rich society can be so easily solved. The solutions are more costly in effort and in reorganization, though sometimes less costly in dollars. To put the matter briefly, if secondary education is to be successful, it must successfully compete with cars and sports and social activities for the adolescents' attention, in an open market. The adolescent is no longer a child, but will spend his energy in the ways he sees fit. It is up to the adult society to so structure secondary education that it captures this energy.

---

[16] See R. H. Knapp and H. B. Goodrich, *Origins of American Scientists* (Chicago: University of Chicago Press, 1952).

3-6 Obligations to self and society in the United States and Germany *

Much has been written about the conscious ideals and unconscious motives of both Germans and Americans (3, 4, 5, 7, 8, 9, 11, 13, 14, 16), but little of it has been based on factual evidence systematically gathered for comparative purposes. The present study does not pretend to be complete or definitive because it is based on a very limited sample of upper middle-class male adolescents, but it does attempt (*a*) to see the value systems of the United States and Germany as functioning wholes and to compare them without prejudice as to which is better, and (*b*) to make the comparisons on the basis of actual measurements taken from individual subjects.

While it is fair to state that it was the intention to make the comparison without prejudice, it is also true that no study can be made without preconcep-

* David C. McClelland, J. F. Sturr, R. H. Knapp, and H. W. Wendt, "Obligations to Self and Society in the United States and Germany," *The Journal of Abnormal and Social Psychology*, Vol. 56, No. 2 (March, 1958), pp. 245-255.

David C. McClelland
J. F. Sturr
R. H. Knapp
H. W. Wendt

tions. So it would be well to state these in advance as explicitly as possible: the general assumption which guided the study was that every society has to strike some kind of a balance between freedom and order, between the wishes of the individual and the obligations of social living, between egocentricism and sociocentricism. Such an assumption has particular value for this study for two reasons. First, two of the best-developed measures of human motivation—n Achievement and n Affiliation—fall easily into one orientation or the other: n Achievement into the egocentric and n Affiliation into the sociocentric orientation. And, second, previous research as well as popular stereotype has tended to picture Americans as "individualistic" (with over-tones of "other-direction" and conformity, to be sure) and the Germans as "sociocentric" (again with a highly individualized sense of honor). So, while this study was designed to be an exploratory inductive enterprise, it was guided by the very general notion that measures should be used that would contrast the two cultures on the obligations to self and to society, although, as the ensuing section will show, many measures were also taken that did not fit precisely into this scheme.

Method

Measures

The materials used consisted of a picture-story test of n Affiliation and n Achievement and a questionnaire. The method of deriving n Achievement and n Affiliation scores from brief written stories to pictures has been fully described elsewhere (12, 17). In this study, the pictures used to elicit stories related to achievement were: a male adolescent at a desk, a foreman and worker in a factory, a "father" talking to his "son" with a farm background, and a man working at a desk in his office. The pictures used for measuring n Affiliation were: seven men seated around a table, a mother-son scene (TAT 6BM), a man standing alone looking out through a door, and a figure underneath a lamp post at night (TAT 20). The instructions for eliciting the stories were standard (12) and so far as possible identical in the two countries. The coding of the German stories was done in German using a translation of the English manuals for scoring n Achievement and n Affiliation.

The questionnaire consisted of 38 items of the F-scale type (1) to which the subject (*S*) was to express the degree of his agreement or disagreement on a scale +3 (for complete agreement) to −3 (for complete disagreement). After the questionnaires were returned, the scale was changed to run from +1 for −3 to 7 for+3, as is common practice, all the results being reported in the latter terms. Three basic orientations influenced the choice of items for inclusion in the questionnaire—the self vs. society dimension already mentioned, previous speculative or research findings on differences between Germans and Americans, and the framework set up by F. Kluckhohn (10) for the comparative study of values. The variety of sentiments covered is illustrated by the fact that at least two items touched on each of the following ideas: achieved vs. ascribed status, loyalty to family and country, emotional control or pride, self-development, kindness and love, community service, affiliative values (friendship), achievement values, other-directedness, man's relationship to nature (e.g., as "over" or "under" nature), the importance of fate and destiny, orderliness and rational planning, and will power. In some cases, a single item was believed to tap more than one of these ideas so that the categories were in no sense conceived as mutually exclusive. In fact, since the categories will play very little part in our analysis, the chief point in mentioning them is to demonstrate how wide a net was cast and to make it easier for subsequent investigators to find obvious areas for comparison that were overlooked.

There were also three open-ended questions at the end of the schedule. The first asked the student to list his extracurricular activities (clubs, hobbies, sports, etc.), which were then simply counted and coded as involving either group or individual activities. The former included all clubs and team sports (soccer, football, basketball), and the latter individual hobbies (e.g., stamp-collecting) and individual sports (hiking, playing chess or tennis). The second open-ended question asked "What are the three things you would most like to teach your children?" and the answers were coded as being either egocentric (e.g., to do well in school, to appreciate music, to enjoy life) or sociocentric (e.g., to be kind, respect others, to be loyal to one's friends). The final open-ended question asked them to list the "six students in your class who you think are most likely to be leading members of their community 30 years from now." The purpose of this item was to break the students roughly into two groups—one consisting of "leaders" and the other of "nonleaders" at least from the point of view of their peers. In all classes tested, both in Germany and the United States, it turned out that roughly half the *S*s received three or more votes and so this cutting point was used to divide the *S*s into "leaders" and "nonleaders," although it should be clear that the categorization is very crude, and that the term "leadership" is being used in a very restricted sense in this context.

Subjects

The *S*s used were males nearly all between the ages of 16 and 19 (mode 17, median nearly 18 in both countries). Furthermore, all of them belonged to what might be called the educational élite who were preparing to go on for higher education either in a college or university. The nature of the sample was dictated to some extent by the way the German educational system is organized. Beginning at the age of 10, German students who are going on to the university tend to be segregated from students with lesser educational or occupational goals (who go to *Volksschule* or *Mittelschule*), so that a sample of German students tested in the "higher" schools around the age of 18 tend to be a more highly selected group than one would find in the ordinary United States high school senior class. Since it was difficult to get a cross-section of German students at this age, it was decided to limit the comparison to the relatively élite group to be found in German higher schools. Fifty-one students were obtained from a Neuprachliches Gymnasium and 36 from an Altsprachliches Gymnasium, in Kaiserslautern, Germany. To match this sample, *S*s were drawn from college preparatory classes in a high school in Utica, New York ($N = 35$) and from a New England private school ($N = 39$). The private school students were tested to provide a group more nearly comparable to those in the Altsprachliches Gymnasium which emphasized a classical curriculum, and also to make certain that the sample of United States *S*s was as highly selected as the German one. They also make the American sample unrepresentative because private schools exist in large numbers only in the northeastern section of the United States, but the purpose of

TABLE 3-1. DISTRIBUTION OF OCCUPATIONAL LEVELS OF FATHERS OF BOYS IN UNITED STATES AND GERMAN SAMPLES

Occupational Level	*U.S.* ($N = 70$) [a]	*Germany* ($N = 85$) [a]
6. Major professional and business executive	32%	24%
5. Minor professional and medium business	26	39
6 and 5 combined	58%	63%
4. Clerical and sales	24	22
3. Skilled mechanical and public service workers	17	14
2. and 1. Semi and unskilled workers	1	1
4 to 1 combined	42%	37%

[a] Information not available on all fathers.

the study is not primarily to get representativeness of each culture but to contrast the value orientations of comparable young male élites within the two cultures. The testing was done in December, 1954 in the United States and in March, 1955 in Germany.

The attempt to obtain boys in the two countries from the same backgrounds was quite successful, as Table 3-1 shows. As expected, the students came predominantly from the upper middle class and therefore constitute an "élite" group in each country, but the proportion of them from different backgrounds was roughly the same in both countries. The difference between Levels 6 and 5 is not significant and, in any case, is more apparent than real because there were 12 students in the German sample whose fathers were teachers in *Höhere Schule*. According to the coding system, high school teachers in the American sample were classified as minor professionals and placed in Level 5, but the fact of the matter is that such teachers in Germany have a considerably higher status than high school teachers in this country and probably belong at the very least somewhere between occupational Levels 6 and 5. If, to take account of this, half of them were classified in Level 6 or Levels 6 and 5 are combined, as in Table 3-1, then the distributions of backgrounds of the boys in the two samples become very nearly identical. Furthermore, the percentages of Protestants and Catholics were around 65% and 28% in both groups. In short, any nationality differences found cannot readily be attributed to differences in the socioeconomic level of the two groups of *S*s, or to age differences (since they were matched for age), or to differences in educational plans (since they were all preparing for college), or to differences in religious background.

Results

The mean score for each of the 38 items on the questionnaire was computed for both the German and American *Ss.*[1] About one half of the items revealed differences between the means for the two nationality groups that were significant at or beyond the .05 level. It would be easy and tempting to work out *post hoc* interpretations of these differences, but probably unwise to do so. Even though great care was taken to make the German translations as precise as possible, it is still highly likely that with emotionally toned sentiments such as those used in the questionnaire, the immediate impact on the statement would not be exactly the same on German and American audiences. So at least some of the differences might be attributed to differences in the way the sentiments were expressed. Furthermore, several of the items that on the surface looked as if they should be tapping the same sentiments yielded contradictory results. For example, the Germans agreed much

[1] These average scores together with the German and American version of each question have been deposited with the American Documentation Institute. Order Document No. 5423 from ADI Auxiliary Publications Project, Photoduplication Service, Library of Congress, Washington 25, D.C., remitting in advance $1.25 for microfilm or $1.25 for photocopies. Make checks payable to Chief, Photoduplication Service, Library of Congress.

more with Item 29, "There is no satisfaction in any good without a companion" ($p < .01$), but agreed less ($p < .05$) than the Americans with Item 2, "No same, normal, decent person would ever think of hurting a close friend." Both items deal on the surface with the importance of friendship, but the Germans subscribe more to the former and the Americans to the latter, which incidentally is one of the items drawn (without the final words "or relative") from the F scale on which Germans generally score higher (4). With such variable results, how can one draw general conclusions as to which country values friendship more highly?

For these reasons it was decided to perform a factor analysis on the questionnaire to pick out those items which belonged together in each country. Such a procedure ensures that the items to be combined are chosen beforehand on the empirical basis of covariation, rather than afterwards, in order to explain the particular grouping of results on individual items. Factor analysis also tends to minimize the importance of the translation factor by yielding groups of items that must have been reacted to in somewhat similar ways in the two countries if matching factor patterns can be obtained. A correlation matrix was set up for each country [2] consisting of 36 of the 38 objective items, the two measures of motivation (n Achievement and n Affiliation), plus the number of egocentric virtues mentioned as being desirable to teach children and the total number of activities the *S* listed. Inspection of the matrices showed that practically none of the a priori clusters hung together. That is, items that had been written to tap the same sentiments were not intercorrelated consistently in both countries. So a factor analysis became all the more urgent. It was clear from inspection that certain items showed what appeared to be only random relations with other items. It was therefore decided to include in the factor analysis only those items whose average intercorrelation with the other items departed from zero at the .05 level or better, or those items whose correlations with other items showed a rate of dispersion exceeding the .05 level of probability. However, in order to make matching of factor patterns in the two countries easier, any item was included in both analyses if it met either criterion or significance in *either* country. Rotation to simple structure was performed blindly on the matrix of 19 items chosen by this method and yielded results readily interpretable in terms of two matching factors plus a set of items that shifted from

---

[2] We are especially indebted to Ralph Haber who ran off the correlations on a high-speed computer.

TABLE 3-2. MATCHING FACTOR PATTERNS OF ITEMS FROM A QUESTIONNAIRE ADMINISTERED TO UNITED STATES AND GERMAN MALES OF HIGH SCHOOL AGE

(Saturations less than ±29 omitted)

	Factor A		*Factor B*	
	U.S.	*Germany*	*U.S.*	*Germany*
Factor A: Rational striving, rationality				
34. I work like a slave at everything I undertake until I am satisfied with the results	43	47	—	—
8. I set difficult goals for myself which I attempt to reach	52	35	—	—
28. Respect is due an older man no matter what kind of a person he is	38	37	—	—
35. A child should never be asked to do anything unless he is told why he is asked to do it	34	38	—	—
6. Nowadays with world conditions the way they are, the wise person lives for today and lets tomorrow take care of itself	−30	−41	—	—
Factor B. "That's life," resignation				
16. There are some people like great artists and musicians who can be forigven for not being considerate of others, kind to the poor, etc.	—	—	33	56
12. Planning only makes a person unhappy since your plans hardly ever work out anyway	—	—	36	43
23. When a man is born, the success he's going to have is already in the cards, so he might as well accept it and not fight against it	—	—	31	37
13. There is no such thing as a really permanent friendship. Your friends change with circumstances	—	—	40	(25)
C items: (those which shift from Factor A to Factor B) Idealistic concern for others, for "decent" social behavior				
27. A man with money cannot really learn how to behave in polite society if he has not had the proper upbringing	—	48	47	—
2. No sane, normal, decent person would ever think of hurting a close friend	—	38	39	—

TABLE 3-2 *(Continued)*

	Factor A		*Factor B*	
	U.S.	*Germany*	*U.S.*	*Germany*
C items—(*Cont'd.*)				
7. It is better to go without something than to ask a favor	—	30	31	—
18. There is hardly anything lower than a person who does not feel a great love, gratitude, and respect for his parents	—	29	40	—
Items with unique patterns				
40. Egocentric values mentioned more often than sociocentric as desirable for children	38	−40	—	—
22. It would irritate me very much to have a watch or clock which was off by several minutes every day or so	−32	46	—	—
24. My political opinion is easily swayed by editorials I read	—	−40	—	—
11. When I see a man working in an ordinary unskilled job, I often wonder why he doesn't try to do better in life	—	—	—	−52
15. If you get bad news it is better to hide what you feel and behave as if you didn't care	—	—	—	33
38. A man who gives his life to helping others in trouble is better than a man who spends his life trying to work out schemes so that there will be less trouble in the world	—	—	—	—

one factor to the other in the two countries, as shown in Table 3-2. Factor A includes five items in each country that saturate ± 30 or more, most of which appear to deal with striving, rationality, and planning. The two most highly saturated items are from the so called v Achievement scale (6), which reflects for the most part the extent to which a person consciously subscribes to achievement sentiments for himself. For simplicity, this factor has been named "rational striving" and perhaps even the one deviant item dealing with the respect due an older man can be thought of as belonging under this heading in the sense that the older man (father figure?) is a kind of symbol or identification figure for people with these sentiments. Factor B contains four items that saturate fairly highly in both countries. It seems to reflect a somewhat passive or resigned attitude toward life with a touch of cynicism, an attitude perhaps best summed up in a shrug of the shoulders and the French phrase "c'est la vie." The interesting thing is that four items switch from being saturated on Factor A in Germany to being saturated on Factor B in the United States. All of them seem to involve a kind of formal concern for the "proprieties," for the abstract code of politeness and obligation to others. As would be expected from this, score on the C items is correlated +.40 ($p < .05$) with Factor A score in Germany but only .06 in the United States. In contrast, the score on the C items is correlated +.28 ($p < .05$) with the score on Factor B in the United States and —.13 in Germany. In other words, explicit concern for "decency" goes with resignation and cynicism in the United States and with rational striving in Germany. The difference is nicely highlighted by the saturations for Item 40, which shows that frequent mention of egocentric virtues is negatively related to Factor A in Germany and positively related in the United States; or to put it more understandably, frequent mention of sociocentric virtues (e.g., loyalty, kindness, honesty) is positively associated with rational striving (Factor A) in Germany but negatively in the United States.

Some of the remaining items with unique factor loadings in the two countries also add to the clear-cut total picture that emerges. For example, perhaps having an inaccurate watch is irritating to Germans high in Factor A because it keeps them from being orderly in fulfilling their obligations, whereas in the United States where orderliness is not a part of the Factor A pattern, being irritable about a watch is not part of the self-picture of the "rational striver." In short, in Germany Factor A is definitely sociocentric: conscientious striving is included in a network of idealistic sentiments relating to decent social behavior. In the United States, rational striving is part of no such framework. On the contrary, sentiments of idealistic concern for "decency" are related to a kind of "un-American" passivity, resignation, and cynicism. In passing, it is perhaps worth noting that two of the C items are from the F scale (one slightly modified) and the other two have an F-scale flavor, a fact which suggests that F-scale-like sentiments may be part of a deviant, rather cynical attitude toward life in the United States, whereas in Germany they are organized into an idealistic pattern dealing with order, efficiency, and striving.

More light on the German-American contrast is shed by Table 3-3 which shows the mean scores for each nationality group on each of the three sets of items derived from the factor analysis, the two

TABLE 3-3. MEAN SCORES FOR VALUES, MOTIVES, AND OUTSIDE ACTIVITIES OF U.S. AND GERMAN MALES AGED 16–19 PREPARING FOR COLLEGE

Variable	*U.S.* (*N* = 74)	*German* (*N* = 87)	*Diff.*	*t*	*p*
Acquiescence score: (36 items) [a]					
M	3.74	3.91	−.17	.58	NS
SD	1.12	1.33			
Factor A: (*S* items) "Rational striving"					
M	15.45	17.30	−1.85	2.40	<.02
SD	4.83	4.81			
Factor B: (4 items) "That's life"					
M	8.36	9.01	−.65	1.08	NS
SD	3.50	4.09			
C items: (4 items) "Concern for decency"					
M	17.92	20.90	−2.98	4.13	<.001
SD	4.88	4.14			
n Achievement					
M	4.69	2.70	1.99	2.93	<.01
SD	4.45	4.01			
n Affiliation					
M	5.34	5.48	−.14	.24	NS
SD	3.70	3.67			
Group activities					
M	5.18	.97	4.21	12.76	<.001
SD	2.60	1.01			
Individual activities					
M	1.45	2.33	−.88	3.52	<.001
SD	1.78	1.24			

[a] Two items dropped, one because it was too complex to be understood, the other because nearly everyone in both countries agreed fully with it.

measures of motivation, and the two kinds of extracurricular activities in which the students said they were engaged. The Germans score significantly higher on Factor A ("rational striving") and the C items ("concern for decency") as expected, and as the first line in Table 3-3 shows, the difference cannot be attributed to a general tendency of the Germans to acquiesce more to items of this sort. That is, since the Germans tend to agree more with all three sets of items included in Table 3-3, it was necessary to check their acquiescence to all items in the questionnaire to make sure that the differences on these sets of items were not due simply to a stronger tendency for Germans to go along with or acquiesce in emotional sentiments of all sorts (2). No such tendency appeared. The German students further list themselves as being engaged in more outside activities of an individual nature—that is, in activities that do not require group organization or participation.

The Americans, on the other hand, score higher on n Achievement and much higher in the number of extracurricular *group* activities that they list. Since the difference in n Achievement score is of considerable importance in subsequent interpretation, and since it might have arisen from coding differences or the "pulling power" of the pictures used, it was carefully checked by comparing subcategory frequencies for each of the pictures used. The German students gave less achievement imagery for each of the pictures used, the smallest difference being for the picture of the student and the largest for the "father-son" picture, which may have been somewhat inappropriate for the Germans since the cattle in the background rather suggested to them an American scene. Nevertheless, even among the Americans this picture evoked the least amount of achievement imagery, and even with it omitted, the difference between the two groups is still significant. So it would be hard to attribute the results to differences in the appropriateness of picture cues for the two groups.

However, it was found that the German scorers had used the category, "task imagery," [3] significantly more often than the American scorers had because, being less familiar with the achievement motive scoring system, they tended, when in any doubt at all, to use this category, whereas the American scorers had been instructed to use it only as a last resort. Consequently, the German mean score might be lower than the American because more real instances of achievement imagery had been classified as doubtful in Germany, which would also mean according to the scoring system that further subcategories could not be scored in such instances. For this reason, a random sample of 46 of the German protocols was rescored in German in the United States by someone with considerable experience in scoring n Achievement in English. The correlation between these scores and the original

[3] In the scoring system for n Achievement (12) "task imagery" has a value (= 0) between "unrelated" (= —1) and "achievement-related" (= +1) imagery.

scores was .70, which is lower than desirable, probably because of the difference in the use of the "task imagery" category. Still, the revised mean score for the German sample was actually *lower* (2.30) than the one given in Table 3-3, indicating that most of the instances of "task imagery" in the German sample should really have been classified as unrelated to achievement at all. So there seems little doubt that so far as this comparison is concerned, the German students are significantly lower in n Achievement score.[4]

The American boys, then, think more frequently in terms of doing well, a finding that is also supported by the greater frequency with which they mention egocentric rather than sociocentric virtues as desirable to teach to children. "Egocentric" is, of course, not meant in an evaluative sense, but refers to the development of individual capacities (to be intelligent, to appreciate music, to enjoy life, etc.). Unfortunately, the German coders did not force all virtues listed either into an egocentric or sociocentric category as the American coders did, but a comparison of the differences in frequency of mention of the two kinds of virtues in the two countries is still legitimate. That is, in both countries egocentric virtues were mentioned more often, but the difference in favor of them over sociocentric virtues was significantly larger ($t = 2.52$, $p < .02$) in the United States than in Germany.

If the Americans are so concerned with achievement, what keeps them in line? What prevents unbridled individualism? How are they to fulfill their obligations to society? The answer apparently lies in their much greater participation in group activities. They are not brought up on sentiments of obligations to others as the Germans are, but from kindergarten on they regularly participate in many more extracurricular functions of a group nature. In fact, by far the most impressive result in Table 3-3 is the low number of group activities listed by the Germans (about 1, on the average) as compared with the Americans (about 5, on the average). In these activities the American student must learn a good deal more about getting along with other people and doing things cooperatively, if these clubs are to function at all. If there is any doubt on this point, there is an interesting pair of items correlated positively both in Germany (+.20) and the United States

[4] Ordinarily such protocols would be scored without knowledge of which group they belonged to but since they were written in different languages, this procedure was not possible in the present case without translating one set into another language. In our view, translation was more objectionable methodologically than the procedure followed here, especially since coding for n Achievement by highly trained scorers is ordinarily done with a re-score reliability of .90–.95, which does not leave much room for unconscious bias to operate.

(+.27) on which the two groups of students differ considerably. They are the following:

Mean scores		
U.S.	*Germany*	
3.30	2.37	#9. The negative opinion of others often keeps me from seeing a movie or play I had planned to attend.
2.84	2.15	#24. My political opinion is easily swayed by editorials I read.

Both groups tend to disagree with these items, but the Germans much more than the Americans ($t = 3.77$, $p < .001$). What is clearly suggested here is the American's greater sensitivity to public opinion, to being guided or directed by others as Riesman has so persuasively put it (15). The American's obligation to develop himself, to achieve, is checked and channelled by the opinion of others in the groups in which he participates so that individualism does not run rampant.

The German is also "individualistic" but in a somewhat different way. He subscribes more than the American to sentiments about rational striving (Factor A) and engages in more individualistic outside activities. Furthermore he agrees more with two other items on the questionnaire which shed light on the nature of this attitude toward the self even though, as evidence, answers to the items do not rank high because they are uncorrelated in either country. The items are as follows:

Mean scores		
U.S.	*Germany*	
3.28	4.88	#7. It is better to go without something than to ask a favor.
3.09	4.92	#15. If you get bad news, it is better to hide what you feel and behave as if you didn't care.

In both cases the Germans agree much more with the item ($p < .001$) than the Americans do, suggesting that they have more pride in self-control and perhaps think of the self as having the will power to exercise restraint in such cases. How is this kind of self to fulfill its obligations to society? Clearly not by "learning from acting cooperatively in groups" as in America but from a strong sense of social obligation, of one's *duty* to others and of the necessity to put such an obligation above selfish interests.

Evidence was also sought for linkages between the two motives measured and the three groups of value items or the extracurricular activity patterns, but none was found. In correlating the two motive scores with the three types of value scores (Table 3-3) and with the total number of individual or group activities in each of the two countries (16 different correlations) only one correlation reached the .05 level of significance and it might well have been obtained by chance. The correlation was between n Affiliation and Factor A ("rational striving") in Germany ($r = -.22$). It gains added significance only because the same correlation in the United States was +.21 and the difference between the two correlations is highly significant. If anything, this result would appear to mean that spontaneous concern for others (n Affiliation) may make it harder to subscribe to an ideological code of individualistic achievement in Germany, whereas n Affiliation may be positively related to rational striving in the United States because achievement values there are more connected to working with others. Nevertheless, the overwhelming impression of this analysis is that motive scores (as obtained from fantasy) and value scores (as obtained from questionnaires) are not correlated and are essentially independent variables. Consequently, great care should be taken to specify the method of measurement when one speaks about such things as an "interest in achievement," which may refer either to the n Achievement score and its correlates or something like Factor A with its correlates.

Finally, an analysis was made to see if the students nominated by their peers as future outstanding citizens differed in any systematic ways from those not so nominated. For the most part they did not. As far as item or factor differences on the questionnaire are concerned, the two groups of "leaders" did not differ significantly from the "nonleader" groups within either country or from each other between countries. Only one finding of possible future interest emerged: in both countries nominated "leaders" had higher average n Affiliation than "nonleaders" ($p < .05$), a fact which suggests that among peer groups, even across nationality differences, it is the spontaneous interest of individuals in others (n Affiliation) that tends to make them "stand out" as potential leaders in the perception of the group members. Further interpretation of these results is not justified in view of the large number of insignificant findings and the possibility that such a "nomination" procedure may not actually select "leaders" in a very stable or meaningful way.

Discussion

The findings of the present study may be most simply discussed in terms of the following table which has been organized in terms of the double obligation of "the individual in society" to fulfill some of his own needs and also to satisfy some of society's needs:

	Obligation to self	*Obligation to society*
United States	High n Achievement, concern for egocentric, "self-development" virtues	High participation in group activities, greater sensitivity to the opinions of others
Germany	High v Achievement (concern for rational striving), greater participation in individualistic activities, more emphasis on power of self to exercise restraint	Greater concern over obligations to an idealistic code of decency (governing interpersonal behavior)

Presumably every culture develops more or less patterned solutions to these two problems if it exists for long, and the individual member learns these norms and reflects them in his behavior and attitudes. The point to notice is that according to this analytic scheme, *both* obligations must be at least in part fulfilled by a majority of its members if the society is to function at all. If society should demand too much of its members, it should eventually collapse through *apathy* or *rebellion* because its members can no longer satisfy their needs. On the other hand, if society is neglected through exclusive concern with individual satisfaction, it should eventually collapse through *anarchy*. No one is interested in the welfare of others and society degenerates into the "war of all against all." Between these two theoretical extremes, there should be all sorts of ways of structuring the two sets of obligations which produce working social systems of greater or lesser efficiency. The data of the present study suggest that the scheme is of some value in presenting the somewhat different ways in which morality is structured in the United States and Germany. In the United States a high spontaneous interest in achievement is counter-balanced by much experience in group activities in which the individual learns to channel his achievement needs according to the opinions of others. In Germany a strong sense of self as a striving, controlling entity is offset by an equally strong sense of obligation to a *code* of decency. Interestingly enough, the American "value formula" appears to be largely unconscious or informally understood, as compared to the German one, at any rate. That is, the American boys have higher n Achievement, which is *uncorrelated* with a conscious value placed on striving, and they participate in many group activities without, it is fairly safe to say, having a very explicitly formulated *moral* justification for such behavior. Yet we are arguing that functionally group activities have just such a moral basis in checking excessive individualism. For the Germans, on the other hand, the whole matter appears to be much more consciously worked out. The moral code is more formal and ideological, as other students of German character have observed (14). Individuals are taught and "know" they have a great obligation to the group and strong egos, which are, however, capable of making sacrifices of personal feelings to meet this obligation. In the present study, the German value pattern appears most clearly in the sentiments expressed on the questionnaire, while the United States value pattern appears most clearly in the projective material and the kind of activity the students engage in.

The present study is obviously of very limited scope. It is based on small samples of German and American boys of predominantly upper middle-class status. But the generalizations drawn from it suggest a much wider application to the cultures involved. What evidence is there from previous studies that our conclusions do or do not apply more generally? Has anything been added or subtracted to what is already known about German and American "national character"? In the main, our results are supported by what others have found previously, with one possible change in emphasis to be noted below. Probably the most sensitive clinical or anthropological comparison of the two countries was made by the social psychologist, Kurt Lewin (11), shortly after he immigrated to the United States from Germany. His observations agree at almost every point with our conclusions. He found "probably no other people as interested in *individual accomplishment* . . . as the Americans" (11, p. 277). On the other hand, he calls attention to the flexibility of Americans, to the ease with which they meet strangers, or appear to change their "personality" (opinions and attitudes) to adjust to new situations. In short, he recognized what Riesman has called the *other-directedness* (15) of many Americans which clearly appears in the data of this study.

So far as the Germans are concerned, he described them as carrying more of their "specific individual characteristics to every situation," as having a greater sense of their own identity as separate individuals than Americans do. This kind of "individualism" we have also met in the reports of our German students with the additional note that the self-concept carries with it connotations of personal striving and self-control. Lewin sees the German's sense of obligation to society largely in terms of his tendency to obey orders from higher authority without question. He says, for instance, "In Germany it seems to be the natural right of the adult to rule and the duty of the child to obey" (11, p. 270). In this respect his opinion is supported by a large number of research workers (1, 3, 4, 8, 13, 16). Their point of view is perhaps best summarized by McGranahan as follows: "The German is noted for his unquestioning obedience to authority, his failure to exercise individual responsibility and act on the basis of independent moral judgment" (13, p. 248).

It is at this point that our study differs most from previous ones, and even here the difference is not so much one of fact, but of interpretation. There seems to be no reason to doubt the evidence that Germans are more obedient. The problem arises when attempts are made to explain why they are so obedient, even when such obedience causes great personal suffering or pain to others. Explanations have frequently been given in terms of such motivating factors as "identification with the aggressor," "authoritarian-submission," "sadomasochistic trends," and the like. All such explanations suffer from doing little more than naming the behavior (i.e., Germans obey because they *like to submit*) and from interpreting it in ways which, however acceptable they may be to outsiders (particularly if they dislike Germans), do not make sense to Germans as the rationalizations that at least consciously lead them to obey. The present study does not pretend to get at unconscious factors behind German behavior, but it does shed some light on why they behave as they do *from their point of view.*

To point up the issue as sharply as possible, compare the average agreement with the following item by our United States and German boys:

Mean scores		
U.S.	*Germany*	
3.50	5.12	#35. A child should never be asked to do anything unless he is told why he is asked to do it.

German boys want explanations significantly more ($p < .01$) than American boys do. On the surface at least, this finding would appear to contradict the notion that Germans are noted for "unquestioning obedience," but one must distinguish between behavior and the attitudes behind it. Suppose we assume that other investigators are correct, that German boys do obey more promptly than American boys, then our problem is to understand why they demand explanations for orders.

Here lies the key to the difference between our interpretation and some others. We believe they obey not because they in some sense like obedience and therefore "obey blindly" but because they have some reason, preferably some idealistic reason, for obeying. Without the reason, without the ideal, obedience is meaningless. Hence, we believe, the German emphasis in our data on obligation to an idealistic code of decency.

To make the contrasting interpretations even clearer, consider the following item from McGranahan's study (13) of German and American high school students:

> Do you think a boy is justified in running away from home if his father is cruel and brutal?

Three out of four of the American boys said they felt the boy was justified in running away, whereas the German boys split about 50-50. McGranahan is inclined to interpret this finding as supporting the hypothesis that Germans are more submissive and more used to obeying family authority without question no matter how cruel it may be. But our previous analysis suggests that the item does not properly distinguish between what Germans do and why they do it. They may in fact be more submissive to cruel fathers, but not, if our interpretation is correct, because it is good per se to submit but because it is a way of discharging one's duty to an ideology of proper behavior to others (including parents as a very special case). In other words, the German boy may understand the question about running away from a cruel father in terms of whether he is willing to endure personal discomfort to follow the code governing children's obligations to their parents, which is seen by him to be clearly correct in the abstract so that not living up to it for personal reasons seems like a form of selfishness. In fact, the overriding importance of this code of social obligation is frequently stressed in German literature by pointing out that it not only may cause suffering to one's self (thus overriding selfishness) but to others as well. McGranahan and Wayne in an interpretation very similar to ours note that in German plays "we find . . . various murders of beloved persons consciously carried out by sympathetically portrayed characters" (14, p. 454). The characters are sympathetic because they *must* sacrifice even their "nearest and dearest" in the interests of a "higher," more idealistic goal. The same theme appears in a popular German fairy tale, *Der treue Johannes*, in which a father must cut off the heads of his twin sons to fulfill an obligation to a servant whom he has wronged. Apparently, Germans learn in this way that the ultimate test of the sincerity of one's commitment to a code of idealistic obligation is the extreme to which one will go in the sacrifice of personal interests or even the interests of *particular* others. It is in this latter sense that the German concern with decency to others is "ideological" rather than "personal," as McGranahan and Wayne (14) point out.

Outsiders may well wonder how a people so concerned ideologically with what we have called "decency" were also capable of so much cruelty to others under the Nazis. Many have struggled with this problem at deep psycho-dynamic levels, but a clue to its solution may lie in the two characteristics of the code of obligation just mentioned. First, it seems to be ideological rather than personal. It applies to "others" in the abstract, not to "particular others," so that it doesn't seem so inconsistent to sacrifice particular others in the interest of an abstract code of right conduct designed for the welfare of the whole group. It is perhaps worth noting in passing that the negative correlation in Germany between n Affiliation and Factor A (sentiments of rational striving and decency) may reflect the conflict between the "ideological" and the personal. It may be harder to subscribe to an *ideology* of personal striving and decency if one has much spontaneous interest in *particular* others (n Affiliation) in a country where particularistic interests are often thought of as conflicting with one's larger obligations.

Second, cruelty may actually appear as the validating sign of the strength of one's commitment to the code, as in *Der treue Johannes.* One must show that he can "take" even doing horrible things to *prove* [5] his commitment to a higher end. Since on this point McGranahan and Wayne's study came to the same general conclusion based on pre-Nazi data as ours does on post-Nazi data, it appears that what the Nazis did was to play up a tendency to idealistic sacrifice of personal interests, even of affiliative ones, always present in German character.

In the main then, our conclusions are supported by other students of German and American character. We differ chiefly in seeing German obedience as a response that at least from the internal point of view is dictated not by a liking for obedience but by a strong belief in the importance of sticking to an abstract, ideological code of right conduct in society. As confirmation of this alternative interpretation, McGranahan and Wayne (14) found that obedience is *not* always good in German plays: but the one time rebellion is legitimate is when it is in the

---

[5] One may even wonder, somewhat paradoxically, if the Germans are forced, functionally speaking, to emphasize self-sacrifice so much just because they have such a strong sense of self. Perhaps the problem is less acute for the American whose sense of personal identity is less well-developed in the sense that he talks more freely to others (Items #7, #15) and is more easily guided by others (Items #9, #24).

interest of some higher good of society as a whole. In short, it is not obedience per se which is good. It is seen as instrumental to an ideology of right social behavior that may on occasion demand rebellion.

Summary

A questionnaire covering various value sentiments and a picture-story test for measuring n Achievement and n Affiliation were administered to 87 German and 74 United States male students preparing for college who had been carefully matched for age (around 18 years) and socioeconomic background (largely upper middle class). A factor analysis of the questionnaire results yielded two factors that could be matched in the two countries and a third set of items that shifted from one factor to the other across countries. The "switch-over" items which dealt largely with decency and obligation to others were associated with Factor A ("rational striving") in Germany and were more strongly accepted by the Germans than by the Americans, as were also the Factor A items. In the United States, the switch-over items were associated with Factor B ("resigned cynicism") suggesting that acceptance of statements about strong obligations to others tend to be associated in the United States with a kind of deviant "un-American" passive resignation. Further analysis showed that the American students were significantly higher than the Germans on n Achievement, on participation in group activities, and in the extent to which they said they were guided by the opinions of others. The Germans for their part reported a greater number of individualistic outside activities and subscribed more to sentiments picturing the ego as independent of others. These results were interpreted to mean that in the United States obligation to self appears as a strong unconscious need for Achievement, and obligation to society as participation in many group activities, and that in Germany obligation to the self appears as a stress on the ego as a separate, unique, willing entity and obligation to society as a moral imperative to place obligation to the "impersonal other" as an abstract code above particularistic, "selfish" considerations. An attempt is made to interpret German "authoritarianism" in terms of duty to such an abstract code rather than in terms of the more usual, somewhat unanalytical and ethnocentric assumption that Germans "like" to dominate and submit more than other people.

References

1. ADORNO, T. W., FRENKEL-BRUNSWIK, E., LEVINSON, D. J., & SANFORD, R. N. *The authoritarian personality*. New York: Harper & Row, Publishers, 1949.
2. BASS, B. M. Authoritarianism of acquiescence? *J. abnorm. soc. Psychol.*, 1955, 51, 616–623.
3. BRICKNER, R. *Is Germany incurable?* Philadelphia: J. B. Lippincott, 1943.
4 COHN, T. S., & KARSCH, H. Administration of the F-scale to a sample of Germans. *J. abnorm. soc. Psychol.*, 1954, 49, 471.
5. COMMAGER, H. S. *America in perspective*. New York: Random House, 1947.
6. DECHARMS, R., MORRISON, H. W., REITMAN, W. R., & MCCLELLAND, D. C. Behavioral correlates of directly and indirectly measured achievement motivation. In D. C. McClelland (Ed.), *Studies in motivation*. New York: Appleton-Century-Crofts, Inc., 1955.
7. DE TOCQUEVILLE, A. *Democracy in America*. (1833). New York: Alfred A. Knopf, 1945.
8. FROMM, E. Hitler and the Nazi authoritarian character structure. In T. M. Newcomb & E. L. Hartley (Eds.), *Readings in social psychology*. New York: Holt, Rinehart & Winston, Inc., 1947.
9. GORER, G. *The American people*. New York: W. W. Norton & Company, 1948.
10. KLUCKHOHN, F. R. Dominant and substitute profiles of cultural orientations: Their significance for the analysis of social stratification. *Social Forces*, 1950, 28, 376–393.
11. LEWIN, K. Some socio-psychological differences between the United States and Germany. *Charact. and Pers.*, 1936, 4, 265–293.
12. MCCLELLAND, D. C., ATKINSON, J. W., CLARK, R. A., & LOWELL, E. L. *The achievement motive*. New York: Appleton-Century-Crofts, Inc., 1953.
13. MCGRANAHAN, D. V. A comparison of social attitudes among American and German youth. *J. abnorm. soc. Psychol.*, 1946, 41, 245–257.
14. MCGRANAHAN, D. V., & WAYNE, I. German and American traits reflected in popular drama. *Hum. Relat.*, 1948, 1, 429–455.
15. RIESMAN, D., WITH GLAZER, N., & DENNEY, R. *The lonely crowd*. New York: Doubleday, 1953.
16. SCHAFFNER, B. *Fatherland: A study of authoritarianism in the German family*. New York: Columbia Univ. Press, 1948.
17. SHIPLEY, T. E., JR., & VEROFF, J. A projective measure of need for affiliation. *J. exp. Psychol.*, 1952, 43, 349–356.

3-7 French parents take their children to the park*

Some of the observations upon which this study is based were made in Paris in the summer of 1947 as preliminary work for a group project on French culture which began in the fall of that year as part of Columbia University Research in Contemporary Cultures (under a grant from the Human Resources Division, Office of Naval Research). Some of the results of that project appear in Themes in French Culture *(Métraux and Mead, 1954). The material presented here has drawn on those findings; also on ideas derived from analysis of French films (Wolfenstein and Leites,* 1950)*; and on Nathan Leites' current, as yet unpublished, researches on France.*

IN PARISIAN FAMILIES IT IS A REGULAR ROUTINE TO TAKE the children to the park. This is a good situation in which to observe how French children play, their relations with one another and with the adults who bring them to the park. In the summer of 1947 and again in the summer of 1953 I had occasion to make such observations in various parks in Paris. As an American watching French children and their parents, I was continuously aware of how they contrasted with American

---

* Margaret Mead and Martha Wolfenstein, *Childhood in Contemporary Cultures,* Chicago: University of Chicago Press, 1955, pp. 99–117. Reprinted with permission.

Martha Wolfenstein

parents and children. I have included these points of contrast in the following account of my observations. The hypotheses about the French which I present draw upon more extensive researches on French culture, of which these observations formed a part.

The "Foyer" in the Park

For the French each family circle is peculiarly self-inclosed, with the family members closely bound to one another and a feeling of extreme wariness about intrusion from outside.[1] This feeling is carried over when parents take their children to play in the park. The children do not leave their parents to join other children in a communal play area. In fact, there are few communal play facilities—an occasional sand pile, some swings and carrousels, to which one must pay admission and to which the children are escorted by the parents. The usual procedure is for the mother (or other adult who brings the children to the park) to establish herself on a bench while the children squat directly at her feet and play there in the sand of the path. Where there is a sand pile, children frequently fill their buckets there and then carry the sand to where mother is sitting and deposit it at her feet. What one sees in the park, therefore, is not so much groups of children playing together while the adults who have brought them for this purpose sit on the side lines, but rather a series of little family enclaves. In a similar spirit the adults bring food from home for the children's mid-afternoon snack (*goûter*); it is rare for them to buy refreshments in the park (and, in keeping with the small demand, there are few facilities for this).

The adults do not seem interested in friendly overtures between children of different families, showing little of the usual eagerness of American parents that their children should make friends and be a success with their age mates. French adults seem to be much more on the alert for negative behavior of other children toward their charges.

These tendencies are illustrated in the behavior of a grandmother and her two-and-a-half-year-old grandson, Marcel. The grandmother seats herself on a bench facing the sand pile, to which Marcel goes, waving back at her across a few feet as if it were a long distance. He keeps looking at her while he plays, and she praises his sand pies. When a little girl steps on one of them, the grandmother scolds her roundly. Repeatedly the grandmother enters the sandbox and takes the little boy away from the others, telling him to stay in his own little corner. She

[1] Cf. Métraux and Mead, 1954, Part I.

makes frequent negative comments about the other children, remarking to me: "Have you ever noticed in children how some of them have the spirit of evil [*l'esprit du mal*]? Marcel, however, never destroys other children's things; he is very well brought up [*très bien élevé*]." The little boy, though on the whole he seems friendly toward other children, has the idea of demarcating his own little space and safeguarding it from intrusion. Thus, when another boy sits down on the cement edge of the sandbox where Marcel has a row of prized sand pies that grandmother has helped him make, he is anxious about the other boy getting too close and makes a barrier with his hand between the other boy and the sand pies; then, becoming increasingly uneasy about these fragile possessions, he starts gently pushing the other boy away (Sèvres-Babylone, July 23, 1953). In such little daily experiences the child learns from the attitude of the adult to carry over into the world outside the home the feeling of separateness and the need to guard one's own against possibly dangerous intruders.

There seems to be a continual mild anxiety that possessions will get mixed up in the park. Mothers are constantly checking on the whereabouts of their children's toys and returning toys to other mothers. One woman hands a toy shovel to another, saying: *C'est à vous, madame?* (Sèvres-Babylone, July 21, 1953). Toys seem to be regarded as the possessions of the parents, and mislaid ones are usually restored to them. While parents are concerned to keep track of their own child's toys, they seem particularly upset if their child has picked up something belonging to another and are apt to slap the child for it. This happens regardless of whether there has been any dispute and where the owner may be quite unaware that another child has picked up something of his.

The following incidents illustrate these attitudes. A girl of about two is holding a celluloid fish belonging to a boy of about the same age. Though the boy makes no protest, the attendant of the girl scoldingly tells her to give it to him, pushes her forward, and after the girl has handed the fish to the boy, hustles her back to her own bench (Parc Monceau, September 10, 1947).

A girl of about two has picked up a leather strap from a neighboring group. Her nurse reproves her, takes her by the hand, and returns the strap. A little later a boy of about the same age, belonging to this neighboring family, plays with the little girl, picks up her pail, and keeps it while the little girl is fed by her nurse. The boy's grandmother becomes aware that he has the pail, hits him on the buttocks, scolds, and, taking him by the hand, returns the pail to the girl's nurse. In front of the nurse she repeatedly hits the boy about the head and ears (Parc Monceau, September 10, 1947).

A three-year-old boy has been playing with a borrowed scooter, when his mother notices that the handlebar grip is torn. She takes hold of the scooter with one hand and the child with the other, goes over to the mother to whom the scooter belongs, apologizes, and scolds the boy in front of her (Luxembourg, September 11, 1947).

Among American children issues of ownership versus sharing tend to arise when two children dispute about the use of a toy. What is considered desirable is that the child should learn to share his playthings, which are his property, with others. French children seem to be taught something quite different. Toys are familial property, and those belonging to each family must be kept separate. Just as the children with their parents or other familial adults form a close little circle in the park, so their belongings should remain within this circle. The child who brings into this circle something from outside seems to be introducing an intrusive object, which arouses all the negative sentiments felt, but from politeness not directly expressed, toward outsiders. At the same time it is an offense to the outsiders, whose belongings are thus displaced, and restitution and apologies to them are required. Also, as French adults are much preoccupied with property and with increasing their own, they have to ward off the temptation to do so by illegitimate means. The child's easy way of picking up others' things may evoke in adults impulses to take which they strive to repress in themselves and which they therefore cannot tolerate in the child.

Friendly behavior between children of different families is not encouraged by the adults. A pretty nine-year-old girl is playing with a boy of the same age and his sister, about a year older. The boy clowns a great deal to impress the girl, who is rather severe and unamused. Having finally won a smile from her, he flirtatiously pinches her chin and asks her name. She does not answer. Her grandmother, watching this, remarks humorously to the boy: "She didn't tell you?" The grandmother seems quite content with the girl's aloofness and a bit mocking toward the frustrated little boy [2] (Luxembourg, July 21, 1953).

Adults also seemed apt to interpret children's approaches to one another as more negatively motivated than they were. The mother of a five-year-old boy who is approaching a three-year-old repeatedly calls to him: *Claude, laisse le petit garçon!* It is not clear at first whether Claude is more interested in the other boy or in a ball which he is holding. However, when the ball has been taken by the younger boy's mother, the two children sit in the sand and play together quite amicably. Claude makes the younger boy laugh. At no time had the little

[2] Cf. in *The Remembrance of Things Past,* Proust's account of Marcel's long-term childhood attachment to Gilberte, whom he used to see only in the park.

one shown any sign of not wanting Claude to play with him (Luxembourg, September 11, 1947). In thus underestimating the children's positive impulses toward one another, the adults may be projecting their own negative feelings toward strangers. It would be mistaken to infer, on the grounds of this adult discouragement, that the capacity for friendship fails to develop in children and adolescents. Other evidence suggests that just the opposite is true.[3] Parental approval or urging does not constitute the only auspices under which the child can find a friend. Sometimes the most intense friendships develop without the encouragement or against the discouragement of the older generation.[4]

Secret Solidarity of Brothers

In the following incident one can observe the friendly relation of two brothers which becomes more outspoken when they get by themselves, away from the adults.[5] The two boys, of about six and seven, very neat, dressed alike in blue jerseys and white shorts, are playing together in the sand of the path. Their father sits talking with two women, who appear to be friends of the family, and the boys' sister, about a year older, sits on a bench with her doll. As the younger boy moves into the father's field of vision, the father slaps his hands and face, presumbly because he has got himself dirty. This puts an end to the sand play; the two boys sit down, subdued, on the bench, and, as the father turns away, the older presents the younger with a cellophane bag —a gesture of sympathy and compensation. After a time the father suggests to the girl that the children take a walk around the park, and they immediately set out. On their walk the boys keep close together, leaving the girl to herself. As they get farther away from the father, the boys begin putting their arms around each other's shoulders. They become much more animated and point things out to each other as they go. As they get nearer to the father again on the return path, they drop their arms from each other's shoulders, drift apart, and again become more subdued. Having returned, they seat themselves quietly again on the bench (Parc Monceau, September 4, 1947).

[3] Métraux and Mead, 1954, Part I.

[4] Roger Peyrefitte's *Amitiés particulières* (1945) recounts a special case of intense homosexual attachment in a strict Catholic school where any meeting of two boys alone together was taboo.

[5] The importance of dyadic relations in the family is indicated in Métraux and Mead (1954), Part I.

Acceptance of the Little Ones

French children show a great readiness to play with children younger than themselves, in a way which contrasts strikingly with the behavior of American children. It is typical of American boys particularly to be intolerant of the "kid brother" who wants to tag along and get into the big boys' game when he isn't good enough.[6] An American boy of seven will complain that he has no one of his own age to play with; the neighbors' little boy is six. In America there tends to be a strict age-grading, which the children themselves feel strongly about.

In contrast to this, French children appear interested in younger children and ready to accept them in their games. A boy of eight or nine will play ball with a smaller boy, a five-year-old or even a two-year-old, without showing any impatience at the ineptitude of the younger one. The two children may be brothers or may belong to families that know each other (Sèvres-Babylone, July 21 and 23, 1953). A slender blond boy of about seven seems completely absorbed in a little girl of two or three whom he follows around, bending over to speak to her. The mothers of the two children are acquainted with each other, and the boy and his mother both shake hands with the little girl's mother when she leaves the park. The boy looks quite disconsolate without his little friend; eventually, at his mother's suggestion, he picks up his scooter and slowly pushes off on it (Parc Monceau, September 18, 1953).

Such interest, particularly on the part of boys, in younger children differs markedly from the American pattern, where interest in babies becomes strictly sex-typed for girls only and out of keeping with the boy's ideal of masculine toughness.

On another occasion I observed a group of seven children, ranging in age from about nine to under two, who had been brought to the park by two nurses. They played a number of group games in which the six- to nine-year-olds regularly included a three-year-old little girl, who was given her turn like the rest. In an interval of play, the children sat on a bench, and a couple of the older girls and a boy of about eight took turns in holding and cuddling the baby boy, who was less than two and

[6] Margaret Mead has pointed out the position of the American "kid brother," whom the older boys regard as a nuisance because he tries to get into their games and he isn't good enough. The recent film, *The Little Fugitive,* gives a vivid instance of this.

who accepted their embraces quite complacently (Luxembourg, September 22, 1953).

This sort of grouping which includes a considerable age range may derive from the requirement of staying within the family circle or the circle of children whose parents know one another. Where the American child is expected from an early age to become a member of a peer group outside the family, for the French child the family and the contacts which the adults make with other families remain decisive. While, from the American point of view, this may appear restrictive, it also facilitates friendly relations between older and younger children, including notably affectionate quasi-paternal feelings of older boys toward small children.

It should perhaps be added that in school there seems to be a sharp awareness of small gradations of age. Thus a six-year-old little girl, the child of some friends of mine, informed me that in her class in school the children were seated according to age and that it was mainly the "babies" who were punished by the teacher (who put them in the wastebasket, according to my young informant, or consigned them to the place under her desk). The little girl telling this was evidently not one of the "babies." However, the order of precedence prevailing in the classroom does not seem to carry over outside it.

To the extent to which I was able to observe exclusive groupings, these seemed to be more in terms of sex than of age, though this also appeared much less sharp than among American children. The pair of brothers, of whom I spoke earlier, who were so closely allied but excluded their sister illustrate this. On another occasion I observed a group of girls of various ages (from about four to about seven) playing together at making a garden in the sand of the path (laying down rows of pebbles, etc.) and brusquely throwing out any little boy who intruded ("Boys aren't allowed in the garden. Only girls are allowed in, because we made it.") (Luxembourg, September 11, 1947). This, however, was not frequent; usually boys and girls played quite readily together.

Grownups Stop Children's Aggression

French children are not taught to fight their own battles, to stick up for their rights, in the American sense of these terms. If one child attacks another, even very mildly, the grownups regularly intervene and scold the aggressor. The child who is attacked is likely to look aggrieved or to cry, to look toward his mother or go to her. He does not hit back, nor is he encouraged to do so. An attack is thus not a challenge which must be met by the attacked to save his self-esteem. It is a piece of naughty behavior to be dealt with by the adults.

In the following instances one can see how quickly adults intervene in even very slight manifestations of aggression. Among a group of small children playing on a sand pile, a girl of about two and a half takes a shovel away from her four-year-old sister and walks away with it, looking back in a mildly provocative way. The older girl remains seated and simply looks dismayed. The younger one is already going back to return the shovel when the mother comes over and scolds her, calling her *vilaine*. The little one gives back the shovel, and the two resume their digging (Parc Monceau, September 4, 1947).

Two girls about three years old are seated on the sand pile. One takes hold of the other's pail, not removing it but only holding on to the rim. The owner of the pail cries but makes no other defense. An elderly woman, grandmother or nurse of the attacker, intervenes, reprimands, and the girl lets go. The woman reassures the victim, who stops crying. The woman continues to scold her charge, who moves away from the sand pile (Parc Monceau, September 4, 1947).

In an incident cited earlier, where a little girl stepped on a little boy's sand pie, the boy looked toward his grandmother with an expression of amazement and distress. The grandmother promptly launched into a biting verbal attack on the little girl: *Vilaine! Vilaine fille! Tu commences maintenant à faire des sottises!* A little later when another girl was throwing sand into the sand pile, the grandmother scolded her repeatedly, telling her it could get into children's eyes. The girl's mother, a little way off, then chimed in and told the girl to stop. Protective as she was of her little grandson, the grandmother was equally ready to interfere in an aggressive act of his. Thus, when he was pushing another boy, who did not even seem to notice the rather gentle pressure, the grandmother called to him to stop, that he would make the other boy get a *bo-bo*, and the grandson stopped (Sèvres-Babylone, July 23, 1953).

Thus what French children learn is not the prized Anglo-Saxon art of self-defense or the rules that determine what is a fair fight.[7] What they learn is that their own aggression is not permissible.

A consequence of the prohibition against physical aggression is that verbal disputes are substituted for it.[8] Also, in the case of any

[7] Margaret Mead describes how, on an American playground, mothers keep admonishing their children to stick up for their rights, to fight for themselves, and to fight fair (Mead, 1942, pp. 141–42).

[8] A stock French parental injunction is: *Disputez, mais ne vous battez pas.*

serious conflict there is a tendency for everything to come to a standstill, for all involved to become immobilized.[9] This was illustrated in a family of five children whom I observed, where a quarrel between two of them brought their play to a complete stop. The four older children (three boys of about twelve, nine, and eight and a girl of about seven) were playing hide-and-seek, while the youngest girl (about six) sat beside her mother, who was knitting. The goal was the chair on which the youngest child was sitting. It happened repeatedly that the second oldest boy, Philippe, a snub-nosed mischievous-looking fellow, did not come out of hiding when he was called. The eldest, a slender, quick, excitable boy, became quite desperate about this, shouting repeatedly: "Philippe! Philippe!" when his brother refused to appear, but not running to look for him. The mother chided him for his shouting, saying, *C'est suffisant.* (Shouting, incidentally, is very rare in Paris parks.) When Philippe finally showed up, in his own good time, smiling provocatively, his elder brother scolded him. Philippe disappeared behind a pedestal against which his mother was sitting; the older boy followed, and evidently hit him, because Philippe was crying when they emerged. The mother appeared to rebuke the older boy. There then followed a prolonged acrimonious dispute between the older brother and Philippe, the game giving way entirely to this dispute. The younger girl and boy, who had participated in the game in a gay and likely way, now became immobile, not joining in the argument or demanding that the game go on or instituting a game of their own, but just standing and gazing abstractedly into the distance. The mother continued to knit, and the father, who had joined them, read his newspaper.

I had the feeling that American children in similar circumstances would, out of a greater urgency for physical activity, have managed to get their game going again. The aggressive feelings would have become dissipated in strenuous action. For the French, the prohibition of fighting seems to extend itself to a general inhibition of motor activity where a conflict has arisen. Everyone becomes immobilized, while protracted and inconclusive verbal hostilities ensue. (This paralyzing effect of conflict is also exemplified in French politics, where *l'immobilisme* in the face of contradictory demands from opposing sides is acknowledged as a central reality.[10])

---

[9] Abel, Belo, and Wolfenstein, 1954.

[10] Nathan Leites, unpublished research in French politics.

Restraint in Motor Activity

To an American visitor it is often amazing how long French children can stay still. They are able to sit for long periods on park benches beside their parents. A typical position of a child in the park is squatting at his mother's feet, playing in the sand. His hands are busy, but his total body position remains constant. Children are often brought to the park in quite elegant (and unwashable) clothes, and they do not get dirty. The squatting child keeps his bottom poised within an inch of the ground but never touching, only his hands getting dirty; activity and getting dirty are both restricted to the hands. While sand play is generally permissible and children are provided with equipment for it, they seem subject to intermittent uncertainty whether it is all right for their hands to be dirty. From time to time a child shows his dirty hands to his mother, and she wipes them off.

Among some children between two and three I noticed a particularly marked tendency to complete immobility, remaining in the same position, with even their hands motionless, and staring blankly or watching other children. A French child analyst suggested that this is the age when children are being stuffed with food and are consequently somewhat stuporous. Occasionally one could see children of these ages moving more actively and running about. But the total effect contrasted with the usual more continuous motor activity which one sees in American children. Also, French children seemed more often to walk where American children would run.

The same French child analyst told me about a "hyperactive" six-year-old child who had been referred to her for treatment. The teacher had brought it to the mother's attention that he was never seated, but constantly moving around at school. I asked whether this was so unusual and was told that the teacher had never seen anything like it, so she knew the boy was ill. Ordinarily, children of this age sit quite motionless in school; as the analyst put it, it is so quiet you can hear a fly flying. As we spoke of the greater activity of American children, the analyst, who had lived for some time in America, remarked that she found many American children *insupportable* in their tendency to keep incessantly in motion.

Thus there appears to be considerable adult intolerance for children's motor activity, which is effectively communicated to the children. The requirement of keeping clean and the inhibition on physical aggression contribute to the restriction of motor activity, and so does the distrustful feeling about alien space, outside the family circle. The relation between restraint on aggression and on large-muscle activity was remarked upon by another French child analyst, who had treated both French and American children.[11] She observed that an American child in an aggressive mood would throw things up to the ceiling, while a French child would express similar angry impulses by making little cuts in a piece of clay.

Forceful activity on the part of children is apt to evoke warning words from the adults: "Gently, gently." Two brothers about nine and six were throwing a rubber ball back and forth. The younger had to make quite an effort to throw the ball the required distance; his throws were a bit badly aimed but did not come very close to any bystanders. His mother and grandmother, who were sitting near him, repeatedly cautioned him after every throw: *Doucement! Doucement!* I had the feeling that it was the strenuousness of his movements which made them uneasy, though they may also have exaggerated the danger of his hitting someone (Sèvres-Babylone, July 23, 1953). Similarly, when two little girls about four and five were twirling around, holding each other's hands, an elderly woman seated near by kept calling to the older girl: *Doucement, elle est plus petite que toi.* To which the child answered that they were not going very fast (Parc Monceau, September 18, 1953). The implication here seems to be that any rapid or forceful movement can easily pass into a damaging act.

The tendency to talk rather than act appears not only in substituting verbal disputes for fighting but also in prolonged talking, which postpones activity, where the activity is not of an aggressive nature. The preponderance of talk over action was striking in the following incident. The younger of two brothers, about six and eight, has a toy airplane of which he is winding up the propeller. The older boy reaches for the plane, but the younger one keeps it, and the older does not persist. Several slightly bigger boys gather around interestedly (this airplane was the only toy of its sort which I saw in the park). A prolonged discussion ensues about how to launch the plane, whether at this angle or at that. They talk and talk, and the boy with the plane continues to wind the propeller. Watching them, I began to feel rather acutely that there was no action: how about trying actually to fly the plane? Finally, it was set off and was a complete failure, nose-diving about four feet from the takeoff. The interest of the boys, however, did not diminish; they continued their discussion while the owner of

---

[11] Cf. Françoise Dolto, "French and American Children as Seen by a French Child Analyst," in this volume (p. 408).

the plane again began winding up the propeller. Though a subsequent flight was as bad as the first, no one seemed to draw the conclusion that the plane was incapable of flying. Interest continued, despite failure in action; one of the older boys took the plane out of the hands of the younger one; and the discussion did not lose its zest, despite its lack of practical results (Parc Monceau, September 18, 1953).

On the same occasion the play of another boy whom I observed, with a paper airplane, seemed to demonstrate very nicely the feeling about remaining within a small space. When American boys make planes out of folded paper, these planes are generally long and narrow, with a sharp point, with the aim of their being able to fly as fast and far as possible. In contrast to this prevailing American style, the French boy had folded his paper plane in a wide-winged, much less pointed shape. It moved more slowly through the air and did not go any great distance, but within a small space described many complicated and elegant loops.

Another time I observed a game where an active chase was led up to by elaborate preliminaries in which action was slight. This seemed comparable to the protracted talk postponing action. Five children (of about six to nine) were playing together with a young nursemaid. The nursemaid sat on a bench while the children performed charades in front of her, the performance being preceded by considerable consultation among themselves as to the subject they would enact. As the nursemaid ventured various guesses, the children interrupted their act several times to explain the exact rules of the game to her. When she finally uttered the right word, this was the signal for them to run and her to chase them. Any child she caught before they reached a certain tree then joined her on the bench and helped to guess and to chase the next time round. But before the next brief chase there were again the consultations and the pantomime. Other children's games in which an introductory ritual precedes a chase are common, but I am not familiar with any in which the less active preparatory phase is so elaborate, where talk and small movements occupy such a large part of the game and the chase comes only as a brief finale.

The Child Alone

French children manifest a greater tolerance for being alone than American children do. Just as they do not show the urge to be incessantly in motion, which one sees in American children, so also they do not show the need to be constantly with other children. When I speak of a child being alone, I mean alone with the adult who has brought him to the park. But this may mean in effect being very much alone, since, as a rule, the adult pays little attention to him. There is usually little interchange in the park between adults and children over one and a half. While mothers and nurses direct a good deal of affectionate talk to a baby in a carriage, they tend to ignore the three-year-old squatting at their feet or sitting on the bench beside them. The child who is able to walk around is, as it were, on his own, even if he is moving around very little. Most of the time the adults read, or knit, or just sit, or talk with other adults of their acquaintance. The child who does not have siblings to play with or other children of families with whom his parents are acquainted may play with a doll or play in the sand or sometimes just sit beside mother without a word being exchanged. There were instances where a mother or a father, a grandmother or nurse, kept up a more lively contact with a child, talking and even playing with him, but this seemed to be the exception rather than the rule.

Where children have others to play with and participate eagerly in common games, they still do not show the need for unbroken social contact. There are intermissions in their play when each may go off by himself. In the group of children of whom I spoke before, seven children of various ages, accompanied by two nurses, a series of organized games (such as charades) were played, which the children seemed to enjoy very much. They could also play in a less organized way, as when they took turns in cuddling the baby or carrying him around. But there came an interlude when they separated. One of the older girls had gone off to take the baby to the toilet, having been given five francs for this purpose by the nurse (this, incidentally, showed an exceptional scruple, as generally children up to six or seven were permitted to urinate in the open). The boy of eight then went a little apart and stood on a chair. He gazed around, looked toward the tennis courts, fingered his collar and his lips, and picked his nose. While in the games he had been lively, smiling, agreeable, and occasionally clowning, he now appeared immobile and abstracted. At a little distance his older sister leaned against a tree, watching one of the younger girls play with a toy that was thrown into the air and caught with a string. While these children came together again shortly afterward, they had chosen for a while to be detached and alone. The moments of detachment, particularly clearly in the case of the boy who was fingering his nose and lips, suggest that the child does not feel so uneasy about autoerotic activities or solitary fantasies that he must be constantly with others to guard against them (Luxembourg, September 22, 1953).

Where there is a choice of either playing alone or with others, playing alone may be preferred (which again I think would be very rare among American children). Three girls of about thirteen were playing near one another, each with the kind of toy which is whirled into the air from a string and caught again, a game requiring considerable skill. The three of them, all quite proficient, continued this play, each by herself, for at least an hour before they joined together and began passing the whirling object from one to another (Luxembourg, September 22, 1953).

For the French child, being alone is partly enforced by the closed family circle, where he is confined with adults, who are often aloof from him. There is some evidence that the child in the circle of adults, preoccupied with their own affairs, may feel painfully abandoned.[12] However, he also seems to achieve a certain tolerance for being by himself, so that, where various possibilities are open to him, he exhibits a range of activities, alternately social and solitary.

It may be added that for the French the mere presence of others, even if there is no overt interaction with them, appears to constitute a valued form of sociability. This would apply to the child who plays by himself alongside other children in the park as well as to the adult who sits alone with his drink and his newspaper at a café table.

Looking

Children frequently become absorbed in watching other children. A child walking past where others are playing will come to a standstill and watch. Children sitting on a bench watch others playing ball. A child in the sand pile becomes immobile, forgets the shovel in his hand and his half-filled pail, as he watches other children. This absorption in looking seems in part related to the obstacles in the way of free contact with others. Sometimes the closest the child can get is to stand a little way off and look. Then, with the inhibition of motor activity, looking may become, in a compensatory way, intensified.[13] But also French children learn by looking more than by doing. They are taught to watch activities for which they are not yet ready but which they will be able to perform later on.[14] This was expressed, for instance, in the

---

[12] Cf. Prévert, 1951.

[13] Abel, Belo, and Wolfenstein (1954) suggest that prohibitions against nocturnal looking intensify the wish to look.

[14] French girls, for instance, learn to cook by watching their mothers (cf. Métraux and Mead, 1954, Part I).

way in which parents held up small children to watch older ones on the swings. A mother with a one-year-old boy in her arms stops by the swings and says: *C'est la balançoire, mon petit chéri,* and holds him so that he can watch. A father with a baby of about six months holds the child up to watch, saying, *Regarde. C'est bon?* (Luxembourg, September 23, 1953).

Adults Are Above the Emotions of Children

Adults seem to look down from a considerable height on both the griefs and the joys of children. Childhood and adulthood are two very distinct human conditions. From the vantage point of the adult, the emotions of the child do not seem serious: they are not, after all, about anything very important. The adult is likely to be detached in the face of the child's distress. Where the child is elated, the adult, though sympathetic, may regard the child humorously, perhaps a bit mockingly: how he overestimates these little childish things!

On an occasion when a mother punished a little boy, she appeared quite unconcerned about his rage and grief and was amused when he later came to fling his arms around her. I did not see what it was that provoked the mother's punishment. My attention was attracted when I saw the boy, of about six or seven, running, with his mother, a sturdy, athletic-looking woman, hard at his heels. When she overtook him, she gave him several hard whacks on the behind, and the boy burst into tears. The mother then sat down on the bench beside her husband, who was holding the baby; for her the episode seemed finished. The boy, however, continued crying, his posture very tense, with an expression of raging protest. He stalked off, still crying, looking helplessly angry and hurt, and walked around the playground, where several other children and mothers turned to look at him. His own mother was not looking but after a while glanced in his direction, smiling, seemingly not at him but about him. The boy returned to the parents' bench, stood first in front of his father, then threw his arms around his mother and put his head in her lap. The mother put her arms around him and turned to a woman on the other side of the bench and laughed. The other woman laughed back. The boy remained for some time with his head buried in his mother's lap. The mother had apparently been unperturbed by the boy's stormy tears and by his gesture of walking away, while his return to her, as his love and longing overpowered his angry feelings, seemed to her humorous. In laughing with another adult about it, she seemed to express: that's the way children are; that's all that comes of their little scenes (Sèvres-Babylone, July 24, 1953). Such discrepancies between the feelings of children and adults, where the adults remain detached while the child is undergoing violent emotions, may produce in the child a sense of painful abandonment.

Where the child is pleased with himself over some achievement, the adults may be more sympathetic, but with a nuance of gentle mockery, expressing a feeling of the smallness of these childish feats. This was the case with the grandmother of the little boy, Marcel, whom I mentioned before. The boy had been trying very hard to make sand molds with his pail. When, after numerous less successful attempts, he turned out a complete one, he threw back his head, beaming with elation. The grandmother was greatly amused by this, laughing and remarking to me: *Il est fier! Comme il est fier!* She was very sympathetic to the little boy, but at the same time found the child's great pride in having made such a thing as a sand pie humorous (Sèvres-Babylone, July 23, 1953). The nuance here is a delicate one. I would say it consists in the adult's never quite putting himself in the child's place but retaining a double position: in part empathizing with the child, but in part seeing the child's concerns as such a small matter that the child's strong feeling about them appears disproportionate and hence comic.

At other times, when children are having fun together, an adult who is with them may be simply unamused, not feeling at all impelled to participate in the children's mood or to smile at what makes them laugh. I observed such a discrepancy of mood where two boys were playing together very gaily while the mother of one of them sat on a bench beside them, reading, very unsmiling, addressing to her son from time to time a slight reprimand and then turning back to her book. Jean, her son, and Michel, his friend, both about seven, were chattering and laughing as they built a sand fort. Jean jumped up to show his mother his muddy hands (he remained otherwise immaculate), saying, *Regarde, maman!* His mother looked up briefly to say in a perfunctory tone, *Quelle horreur*, and continued reading. Jean returned to the fort, jumped up now and then to prance around in a clowning way, then seated himself on the shoulders of Michel, who was squatting over the fort, and playfully bounced up and down. Michel giggled. The mother repeatedly, unsmilingly, told Jean not to do this, without, however, interrupting the play or the good humor of the boys. When the mother announced it was time to leave, the boys began by slow stages to demolish their fort, the operation ending with Michel sitting down on it. The boys thought this very funny (probably the more so since throughout their play they had carefully squatted with their behinds poised an inch or so above the ground). At this final foolishness, the mother smiled for the first time, saying: *Michel, tu es bête* (Parc Monceau, September 18, 1953). In such circumstances as these, the adult's detachment is mingled with disapproval. The children's way of having fun, which here included getting dirty and physical contacts which produced giggles, seems to the adult slightly naughty or at best silly.

I think this latter instance particularly contrasts with the way in which American adults are likely to respond to children's play. For Americans, there is not such a cleavage between childhood and adulthood, nor is adulthood so decidedly the advantageous position. To be able to play like children and with children is a highly valued capacity. The sour-faced adult who is a killjoy to the children's sport is likely to arouse negative reactions not only in children but in adults as well. Adults generally do not like to think of themselves in this role. They are eager to show children that they are good sports, that they have a sense of humor, and this involves falling in with children's playful moods.

Children Mimic Adults

I observed very little of the sort of make-believe play in which children assume the roles of imaginary characters of drama or story, such as the frequent cowboy play of American little boys. Perhaps such dramatic play is carried on more at home than out in the open. I saw a few little boys with toy guns, but their play was far from aggressive by American standards, and if shooting noises were simulated, they were quite soft. A boy of about seven or eight, holding a gun, told a playmate, *Haut les mains*, in a tone of instructing him how to play the game rather than as a convincing dramatic threat. The second boy obligingly put up his hands and walked smilingly in front of his friend, who held the gun pointed at the other's back (Parc Monceau, September 18, 1953).

More often children mimic the familiar gestures and intonations of adults. Here they show excellent observation, combined with mockery. Their performance has much more zest and vividness than the mild *Haut les mains* of the friendly little gunman. The handshaking ritual of the adults is repeatedly imitated. For instance, as a group of boys pass a brother and sister, one of the boys calls: *Salut!* and the girl takes his hand and shakes it rather hard. Her brother starts shaking hands with the other boys with more show of politeness, saying, *Bonjour, Monsieur* (Parc Monceau, September 18, 1953).

A group of six- and seven-year-old girls who have been working at laying out a garden in the sand of the path take time out to sit on a bench and gossip. After a while, one of them interrupts their talk, exclaiming, like a busy woman who has let herself be distracted from her tasks: "But what are we doing chattering [*bavarder*] like this?" They laugh and return to their work. When smaller children unwittingly get in their way, the girls pick them up and put them to one side, with a *Qu'est-ce que tu fais, petite?* uttered in a tone of simulated amazement, combined with resignation, well imitated from the adults (Luxembourg, September 11, 1947).

At a band concert, a boy of nine, showing off to a pretty little girl, applauds exaggeratedly and cries, "Bravo! bravo!" after every piece. Later, when the concert is over, he mounts the bandstand and imitates the conductor, with autocratic gestures and a grandiose air, while a few other little boys sit in the places of the musicians and pretend to play different instruments (Luxembourg, July 21, 1953).

For the French, adulthood is decidedly the desirable time of life. Simply assuming the role of adults as he knows them is gratifying to a French child; no extraneous glamour need be added. At the same time, the adults in their role of authority rouse impulses of rebellious mockery in children, which they express in parodying the adults among themselves. This motive is liable to persist and to be permitted much stronger expression when the children grow up, in the mockery of authority figures, particularly in the political sphere, which is so prominent in French life.[15]

In contrast to this, for American children the adults they know are far from glamorous. Father is no superman.[16] Cowboys and spacemen provide models that better express the children's aspirations to strenuous and violent activity. The choice of models for children's make-believe play is perhaps reflected in the different styles of adult acting which we find in American and French films. There is little fine mimicry in facial expression, gestures, or tone of voice on the part of the American film hero. As the man on horseback, the man with the gun, fast-moving, triumphant in violent action, he fulfils the small boy's dream, at the same time exemplifying the heroic qualities which daddy lacks. In French films the actors show rather a mastery of small nuances of voice and manner, expressive of different characters that seem to have been unerringly observed. Such acting appears to be the highly elabo-

---

[15] Cf. the peculiarly irreverent political satire of *Le Canard enchaîné*.

[16] Mead, 1942, 1949.

rated sequel of the children's keen mimicry of adults. The contrast previously indicated between American and French children in respect to large and small movements is also relevant here.

Childhood Is Not for Fun[17]

For the French, enjoyment of life is the prerogative of adults. Childhood is a preparation. Then everything must be useful, not just fun; it must have an educational purpose. The hard regime of French school children, with its tremendous burden of work, is well known. Probably nothing in later life is such a terrible ordeal as the dreaded *bachot* (the examination at the conclusion of secondary school). It is a real *rite de passage*, a painful test to which youths on the verge of maturity are subjected by their elders.

The attitude that everything for children, even the very young, must serve a useful purpose and not be just amusing is well exemplified around the carrousel in the Luxembourg Gardens. There are various rides for the children, among them rows of large rocking horses. A sign describes these as: *Chevaux hygiéniques. Jeu gymnastique pour les enfants développant la force et la souplesse.*

At the carrousel, as soon as the ride began, an old woman with spectacles and red hair done up in a bun on top of her head and wearing an old-fashioned gray coat (she seemed to me a benevolent witch), handed out to each child in the outer circle a stick (*baguette*). She then held out to them a contraption which dispensed rings and encouraged them to catch the rings on their sticks. Throughout the duration of the ride, the old woman directed to the children an incessant didactic discourse, urging them to pay attention and work very hard to catch the rings. *Attention! Regarde ton travail! Regarde bien, chou-chou! Au milieu,* indicating with her finger the middle of the ring at which the child should aim. *Doucement!* When a child used his stick to beat time instead of to catch the rings, the old woman scolded him for this frivolity. At the end of the ride, she commended a boy who had caught many rings: *Tu as bien travaillé. Tu es gentil.* There was no other premium for catching the rings. On the next ride, a girl of about seven who failed to catch the rings where younger children were succeeding smiled with self-conscious chagrin. The elderly woman who had brought the girl there urged her to do better: *Attention! Regarde bien,*

[17] Cf. Françoise Dolto, "French and American Children as Seen by a French Child Analyst," in this volume (p. 408).

Françoise (Luxembourg, September 23, 1953). Thus, even on the carrousel, children have a task to perform. The elders direct, commend, and rebuke them. They are not there just for fun.

The paradox from the American point of view is that the French grow up with a great capacity for enjoyment of life. The adult enters fully into the pleasures which have not been permitted to the child. There seems to be a successful realization that pleasure is not taboo, but only postponed. The song of Charles Trenet, *Quand j'étais petit*, ends with the triumphant, *On n'est plus petit!*—everything is now permitted. It remains one of the puzzles of French culture how this effect is achieved: that the restaints to which children are subjected have only a temporary influence and do not encumber the adult with lasting inhibitions.

If we compare Americans and French, it seems as though the relation between childhood and adulthood is almost completely opposite in the two cultures. In America we regard childhood as a very nearly ideal time, a time for enjoyment, an end in itself. The American image of the child, whether envisaged in the classical figures of Tom Sawyer and Huckleberry Finn, or in the small hero of the recent film *The Little Fugitive*, who achieves a self-sufficient existence at Coney Island, is of a young person with great resources for enjoyment, whose present life is an end in itself.[18] We do not picture children as longing for adult prerogatives from which they are excluded. Adults tend to feel nostalgic for the carefree times of childhood, or at any rate adolescence. Young adults in their middle twenties may feel old and wish they were back in college. It is in adulthood that the ceaseless round of activities which are means to further ends sets in: the job which is a steppingstone to a better job, the social entertainments which may lead to some advancement, etc. In this continual planning ahead which absorbs adults, the capacity for immediate sensuous enjoyment is often lacking. With the French, as I have said, it seems to be the other way around. Childhood is a period of probation, when everything is a means to an end; it is unenviable from the vantage point of adulthood. The image of the child is replete with frustration and longing for pleasures of the adults which are not for him.[19] It is in adulthood that the possibility of living in the moment is achieved. Not that this precludes much scheming and planning as far as careers or business advantage is concerned. But this is not allowed to interfere with sensuous pleasures, which are an end in

[18] Cf. Martha Wolfenstein, "The Image of the Child in Contemporary Films," in this volume (p. 277).

[19] *Ibid.*

themselves. The attainment of these end-pleasures, notably in eating and in lovemaking, is not a simple matter. Much care and preparation are required, and changing stimuli may be needed to keep pleasure intense. Concern with such pleasures and ingenuity in achieving them are persistent in adult life. It is with the prospect of these pleasures that the individual has served his hardworking childhood, and it is now, as an adult, that he can lose himself in the pleasures of the moment.

References

ABEL, THEODORA M., BELO, JANE, and WOLFENSTEIN, MARTHA. 1954. "An Analysis of French Projective Tests." In *Themes in French Culture: A Preface to a Study of French Community*, ed. RHODA MÉTRAUX and MARGARET MEAD, pp. 103–20. ("Hoover Institute Studies.") Stanford, Calif.: Stanford University Press.

MEAD, MARGARET. 1942. *And Keep Your Powder Dry*. New York: William Morrow & Co.

———. 1949. *Male and Female*. New York: William Morrow & Co.

MÉTRAUX, RHODA, and MEAD, MARGARET (eds.). 1954. *Themes in French Culture: A Preface to a Study of French Community*. ("Hoover Institute Studies.") Stanford, Calif.: Stanford University Press.

PEYREFITTE, ROGER. 1945. *Amitiés particulières*. Paris: Jean Vigneau.

PRÉVERT, JACQUES. 1951. "L'Enfant abandonné." In *Spectacle*. Paris: Gallimard.

PROUST, MARCEL. 1934. *The Remembrance of Things Past*. New York: Random House.

WOLFENSTEIN, MARTHA, and LEITES, NATHAN. 1950. *Movies: A Psychological Study*. Glencoe, Ill.: Free Press.

Introduction to

Contributors to section four:

Barbara Biber

Jerome S. Bruner

Norma Haan

OVERVIEW Magazine

Explorations in moder

section four

THE FIELD OF EDUCATION IS IN FERMENT. THE DEVELOPment of new learning conceptions, new methods of teaching, new organization of material, new aids to teaching, increased public anxiety and criticism, and the rapidly growing knowledge of mental hygiene have all served to stimulate the profession. The six selections in this Section by no means exhaust the list of changes and experiments going on, but they do represent important events in the profession. Although the editors do not agree that all these things are wise or good, they do agree that it is encouraging to see wider and more intense experimentation and trial in the business of educating children. The reader will need to use the basic data furnished in the previous sections and in many other sources to help him make judgments as to the merits of the new proposals and experiments.

Among the most significant studies in education are those dealing with the mental health of the teacher and the importance of teacher personality in the education of the child. Among the leaders in this movement are the directors of the Bank Street College of Education in New York. Dr. Biber, who is Director of Research at the College, is probably better qualified to write about teachers' mental health than anyone in the field. Her selection, "Teacher Education in Mental Health," is of importance to the student contemplating teaching, to persons in teacher education and particularly to parents who are puzzled and confused as to the meaning of new research for teacher education and teacher functioning in the classroom. This is one of the

n education

SECTION IV

frontiers of teacher education that we expect to develop into the most significant change in education in this century.

The selection from Dr. Bruner's immensely stimulating volume, *The Process of Education*, presents a balanced point of view toward the use of teaching machines. As we pointed out in the introduction to Section III, the advocates of a simple reinforcement theory of learning are those who find the most value in the teaching machine idea. Dr. Bruner, on the other hand, takes a much broader view of the theories of learning. Interpolated between those who claim that machines can take over nearly all educational functions and those who fear that the machine will rob children of full comprehension at both emotional and ideational levels, Bruner's viewpoint is sane and useful.

A rapidly developing field, well established in many states, is that of programs for the handicapped. The mentally retarded, orthopedically handicapped, the blind and deaf, and now the emotionally disturbed, have all received special financial aid and program development. We have also moved away from the idea of segregating these children any more than their safety and special educational needs require. Integration of blind and partially blind, for example, into the regular classroom at least part of the time is most desirable. The integration of those who have been mentally ill back into the classroom also presents a special problem. This is discussed in Norma Haan's article, "When the Mentally Ill Child Returns to School." As classes for the emotionally disturbed become more common, the reintegration of these children into regular classrooms will be a persistent problem for which teachers will need some preparation.

A book of readings can only scrape the surface of new developments in education. The use of educational television, organization of the staff for team teaching, modern language instruction, outdoor education, general education in the use and meaning of the big computers, ungraded classrooms, multi-graded classrooms, flexible scheduling, parent helpers in the classroom, these and many others testify to the ferment in modern education. Not all are good but they all cry for experimentation, acceptance or rejection on scientific bases. The educator of tomorrow will need a much broader education than his predecessor.

See Section Bibliographies, page 361.

4-1 Teacher education in mental health (from the point of view of the educator)*

There is much talk about "closing the gap" between education and mental health, but it is not often that a comprehensive program of education, in which mental health and child development concepts and practices assume their appropriate places, is described. In the accompanying paper, Dr. Biber not only accomplishes this, but she also succeeds, at the same time, in formulating the role of the modern teacher in a way that educators will find new, sensitive, refreshing and sound, and that clinicians will accept as clinically substantial without pretending to be clinical.

It is easy to forget how far we have come from the beginning. By the beginning I mean the recognition that the principles of dynamic psychology are requisite foundation for school practices if such terms as "the education of the whole child," or "dynamics of the learning process," are to have more than semantic significance. This was brought to me sharply during a class discussion recently. I was leading a discussion for grad-

---

* Barbara Biber, "Teacher Education in Mental Health (From the point of view of the educator)," in Morris Krugman (ed.), *Orthopsychiatry and the School,* New York: American Orthopsychiatric Association, Inc., 1958, pp. 169–83. Dr. Biber is Director of Research, Bank Street College of Education, New York City.

Barbara Biber

uate level student-teachers whose professional training had begun last fall, about six months ago. The content of the discussion had to do with the specific ways in which the projective approach to personality study could be useful to a teacher. The students had raised important critical questions which showed they were troubled about the complex problem of how projective technique interpretations could be validated although they were not using research nomenclature.

How, they were considering, had Alschuler and Hattwick arrived at the relation which they postulate between predominant use of black and underlying anxiety? In the midst of this, one of the students asked: "But what if a child just happens to like black?" The class fell suddenly silent. So did the leader of the discussion, for a moment, until, noticing the register of amused and patronizing surprise on a few faces, she recognized the responsibility to give a dignified answer to the question. But, in that moment, there was time to realize what the surprise meant. With rare exception, of which this question was an example, it could be taken for granted that these student-teachers had absorbed the concepts that behavior is determined, that conflict is part of the growth process, that the cognitive and affective spheres of experience are interdependent, that successive periods of a child's development are to be understood in terms of the basic life challenges which the child faces as well as his growing capacities to understand, act and react.

If this represents progress in the concept of what the material of educational psychology should include in the education of teachers, and I think it does, then it is appropriate to ask what assumptions concerning the function of the school in relation to mental health are related to this progress. More particularly, the question becomes, What is the teacher's role in this context? And then inevitably, Who shall teach, how shall he (she) be prepared to teach and be kept "refreshed" for teaching, as thus conceived?

In the short space of this paper I have not found it possible to cover the last question, namely, the area of in-service development, but will restrict myself to the questions of the teacher's role, selection and preservice preparation. I shall make no attempt to review the literature in this broad field, recently covered in a volume issued by the National Society for the Study of Education entitled *Mental Health in Modern Education*. Rather, I shall draw on my own research and teaching experience in teacher education and, thus, on the particular program of research and graduate teacher-training of the Bank Street College of

Education, which includes the nursery-primary-elementary levels but does not extend to the secondary school.

This we assume: that part of a child's life that is spent in school significantly influences his total growth as a personality and that this contributes to his potential good mental health or ill health; that this influence will make an impact on attitudes toward himself, toward people, toward work, and will condition his potentialities for becoming a productive, adaptable individual whose self-realization is integrated with responsible, effective functioning in his environment.

Also, the influence of school cannot be isolated but rather is compounded of the qualities that characterize the whole complex of the learning-teaching situation. In this sense, if one were attempting to analyze how a given school influences personality, it would be feasible, more than that, necessary, to look at the way the children's tables are arranged with respect to the teacher's desk; to see whether the teacher spares the rod but uses words as poisoned arrows; to make a mental estimate of the quotient of boredom for teacher and children; to think whether this classroom by its appurtenances could be as readily located in a rural region of Oklahoma as in a Puerto Rican district of Manhattan; to note when someone laughs, at what, at whom; and in countless other ways to examine the undersides of the everyday events, appearances and relationships of the school life. It follows that attempts to alter the school's influence by vest-pocket devices or programs for improved mental health can only be expected to remain tangential and to prove ineffectual alongside the basic influences of the mode of learning which the child is experiencing and the quality of his relations to the people in his school world.

Sufficient experience is already behind us in efforts along these lines to permit and require recognition of errors. We are all familiar with the misinterpretation of what constitutes freedom, psychologically, for a child, and with the accompanying distortion of the teacher's role in the direction of passivity due, in part, to confusion of ideas, and in greater measure to the fact that most teachers were not ready, personally, to carry the balanced guiding role which the new concept required.

Another error, not so widely recognized or accepted, appears in the *exaggerated* emphasis placed on the human relations aspects of school life as *the* mainline to mental health. I have no wish to engage in another pendulum swing error and so feel quite reluctant to make such a statement for fear that it will place me with some who think the time has come to return to some antediluvian era when what went on in a classroom was correctly called "deportment." Human relations in school as elsewhere, are indeed *a* mainline to mental health. The error in school practice lies in taking the teacher-child relationship and the child-child relationship to be the content rather than the medium of learning, and in the failure to recognize that, in the interest of positive personality development, it is essential to rethink and reorganize the content and the process of the learning experience, per se.

There is reason to be optimistic that this error is in line for correction if we do not allow ourselves to be pressured into reactionary regressions to old stereotypes. The current interest in theory of ego development should be a healthy protection in this regard as well as the critical thinking of practitioners in education, psychology and psychiatry. As one example of such critical thinking one can cite the paper by Kotinsky and Coleman, delivered to a meeting of this society in 1954, in which they argue that the school has a specific and unique role in fostering healthy personality development, namely, to support the child's basic growth needs for adequacy and achievement in the particular way it helps each child acquire understanding of his world and ability to cope with it creatively.

Above and beyond all reference to the changing practices of schools and the rationale which underlies them, it is important to remember that we cannot offer systematic proof that what is claimed for the school's influence on mental health is indeed true. Nor are we anywhere near being able to document the advice, frequently given, that for this kind of child, that kind of school would be preferable. Systematic proof for a problem of this kind is hard to come by. Obviously the research difficulty here lies in the fact that the school influence cannot be examined independently of a whole series of other influences, most notably, the home and family factors.

This leads to another point which can be made briefly: If it is true, as we now assume, that there is a kind of school experience which holds positive potential for mental health, then this potential can best be realized by adapting every aspect of school life, and most especially the learning process, to a psychodynamic concept of child development. Every part of the setting—the things, the people, the ideas are part carriers of this influence. However, to hold this assumption with conviction, based on the cumulative experience of thinking people, while we lack other forms of evidence does not imply any bias as to how strong an influence school can or should have vis-à-vis home and family.

Mental Health Aspects of the Teacher's Role

For today we turn our attention to the teacher who is no longer willing to be a schoolmarm, who has not settled for being a poor substitute for a mother and does not yearn to be a therapist. What can she give and be to a child that can constitute the enabling ingredients for positive growth?

She can lead him to become skilled, knowing, perceptive and effective in his world; to master confusion; to reorder experience through his own invention; to communicate in the modes of his culture and sustain the idiom of himself; to extend his "interest" world to far places and times; to act, to organize, to accomplish, to reason, to reflect. For this exciting and challenging task there are special techniques, some old, some new. It is the teacher's choice of techniques and skill in using them that determines the extent to which the child's learning, achievement and mastery become the framework for positive ego-growth, and contribute to the child's growing feeling as a knowing, doing, confident self in relation to a knowable, manageable world.

She can be to the child a member of the adult community, one of the most important ones in his life, who can connect with him as a person, respectful of his distinctness, attuned to his feelings as well as to his capacities and aware of the importance of his private world to him. Through her he will experience again, but differently, what he has already lived through with his parents: the taste and the boundary of freedom; the comfort and the irritation of being controlled; the safety and threat of being known. By the way these relations are mediated for each child and by the kind of climate she creates for the "yeast" of the children's relations to each other, the teacher is in a position to make an impact on the child's image of the adult world into which he is growing. She can also be a force in determining how safe and nondefensive he will feel with people, how benign and without hostility toward himself.

To fill this role even approximately the teacher needs skills and knowledge. She needs training in how to perceive children in all their individuality; she needs knowledge to place each child against the context of a stage of growth, behaviorally and dynamically conceived; she needs scope to comprehend how the myriad factors of the child's life-environment condition how he, individual that he is, lives through a particular stage of growth. She needs experience and the help of specialists to judge when a child's potential for growth is so seriously obstructed that he can no longer learn or grow through the processes of the classroom.

Who Shall Teach?

Our next question intrudes quickly: Who are the people whose capacities, proclivities and life stories have readied them for this role, who could find healthy growth for themselves in constructing this kind of child world of learning? By what considerations of personality shall we be governed in selecting candidates for professional training or placement in the teaching field? How specific to the teacher's functioning in her job can or should these considerations be?

I think I can best answer these general questions by presenting a sampling of those characteristics, attitudes and dimensions of personality which we have taken to be most relevant to the teacher's role. This list is actually a synthetic one, drawing on formulations (in the form of scales) now in use in our research program as well as on more general reference guides which govern the content of the personal interviews conducted with candidates seeking admission to our graduate training program.

It is important to remember that this line of inquiry does not intend to be comprehensive, omitting for example any assessment of intellectual capacity, per se, or extent of information, and stressing only those elusive qualities which are increasingly regarded as important for selection and job placement of teachers and student-teachers, but for which conceptual orientation is often either vague, undifferentiated or bound to a form of trait psychology. For ease of expression I prefer to put these considerations in the form of questions.

1. *Relatedness to children.* What aspect of childhood is responded to: spontaneity, ignorance, powerlessness? Would communication be on child level? Dependent on verbal articulation? Would the child's view be seen empathically? Taken defensively? Are children enjoyed? In what way?

   How strong is impulse to protect and support children? To emphasize values of independence? To censor? To retaliate? To punish? To protect adult self against child exploitation? To submerge adult self for child needs?

   Is childhood apperceived sentimentally, patronizingly? As continuous or discontinuous with adult life?

   Is there tendency to support mutuality among children? Competitiveness? Rivalry?

How accepting of different children? Race, class, temperament, brightness? Are children perceived as individuals? As group stereotypes?

2. *Orientation to the psychology of growth.* How much is child behavior seen as determined by multiple factors? How much identified with fixed character structure? How much is behavior seen in context of motivation?

   How much awareness of developmental stages? In terms of capacity? Of dynamics of conflict? How much acceptance of conflict as part of growth process? How tolerant—resistant—devoted to depth approaches?

   Is there stress on social conformity? Are childish impulses to be expressed, repressed, modulated, redirected, retrained? How are self-fulfillment and social adjustment balanced?

3. *Relation to authority* (freedom and control). What kind of authority models are accepted, rejected, idealized? Benign, arbitrary, reality-adjusted?

   Is authority identified with position, function, status, experience?

   Is there tendency toward permissiveness as being identical with freedom?

   Is there prospective fear, delight, ambivalence in retaking an authority role?

4. *Emotional strength.* How much ease and depth in expressing feeling, in responding to feeling? Tendency to become emotionally involved? How would aggression or hostility be received? Would they arouse guilt, weakness, fear, anger, impulse to do battle? How much equilibrium and vigor in the face of frustrating circumstance? How able to accept help as needed? How much primacy placed on self-sufficiency? How self-accusing? Self-effacing? Self-adulatory? How much need for façade? How able to act with effectiveness?

5. *Motivation toward teaching.* Does teaching appear as a way of serving people? Of assuring children a good start? As a means of achieving status? As a pleasant remunerative occupation?

   Does teaching represent an opportunity to nurture thought, wonder, inquiry? To enjoy at first hand the reality of the learning process? To re-experience freshness, creativity? To withdraw from the complexity of adult living?

Let us suppose, at this point, that we are agreed that this sampling of characteristics, related to general personality as it is, is significantly meaningful with respect to the psychological role of the teacher. By what techniques can they be assessed? Where there is time and opportunity a combination of methods are available and are, in fact, in use. In our own institution each candidate, in addition to usual factual vitae, college transcript and references, submits an autobiography, takes a projective test structured toward the teaching profession, and is interviewed by two members of the college staff. This multiple approach to assessment provides some degree of validity to the final judgment made (which matters not only for selection but for the subsequent course of guidance for each individual).

We are well aware, however, that true validity rests on how these initial judgments align with ultimate performance as a teacher. The pursuit of that level validity involves complex and difficult research problems, which, you will be pleased to hear, I have no intention of discussing at this point, except only to say that the subtler the characteristics chosen as variables, the harder the research becomes.

The Bank Street Research Division is now engaged in a pilot study of this kind, successive to the one that originated in a subcommittee of Citizens Committee for Children, several years ago. For assessment purposes, this study employs a battery of written tests, relying upon projective type instruments to substitute for the insights of interview in the complex selection procedure already referred to. If such a battery or parts of it can indeed be validated, these findings may prove a steppingstone to a time when even large school systems or large teacher training institutions can include reliable judgments of significant characteristics in their selection procedures. It would be premature to expect too much too soon, especially since there have been disappointing results from similar work in education and in related fields. There is, however, no turning back. If this is our concept of teaching, we must continue to seek methods for finding the people for whom such teaching is congruent with personality organization.

In a time of teacher shortage, this whole approach may sound fantastically idealistic to many people. It sounded just that to an executive of one of our larger foundations when I described this project to him, recently. However, he was inclined to agree with me, and I hope you will too, when I made the point that, if a changed concept of the teacher's role could filter through to the keen minds and good spirits of this country's undergraduates, we might not be faced with a desperate shortage problem. In this sense, the work that one does on a technique has a purpose beyond the practical—namely, to demonstrate by the underlying conceptual approach the nature of the function which is being examined. We have had applicants take a deep weary breath, after completing the admissions procedure, and say: "Now, I am really sure I want to teach—I never realized—etc." This individual experience could be multiplied many times over.

I must not let my enthusiasm carry me away. There is still another point with which to make peace before we can leave this topic. It was stated beautifully by Dr. Sibylle K. Escalona at a conference in Boston last fall. It goes something like this. A technique is only a technique.

Good enough if it can help us assess a situation, a teacher or a candidate. It cannot tell us how to act, whom to choose. At that point a new set of factors enter in—the factors of purpose, goals and values. In this connection, I want to take a clear position: There is no unitary good teacher; instead there is a broad range of ways of doing good teaching. There are of course limits to this range that suggest themselves readily: Chronically angry, sluggish, withdrawn, overmanipulative people are outside the pale of eligibility. The school's contribution to healthy personality will take a great forward leap when we are in a position to place teachers in jobs with intelligent consideration of their psychological suitability for working with children at one stage of development or another, with deprived or protected children, under close supervision or with great autonomy, and so on.

Preparing the Teacher

And now quickly, though belatedly, to the question of how to prepare teachers for a way of teaching that will contribute to the healthy personality of children. I can only attempt to present general principles with a few illustrations to make them concrete. Any kind of coverage of a whole curriculum would obviously be a foolish attempt. One prime principle has become clear to us: What any student-teacher learns is a product of the design of the curriculum in its several parts, the infusion of an integrated point of view through all parts, and the nature of the relations with the people through whom the learning is happening.

A concept of teaching, from a mental health point of view, needs to be learned and clarified. What that concept is, has been sufficiently developed already in this paper, not to need repetition. In any week of her training a student might be gaining insight into this concept through various sources: in the curriculum principles seminar, where the problem arises of how to handle a discussion with ten-year-olds who are expressing excited opinions on a forthcoming election so that the family origins of these opinions are not violated while the teacher develops with the children the concrete issues which are suitable content for their level; in a child development class where the question arises of what the teacher's role is (and why) when the five-year-olds' dramatic house play develops into an orgy of fire fighting in which most of the babies but not all are successfully rescued; in her own spontaneous joining with the eight-year-olds' pleasure and relief when they finally manage to get their electrical rig-up to work; in a conference with her adviser where she realizes that she has taught the arithmetic lesson according to her preplan, which was remarkably similar to the way she had been taught, and had missed the cues that could have told her she was at least three steps ahead of most of the children.

There is not only a concept but a content to be learned. What are children like? How do they feel, what do they think? How is the ability to generalize related to direct experience? Are there inevitable conflicts in the process of growth? What major changes take place in their drives at different stages of growth? How is social development related to the thinking process, to self-fulfillment? What is latent in the latency period? What isn't? When are fantasy solutions part of a stage of growth, when a sign of anxious individual retreat? How are psychosexual and psychosocial sequences related? How can we know children in school? Is there a "language of behavior"? How useful can acquaintance with projective methods be to teachers? How can you hear a child think when you don't know his language?

And there are techniques to be learned. When and how to teach children to read, to write, to talk, to spell, to handle number system? How is play a form of study? How to select what they need and want to learn? How to make a group discussion an experience in thinking and communicating? How to use the physical and social environment to develop concepts of how things work and how people live? How to turn a classroom into a workshop? How to keep a level of order (of things and children) that supports expression, thinking, work? How to lead natural curiosity to structured pursuit of understanding?

Then, there is the large question of knowledge—how much, what kind—for, contrary to the overused adage about those who know, do, and those who don't know, teach, a teacher needs knowledge. The modern teacher needs a body of knowledge to be used, flexibly, as a resource, which she can organize and reorganize intelligently and imaginatively according to the interests, capacities and needs of children. Her job is no longer to transmit easily digestible units of information, but to communicate effectively with the young learner and stimulate his independent thinking. To do this, it is not enough to add understanding of the dynamics of the cognitive-affective growth of children to the body of information acquired in a liberal arts education. The compartmentalization of knowledge in the liberal arts fields is not the appropriate organization of information for the teacher of children in the earlier stages of intellectual development. She needs to learn, in the course of teacher preparation: how to work and rework information so that it shall serve as sound, relevant, raw material for the conceptual growth of young thinkers; how to use her understanding of emotional life in selecting the facts, the themes, the principles which the children's minds are ripe to grasp and control; and finally, how to appreciate the service that intellectual mastery contributes to healthy, psychological growth.

To acquire this knowledge and these skills, students need several levels of learning experience themselves. The lecture-discussion remains an important medium especially when the leader of the discussion is aware of the relationship factors that are enmeshed with the intellectual activity in progress. There is the question of how much mergence of thinking between the group and the teacher can be achieved without interfering with presentation of organized information; how receptive or denying to be of the questions that come from the least-respected members of the group; how to communicate conviction and leave the atmosphere open for disagreement; how to maintain high work standards when students overreact to lessening of teacher-student distance.

Another level of learning is provided in the direct experience in working with children in classrooms at different stages of growth. Nothing can take the place of this firsthand taste of children and of one's self as a teacher, if only a helping one. But for student-teaching practice to be optimally useful, certain conditions need to be provided. Most important of all is that the experience be worked over, thought over, critically reviewed. This can partly be accomplished by using student experience as live material for seminars where the practical can be sieved through theoretical considerations and theory thus gain functional meaning.

The third level of learning takes place through individual guidance for which principles and procedures, as it is applied in teacher education, are at an early stage of development. Knowledge, skills, direct experience with children are not sufficient preparation for carrying a stimulating, guiding, supporting relation to children in the orbit of the classroom. This role requires a facility that derives, in part, from understanding of one's self in relation to the reality of becoming a teacher. To individual conferences with an adviser (in the program I am referring to) the student brings her personal response to the experience of being a teacher with children as well as her individual needs for improving concrete teaching skills. This relation becomes a core experience for each student's need to arrive at her own teaching role, through a process of integrating new knowledge with an old self. The definition of this process, as well as the limits to be set on it, calls for clinical insights and represents a distinct area in which teamwork between clinician and educator is necessary. The development of this topic I will leave to Dr. Bernard. I would like to make only one comment in this connection. Many students, most probably, were not taught as they are now learning to teach. They are in the same position as are parents whose own childhoods do not provide them with subjective experience to serve as a floor for their intellectual beliefs about modern child-rearing. The experience the student-teacher has in feeling herself helped, guided and understood as she tries to learn provides her with a model of what the learning experience can be for children.

At this point, my critical teacher-self protests. This is all very important, granted, but serious to the point of monotony. Where is the rhythm—the movement from the heavy to the light, from the concentrated to the diffused, from the verbal to the sensed, from the specific to the symbol—that makes learning, like love, a "many-splendored thing." In reply, I can make only a few brief references to two essential leavening aspects of teacher education: first, experience in the creative arts at the adult level whether it be painting, creative writing, music or dance; and second, the vitalizing experience of perceiving and apperceiving the world around with the naïveté and curiosity of children, an experience rendered teachable through the creative techniques of study of the environment developed by one of our great teachers, Lucy Sprague Mitchell.

And now, the question of questions: Are we conjuring up an extremely ambitious role for teachers? What toll in guilt and anxiety will this take? What insidious effect will this have on the mental health of children? This calls for careful examination of the total teacher-training curriculum. Built-in correctives can and should be provided, of which the most important is the individual guidance program. In addition, there are subtleties of attitude which can be transmitted to students: Children are resilient, they can't be ruined in a day; the sacrifice of uniqueness that the social situation of school requires is compensated by the pleasures of communing with friends; there are some children who cannot be really helped by what any teacher alone can do and it is good accomplishment if they can just live and let live in a classroom; no teacher can or needs to be all these things to all children; sensitive appreciation of children and capacity to have fun with them will be deeply appreciated even while the new teacher is just getting off the ground with techniques and procedures.

And yet, on the basis of experience, we must honestly report that there are many instances in which young well-prepared teachers find it very difficult to stand up to the impact of their first jobs, especially where the teaching conditions, the quality of administration, the life backgrounds of the children are in sharp contrast to what they experienced in their own backgrounds or during the training period. It is for this reason that many teacher-training institutions, Queens College and Bank Street College in this vicinity, are experimenting with programs that provide a continuous supervisory-consultant relation with the student after she has been placed in her first, salary-earning teaching job.

Now, by way of summarizing briefly, I would like to restate three points: 1) It is essential that we strive to apply the concept of the unified nature of cognitive and affective development, which we have accepted as basic to the education of children, on the teacher training level. 2) That the training period for the student-teacher shall provide a meaningful subjective experience of what a dynamically integrated learning process is at any level. 3) That it is not expected or necessary that any student master the whole rationale of mental health and education; but that it is of the utmost importance that she be educated in a situation where it is being continuously thought through and applied.

Thus, to become a teacher takes learning and growth. This is far too important a skill to be trusted to the ingenuity of the individual mind or the general qualities of stable personality. That is why liberal arts training, on the intellectual plane, like love, on the emotional, is not enough.

4-2 Aids to teaching*

THERE HAS BEEN A GREAT DEAL OF DISCUSSION IN RECENT years about the devices that can be employed to aid in the teaching process. These devices are of many kinds. Some of them are designed to present material to the student of a kind that would not be available to him in his ordinary school experience. Films, TV, microphotographic film, film strips, sound recordings, and the like are among the devices ordinarily employed in such work. Books also serve in this role. These are the tools by which the student is given vicarious though "direct" experience of events. It does not serve much to dismiss such materials as "merely for enrichment," since it is obvious that such enrichment is one of the principal objectives of education. Let us call these *devices for vicarious experience.*

A second type of teaching aid has the function of helping the student to grasp the underlying structure of a phenomenon—to sense the genotype behind the phenotype, to use terms from genetics. The well wrought laboratory experiment or demonstration is the classic aid in such activity. A closer look at our efforts to get students to grasp structure indicates that there are many other devices and exercises that have the same

---

* Jerome S. Bruner, "Aids to Teaching," in *The Process of Education,* Cambridge, Mass.: Harvard University Press, 1961, pp. 81–92.

Jerome S. Bruner

function. The effort to give visible embodiment to ideas in mathematics is of the same order as the laboratory work. The Stern blocks, Cuisenaire rods, and Dienes blocks, as well as the demonstrations of Piaget and Inhelder mentioned earlier, have the same function. So too do certain kinds of charts and representations, either in animated or still form. Models, such as a model of the molecule or an idealized model of the respiratory system, serve a comparable function. Needless to say, films and television as well as adroitly illustrated books can be adjuncts to the effort at producing clarity and concrete embodiment.

But there are other, more subtle devices that can be and are being used to lead the student to a sense of the conceptual structure of things he observes. Perhaps the best way to characterize them is to call them "sequential programs." There are certain orders of presentation of materials and ideas in any subject that are more likely than others to lead the student to the main idea. The courses being devised by the University of Illinois Committee on School Mathematics, the School Mathematics Study Group, the Physical Science Study Committee, and others are excellent instances of the well conceived sequence designed to lead the student to an understanding of basic ideas and structures.

The whole range of aids from the laboratory exercise through the mathematical blocks to the programmed sequence we shall, for convenience, speak of as *model devices.*

Closely related to these are what might be called *dramatizing devices.* The historical novel that is true in spirit to its subject, the nature film that dramatizes the struggle of a species in its habitat, the exemplification of an experiment executed by a dramatic personality, exposure to greatness in government by a documentary on the life and service of a Winston Churchill—all these can have the dramatic effect of leading the student to identify more closely with a phenomenon or an idea. Undoubtedly, this "aid" in teaching can best be exemplified by the drama-creating personality of a teacher. But there are many additional dramatic aids upon which teachers can and do call—and one wonders whether they are called upon often enough.

Finally, the past decade has witnessed the emergence of various *automatizing devices,* teaching machines, to aid in teaching. While such devices vary quite widely, they have certain features in common. The machine presents a carefully programmed order of problems or exercises to the student, one step at a time. The student responds selectively in one form or another to the alternatives presented in a problem or exercise. The machine then responds immediately, indicating whether the response was or was not correct. If a correct response is made, the machine moves to the next problem. The progression in difficulty from problem to problem is usually quite gradual in order to keep the student from the discouragement of excessive failure.

What one teaches and how one teaches it with the aid of such devices depends upon the skill and wisdom that goes into the construction of a program of problems. The art of programming a machine is, of course, an extension of the art of teaching. To date, most of the programming has been intuitive and has been entrusted to a teacher of known reputation. It has been remarked by teachers who have written tapes for teaching machines that the exercise has the effect of making one highly conscious of the sequence in which one presents problems and of the aims of the sequence—whether, for example, one is trying to get children to memorize material or use material cumulatively in doing progressively more difficult problems.

Perhaps the technically most interesting features of such automatic devices are that they can take some of the load of teaching off the teacher's shoulders, and, perhaps more important, that the machine can provide immediate correction or feedback to the student while he is in the act of learning. It is still far too early to evaluate the eventual use of such devices, and it is highly unfortunate that there have been such exaggerated claims made by both proponents and opponents. Clearly, the machine is not going to replace the teacher—indeed, it may create a demand for more and better teachers if the more onerous part of teaching can be relegated to automatic devices. Nor does it seem likely that machines will have the effect of dehumanizing learning any more than books dehumanize learning. A program for a teaching machine is as personal as a book: it can be laced with humor or be grimly dull, can either be a playful activity or be tediously like a close-order drill.

In sum, then, there exist devices to aid the teacher in extending the student's range of experience, in helping him to understand the underlying structure of the material he is learning, and in dramatizing the significance of what he is learning. There are also devices now being developed that can take some of the load of teaching from the teacher's shoulders. How these aids and devices should be used in concert as a system of aids is, of course, the interesting problem.

The matter of "integration" is nicely illustrated in a report on the teaching films used by the Physical Science Study Committee. "Until quite recently, most educational films were enrichment films, designed primarily to introduce phenomena or experiences that would otherwise be unavailable inside the classroom. Such films are necessarily self-contained, since the producer is ignorant of what his audience has previously learned or what it will go on to learn; he can neither build upon the student's immediate past nor lay the groundwork for his immediate future. In the last few years, another kind of educational film, stimulated to a large extent by television, has made its appearance. These films present the entire substance of a course, and are designed to minimize the need for a teacher. Clearly, it is possible to make extremely useful films in either of these forms, and such films have indeed been made." Stephen White, who has had a major part in producing the films used in the high school physics course prepared by the PSSC, then goes on to say in his report on the film work of that group, "Every film produced by the PSSC must meet two conditions. It must (1) further the presentation of the PSSC course as a whole, and (2) set the tone and level of the course. For the PSSC film is part of a complex that includes also the text, the laboratory, the classroom, the student, and the teacher."

White describes some of the problems of making the film fit. "The film must fit into this complex and never disrupt it. Obviously, this principle imposes serious restrictions on the producer. The most important of these for the PSSC films lies in the relation between the film and the laboratory. Only at his peril may the producer include in a film experiments which the student should and could do in the laboratory. Occasionally such an experiment will be included because it is essential to the logical development of the film's theme, in which case it is done briefly and allusively. More often, it is considered desirable to repeat on film, with more sophisticated apparatus, an experiment that is suitable for the school laboratory; in such cases the film is made in a manner which indicates clearly that it should be shown *after* the student has done the lab work, and the teacher is strongly urged to defer it until that time."

Other elements in the complex must also be taken into account. "Other restrictions on the film require it to follow the logical development, the spirit, and the vocabulary (where it exists) of the text. Finally, the film must always respect the position of the teacher; it must leave for him those activities which are necessary for him if he is to retain the respect of his class. All these are negative, but the film makes positive contributions to the complex as well. It serves the classroom by directing attention to those aspects of the subject which will best stimulate classroom discussion. Thus, the PSSC film on 'Work and Mechanical Energy' deliberately calls attention to the temperature rise in a nail on which work is being done, and thus opens discussion of thermal energy, which the class will meet next. And the film, wherever possible, serves the individual student directly by suggesting work he himself can carry on outside the school; it is for this reason that many PSSC films contain sophisticated experiments performed with simple apparatus."

The writer discusses a second function performed by the integrated teaching film: "The second condition that every film must meet—that of setting level and tone—may well be the most important contribution that the film medium can make. By directing attention to the important questions and the important problems, the film can help assure that all the great mass of fact and concept and theory and application that constitute any field of knowledge will fall into a coherent pattern in which the more important aspects will be clearly differentiated from the trivial. This is most difficult to achieve with the printed word; on film it can be accomplished at times with a gesture. Beyond meeting these two conditions, PSSC attempts in each film to make other substantial contributions to the learning process. Each film shows a real scientist in action, presenting him not as a disembodied intellect but as a normal, active, occasionally fallible human being, dealing rigorously and respectfully with real problems and deriving not only satisfaction but at times excitement from the intellectual pursuit in which he is engaged. It is in this implicit fashion that the films attempt to elucidate the nature of scientists and of the scientific life. . . . The films are scrupulously honest. Experiments that are seen on the screen were carefully performed and are accurately reported. The temptation to use the legerdemain inherent in film processes has been steadily resisted, and in those rare cases where it is used to produce a desirable effect, the student is told explicitly how it is used and why."

The task of the PSSC—the creation of a single high school course in physics—was a specialized one, and the particular problems of the course may not relate to all forms of curriculum construction. Yet there is always a question as to the purpose of any particular device—be it a film of paramecia or a slide projection of a graph or a television show on the Hoover Dam. *The devices themselves cannot dictate their purpose.* Unbridled enthusiasm for audio-visual aids or for teaching machines as panaceas overlooks the paramount importance of what one is trying to accomplish. A perpetual feast of the best teaching films in the world, unrelated to other techniques of teaching, could produce bench-bound passivity. Limiting instruction to a steady diet of classroom recitation supported only by traditional and middling textbooks can make lively subjects dull for the student. The objectives of a curriculum and the balanced means for attaining it should be the guide.

A discussion of teaching aids may seem like an unusual context in which to consider the teacher's role in teaching. Yet, withal, the teacher constitutes the principal aid in the teaching process as it is practiced in our schools. What can be said of the teacher's role in teaching?

It takes no elaborate research to know that communicating knowledge depends in enormous measure upon one's mastery of the knowledge to be communicated. That much is obvious enough—whether the teacher uses other aids or not. It is also quite plain from recent surveys that many primary and secondary school teachers are not, in the view of various official bodies, sufficiently well trained initially to teach their subject. It is also the case that, with the present high turnover in the teaching profession, even relatively well prepared teachers do not have sufficient opportunity to learn their subjects in that special way that comes from teaching it. For teaching is a superb way of learning. There is a beautiful story about a distinguished college teacher of physics. He reports introducing an advanced class to the quantum theory: "I went through it once and looked up only to find the class full of blank faces—they had obviously not understood. I went through it a second time and they still did not understand it. And so I went through it a third time, and that time *I* understood it."

There are certain measures that must be taken to improve the quality of teachers, steps that have been proposed many times and that need no elaboration here. Better recruitment and the possibility of better selection, better substantive education in teacher training institutions, on-the-job training of younger teachers by more experienced ones, in-service and summer institutes, closed-circuit television to continue the education of teachers, improvement in teachers' salaries—all of these must obviously be pursued as objectives. But equally important is the upgrading of the prestige of the teaching profession. This upgrading will depend upon the degree to which we in America are serious about educational reform and the degree to which efforts are made to improve not only the facilities and salaries available to teachers but the support they can count on from the community and from our universities.

One special matter concerning the teacher as communicator of knowledge must be mentioned: the training and qualifications of the elementary-school teachers. Several references have already been made to the training of children concretely and intuitively in logical operations that will later be taught more formally in upper primary and secondary school. Such teaching requires special training, and it is not clear what the most effective form of training is. Special emphasis should very likely be given to such work—research on how to train teachers for such teaching along with research on the actual teaching of younger pupils.

The teacher is not only a communicator but a model. Somebody who does not see anything beautiful or powerful about mathematics is not likely to ignite others with a sense of the intrinsic excitement of the subject. A teacher who will not or cannot give play to his own intuitiveness is not likely to be effective in encouraging intuition in his students. To be so insecure that he dares not be caught in a mistake does not make a teacher a likely model of daring. If the teacher will not risk a shaky hypothesis, why should the student?

To communicate knowledge and to provide a model of competence, the teacher must be free to teach and to learn. We have not been sufficiently mindful of the ways in which such freedom can be achieved. Notably, we have been neglectful of the uses to which educated parents can be put. Various schools have experimented successfully with plans that use parents for the semi-professional tasks that keep teachers pinned down. Parents can certainly help in supervising study halls, in grading routine quizzes, in preparing laboratory materials, and in the dozens of routine operations necessary in a school. The effect would be to free the teacher for teaching and study. If the teacher is also learning, teaching takes on a new quality.

The teacher is also an immediately personal symbol of the educational process, a figure with whom students can identify and compare themselves. Who is not able to recall the impact of some particular teacher—an enthusiast, a devotee of a point of view, a disciplinarian whose ardor came from love of a subject, a playful but serious mind? There are many images, and they are precious. Alas, there are also destructive images: the teachers who sapped confidence, the dream killers, and the rest of the cabinet of horrors.

Whitehead once remarked that education should involve an exposure to greatness. Many of us have been fortunate. But there is no simple plan for attracting greatness to the teaching profession. Emphasis on excellence is still the slow but likely way. Might it not be the case, however, that television and film might expand the range of identification figures—models of greatness—within the special limits imposed by one-way communication? We know relatively little about effective identification figures for children at different ages and in different circumstances. Are Olympian models the only ones or the best ones for engaging a child's sense of competence or greatness? Perhaps promising high school students as guest teachers from time to time would do better? They might also lure more talent into teaching.

In sum, then, the teacher's task as communicator, model, and identification figure can be supported by a wise use of a variety of devices that expand experience, clarify it, and give it personal significance. There need be no conflict between the teacher and the aids to teaching. There will be no conflict if the development of aids takes into account the aims and the requirements of teaching. The film or television show as gimmick, the television system without substance or style in its programs, the pictographically vivid portrayal of the trivial—these will help neither the teacher nor the student. Problems of quality in a curriculum cannot be dodged by the purchase of sixteen-millimeter projection equipment. The National Defense Education Act provides considerable sums of money for the development of audio-visual aids. The intelligent use of that money and of other resources now available will depend upon how well we are able to integrate the technique of the film maker or the program producer with the technique and wisdom of the skillful teacher.

4-3 When the mentally ill child returns to school*

SINCE THE PSYCHOLOGICAL PROFESSIONS HAVE ONLY RE-cently recognized the widespread incidence of mental illness in children, it is not surprising that the education profession is unclear about the help which schools can give in the treatment of mentally ill children. In the past, such children were apparently labeled "feeble-minded," "brain-injured," "queer," and so on, and they were either kept at home or placed in special classes or institutions. Now, however, increased sophistication and understanding on the part of psychiatrists and psychologists give hope of recovery for many mentally ill children, and a school experience for them is considered an important part of the treatment plan.

In the past several years the Berkeley public schools have successfully integrated a number of formerly severely disturbed children into a regular elementary-school setting. This integration has been a cooperative venture, and at every step the planning has involved the teacher, the principal, the school psychologist, the child's therapist, and the parents. Although the particular aspects of school plans for mentally ill children will vary in number as greatly as do the number of children involved, there are probably common aspects of such plans that would have general application.

---

* Norma Haan, "When the Mentally Ill Child Returns to School," *Elementary School Journal* (April, 1957), pp. 379–85.

Norma Haan

It is not our intention to go into the facts and theories of why children or adults become mentally ill (1, 2, 4). Suffice it to say that mental illness does occur in children and that some of these children now sit in public school classrooms without being recognized as ill. There are others who are never brought to school. Some children may be removed from school during an acutely disturbed phase but will return later after psychiatric treatment and experience in a special school. This article is concerned with the educational experience of these latter children.

The magnitude of the problem of severely disturbed children is indicated by the statistical report entitled *Outpatient Psychiatric Clinics of the California State Department of Mental Hygiene* (3) for the year ending June 30, 1954. Although this report does not include the many ill children who are never brought to psychiatric clinics, it reports accurately the number of mentally ill children who are brought to such facilities. According to this report, 10.6 per cent of the children discharged from California state psychiatric clinics during 1954 were mentally ill. This figure does not include children whose illness or home situation was such that hospitalization was necessary. The children reported on are those whose social, emotional, and intellectual development has been atypical and who have not come to feel at home in the world or with themselves, for reasons known or unknown. Generally, many of them appear to have great areas of inhibition or pseudo dulness, coupled with a few areas of amazingly sensitive insight. For many of them, the body and its co-ordination are involved in their inhibition, and all of them feel uncomfortable with others, particularly strangers.

The school's part in all this is related to the developmental tasks of childhood, and in this respect mentally ill children are no different from other children. The job of childhood, if not of all mankind, is learning, formally and informally, from parents, teachers, and peers. Children who are mentally ill have been unable, for one reason or another, to utilize effectively the earlier informal education given them by their parents or have found it necessary to utilize it in an atypical way. As a result the imparting of society's teachings in the classroom by peers and teachers becomes all the more vital for them. In our work with disturbed children we have seen that the informal learnings which result from peer-peer interaction and teacher-pupil interaction aid disturbed children to normalize themselves. However, socialization has not been our only goal because all humans find inherent gratification and reassurance in being able to master the facts, reading materials, and figures suitable for one's age group.

A neurotic child can loosely be thought of as a child who has assiduously overlearned some aspects of society's "do's" and "don't's" in order to reduce his anxiety, while a mentally ill child avoids anxiety by underlearning most of the "do's" and many of the "don't's." The child psychiatrist can sometimes successfully treat the neurotic child without co-ordinating his work with his patient's classroom experience. But, with children such as ours, the co-ordination of teacher and therapist seems indispensable; for learning to trust the world—the most primitive and earliest learning experience—goes hand in hand with the usual later learning of the elementary-school child; indeed, they appear inextricably intermixed. Such co-ordination between school and therapist was always present in the case of the children with whom we have had these experiences, and we feel this co-ordination has contributed to the success of our venture.

It is recognized that there are many degrees and stages of disturbance. There are children whose disturbance is so great that they do not belong in public school, not only for the sake of the equilibrium of the school, but also for the reason that adjusting to the irreducible minimum of control and standardization necessary in the public school classroom may constitute too complicated a problem for the ill child to handle. However, we are concerned here with children who, though they had been considered at one time too disturbed to attend public school, came to need the experience that a regular classroom can provide. The decision that the children were ready for such an experience was made by those who had the experience to offer (the teacher and the principal) and by those who had previously been responsible for the development of the child (his parents, his psychiatrist, and special school personnel).

We shall examine our experiences from the standpoint of (1) control and permissiveness, (2) relations with other children, and (3) academic work. We shall try to summarize what seems incredibly intangible, that is, the benefits to the disturbed child.

Control and Permissiveness

One of the chief sources of anxiety for any teacher who receives mentally ill children in his classroom is the problem of classroom order and management. Each teacher who has had experience with these children has reported an initial period of experimentation in the process of finding out how much conformity can be required and how much permissiveness must be granted. We have come to call this "playing by ear," because there seems to be no way to communicate from teacher to teacher or from therapist to teacher the amount of conformity that can be expected from any particular child. This we have found true for all such children, not only in the beginning of their school experiences, but also when they are being passed from one teacher to the next. It is evident that the interaction among the personalities of the child, the teacher, and the group is a complicated process. For the psychiatrist or psychologist to lay down ground rules in advance may make for constriction and artificiality in this interaction, which is most productive when it is genuine and natural. Furthermore, the amount of conformity that can be expected from these children seems to change with the day, the hour, and the situation. One teacher said that on some days she suggested to a primary-grade child that he put a puzzle away; on another day she requested that he put the puzzle away; and on other days she demanded that he put the puzzle away.

Another variable that obviously affects the polarities of conformity and permissiveness is the nature of the particular activity involved. Climbing on cupboards can be dangerous, but talking to one's self is not and only becomes important as a long-range indicator of one's social growth. The question is obviously related to the values placed on classroom behavior, not only in terms of the individual child's safety, but also in terms of his growth, when growth is seen as his increasing ability to relate himself harmoniously and meaningfully to others. Rules and controls are to be learned, not imposed, as part of growth, and the fact that abiding by the rules brings greater adult peace of mind is one of the happy facts of life. We are focusing this discussion largely on the disturbed child and are not thinking of conformity in terms of the group's standard because we have discovered that the group, even when composed of kindergarten children, does not demand conformity from the disturbed child which is identical to that demanded of the group.

Underlying the ups and downs of the disturbed child's conforming or his failure to conform are the slow-moving, but persistent, gains in being willing to do what the teacher asks. Many of these children have found survival in inexorably thwarting the educative attempts of their parents, but in the schoolroom the teacher has powerful allies, not possessed by the parents, in the form of thirty-five children of the same age. Time and again we have seen the other children expect conformity and accomplishment, and win, where an adult would fail. It is evident that the children's unabashed astonishment at nonconformity cannot be effectively operative in a teacher-centered classroom. The effect of other children on the disturbed pupil is somewhat stronger in the upper grades. This fact is related to the older children's stronger orientation toward their peers and weaker orientation toward their teachers. At the same time, the children are generous in their recognition of gains made by the disturbed child; we have heard many comments about how "So-and-so is getting much better." One cannot escape the impression that these comments are not directed merely to the disturbed child's increased conformity but are also astute and sensitive observations of increased psychic well-being.

There is no doubt that a disturbed child can utilize the pressure from his normal peers for a multitude of reasons; the cultural, wide, and impersonal expectation that all children shall go to school to learn is a powerful lever. Our disturbed children have been incredibly pleased and gratified when they knew that they were to attend public school "like other kids." Mentally ill children know that they have problems and that they are disturbed, and the increased normality and health that are implied by regular school attendance must be a reassurance of no small importance. The demands of other children and of that somewhat more impersonal and different adult, the teacher, can sometimes be met a little differently, perhaps, from the way in which the demands of parents have been met. One teacher persuaded a child to give up wearing his rubber pants to school and to use the school lavatory, although previous attempts by the home had been rebuffed. No doubt, too, the inevitable competitiveness in the situation and the meeting of new competitors of one's own age hasten accomplishment through imitation.

Almost all these children have some unusual and eccentric symptoms. For the most part, these symptoms are self-directed; that is, they have personal meaning for the child but are not too obnoxious socially, although they may be irritating. We have in mind such things as making funny noises, rocking back and forth, and being obsessed with prehistoric times, cars, television programs, etc. These seem to operate from the very depths of the child's being. Some symptoms appear when things are unusually upset at home or at school, and they disappear when things are again more comfortable. We do not interfere with the symptoms, but sometimes we try to distract and redirect the child. The symptoms are weather vanes, and, as growth progresses in the school and in therapy, the symptoms disappear.

Relations with Other Children

As school is a standardized group situation for the most part, one of the first and most inevitable things a teacher needs to consider is the group's attitude toward the unstandardized, and sometimes unusual, disturbed child. In almost all classrooms we have found it necessary to structure for the group, at some time, something of the nature of the mentally ill child's difficulty and the role of the group members in relation to him. The explanation is best given after the pupils have had some experience with the child. The structuring needs to be done within the specific and limited frame of reference of the particular child and his unusual behavior that is causing anxiety in the group. As seems to be generally true of adult society's fantasized preconceptions about mentally ill people, children's fantasized preconceptions sometimes are far beyond the bounds of reality. Always the teacher's explanations to the group seem best when they are simple, convey his acceptance of the child, and indicate the need for a helping role toward the disturbed child. We have given calm, matter-of-fact explanations, such as, "We are all different, and he hasn't had the chance to learn some of the things, or as many things, as you have yet. Sometimes he gets unhappy, and, when he gets unhappy, he may scream. We must help him."

We have found that intermediate-grade pupils demand more explanations, patricularly in regard to their own role, than do primary-grade pupils, who require almost no structuring at all. At the same time, intermediate-grade children play a more active role with the disturbed youngster. One teacher found that other children in the room were much more successful in quieting the disturbed child after an anxiety attack than was the teacher himself. Older children can be used, too, as protective companions for the child when he must temporarily escape the confines of the room.

We have come to believe that the involvement of other pupils with the disturbed child is a most valuable curriculum experience from a number of standpoints. One teacher said that the effect on the other pupils had been one of producing "better citizens because of the real need to share, practice tolerance, show consideration, and realize the worth of each individual. Not many children have this experience made so real to them." Certainly, the concept of the worth of the individual, upon which our democratic philosophy rests, can be made no more clear to children than it is when a teacher accepts a disturbed child and his behavior because the teacher knows that he can do no other in the school situation—a situation which has been constructed and arranged by cultural agreement to produce a modicum of, and an opportunity for, basic cultural uniformity. One teacher said, "I notice the wonderful attitude they have towards me. I can't help but feel that they appreciate the allowances that I have made for the disturbed one. They seem to have this attitude in all activities, and not just those around the disturbed child, which conveys a feeling that they are all working with me and not just for me." To us there seems to be no dichotomy here between disturbed and normal children with regard to making allowances. Rather, the emotional growth of each child is regarded in the same way that intellectual growth has been for so long: "You take the child where he is and go on from there."

Children seem to sense, sometimes more quickly and accurately than do adults, that the child's disturbed behavior comes because he cannot help it. When a teacher scolded one of our disturbed children for not finishing his work, a little girl said, "But, Miss Jones, Tom is much better about finishing than he used to be." Another value for all the children, although probably more subtle, is the reassurance, implicit in the disturbed child's presence and treatment in the classroom that, if they themselves should find themselves in a situation where they can do no other, people will treat them protectively and kindly. Basically, this is a prophylactic principle, because much disturbance in modern society is, in part, the fear of losing control rather than the actual loss of control. No doubt, too, the presence of mentally ill children in ordinary classrooms will aid in the reduction of the stereotypes and fantasies surrounding psychological handicaps, as has been the result of integration programs involving physically handicapped children.

We have had some parental reaction to the presence of these children in classrooms. The parents' questions have been answered satisfactorily in terms of the gains for the class as a whole. Some parents, to judge from their children's comments, have apparently utilized the opportunity to help their children understand differences in people and to suggest an attitude toward the child based first on his being an ordinary person and only secondarily on consideration of his handicap. Most parents have been satisfied with the teacher's explanations, and seem to believe they need feel no concern as long as the teacher and the principal have had no cause to believe that the majority was suffering. Some parents have, without suggestion, fitted into the school's plan by inviting the disturbed child to accompany their own child in out-of-school activities.

Academic Work

When a neurotic child has an emotional difficulty which affects his school learning, one can hope that, once his emotional problems are resolved through psychiatric treatment, he will quickly catch up. However, with the sort of child we are discussing, the fact of not learning at all is, in a sense, the primary difficulty. He is in some ways a thing unblossomed, and whatever gains he can make in formal learning at school will aid the blossoming and normalizing process. Furthermore, the recovery process, even under the best conditions, is much longer than for a neurotic child, perhaps four or five years, so that a disturbed child could be hopelessly behind and suffering secondary complications if all academic learning were delayed until his recovery. It is a question whether complete, or even partial, recovery could be obtained without the accompaniment of school learning. However, academic learning is secondary to the group experiences. Learning cannot be forced, although, after some experiences with a particular child, we have found there are days when a little judicious pressure pays dividends.

Disturbed children will not learn unless they are emotionally able, at a particular time, to do so. Inducing them to learn requires the greatest persistence and timing. However, most of these children learn a great deal without seeming to have learned anything. For example, one of them reported at home in great detail and accuracy the content of a social-studies lesson but was seemingly not listening or not understanding at school. One day when a primary-grade child felt in a particularly communicative frame of mind, his teacher asked him to respond to a number of flash cards. He knew all the words that had been taught and none of the others. His teacher had thought he had absorbed nothing up to that point.

Roles of Other Adults

The principal of the school plays a vital role in the school's plan for the mentally ill child. It is he who, first and maybe for some years, has helped in establishing a climate of easy and frank human interaction between himself and staff and between staff and children. This quality of human understanding is characterized in one principal's observation: "If we understood enough about any one child, we would then understand that what he is doing is normal for him in terms of the history of his experiences." The principal's influence is first exercised in selecting teachers who will feel challenged by dealing with these children. It is probably true that being a good teacher is not necessarily synonymous with being an effective interactor with mentally disturbed children.

Our principal was sometimes able to give the teacher assistance. For some children the principal's office can become a haven when on a particular day the group is too stimulating and anxiety-provoking. During the early stages of adjustment to school by one upper-grade child, the child and a classmate arrived in the principal's office. The child was obviously severely agitated, and his classmate said that they would like to talk to the principal. A more or less innocuous conversation followed. After a bit, the two left. The child was calm again, and his classmate gave the principal the Churchillian "V for victory" sign as the two went out the door.

The certain assurance that the authority of the principal will set things straight is useful in reassuring frightened children. Some mentally disturbed children become acutely agitated over minor scratches and injuries. Knowing and understanding the child, the principal and the nurse are able to understand and reduce his terror over this body violation. We have seen our children progress from acute agitation over a sliver to casual indifference.

The secretary and the janitor in our school also have known something of the mentally ill child who is just learning that the world is essentially a safe place, and they have, when occasion demanded, dealt with him as an individual. Other teachers, too, who direct special activities have played roles in helping our children widen their horizons of participation and achievement. Some of the children have gone to other classrooms when they could not or would not participate in the necessary activities (an excursion, for example) in their home rooms.

Summary

We feel that we have had the privilege of sharing an unusually gratifying and stimulating experience. We have seen growth processes at work that are not different from, but perhaps more clearly basic than, those ordinarily seen in an elementary school. Our participation in them and our contribution to them have seemed great. We shall continue to work with mentally disturbed children. We feel that we have hardly scratched the surface in finding methods and techniques of providing a public school experience for such youngsters.

References

1. BETTELHEIM, BRUNO. *Love Is Not Enough.* Glencoe, Illinois: Free Press, 1950.
2. BETTELHEIM, BRUNO. *Truants from Life.* Glencoe, Illinois: Free Press, 1955.
3. CALIFORNIA STATE DEPARTMENT OF MENTAL HYGIENE. *Outpatient Psychiatric Clinics of California State Department of Mental Hygiene.* Sacramento, California: State Department of Mental Hygiene, June 30, 1954.
4. CAPLAN, GERALD. *Emotional Problems of Early Childhood.* New York: Basic Books, 1955.

4-4 The administrator and the new curriculums*

MOST ADMINISTRATORS CAN RECALL THEIR TEXTBOOK ACcounts of the great curriculum revisions of a half-century ago: The Committee of Ten (1893), The Committee of Fifteen (1895), The Committee of Nine (1911). However, the revisions now in progress make the present a period of equal or greater historical significance: revisions are far-reaching and often revolutionary, participation is universal within the educational community, and communication betwen the revisers and the practitioners is at a maximum.

There is yet another element lending excitement and importance to the present activity in curriculum. Former revisions helped the schools catch up with a changing industrial America. Today's work attempts to place the schools in a leadership position for social change. Harvard's President Nathan Pusey probably stated it best in 1955, when the first rumblings were heard: "Today it should be transparently clear to all that our first need is less for specialists than for diffused wisdom and reliability in society."

Those two qualities—wisdom and reliability—may be considered the hallmarks of curriculum projects planned or already underway. For the school and college administrator, this means approaching today's curriculum with the utmost seriousness and patience. Certainly new problems and responsibilities will emerge. Teachers must be trained and re-trained in every discipline at every level. New equipment, radical in design

---

* "The Administrator and the New Curriculums," *Overview*, Vol. 3, No. 4 (April, 1962), pp. 33–37, 63.

and exotic in composition, must be acquired. Concepts of classroom space must be re-appraised and buildings put up which can accommodate new methods and materials integral to the new curriculums.

Although all levels of education are feeling the impact of change, the developments in curriculum tend to polarize in the secondary school. From here, theorists work back to the requirements of the primary grades and forward to the expectations of higher education. The following descriptions fall within this framework. OVERVIEW offers them with the hope that its readers will be able to administer change (*i.e.*, promote wisdom and reliability) all the better after having the total picture in mind.

The New Science

Most science curriculum projects have been devoted to single subjects within the field. Three of these projects—the Physical Science Study Committee, the Chemical Bond Approach, and the Chemical Education Materials Studies—are aimed at secondary-school students in the top scholastic half. A fourth—the Biological Science Curriculum Study—is currently limited to secondary education, but will soon reach into the elementary schools. Each project, however, would provide general courses for all students, yet serve as introductions for specialization in each field later on.

Elementary school science studies, largely taking their cues from high school projects, are nevertheless in progress. Several are exploring the general needs and procedures for updating elementary school instruction; others are aimed at discovering just which basic concepts can be taught effectively for a smooth transition to high school power courses.

The Physical Science Study Committee program was the first secondary science project established (1956, at MIT) and is nearing completion. A committee of college professors, high school teachers, and scientific and technical specialists have developed a modern high school physics course and the materials for teaching it. The PSSC course is a study in depth of basic concepts in modern physics. Stress is put on open-ended laboratory work; students gain understanding of scientific methods as well as the conclusions of modern physics through concentrated, individual lab work. (Individual lab work and independent "discovery" studies are keystones of most curriculum revision. The implications for administrators of this emphasis on individual learning are, of course, profound. See March '61 and March '62 OVERVIEW.)

Course textbooks and materials have been exhaustively tested and revised according to teacher suggestions and pupil performance on achievement tests. Commercial editions and models based on PSSC work became available in 1960. Achievement tests are produced by Educational Testing Service, which participates in the project. This school year, more than 1,800 teachers are using the PSSC course with over 50,000 students.

The "new physics"—thermodynamics, quantum theory, space science, solid state physics—poses an enormous challenge to the American teacher. More than 1,300 have attended resident summer institutes to learn the new facts and teaching methods resulting from the PSSC project. Intensive in-service training for physics teachers—as indeed for teachers in all disciplines—will be one of the great tasks of the decade.

The Chemical Bond Approach was organized in the spring of 1959 to develop a modern introductory chemistry course. Believing that present-day high school chemistry is a series of unrelated assignments, CBA researchers developed a new course integrated around the concept of chemical bonds (relationships between atomic structures, fundamental to understanding nuclear physics). Again, independent lab work is stressed.

Materials for CBA were tested and revised during the 1959–60 and 1960–61 school years; further tests are now going on. Course materials should be approved and commercially available in the spring of 1963, according to the CBA group. Achievement tests (again, prepared with the help of ETS) are being used to measure student progress in pilot courses. Results so far show that superior students make excellent progress with the sophisticated CBA program; average pupils, however, have done reasonably well. The CBA staff feels their course will eventually be within the grasp of the average high school chemistry student and are directing current research toward this goal.

A more recent high school chemistry project, begun in 1960, is being worked out by the Chemical Education Materials Study (called CHEM). The CHEM approach is best indicated by the title of its first textbook: *Chemistry—An Experimental Science.* Intensive lab work, through which students "discover" principles and methods of modern chemistry, is the heart of the course; the text and other learning materials are used as study aids. Two-thirds of a student's first two weeks is spent in the laboratory; however, emphasis on learning by experimenting and observing continues throughout the year.

Course materials for CHEM are being tried out in about a hundred schools this year. After a final revision they might be available for general use in 1963–64.

The Biological Sciences Curriculum Study passed its third year in January, the child of the American Institute of Biological Sciences. During the project's first eighteen months, plans were formulated for three new high school biology programs: one would be ecological and evolutionary; another, genetic and developmental; and the third, biochemical and physiological.

Last year preliminary versions of BSCS textbooks and teaching guides were used by 104 teachers working with 14,000 students. Criticisms by teachers and data from a thorough testing program lent direction to last summer's revisions. (Meanwhile, twenty-one summer institutes for biology teachers were also held in 1961.) The newer materials are being widely tested (520 teachers and 52,000 students) during the current school year for the final revision.

In BSCS, the emphasis is also on open-ended lab work. The staff is now developing a series of twelve "laboratory block" programs. These would be sequential experiments related to major biological areas, such as plant growth and development. Each six-week "block" would deepen a pupil's understanding of general scientific methods and specific biological concepts.

The Universities of California and Illinois are carrying on seminar studies in elementary school science. The Californians are emphasizing the teaching of a conceptual framework within which children can perceive and interpret phenomena and organize conclusions. About a thousand pupils from schools in various socio-economic neighborhoods have tested the California units. Results indicate that youngsters can learn basic science, they enjoy using inductive reasoning, and teachers work successfully with the program.

The Illinois project, begun in 1960, concentrates on basic knowledge. The guideline, says co-director J. Myron Atkins, is "not the apparent interests of children . . . not the social utility of science. Children's interests are important. . . . But we feel a deep interest in science can result from a basic understanding [of it]." Initial efforts have gone into an astronomy course (an interdisciplinary subject). From experiments with fourth-graders have come two teaching booklets. These booklets are now being tested by 250 teachers and 7,500 pupils. After revisions this summer, the booklets will go out for further tests and revisions. Concurrently, films, apparatus, manuals, and tests are also being prepared.

The New Math

The mathematics curriculum in American schools and universities has remained virtually unchanged for a century. This is especially the case in the lower schools, where the course sequence was the slave of tradition. However, math is in the throes of revolution.

In 1959, after a three-year study, the College Entrance Examination Board's Committee on Mathematics published recommendations for a program to enable high school graduates to begin college math with calculus and analytical geometry. Prospective college students would thus take at least three—and preferably four—years of high school math.

Whereas the CEEB restricted its study to college-capable students, the National Council of Teachers of Mathematics set to work on new math programs for all secondary school students. Its Secondary School Curriculum Committee supports Dr. Conant's recommendation for at least four years of math for all.

According to the NCTM committee, the "new math" treats traditional elements more thoroughly and from new points of view, introduces new elements, and eliminates some outdated ones. Beneath it all is an instructional approach that helps students understand the unity of all mathematics. The student is to learn this through individual "discoveries." The committee recommends that the repetitive, tedious "social arithmetic" of grades seven and eight be reduced in favor of instruction in basic arithmetical concepts and skills and that simple algebra and geometry be introduced to all junior high students. The NCTM people don't advocate dropping ninth-grade algebra back to the eighth grade (as recommended by some other revisers); but they do feel that a more suitable eighth-grade algebra program is possible.

Ten years ago, the University of Illinois Committee on School Mathematics began working on a new college preparatory math curriculum. Text materials for grades nine through eleven were given extensive trials, and were carefully revised. They are now available in eight units, each with a teacher's guide. (Twelfth grade units are nearing publication.)

Illinois course materials and methods are designed to evoke discovery and the understanding of generalizations. An extensive teacher-training program—summer institutes with supervised follow-ups of all participants—helps teachers gain command of the content and methods. For many instructors, these institutes are jarring; having been sold on the "order and symmetry" of math in their own schooldays, they now are exposed to irrational, unequal, and illogical numbers and must grapple with the meaning of infinity.

Another comprehensive curriculum project is being carried out by the School Mathematics Study Group, now based at Stanford University under the direction of Professor E. G. Begle. The SMSG group is developing improved math programs for college-capable high schoolers, average students, and for fourth- through sixth-graders. SMSG textbooks (for superior students) introduce modern math and give a deeper understanding of traditional math elements. They do not embark on a radically different sequence of study, however.

Among other things, this group is working on a correspondence course for superior students in small schools, programmed materials for teaching machines, and a study of student attitudes toward math in general and SMSG materials in particular.

At the elementary school level, math researchers are creating much excitement. One example is the curriculum being carried on now for some ten thousand first-, second-, and third-graders in Bucks County, Pennsylvania. Called the "Math Workshop for Children" by its publisher, Encyclopedia Britannica Films, it introduces youngsters to fractions, negative numbers, and algebra. Pupils use special texts and workbooks, manipulate a "number line," and juggle sophisticated number sets. The Workshop's originators, Drs. Morton Botel and Robert Wirtz, developed their course on the theory that children can grasp these concepts at an earlier age than was commonly thought possible. Games, cut-outs, counting blocks, and other tactual materials are used extensively. Underlying the Workshop is the feeling that various branches of math—arithmetic, algebra, trigonometry—can be taught together.

The University of Illinois, which has effectively taken leadership as the "home base" for much new curriculum work, also has a comprehensive math program under study for K-6. Stanford is involved in a geometry curriculum for K-6.

Mathematics is evoking new responses from several other sources. Administrators must be warned, however, that parts of one project cannot be usefully "spliced" into another.

The New English

Several major changes have occurred in the English curriculum over the past three decades. Developmental reading has become the rule in junior and senior highs; listening skills are part of every syllabus; and reading, writing, speaking, and listening are recognized as interrelated and are taught together whenever possible. Appreciation of literature and creative writing are widely used to help pupils understand themselves and their society. Critical thinking, propaganda analysis, and evaluation of mass media reflect the impact of current events, as does the growing use of foreign stories and poems.

Many of these changes are outgrowths of two reports by the National Council of Teachers of English. The first, "An Experience Curriculum in English" (1935), states that literature should be taught not only for its practical values, but also for the way in which it can enrich the lives of students. The second report was a massive, three-volume study: "The English Language Arts" (1952), "Language Arts for Today's Children" (1954), and "The English Language Arts in the Secondary School" (1956).

The 1956 volume called for a broad variety of content and instruction to cope with the wide range of student abilities (English classes were among the first to try ability grouping). Among the recommendations: individualized reading programs, study of mass media, and nonchronological study of literature. The report also advocated a functional approach to the teaching of grammar.

But many of these new ideas have not been as widely incorporated into curriculums as their originators hoped. In senior high schools especially, individualized reading programs are not generally accepted as supplements to the class study of literary masterpieces. If it were not for the paperback book, progress in this area would be at a standstill.

In addition, the teaching of grammar by traditional perscriptive methods—learning the rules in a fixed sequence—persists in many schools. The "structural linguistics" movement (hampered by a rather private jargon of its own) has not become the wave of the future either.

The Commission on English was established in 1959 as a function of the College Entrance Examination Board to make recommendations for a modern college preparatory curriculum. In a preliminary statement the Commission held that high school English suffers from "confusion about what legitimate curriculum content should be and too little coordination of its parts," inadequately prepared teachers, and poor working conditions for teachers and students."

The Commission has set forth certain goals for the new curriculum. In Language: attention to spelling, vocabulary enrichment, study of word derivations and changes in meanings, and modern grammar and usage. In Literature: chiefly, but not exclusively, American and English prose and poetry, with specific unabridged masterpieces parcelled out each year for intensive study. In Composition: original student writing to be part of each week's work (exposition rather than creative writing) with subjects derived from concurrent studies in language and literature.

This summer, twenty institutes (forty teachers in each) will be held on as many college campuses. Participants will take graduate courses and prepare materials for their own 1962–63 classes. A follow-up program will enable these teachers to take part in the further development of Commission materials. In addition, the Commission is producing three series of thirty-minute films that show how to teach the "new English."

Last year the NCTE issued a report titled "The National Interest and the Teaching of English." It contained curriculum recommendations, pleaded for an easing of class loads and extracurricular assignments (yearbook, school paper, dramatics, etc.), and cited as the biggest problem of today's English curriculum the lack of a proper year-to-year course sequence. This latter criticism applies not only to the English curriculum, but to all other curriculums as well in today's school. To Dr. Pusey's plea for wisdom and reliability, many revisers would unhesitatingly add "continuity."

The New Languages

During World War II, the armed forces gave language training to students in intensive nine-month doses. Films, recordings, and small-group conversational drill were used extensively and the program was highly successful.

Current trends in foreign language teaching date from 1952. In that year the U.S. Office of Education took a strong position favoring such study on every level, and the Modern Language Association of America began a comprehensive investigation of the place of language study.

Four years later, in 1956, the MLA declared that foreign language study should have these results: (1) skills should be developed for real language mastery; (2) students should gain understanding of a foreign language so as to give them a better perspective of English; (3) students should know the cultural similarities and differences between the United States and the country whose language is studied.

Other recommendations were: learning should begin with hearing and speaking the language ("direct learning"); accurate comprehend without conscious translation; audio-visual aids (especially those combined in a language lab) should be used extensively. Secondary and higher education were encouraged to expand their Near Eastern, Eurasian, and Asian language study programs (January '62 OVERVIEW, page 62).

Figures compiled by the MLA show that the number of foreign language elementary school students soared from about 145,000 in 1953 to approximately one and one quarter millions in 1961, while secondary school enrollments jumped from nearly 740,000 in 1948 to about one and three quarter millions.

Key influences behind the increases, the MLA says, are federal support for foreign language teaching under the NDEA, and the advocacy by Dr. Conant and others of a four year foreign language program in the comprehensive high school.

Despite widespread agreement on the importance of foreign language study, a number of questions have not been answered. Should foreign languages be studied in elementary school? If so, how many years of instruction should there be? Can continuity be assured, whether it begins in elementary or secondary school? Answers are being sought by various Foreign Language in the Elementary School (FLES) programs.

FLES developed slowly after World War II. Then, in 1953, it was given impetus by an MLA report defending elementary school foreign language study. The report called for fifteen-minute classes three to five times a week in kindergarten through grade two, and twenty-to-thirty-minute classes for grades three through six, plus extra work for superior students.

In 1954 the MLA issued a second report expressing reservations about its own initial recommendations. The report said they had been based largely on subjective opinions rather than experimental data, and that time for foreign languages presented difficulties in developing an integrated elementary school curriculum. In 1956 MLA again endorsed FLES but cautioned against "faddish aspects of this movement." The committee declared that no elementary school foreign language program could succeed unless a majority of parents had approved it, adequately prepared teachers were hired, reliable materials had been purchased, and provisions for careful evaluation had been made.

Last year the MLA issued even stronger warnings against mounting an inadequate program. "Hundreds of communities have ignored our admonitions," said the MLA's language advisory and liaison committee; many programs were clearly "wasteful and disappointing, and have misled many persons about the nature and value of such study." The committee has also advised that school systems unable to afford both FLES and a six-year secondary school program should give precedence to the latter.

The MLA is developing achievement tests for modern languages most commonly studied in secondary schools. Tests cover listening, speaking, and writing skills in French, German, Italian, Russian, and Spanish, and are expected to be ready for general use this fall. Proficiency tests are also being developed in a drive to raise levels of teacher preparation, performance, and certification.

The New Social Sciences

The National Council for the Social Studies and the American Council of Learned Societies are co-sponsoring a study of the K-12 social studies curriculum. This joint study—like so many others in the current ferment—has classroom instructors working with university scholars to assure the core of "wisdom and reliability" deemed essential to all new curriculums.

NCSS and ACLS joined forces after preliminary studies had revealed a gap between social science research and course content. They are now engaged in the development of a squence for social studies with emphasis on the cumulative development of knowledge, skills, and attitudes. Another study will delineate the concepts students should know before graduating from high school.

Besides the broad-scale NCSS-ACLS project, there are several specialized programs underway.

The project for Improving the Teaching of World Affairs began at Glens Falls, N.Y., in 1957 under the joint sponsorship of the Glens Falls Board of Education and NCSS. The district was chosen because of its strong professional staff, board of education approval, and a favorable climate of opinion in the community.

The project has been carried out under these conditions: (1) all grades and curriculum areas are involved; (2) the existing curriculum is used, no special courses are introduced; (3) every source of teaching evaluation is being used; (4) the program is related to community activities; (5) the bulk of the program is supported by the district's regular operating budget. An evaluation of the project will be out this fall.

Among the social sciences, economics is forging rapidly ahead as an important element. In 1953 the National Association of Secondary School Principals chose economics as the first project for its Council for the Advancement of Secondary Education. Two research projects were completed out of which CASE published a series of five-unit text-booklets now widely used.

In 1961, another economics study group, the National Task Force on Economic Education, also published recommendations for high school economics teaching. The group was appointed by the American Economics Association and financed by the Committee for Economic Development. The task force called for instruction that intensifies objective, rational thinking about economic problems. It suggested a group of major economic issues and problem areas with which students should be familiar, such as income distribution, economic growth, and international trade. It warns against fostering mere memorization of facts and figures, and advocates discussion of controversial issues related to course content. (The Task Force itself became the subject of controversy when the *Wall Street Journal* labeled its recommendations as anti-free enterprise. See January '62 OVERVIEW, page 23.)

In September 1961, the Association of American Geographers and the National Council for Geographic Education began a study to revise high school courses in that field. The initial project has been a course for classroom film and television use. By January of 1962 a preliminary version of the course had been mapped out. It will be tested during 1962–63, then released.

Bibliographies

Section One: "Educational Decisions in Various Societies"

BEREDAY, GEORGE Z. F., "A Comparative Look at English, French, and Soviet Education." *Educational Leadership,* Vol. 16 (January 1959), 215–223.

CLARK, COLIN, "World Population Growth," *Teachers College Record,* Vol. 63 (March 1962), 418–424.

HOLLINSHEAD, BYRON S., "American and European Education: Why the Differences?" *NEA Journal,* Vol. 48 (February 1959), 56–59.

KING, EDMUND J., *Other Schools and Ours.* New York: Rinehart & Company, Inc., 1958.

KINNE, ERNEST W., "A Fulbrighter Views Dutch Education: A Comparative Study," *Journal of Higher Education,* Vol. 30 (January 1959), 15–26.

LAVES, WALTER H. C. and CHARLES A. THOMSON, UNESCO: *Purposes, Progress, Prospects.* Bloomington, Indiana: Indiana University Press, 1957, 163 pp.

MEAD, MARGARET, *Cultural Patterns and Technical Change.* New York: New American Library, 1955, 294 pp.

MILLER, RICHARD I., "Framework for Education in Newly Emerging Nations," *School and Society,* Vol. 89, No. 2199 (November 18, 1961), 399–401.

PARKER, FRANKLIN, "UNESCO at 15: Young Adam in Troubled Eden," *School and Society,* Vol. 89, No. 2201 (December 16, 1961), 431–433.

SHUSTER, GEORGE, "The Trials and Triumphs of UNESCO," *Saturday Review,* February 24, 1962, pp. 21–22, 63.

SNOWDEN, FRANK M. JR., "A European View of American Education," *Educational Forum,* Vol. 23 (March 1959), 343–349.

U. S. OFFICE OF EDUCATION, *Soviet Commitment to Education: Report of the First Official U.S. Education Mission to the U.S.S.R.; with an Analysis of Recent Educational Reforms.* Bulletin 1959, No. 16, Washington, D.C.: Government Printing Office, 1959, 135 pp.

Section Two: "The Function of Education in a Society"

BORROWMAN, M. L., "Traditional Values and the Shaping of American Education," *National Society for the Study of Education Yearbook,* Part 2, 1960, pp. 144–170.

BRAMELD, THEODORE B. H., *Education for the Emerging Age: Newer Ends and Stronger Means.* New York: Harper and Brothers, 1961.

CURTI, MERLE, *The Social Ideas of American Educators.* New York: Pageant Books, Inc., 1959.

DEWEY, JOHN, *Democracy and Education.* New York: The Macmillan Company, 1961, (Macmillan Paperback Edition).

DEWEY, JOHN, *Experience and Education.* New York: The Macmillan Company, 1944.

EDUCATIONAL POLICIES COMMISSION, *The Unique Function of Education in American Democracy.* Washington, D.C.: National Education Association, 1937.

Educating for Economic Competence. Washington, D.C.: Association for Supervision and Curriculum Development, 1960.

HOFFER, ERIC, *The True Believer.* New York: New American Library of World Literature, Inc., 1958.

LA BARRE, WESTON, *The Human Animal.* Chicago: University of Chicago Press, 1955. (Paperback)

LEE, DOROTHY, *Freedom and Culture.* Englewood Cliffs, N.J.: Prentice-Hall, Inc., 1959.

POPPER, KARL, *The Open Society and Its Enemies.* Princeton, New Jersey: Princeton University Press, 1950.

ROE, ANNE and GEORGE SIMPSON, *Behavior and Evolution.* New Haven, Conn.: Yale University Press, 1958.

ROKEACH, MILTON, *The Open and Closed Mind.* New York: Basic Books, 1960.

SMITH, T. V. and EDUARD C. LINDEMAN, *The Democratic Way of Life.* New York: New American Library of World Literature, Inc., 1951, a Mentor Paperback.

THAYER, V. T., *The Role of the School in American Society.* New York: Dodd, Mead & Company, 1960.

UNITED STATES COMMISSION ON CIVIL RIGHTS REPORT, *Education.* Washington, D. C.: Government Printing Office, 1961.

Section Three: "Contributions of the Behavioral Sciences"

ALLPORT, GORDON, *Pattern and Growth in Personality.* New York: Holt, Rinehart and Winston Inc., 1961.

BRUNER, JEROME, *The Process of Education*. Cambridge: Harvard University Press, 1961.
ERIKSON, ERIK H., *Childhood and Society*. New York: W. W. Norton and Co., Inc., 1950.
Freeing Capacity to Learn. Association for Supervision and Curriculum Development. Washington, D.C.: National Education Association, 1960.
GETZELS, JACOB W. and PHILIP W. JACKSON, *Creativity and Intelligence*. New York: John Wiley and Sons, Inc., 1962.
HAAN, AUBREY, "How Children Grow," Ch. ii in Aubrey Haan, *Elementary School Curriculum*. Boston: Allyn and Bacon, Inc., 1961.
HAMMER, EMANUEL F., *Creativity*. New York: Random House, Inc., 1961. (Paperback)
KRUGMAN, MORRIS (ed.), *Orthopsychiatry and the School*. New York: American Orthopsychiatric Association, Inc., 1958.
New Dimension in Learning, A Multidisciplinary Approach. Association for Supervision and Curriculum Development. Washington, D.C.: National Education Association, 1962.
TRILLING, LIONEL, *Freud and the Crisis of Our Culture*. Boston: Beacon Press, 1955.
WALLACE, ANTHONY F. C., *Culture and Personality*. New York: Random House, Inc., 1961.
WHITING, JOHN W. M. and IRVIN CHILD, *Child Training and Personality*. New Haven: Yale University Press, 1953.

Section Four: "Explorations in Modern Education"

ANDERSON, ROBERT, "Team Teaching in the Elementary Schools," *Education Digest*, XXV (November, 1959), 26–28.
CONANT, JAMES B., *Slums and Suburbs*. New York: McGraw-Hill Book Company, Inc., 1961.
GOODLAD, JOHN I. and ROBERT ANDERSON, *The Nongraded Elementary School*. New York: Harcourt, Brace and Company, 1959.
HAAN, AUBREY, "Teacher Personality and Curriculum," ch. xii in Haan, Aubrey, *Elementary School Curriculum: Theory and Research*, Boston: Allyn & Bacon, Inc., 1961.
HARRIS, DALE B., "Work and the Adolescent Transition to Maturity," *Teachers College Record*, Vol. 63, No. 2 (November 1961), 146–153.
HAUSER, PHILIP M., "Population—gap in the curriculum," *Teachers College Record*, Vol. 63, No. 6 (March 1962), 425–433.
HOLLAND, JAMES, "Evaluating Teaching Machines and Programs," *Teachers College Record*, Vol. 63, No. 1 (October 1961), 56–65.
JERSILD, ARTHUR, *When Teachers Face Themselves*. New York: Bureau of Publications, Teachers College, Columbia University, 1955.
KRUGMAN, MORRIS, *Orthopsychiatry and the School*. New York: American Orthopsychiatric Association, Inc., 1958.

LICHTER, SOLOMON, ELSIE B. RAPIEN, FRANCES M. SEIBERT and MORRIS A. SLANSKY, *The Drop-Outs.* New York: Free Press of Glencoe, 1962.

LUMSDAINE, A. A. and ROBERT GLASER, *Teaching Machines and Programmed Learning.* Washington, D.C.: National Education Association, 1960.

SARASON, SEYMOUR, KENNETH DAVIDSON and BURTON BLATT, *The Preparation of Teachers, an Unstudied Problem In Education.* New York: John Wiley and Sons, Inc., 1962.

Self-Contained Classroom. Association for Supervision and Curriculum Development. Washington, D.C.: NEA, 1960.

Reference Chart Bibliography

(*see next page*)

Callahan, Raymond, *An Introduction to Education in American Society*. New York: Alfred A. Knopf, 1960.

Cressman, George B. and Harold W. Benda, *Public Education in America*. New York: Appleton-Century-Crofts, Inc., 1961.

Crow, Lester D. and Alice Crow, *Introduction to Education*. New York: American Book Company, 1950.

De Young, Chris A., *American Education*. New York: McGraw-Hill Book Company, Inc., 1960.

Haan, Aubrey, *Education for the Open Society*. Boston: Allyn & Bacon, Inc., 1962.

Haan, Aubrey, *Elementary School Curriculum*. Boston: Allyn & Bacon, Inc., 1961.

Hansen, Kenneth, *Public Education in American Society*. Englewood Cliffs, N.J.: Prentice-Hall, Inc., 1956.

Haskew, Lawrence D., *This is Teaching*. Chicago: Scott, Foresman and Company, 1959.

Hillway, Thynus, *Education in American Society*. Boston: Houghton Mifflin Company, 1961.

Thomas, Lawrence G., Lucien B. Kinney, Arthur P. Coladarci, and and Helen A. Fielstra, *Perspective on Teaching*. Englewood Cliffs, N.J.: Prentice-Hall, Inc., 1961.

A Reference Chart

READINGS IN THIS TEXT

AUTHORS OF

NO., AUTHOR	*TITLE*	*Callahan*	*Benda & Cressman*	*Crow & Crow*	*DeYoung*
1-1 **E. Afanasenko**	*Soviet School Reorganization*	**1** (*17, 18*) **2** (*46–50*) **8** (*187–90*) **9** (*212–23*) **12** (*287–89*)	**1** (*4–5*) **5** (*116, 134–36*) **9** (*251–59*) **10** (*265–96*) **14** (*402–3*) *Appendix D*	**3** (*52–3, 60–65*) **4** (*77–80*) **6** (*129–30*) **9** (*223–24*) **11** (*258–72*) **20** (*462–66*) **22** (*488–90*)	**I:** (*2–29*) **II:** (*80, 81, 84, 102, 119, 124, 147, 180*) **III:** (*202–3, 242–44*) **IV:** (*302, 323*) **V:** (*375–76, 387–89, 401*)
1-2 **Irma Salas**	*Education In Latin Countries*	**1** (*17–18*) **2** (*46–48*) **6** (*107–45*) **7** (*146–170*) **8** (*171–190*) **9, 11** (*250–258*) **12** (*287–89*) **18, 19** (*455–456*)	**2, 3, 4, 5** (*134*) **6** (*155–158*) **8** (*232–48*) **10, 17** (*484–88*)	**2, 3** (*55–75*) **4, 5, 11**	**1, 2, 3, 4, 5, 6, 7, 8, 11, 16**
1-3 **L. J. Lewis**	*Education and Political Independence in Africa*	**2** (*46–47*) **7** (*147–53*) **8** (*187–90*) **9** (*212*) **10, 11, 17, 18** (*419–22*)	**1, 2, 3, 4, 6, 8, 17**	**1** (*17*) **3, 4, 5, 8, 22**	**1, 2, 3, 4, 15, 16, 17**
1-4 **Charles H. Dobinson**	*French Educational Reform*	**5, 6, 9,** (*202–3 & 212*) **10, 11, 12, 18**	**1, 2, 3, 4, 7** (*213–15*) **9, 14**	**2, 3, 4, 5, 6, 7, 11, 16, 22**	**1, 2, 3, 4, 5, 6, 7, 8, 9, 15, 16**
1-5 **Edmund King**	*Comprehensive Schools in England*	**5, 9, 10, 11, 12, 13**	**2, 3, 4, 9, 10, 11**	**3, 6, 11, 22**	**5, 6, 7, 8, 9, 13, 15, 16**
2-1 **Educational Policies Commission**	*The Founders of the Republic Exalted Education*	**6, 9, 10, 11, 12**	**1, 2, 3, 4**	**1, 2, 3, 4**	**1, 2, 3, 4, 5, 6, 7, 8, 9**

to Related Texts

KEY: *Bold face roman numeral—Part*
Bold face arabic numeral—Chapter
Italic numbers—pages

RELATED TEXTS (*see p. 365*)

Haan	*Haan*	*Hansen*	*Haskew*	*Hillway*	*Kinney, et al.*
(*Education for the Open Society*)	(*Elementary School Curriculum*)				
1 (*2–42*) **2** (*69–76*) **3** (*132*) **4** (*136–59*) **5** (*170–71, 178–79, 184–85*) **6** (*216, 245*) **7** (*266–82*)	**4** (*84–90, 100–3*) **5** (*124–27, 140*) **8** (*190–222*) **9** (*228–57*)	**1** (*17–18*) **3** (*64*) **4** (*70–85*) **5** (*112–117*) **6** (*129–39*) **7** (*174–76*) **8** (*193–200*) **10** (*260–62, 269–76*) **11** (*320*) **15** (*429–34*)	**7** (*140–44*) **12** (*215–28*)	**1** (*3–5*) **2** (*53–55*) **3** (*83, 98–104*) **7** (*211–14, 225–31*) **10** (*309–12*) **13** (*432*) **15** (*461–73*)	**1** (*11–26*) **2** (*44–53*) **3** (*84–85*) **5** (*127–28*) **7** (*182–83*) **10** (*242–49*) **11** (*275–76*) **12** (*298–99*) **14** (*354*) **15** (*378–79*)
1, 2 (*75–78*) **4, 5** (189–*208*) **9**	**4, 5, 14, 15**	**1** (*19–22*) **2** (*27–48*) **3, 4, 8, 11** (*313–22*) **15** (*429–35*)	**4, 5** (*79–80, 102–103*) **6** (*106–35*) **7, 8, 11**	**1, 4, 5, 6, 7, 8, 15**	**1** (*9–14*) **2** (*35–58*) **3** (*65–68*) **5, 6, 15**
1, 2 (*69–78*) **3** (*132*) **4, 5** (*207–8*) **9**	**5, 14, 15, Epilogue**	**1** (*14–22*) **2, 3, 8** (*216–17*) **10, 11** (*323*) **15**	**4, 7, 8, 11, 12** (*215–26*) Section **2** (*260–73*) Section **3** (*278–95*) Section **4** (*296–302*)	**1, 2, 3, 4, 5, 13, 15**	**5, 6, 10, 11, 16**
1, 3, 4, 7, 9	**1, 2, 3, 4, 12, 14, 15**	**1** (*6–10 & 19–24*) **2, 3, 4, 10, 15**	**4, 5, 7, 8, 12** **Section 2 and 3**	**1, 2, 3, 4, 5, 6, 7, 8, 15**	**3, 5, 6, 10, 11, 13**
1, 2, 3, 4, 9	**1, 4, 5, 6, 7, 13, Epilogue**	**2, 3, 4, 6, 9, 10, 15**	**4, 5, 6, 7, 8** **Section 2 and 3**	**2, 3, 4, 5, 6, 7, 8, 12, 15**	**1, 2, 3, 5, 10**
1, 2, 9	**5, 14, 15, 16, Epilogue**	**1, 2, 3, 4**	**7, Section 2 and 3**	**1, 2, 3, 4, 5**	**5, 10, 11**

READINGS IN THIS TEXT		AUTHORS OF			
NO., AUTHOR	*TITLE*	*Callahan*	*Benda & Cressman*	*Crow & Crow*	*DeYoung*
2-2 William J. Platt	*The Economic Value of Education*	**8**	**14**	**22**	**9**
2-3 Dorothy Lee	*Individual Autonomy and Social Structure*	**2, 3, 4, 5**	**1 (*3–7*) 9 (*14*)**	**6, 7, 11, 13**	**10, 11, 12, 13**
2-4 Herbert Muller	*The Open Society*	**2, 4, 13, 14**	**1, 9, 10, Appendices A, B, C, D**	**3, 5, 20, 22**	**10, 11, 12, 13**
2-5 Julian Huxley	*Cultural Process and Evolution*	**2, 3, 4, 5**	**1, 9, 10, 11, 15**	**1, 2, 3, 11, 12**	**1, [illegible]**
2-6 Sir Aurobindo Ghos	*A System of National Education*	**2, 3, 4, 5**	**1, 2, 9, 10, 11, 12**	**3, 6, 11, 12, 13, 14**	**5, [illegible] 10, [illegible] 14**
3-1 Jacob W. Getzels & Philip W. Jackson	*Varieties of Giftedness in Children*	**4, 12, 13**	**12**	**6, 15**	**6, 7, 10, 11, 13, 14, 17**
3-2 Gordon Allport	*Principles of Learning*	**2, 3, 4, 5, 16**	**9, 10, 11, 12**	**6, 11, 12, 13, 15**	**5, 6, 7, 8, 9, 10, 11**
3-3 J. P. Guilford	*Factors That Aid and Hinder Creativity*	**2, 4, 5**	**9, 10, 11, 12**	**6, 9, 11, 12, 13, 14**	**5, 6, 7, 10, 11, 13**
3-4 Lawrence S. Kubie	*Education for Preconscious Freedom and Relation to Creativity and the Process of Maturation*	**2, 4, 5**	**9, 10, 12**	**6, 9, 13, 14**	**5, 6, 7, 10**
3-5 James S. Coleman	*Adolescence And Secondary Education In Modern Society*	**3, 4, 12, 13**	**9, 10, 11**	**6, 11, 12, 13**	**7, 10, 13, 14**
3-6 David McClelland, et al	*Obligation To Self And Society In The United States and Germany*	**3, 4, 7**	**1, 9**	**3, 6, 9**	**1, 10**

RELATED TEXTS

Haan (*Education for the Open Society*)	*Haan* (*Elementary School Curriculum*)	*Hansen*	*Haskew*	*Hillway*	*Kinney, et al.*
4	15	4	7	12	11
3, 4	1, 2, 3, 4, 5, Epilogue	4, 5, 6, 8, 10	3, 4, 5, 7	2, 3, 9	7, 8, 9, 10, 11
1, 2, 3, 4	1, 2, 5	4, 5, 10, 15	3, 4, 7	1, 2, 3, 12, 15	7, 10, 11
1, 2, 3	1, 2, 4, 5	4, 5	3, 4, 7	1, 2, 3, 4, 15	3, 7, 8, 11
[illegible] 6, 7	1, 2, 3, 4, 5, 6, 13, Epilogue	4, 5, 6, 7, 8, 9, 10	2, 3, 4, 5, 6, 7	1, 2, 3, 9, 10, 12	1, 2, 3, 4, 7, 8, 9, 10, 11
	1, 7, 13, 14	8	3, Section 1	9, 15	2, 9, 12
2, 3, 6, 7	1, 3, 8, 9, 10, 11	4, 5, 6, 7	3, 4, 5, Section 1	6, 7, 8, 9, 10	7, 8, 9, 10, 11, 12
2, 3, 7	1, 2, 3, 12	4, 5, 6	2, 3, 5	6, 7, 8	1, 2, 7, 8, 9, 10
2, 3	1, 2, 3 Epilogue	5, 6	3, 6, 7	6, 7, 9	7, 8, 10
2, 3, 4	1, 4, 5	4, 6, 10	7	2, 7	2, 3, 11
1, 4	1, 2, 5	1, 4	7	1, 2, 3	9, 10, 11

READINGS IN THIS TEXT

AUTHORS OF

NO., AUTHOR	TITLE	Callahan	Benda & Cressman	Crow & Crow	DeYoung
3-7 **Martha Wolfenstein**	*French Parents Take Their Children To The Park*	**3, 4**	**9**	**6, 13**	**5, 6**
4-1 **Barbara Biber**	*Teacher Education In Mental Health*	**18, 19**	**5, 6, 7**	**7, 8, 9**	**11**
4-2 **Jerome S. Bruner**	*Aids to Teaching*	**19**	**13** (*384–99*)	**18, 19**	**11, 15**
4-3 **Norma Haan**	*When The Mentally Ill Child Returns To School*	**4**	**12**	**6, 13, 14**	**13** (*294–95*) **14** (*311–12*)
4-4 **OVERVIEW Magazine**	*The New Curriculums*	**13**	**10, 11**	**11, 12**	**13, 14**

RELATED TEXTS

Haan	*Haan*	*Hansen*	*Haskew*	*Hillway*	*Kinney, et al.*
(*Education for the Open Society*)	(*Elementary School Curriculum*)				
3, 4	**1, 2, 5**	**5**	**3**	**2, 6**	**9, 11**
5	**12**	**11, 13**	**1, 2, 3, 6, 10, 11**	**13, 14**	**7, 8, 13, 14, 15**
7	**12, 13**	**9**	**9**	**10**	**3**
2, 3	**1, 2, 3**	**5**	**3**	**9**	**4**
6, 7, 8	**6, 8, 9, 10**	**6**	**5**	**10**	**3**

Index

A

B

C

M

N

O

P

R

S

T

U

V

W

Y